Believe What?!
Where to?

Believe What?!

Where to?

REV. GEORGE HENRY WARREN

CITI OF
BOOKS

CITIOFBOOKS, INC.
3736 Eubank NE Suite A1
Albuquerque, NM 87111-3579
www.citiofbooks.com
Hotline: 1 (877) 389-2759
Fax: 1 (505) 930-7244

Ordering Information:
Quantity sales. Special discounts are available on quantity purchases by corporations, associations, and others. For details, contact the publisher at the address above.

Printed in the United States of America.

ISBN-13:	Softcover	979-8-89391-647-8
	Hardcover	979-8-89391-649-2
	eBook	979-8-89391-648-5

Library of Congress Control Number: 2025907706

Rev. George Warren
25th Ordination Anniversary - 1996

The contents of this collection of stories calls upon questions of beliefs in search for the truth. It does not answer the profound questions of belief and history but rather seeks the answers.

There are opinions stated which call for further discussion and debate. The search is for the facts, for the truth, in order for the discussion to continue to hopefully and thankfully get resolved.

The major question is, "Does God exist in our experiences?" Who or what might God be if at all? Atheism and Theism have always been in the mix of discussions and debates throughout history. This book calls for belief in who-mever or whatever God may or may not be. It is the truth that we need if it is truth at all.

Major questions today in such problems as climate change, the latest pandemic, and divisive political postures make it critically important to know the facts and to seek the truth in these matters. As all too often, it is the case that such matters of mutual concern become politicized and thereby open the door to misgivings which distort the facts, the truth, leading to misuse, distraction, and poor, if not dangerous outcomes. The end does not justify the means if those means are not of the truth.

Verify, verify, verify!

Quotations

"My hope is that I have not led you astray."
Socrates

"Seek and ye shall find, knock and the door will be opened,
ask and ye shall receive."
Jesus

"If only I could enter the pulpit one more time!"
Father Howard C. Olsen

"We are only one generation away from all we have learned
if we don't teach our children our history."

"Verify, Verify, Verify!"
President Ronald W. Reagan

"We have nothing to fear but fear itself."
President Franklin D. Roosevelt

"Ask not what your country can do for you,
ask what you can do for your country."
President John F. Kennedy

"If God doesn't exist everything is permissible."
Fyodor Dostoyevsky

"I am the way, the truth, and the life."
Jesus

"Evil will persist and win if good men do nothing."
Anonymous

Once asked: "Where is Heaven?" Answer: "It is a state of Being."
John Paul II

"Seek the truth and the truth will set you free."
St. Paul

"We can safely trust a whole lot more than we think we can."
Henry David Thoreau

Table of Contents

DEDICATED

TO

JOEL RIVES, ADDIE ANNALISA,

BRIAN MICHAEL, ETHAN JOEL, OWEN JACE,

WESLEY CHRISTIAN, AND PHOEBE SKYE

My children and grandchildren

In Gratitude

Inside of everyone is a book to be written. I believe there is indeed meaning and purpose to each of our lives. Even the seemingly least important act, or thought, or gesture given becomes the description of who you are or might one day become.

Thank you to Catherine Warren for all her help in placing and organizing the various titled pieces and the table of contents into order; to Joel Warren for the many hours given to help me learn and navigate the computer; to Kristin Allen for designing the cover of this book; and to my family, friends, and colleagues who kindly contributed their thoughts and stories into this collection.

My sincerest thanks to Rachael Barr for her continued dedication and dogged work throughout this project; for typing, organizing, and giving wisdom; and for helping my scribbling and piles of scattered papers to miraculously find order. It was no surprise to me to find Rachael Barr humbly accepting when I asked for her permission to place this page into the beginning and acknowledgements of this collection. Without Rachael's years of help and dedication, I would not have been able to complete this project. The following is one example of the hieroglyphics that she had to translate, transpose, and give commentary to the myriads of pages that I continued to hand over to her. Later in this book is a description of Rachael's own spiritual journey. I would suggest it as one's primary introduction to this book as it so adequately describes the basic intentions herein given.

changes

Insert I   Introduction

"Inside of everyone is a book to be written. There is indeed meaning and purpose to each of our lives. The seemingly least important act, or thought, or gesture given becomes the description of who we are or might one day become. In all of the complexities of living there is that you are special and singularly important. It is you who nurtured the injured body back to health and freedom. It was your smile of love and word of encouragement that will ever be forgotten by the neighbor or passing stranger. And yes, it was during those events, something mistakes or even purposeful courage that forgiveness and learning brought healing. And yes, the Truth and Good need to be the outcome.

My need to write this book says that thoughts, events, people in our lives should be noticed. Most especially it is my desire to give to my children and their children some things to know and my desire to give them the best guidance I can. I do believe that our greatest gifts come to us from our Creator whom we call God. "But by the Grace of God" "Thanks be to God"

My gratitude goes extends to all the people and events of my life that shaped my Spiritual Journey. I beg forgiveness for their Trials. I failed and was not there for you. I've heard it said that the best gifts are forgiveness, to your adversary tolerance; to your opponent, to a friend your heart; to your child, a good example; to your father, deference; to your mother, conduct that will make her proud of you.

The stories and anecdotes written here have been thought as I have experienced them. Some of these were ordinary, some questionable, but all exceptional. My own journey has been informed by them and I'm eager to have you share your journeys with me. Somehow we are able to relate each of our paths to deeper, more profound meanings to our lives.

Later in this book is a description of Rachael's own spiritual journey. I would suggest it as one's primary introduction to this book as it so adequately describes the basic intentions herein given. The intention is

It is important to note that differences of opinions and points of view are expressed here–leaving much room for clearer understanding of our individual and together spiritual journeys. The Holy Bible; the Encyclopedia Of 7700 Quotations; along with sundry books and resources have been drawn upon for help in attempting to better clarify the facts and opinions expressed in this volume.

"Introduction"

In the midst of a war to end all wars, political divide, disease and pandemics, natural disasters, and so much more, it is seen that human beings have continued to survive and advance in remarkable ways. My prompting in writing this book is primarily due to the question, "What, how and why?" My basic premise is that a belief in power greater than ourselves provides principles, values, and Truth that give us the knowledge, power, and will to go forward and advance. I believe that the greater source of this power is God as I have experienced because of my Christian upbringing. This does not negate other religious dimensions wherein such experiences have been described. It has been my observation and experience that the Sin of false human pride has been the primary Evil in which human advancement is detained and even destroyed. The problem of Sin and Evil is elusive as we also learn from our mistakes and are thereby given opportunity to move ahead. The question resides as, "How and why do we survive and also advance?" We are in the midst of the Battle of Ideas! What is the Truth? From whence does it come?

The primary reason for me in writing this collection of stories is to give a legacy to my children and grandchildren. Secondly, I hope that other readers will gain some insights into their own life's journeys in search of Truth. I don't expect readers to compare to my journey but do hope that sharing such journeys will help to enhance our journeys together. Can we find the Truth in each other and then become the best we can be?

It seems to me that a Spiritual Base that can hold us together has been seriously declining during my lifetime since the end of World War II. That spiritual base has been a belief in a higher power whom we refer to as God. It has been my belief that the freedom we enjoy and practice, due to our beliefs, is at risk.

The task of gathering thoughts from one's mind, heart, and soul and placing them into some kind of order began for me in 2008, about fourteen years ago. My need to do this was a desire to offer to my grandchildren some insight into how and why Papa thinks and acts as he does. This book has since evolved into a desire to share with whomever may listen, a belief in God. As far as my family, friends, colleagues, along with my love for our country and mission are concerned, it is hoped that such a book would continue and enhance our conversation about Truth, hope, and future. And, indeed, it has been my good fortune to have such a belief system as given to me by family, friends, teachers, colleagues and Nation that my life has thus far been exceptional. It is my considered belief that the most important gift to us is freedom, aside from the gift of life itself. I believe that the gift of free will is to forward God's plan of creation.

The cover of this collection depicts the individual on the path of life looking towards the future with hope and promises. The previous covers shows an old bi-plane heading into clouds posing the eternal question, "Where are we headed?" Below such an excursion through history is the Roller-coaster ride depicting the ups, and downs, twists and turns, and all the questions we face in each of our lifetimes. I'm reminded of a teacher from the annals of history who so aptly stated his own version of the meaning and purpose of his own life. John Newton wrote in a Hymn familiar and loved by so many of us "Amazing Grace" how sweet the sound that saved a wretch like me. As he thought upon the words: "By the grace of God

I am what I am," he said, "I am not what I ought to be. How imperfect and deficient I am. I am not what I wish to be. Though I am not what I ought to be, I can truly say that I am not what I once was – a slave to sin and Satan. I can heartily say with Paul: "But by the Grace of God I am what I am'!" (Encyclopedia of 7700 Quotations).

Freedom, we may argue, is not available to everyone, especially due to circumstances in a real world. The questions become: "What is freedom?" and "What does freedom mean?" A good example of such a struggle towards freedom is that of Helen Keller, who was born blind, deaf, and mute. Her story is related later in this book and many documentaries have been produced to relate this remarkable story. Another story is that of Kasper Houser. More than a half century ago, Kasper Houser appeared in the streets of Nuremburg, having been released from a dungeon in which he had been confined from infancy, having never seen the face or heard the voice of man, nor gone without the walls of his prison, nor seen the full light of day.

A distinguished lawyer of Germany wrote a legal history of this case which he entitled 'A Crime Against the Life of a Soul'." (Encyclopedia of 7700 Quotations #1778). We can all relate to the myriads of such personal journeys! One question and possible answer can be this: "You ask: 'What is the Will of God? What is it that God gives to us to fulfill His will?' Freedom is the nearest thing that should be done, can be done, through you!" (Encyclopedia #7357)

Everyone has a story to tell. Everyone has a book to share. From birth and throughout our lives, we have experiences and many forms of influence which help to form our stories. As human beings, as opposed to the rest of the Animal Kingdom, we are, for whatever reason, unable to make this journey alone. There are important, essential ingredients needed to help each of us both together and simply alone along the way. For example, a bird is almost immediately cast out of the nest to fend for itself. Humans need continual love, care, and attention throughout the entire life cycle. The key question arises from here: "What are the essentials for our survival?"

Throughout history, individuals and societies have sought the answers for making all things better. We have learned by both good and not-so-helpful solutions to the question of how best to move ahead. It is true that we need to learn from our past to grow in comprehension and thereby make whatever changes are needed to move ahead. It becomes our universal goal to make the world a better place for our children and generations to come. Philosophers and scientists were always on the front lines seeking the primary answers to the questions of making things better. A searching and healthful look at those discoveries and principles' can and do give us a better look at reality in search of truth. Again, what is the reality and is there TRUTH to be found? If there are such answers, we have a hopeful journey ahead. If there are no answers other than a hit or miss reality, then we are doomed to failure into a non-purposeful end.

In What or in Whom are we to believe and to trust? Throughout life, we realize that we are all too often in the midst of important dilemmas that require decisions to be made. More often than not, our decisions are not always clear with choices to be made which require thoughtful consideration. We find ourselves looking for answers to guide such deliberations. This is how we learn and hopefully grow in the process. It was Saint Paul in the New Testament of the Holy Bible who said that, "All things work to the good for those who love the Lord." Is this true? Is there a purpose to it all? How will it all turn out?

My own attempt to search these questions is reflected in the thoughts and opinions I express in these writings. I do believe that there are answers to life's questions and guidance to find them. The greater question in my search is whether or not we have that which many of us call, "A Soul which provides the essence of our being and Being itself." In other words, "Do we have "beingness' beyond ourselves which can guide us forward? How are we connected to that beingness? From whence does it come? Is there TRUTH in the midst of the Good and the Evil?!

It was William E. Gladstone of Britain who gave an answer to a gathering of young students on the question of Good, Evil, and the pursuit of the Truth. His statement nicely summarizes the contents and goals of this book. Gladstone was a British Statesman and had served several terms as Prime minister of England between 1868 and 1894. The following paragraph is from *the Encyclopedia of 7700 Quotations* from which I've utilized throughout this book:

> The British Statesman, W. E. Gladstone who often served as Prime Minister of Britain once sat in Christ Church College and talked at some length about changes he had witnessed during his lifetime in the lot of the English people. His outlook was so radiantly optimistic that it aroused a challenge. One of the students said, "Sir, are we to understand that you have no anxieties for the future?" The grand old man of England answered slowly, "Yes, there is one thing that frightens me———The fear that God seems to be dying out in the minds of men.

Now, in going forward in such a dialogue I suggest that the reader first go to the Holy Bible and read the following passages which are given in the common lectionary of the Church on the 17th Sunday after Pentecost, Year B:

Prayer: Grant us, O Lord, not to be anxious about earthly things, but to love things heavenly; and even now, while we are placed among things that are passing away, to hold fast to those that shall endure."

I suggest here that you read the following Biblical passages from "The Wisdom of Solomon" and "The Epistle of James:"

> But ungodly men by their words and deeds summoned death; considering him a friend, they pined away, and they made a covenant

with him, because they are fit to belong to his party. For they reasoned unsoundly, saying to themselves, 'Short and sorrowful is our life, and there is no remedy when a man comes to his end, and no one has been known to return from Hades, because we were born by mere chance, and hereafter we shall be as though we had never been; because the breath in our nostrils is smoke, and reason is a spark kindled by the beating of our hearts. When it is extinguished, the body will turn to ashes, and the spirit will dissolve like empty air…Let us lie in wait for the righteous man, because he is inconvenient to us and opposes our actions; he reproaches us for sins against the law, and accuses of sins against our training. He professes to have knowledge of God and calls himself a child of the Lord. *(Wisdom of Solomon 1:16- 2:1, 12-22)*

Who is wise and understanding among you? By his good life let him show his works in the meekness of wisdom. But if you have bitter jealousy and selfish ambition in your hearts, do not boast and be false to the truth. The wisdom is not such as comes down from above, but is earthly, un-spiritual, devilish. For where jealousy and selfish ambition exist, there will be disorder and every vile practice. But if the wisdom from above is first pure, then peaceable, gentle, open to reason, full of mercy and good fruits, without uncertainty or insecurity. And the harvest of righteousness is sown in peace by those who make peace *(James 3:13ff)*

"What and Why"

More than ten years ago, I began pouring out thoughts that I could share with my children, grandchildren, and others so that we may, together, consider our journeys in the best possible ways. The best anyone can do, including myself, is to share such experiences as have influenced our direction and thought processes with a goal to share with others our particular journeys and go forward in better ways. A primary goal could and should be to help future generations move ahead. in the best ways possible. It is true that life is a difficult journey likened to a roller coaster ride, but wonderful and exciting as well.

Included in these pages are "Faith Journey" stories of some friends and colleagues with whom I've shared my own journey. Certainly, it is true that we've learned much from one another on this journey both in much agreement but also in points of disagreement with a realization of so much more to learn. As many philosophers have acknowledged, "The more you know, the less you know." It is true that knowledge is so much larger than our own often limited perspectives on the Truth. Much humility is required by all of us in this realm. Much, or more than enough, of my own perspectives and world view may easily be challenged by my friends, colleagues, and relatives- even my own children- and their reasonable responses.

Including all of them in my own perspective does not implicate them as if they lock step. The joy of learning is the joy of growing to a higher place than previously realized. The hope and prayer on our together spiritual journey is that we each individually and together reach a higher plain in our growth and development. In raising our own children as well as each other, it should be our goal towards growth and understanding. Of course, much work needs to be done in the meantime. It was Jesus who said to his friends, "Let your light so shine that they may see your good works and glorify your Father who is in Heaven." *(Mtt. 5;6)* "You are a light of the world. A city built on a hill cannot be hidden. No one, after lighting a lamp, puts it under the bushel basket, but on a lampstand, and it gives light to all in the house." *(Mtt. 5:14, 15)*

The Roman Catholic monk, Thomas Merton, said the following: "If we descend into the depth of our own spirit, and arrive at our 'center,' we confront the inescapable fact that, at the root of our existence we are in immediate and constant contact with God."

Merton wrote sixty books on the human "spiritual journey." Bishop Douglas J. Fisher, in his 2017 address to the Diocese of Western Massachusetts, spoke Merton's thoughts in this way: Thomas Merton said, 'At the root of our existence, we are in immediate and constant contact with God.' As we run from thing to thing, it does not always seem that way. Instead, it seems like we have immediate and constant contact with anxiety. We live in anxious times in our nation, in our world and our Church. We can't think that anxiety away. We can't make it stop by force of our will. We can only be set free to be authentically human by finding the source of our life and the meaning of our life in God. Our God who is as close as our next breath. It is by entering intentionally into that relationship that we are transformed. No one says that better than last night's speaker, my friend, Rob Wright (The Rt. Rev. Robert Wright, Bishop of Atlanta)

'God causes freedom in people. Freedom to be authentic. Freedom from fear. Freedom for improvisation. Freedom to befriend the world. God is a freedom God and God's people are in the freedom business.'

What a vision! I want to live that way. Do you? However, remember what Thomas Merton said. He had an "IF" clause in there. "We confront the fact that we are in immediate and constant contact with God (the freedom God) if we descend to the depth of our own spirit and arrive at the center." (Bishop Fisher)

It was the great musician Hayden who responded positively to the question as to why his compositions were so cheerful. He said, "When I think upon God, my heart is so full of joy that the notes dance and leap, as it were, from my pen, and since God has given me a 'cheerful heart' it will be pardoned that I serve him with a cheerful heart." (Encyclopedia 7700 Illustrations)

It is my hope that this collection of true stories and anecdotes will help readers to recognize God in the everyday events and circumstances of their lives. My own experiences, before and after becoming a priest in the Church, have continued to enhance my search for God.

Recently asked by a colleague if I have any singular objective in writing these pages, my answer is that I need to somehow express why I think the way I do. Secondly, I need the rest of the world to do the same with me so that I can learn from them and perhaps they can learn from me. This should become "healthful communication" and hopefully bring us closer to 'truth' or at least result in some facts being presented to help lead us forward toward clearer and more fruitful perspectives together. Yes, I want to know why you think the way you do, as well as for you to know why I think the way I do...help me! In the following pages, I reveal many extraordinary experiences and learning during my lifetime which have formed me into the one I have been and since become. My story is not all that unusual except to say that I yearn for answers to the questions of who God might be and can the truth be found there?!

Ancient Greek philosophers such as Socrates, Plato, and Aristotle, among so many others, have come up with a word called "sophistry." Sophistry was termed dangerous and destructive in our communication with one another because it means "half-truth," when misuse of actual facts are used to distort actual facts and the truth, the good is not served and the distortion leads us astray. Hence, the reality of evil intent enters in to serve a lesser end.

Sophistry puts the search, discussion, debate into an "I'm right-you are wrong" posture. Socrates made it clear that the truth is outside of all of us, but we can and must participate in that truth to not only survive but also thrive. Tyranny is the result of sophistry – a deterrent to the truth and distortion of our ability to think. My hope, again, as I share true stories and experiences, is to continue the discussion of truth and where such truth is, if it is at all.

During my years of growing up, I recall a two-party political system allowing and calling for honest debate in hopes of moving forward with clearer solutions to both individual and societal problems and questions. We had debating clubs in high school. This always seemed to me a very healthy way of moving towards the Truth and a more perfect union. At least the conclusions raised further questions to be dealt with and answered in better ways. We must begin somewhere in the search for the Truth. It was President Reagan who recently reiterated the warning that if we don't teach our children history as our guide, we are doomed to repeat the same failures, at least in the short run. The question here looms: Can and will the Truth come forward, and ultimately prevail?

As Socrates told his friends soon before he left them to carry on without his loving concern and guidance, "I fear that I may have led you astray," in our search for the Truth. Saint Thomas Aquinas, Doctor of Theology in the Church, soon before he died, asked for forgiveness for the many mistakes he made in his interpretation of theology and the mission of the Church. Before his death he was prompted by a glimpse of the other side.

It was Jesus of Nazareth who told us, "I am the Way, the Truth, and the Life." *(John 14:6)* Both of these humans of history saw Truth as emanating from a higher source.

It has long been an unmet wish of mine that family and friends from before my birth had left written accounts of their lives and beliefs. This book is about experiences I've had which have formed my own belief journey. Yes, some stories of my loved ones were shared with me, photos kept, and memories of their lives have been expressed, which have been a great joy. However, more thorough written accounts from my ancestral past would have been the greatest gift of love to me and those following. Why did they believe the way they did? What were their formative experiences?

1915

Hannah Lawton and John Arthur Warren, my dad's mother and father, died before I was born. I was most fortunate, in my younger years, to have enjoyed my mom's mother and father Helena and Karol Barszcz, who had emigrated from Poland. They came to America in the promise of new life and hope for the future.

Hannah Lawton was a D.A.R. (Daughter of the American Revolution), with her forebears dating back to newborn America. John Arthur Warren was brought here from Wales at the age of two years. My strong desire is to finally meet them in person in Heaven. I do hope there is a Heaven! The accounts given in this book share extraordinary as well as more normal experiences that give wonderful credence to the belief of eternal life with those we have loved and who have loved us from the beginning of time.

1913

Yes, inside of everyone is a book to be written. There is indeed meaning and purpose to each of our lives. The seemingly least important act, or thought, or gesture given becomes the description of who you are or might one day become. Remember the fledgling little bird you took into health and freedom or the smile of love and encouragement you gave that would never be forgotten by the receiver and stranger? It is the pure love of those who have come before us that enhanced our formative experiences. We've also learned from the mistakes that inevitably happen on the human roller-coaster ride. What and where is the truth that makes all this okay? It is during those events of both sinfulness, and mistakes, or even purposeful revenge, that forgiveness and learning brought healing. And yes, the Truth and Good are to be the outcome.

My need to write this book says that thoughts, events, and people in our lives, should be shared. Most especially it is my desire to give to my children and their children some things to know about me and my desire to give the best guidance that I can, for their own growth experiences. I do believe that our greatest gifts come to us from our Creator whom we call God. "But by the Grace of God."

My gratitude extends to all the people and events of my life that shaped my own spiritual journey. I beg forgiveness for those times I failed and was not there for ones who may have needed my help and understanding. It has been said that the best gifts are forgiveness to your adversary, tolerance to your opponent, comprehension of the wider picture; your heart to a friend; a good example to your child; deference to your father; conduct that will make her proud of you to your mother!

The stories, anecdotes, and other personal experiences written here are true and not embellished. Some of these experiences were ordinary, many questionable, but all exceptional. My own journey has been informed by them, and I'm eager to have you share your journeys with me. Somehow, we are able to relate each of our paths to deeper, more profound meanings to our lives.

Here I remind myself of the method of Socrates who taught, mentored, and made Truth the ultimate goal of humans and civilization. The Socratic Method was to share one's knowledge and experience in order to draw from within his students a likewise and even more profound response. Teaching is fruitless if the other cannot relate. The Bible informs us that our teacher, Jesus, asked his disciples to go forth and share the light they've been given. "Let your light so shine before men that they may see your good works and glorify your Father who is in Heaven."

It is my hope that in sharing these experiences, others will be able to relate and do the same to their followers for the good of all and for enlightenment toward the Truth.

The famous aviator and science buff, Charles Lindbergh, shared his perception of truth in saying that:

> In my youth, science was more important to me than either man or God. I worshipped science. Its advance had surpassed man's wildest dreams. It took many years for me to discover that science, with all its brilliance, lights only a middle chapter of creation. I saw the aircraft I loved destroying the civilization I expected it to save. Now I understand that spiritual truth is more essential to a nation than the mortar in its city walls. For when the actions of a people are undergirded by spiritual truths, there is safety. When spiritual truths are rejected, it is only a matter of time before civilization will collapse.

We must understand spiritual truths and apply them to our modern life. We must draw strength from the almost forgotten virtues of simplicity, humility, contemplation, and prayer. It requires a dedication beyond science, beyond self, but the rewards are great and it is our only hope." (From the Encyclopedia of 7700 Illustrations)

> Jesus said, "Set your troubled hearts at rest. Believe in God, believe also in me. In my Father's house are many rooms, if it were not so, would I have told you that I go to prepare a place for you? And when I go and prepare a place for you, I will come again and take you to myself, that where I am, there you may be also. And you know the way where I am going." Thomas said to him, "Lord, we do not know where you are going; how can we know the way?" Jesus said to him, "I am the way, the truth, and the life; no-one comes to the Father but by me. If you had known me, you would have known my Father also; henceforth you know him and have seen him." *(John 14:1-6)*

Oftentimes, Jesus was confronted with the most profound of questions dealing with who we are and from whence do we come?! The Bible says that those listening to Jesus, "marveled at His teaching." They asked one another, "How is it that this man has such learning, when he has never studied?" Jesus answered them, "My teaching is not mine, but His who sent me; if any man's will is to do His will, he shall know whether the teaching is from God or not." *(John 7:15)*

In the fear that God and hope might get forgotten with despair and doom to follow, our own President Buchanan in 1860 said as he was in the midst of critical decisions for the good of the nation; "Indeed, all hope seems to have deserted the minds of men." (Encyclopedia of 7700 Illustrations) At the last minute, I changed the title of this book to *Believe What?!* from *Really- That Happened?!* Both titles capture my purpose and intent in these writings. In the current climate of disruption and disease (political and medical), I believe that God is always present and with us no matter what. The Judeo-Christian Holy Bible clearly testifies to this belief. This collection of stories and experiences also testify to such a belief.

The greatest question of all time is: Are we simply material beings in a very brief lifetime? Or, is there something more than the material universe such as we might call, the Soul? This book poses this question. Hence the title, Believe What?!

Experiences and education over my lifetime have brought me to belief in the Soul, i. e. that which belongs to the spiritual and that which is above, within, and beyond ourselves, and that which animates us. It is stated in the Holy Bible that, "God breathed life into the valley of the dry bones." *(Ezekiel 37:9)* For me, the Bible has become the guidebook for and about the human soul. The following stories, experiences, and witnesses are testimony to such a belief, and thereby learning and growth to a greater end, and therefore, a greater beginning. I suggest here that the reader look up the prophet Jeremiah in the Old Testament and read chapter thirty-one. The chapter nicely relates our spiritual connection to God and the results of that connection.

My intention is that these pages will help readers to recognize God in the everyday events and circumstances of their lives. My own experiences as a priest in the Church has continuously enhanced my search for God in such events. As my own world has been shaped over these decades, the important beginnings were from a loving and devoted family only wanting the best for me. I am truly grateful for this opportunity and much learning over time. My own faith in God was given to me by my family, friends, teachers, and this awesome country in which I was raised.

Ever since early childhood I have observed with curiosity but then more so with dismay that which appeared to be a gradual breakdown of the many principles that have formed and informed a great nation of high character based on those principles. The Constitution and Bill of Rights provided the framework for the idea of freedom by which we could guide and protect that idea. The framers of these principles believed that freedom was primarily based on the conviction of higher TRUTH within which such freedom exists. Their understanding of the Holy Bible was the basis of these principles. With a troubling dismay I have watched what appears to be a gradual dismantling of those basic principles which have led us forward as a well-formed and hopeful people.

The contents of this book convey many of the reasons in which we, as a culture and a People have been losing touch with our belief in those principles which have guided us into being a remarkable republic. A serious loss of our belief and understanding of God's Will for all peoples is, I believe, the primary reason for the weakening and potential destruction of our beloved republic. The incursion and infusion of contrary philosophies, with determination and much success have, forthrightly led us in this direction. For example, the teaching of the Atheist Society of America has forwarded Atheism and similar philosophies into our culture as an alternative to long held belief-based way of thinking and acting. Recently the new "Woke Culture" has entered with high intensity. There is nothing new about this interruption as it has been brought to other cultures and countries long before now.

History has shown the results. The purpose of the "Woke Culture" is to cancel, erase, disregard, teach against, dismantle, and so on the entire belief system by which our forebears have designed our culture. We need to know about such history in order to reenter these discussions into our ongoing debates on how best to factually, and truthfully help us move forward. It is my sincere hope that the belief experiences included in these writings will reopen our debates so that we can continue as a People and society.

2018

1955

1891

1962

1953

1996

"Andrew"

Andrew's life on this fragile island home we call the Earth began after WWII had ended. He says now that he can remember to this day in 2017 his first awareness of his mother's embrace and touch. I try myself to think of my own first awareness. It is a difficult thing to do, I think, for most of us. For Andy his life evolved from that moment to awareness after awareness. He says he can't recall the things, events, or people who immediately followed that first moment, but it was good.

Andy asked that he remain anonymous and that his story be told as he remembers. From his perspective the evolution of his life was normal. In this account he reveals a split second in time that changed and informed his entire world view and the decision-making process throughout his journey. I shall do my best here to relate his story.

Andy was born into a hard-working, middle class family in a neighborhood of lower to middle class families. He was the third born of three brothers. Each brother was some years older and, as far as he knew, very advanced in their own experiences of growing up. As a third child, in these early years Andy thought he would never be able to catch up to their amazing accomplishments. He was distressed by the fact that schoolteachers would call him by their names, depending upon which one they knew best. He often had to say, "I'm Andy," or just stay silent until they finally figured out that as proud as he was of them, he was not one of them. He adored his older brothers as he knew how much they loved him most of the time. In many ways he would try to emulate them. They loved him to pieces, spoiled him and taught him well. Andy felt privileged to be the third born in his wonderful family and fun place to be.

He relates that the 1950s was a great time to be living and growing. Thinking back, he believes it was a simpler time, in a good place, with much to promise toward a happy and successful future. There were values to learn and live by and everyone else throughout the universe lived by the same rules of the road and hopes for the future.

It took a long time to realize that everything wasn't always perfect and not everyone played by the same rules. In those days, Mom was home and Dad earned the money to keep home afloat. There were many lean times, but they were all fed and clothed. There were also the better times, and a meal at the local restaurant occasionally happened. His family always had specific meal-times and ate together. Holidays were always special with larger family and friends. Television was just coming into living rooms. Times were good. Even the doors were kept un-locked with no fear of robbery and allowance for neighbors to enter if they needed something.

Skipping a few years into the later grammar school drudgery, Andy relates his experience into the direction he later followed. It was initially begun by a promise made to him in Sunday School. He says that he didn't care for being sent to church and often found ways to skip. His fishing pole was hidden at a nearby pond and playing hooky was the thing to do. He didn't tell anybody about his ruse until he got caught and was thereafter ushered into the Sunday services and Sunday School. He learned there, for the first time, that God hears all our prayers and answers them. He wanted to believe this but clearly wasn't so sure.

One day, at about the age of ten, Andy peered out his bedroom window, looked up into the sky, and prayed, "God, if you are real, please let me know." It was as simple as that.

Prayer completed and almost immediately forgotten, he left his room and went out to normal playtime with friends. He had a bunch of friends who enjoyed being together and getting into all kinds of mischief, as children do. Years went by with no memory of the prayer and no special answer. That was ok! It just didn't come back to mind. Life was normal, good, existing in playtime as he and his friends and family went on as usual. Here is Andy's account of what he considers and says he knows was the first answer to the childhood prayer of nearly five years earlier:

The Vision
"It was a fairly long day of school, and after school – job, dinner, homework, and bed. Feeling rested after a tiring normal day as he was lying on his back and drifting toward sleep, he became unusually peaceful. He says that, "In an

unusually peaceful state he was being lifted out of his body and into an indescribable weightlessness. A very bright but soft light appeared above that state of transition. There are no words that can describe the light except that "all knowledge" entered his being. Again, there are no words that can describe the "all knowledge" entrance except that it was real and a gift beyond any physical comparison and meant everything likened to a mystical consumption. There is no way to explain it except that he knew it would inform him for the rest of his life.

Within a very short span of time, less than one minute, all became normal again. He was returned to his body in sheer wonder, and started to go to tell his Mother, then asleep. But then he stopped in his tracks and says, "Even my Mother would not understand any attempt to explain. No one would! I realized then that this was the answer to my genuine childhood prayers. As in the earlier days, I went to normalcy." It was realized to be time again to return to normalcy as life would be going on as usual. But Andrew recalls that, "I knew that God and Heaven were absolutely real, in another dimension, and comes to all of us at one time or another."

Andrew went on to say that, "At one point soon after I asked God to help me to understand the Bible. He did! The light from that other dimension enters into the mortal soul." The light never stopped informing him from then on. His inquiries continue to this day in all the circumstances, thoughts and prayers of immortal soul. There have been no more dramatic experiences although he has often thought another would be great. Come to find out through the rest of normal life of circumstances and growing that such another occurrence was not necessary nor warranted. He says, "It is my belief, from that experience, that everyone is destined at one time or another for that prayerful answer from God." St. Augustine of Hippo, who traveled through his life full of questions and always in need of answers said at the end of his searching, "I have not rested until I rested in Thee, O Lord!"

Andy related how, one day, at undergraduate school he thought he could and tried to share this story with one of his philosophy professors. The short of it is that the professor was disrespectful and asked him, "What kind of drug or mushroom are you taking?" That was the end of the conversation and the experience; he went back into hiding!

I am grateful to Andy for this sharing, especially at a point in time where we both still believe that God is there for everyone. They simply need to let Him in. I write this book in order to share stories that might show others the truth of Andy's account and that those who read them and struggle with questions of Faith. All the stories here are real, un-embellished accounts of extraordinary events of ordinary people where the gifts of God have entered in. These are accounts of my experiences of God's love and actions in my life through my own interactions with others in the belief that all answers to prayer belong to all of us. We simply need to be open to those answers.

I love to hear the sounds that give me peace and quiet all around when the world is moving fast I love to stop and take a rest remember all the time to quiet your mind if you try it you will find thoughts and dreams come to rhyme stop and listen to whispers of the wind stop and listen songs birds are to of the with they me in my here place favorite down slowing pace my sounds the outdoors of the and stop to listen of the whispers stop wind listen and songs to birds of the to I love the hear that sounds me give that peace me and quiet all around when the world is moving fast I love to stop and take a rest remember all the time to quiet your mind if you try it you will find thoughts and dreams

My son Joel

Andrew's World View

We can define "World View" as: "The way in which one sees the World and thereby makes decisions accordingly." The world view of every individual on the planet is influenced and determined by his/her upbringing, surroundings, education, and speculation into the future! It is important to note here that human beings are the only creatures in the animal kingdom who need nurturing throughout his/her life. Animals are instinctively set into the wild soon after birth. The human cannot survive without love and care throughout life. Here is the "how" of creating the human World View. These forthcoming stories, anecdotes, testimonies, and quips point to a particular World View determined by belief in God.

In Atheism, a human is sent into the World – the wild – with a World View that he/she has only oneself to count on for the ultimate answers to all questions. The World View of a Believer is based on information that one's belief and faith come from and is in connection with the Creator whom we call God.

According to the following stories, the writers' World View looks to God and to reliable resources for inspiration, information, and there-by speculation, and guidance into the future. In the Judeo-Christian tradition, Truth emanates from the Creator and through our experiences of that Truth – and thereby a healthful future which translates into progress towards the "building of the Kingdom". The term "Kingdom" refers to the belief that God has a purpose and meaning into which we are called. It is the Holy Bible which gives credence to a Believer's World View. It is interesting to note here that the Holy Bible is built upon experiences which lead us to the Kingdom. It is our experience of God which propels our World View. For example, love is an experience and it comes from God. Love cannot be seen except through experience and then comprehension of its real existence.

In the previous experiential testimony we see that Andrew recognized his other-worldly spiritual experience" as a gift from God. It was from such an experience that his World View was established. It had become Andrew's belief that the Gifts of the Holy Spirit are the experiences which form a World View and thereby a Truthful World View. Upon studying the Holy Bible, we discover and believe that Jesus of Nazareth was indeed the Incarnation of God as he taught, lived, died, and rose again by that same experience.

Likewise, my thank you is to a loving God, and then to friends like Andrew, along with family, teachers, and those of history who have purposely contributed to my own sense of a World View for my own good and for the sake of the future of us all. There is a prayer before the Readings of the twenty-third Sunday after the Pentecost which appeals to our need to read, understand, and live by the Holy Bible:

Prayer: "Blessed Lord, who caused all holy scriptures to be written for our learning: Grant us so to hear them, read, mark, learn, and inwardly digest them, that we may embrace and ever hold fast the blessed Hope of everlasting life, which You have given us in our Savior, Jesus Christ, who lives and reigns with you and the Holy Spirit, one God, for ever and ever, Amen." *(Book of Common Prayer, page 236)*

Andrew expressed that his experience was a gift of the Holy Spirit, therefore a spiritual event. The writer, A. J. Gordon compared the spiritual experience with the regular experience of the world around us. He told a story to express the meaning of such a belief:

An American with an English gentleman were viewing the Niagara whirlpool rapids, when he said to his friend, "Come and I'll show you the greatest unused power in the world. "And taking him to the foot of Niagara Falls, "There," he said, "is the greatest unused power in the world!". "Ah, no, my brother, not so!" was the reply. "The greatest unused power in the world is the Holy Spirit of the living God!" *(Encyclopedia of 7700 Illustrations, #2232, page 555)*

In closing, and going forward into the following "World View" and experiences of this book, I utilize here the "Proclamation of President George Washington in Establishing a National Day of Thanksgiving:"

WHEREAS, it is the duty of all nations to acknowledge the providence of Almighty God, to obey His will, to be grateful for His benefits, and humbly to implore His protection and favor;

WHEREAS, Both the houses of Congress have, by their joint committee, requested me to recommend to the people of the United

States a day of public thanksgiving and prayer, to be observed by acknowledging with grateful hearts the many and signal favors of Almighty God, especially by affording them an opportunity to peaceably establish a form of government for their safety and happiness!"

Now, therefore, I do recommend the next, to be devoted by the people of the states to the service of that great and glorious Being, who is the beneficent Author of all the good that was, that is, or that will be, that we may then all unite in rendering unto Him our sincere and humble thanks for His kind care and protection of the people of this country. *(George Washington, #6585 of Encyclopedia of 7700 Illustrations, page 1458)*

Andrew's World View not only depends on a continuing search for the TRUTH but most especially that the TRUTH actually exists and that TRUTH comes to us from God.

Intelligence

Many of us remember the famous Steven Spielberg movie entitled "A. I." (Artificial Intelligence). I remember it well as I saw it in a movie theater in Santa Monica, CA, with my daughter, Addie. It premiered, I think, in the late 90s. If you did not see this pertinent, right up to date warning of the expanding science of creating intelligence machines, I hope you do. I use it regularly in Confirmation class preparation for understanding our relationship with the Divine Creator we call God.

Without giving away the contents of this production I mention here its 'key' beginning. The opening scene shows a boardroom filled with scientists and producers of robots as 'thinking and acting' machines. The dramatic and critical question of the viability and/or destructive power of such a machine that is now, in the new century, being produced, was brought up in that boardroom by one of the perceptive scientists. She said:

I believe we are on very dangerous ground in this project for several reasons:

1. A machine is unable to love.
2. The machine cannot know, as does the human being, that which it is doing.
3. A machine does not have a soul that is, the capacity to actually experience oneself.
4. The machine can only do that which is programmed into it.
5. The programmer or Soul, is the human being from whom the machine is given power to act.
6. The two major questions arise:
   a. What is our Soul?
   b. What creates our Soul which in turn gives power to the robot?"

The above description of the scientist's questions is a paraphrase of the actual words given in the movie A. I. It is clear to each of us that we are aware of ourselves and our ability to process our thoughts. We are not machines, but we are Soul. It is our Soul, spiritual beingness which gives us the power to create and destroy by our own free will. This opens the door to the reality of Evil as well as the reality of Good, or Love, or God. What are they? How do we know and experience their reality? What can we do as choices are presented and we act upon them for the good and for the evil? Well and truthfully directed education will bear out in intelligence with integrity. Again, what is the truth and where does it come from?

Integrity is defined as 'strict adherence to a standard of value or conduct. 2) Personal honesty and independence. 3) Sound thought. 4) Proper direction

People of the past have bequeathed us statements that have become keystone mottos such as this following story about Presidential candidate Henry Clay: "History declares that Henry Clay was about to introduce a certain bill in Congress when a friend said, 'If you do, Clay, it will kill your chance for the presidency.' 'But is the measure, right?' Clay asked, and on being assured it was right, said, 'I would rather be right than be president.' (Encyclopedia of 7700 Quotations)

Before WWII, Nora Waln wrote a book exposing Hitler and his Nazi plotters. The manuscript, *Reaching for the Stars*, was intercepted in the German mail on its way to an American publisher. She fled to London, re-wrote the book from memory and sent copies to Heinrich Himmler, the Nazi hangman.

Himmler took vengeance by imprisoning seven of the author's anti-Nazi friends. Ms. Waln came back to Germany in 1939 and offered her life for the freedom of her friends. Himmler offered to empty a whole prison if she would re-write the book to make Hitler appear good. In refusing she said, "I am willing to forfeit my life, but not my beliefs." (Encyclopedia of 7700 Quotations)

The Keys

As previously mentioned in my friend Andrew's testimony, a World View becomes integrated with our own experiences and learning. We can only see the world around us as per our experiences of it and that which informs those experiences. Any changes in such a world view could only come from further enlightenment. The key to any world view, if it has accuracy, must depend on the truth that informs that view. Any form of deceit or inaccuracy or half-truth could and would inevitably distort the picture. So, we search for the KEYS of the truth and correct the mistakes of the distorted. This is called discernment. This begs the question in that it assumes a rightful and wrongful way of trying to reach a, or the TRUTH that does exist. Distortion here means an inaccurate and misleading account, such as that the world is flat.

It is important that I begin with a simple example of a world view which I share in this collection of documents. I can only enter any discussion or debate from a shared but also personal point of view. Push back or more wise input is welcome!! In a climate these days of wide divergence of opinion and philosophies about TRUTH we recognize the need for solutions to many problems and issues. We seek keys of Truth and hope to rise to a higher level of understanding, and thereby, at least reasonable solutions at the other side of the debate at hand. Even if there are only two individuals duking it out in the ring, the observers are numerous.

The outcome of the match clearly affects all the observers as well as the entire populace. This is why we can safely depend on the view of the wider populace. Thereby the process of voting. Can we rise from our discussions and experiences with a clearer picture of that which brought us into the ring in the first place? A bigger question would be, why are we having such a discussion in the first place? Could it have been handled differently? Is there an ultimate battle between the Good and the Evil? Is there a reality known as The Good, the Truth, the correct answers? Wrong answers as well as right: is Evil a reality? How might Evil distort the truth? What helps the dilemma?

Required in one of my under-graduate philosophy courses was the reading and discussion of the book *History as Myth* by Laura E. Cruz and William Frihoff. I can't recall the name of the course except that it was in the category ethics, law, and historical perspective. This course sought systematic research in pursuit of the facts and Truth. In essence the author of *History as Myth* points out that history is a matter of factual happenings but then recorded by human interpretation. Here is where the problem lies.

Human observance is tainted by or added onto by opinion. What is the opinion and from whence does it emanate? For example, two cars collide at an intersection. Observers surrounding the happening view it from a variety of angles or perspectives. The drivers of the cars also have perspective on how, why, and what happened? So, where do the facts and the Truth enter into this situation? Hence, history is interpreted according to the observer. Where do we go from there? We must draw upon the actual facts of the situation such as the weather, condition of the road, condition of the drivers and so forth. How do we arrive to at least a reasonable conclusion?

As I said in my introduction, the writings here may, at best, help us in this journey we know as our lives, or better said, our Being. At worst, my own observations and actual practice of living are way off track and in need of correction. I've learned that I need a lot of help! One conclusion, for me, over time, has been BUT BY THE GRACE OF GOD! Can this be true?

We can ask if or not this collection of stories of real experiences be interpreted differently than I have perceived them? I look for feedback from anyone concerned with my considered conclusions. My own search for truth requires corrective, new, and more thorough insights for positive conversation and further growth. Of course, our individual interpretations of ideas and events beckon further light. Again, these accounts are as observed with no embellishments. Names of some personalities have been changed 'to protect the innocent' – the privacy of any involved.

Since the beginning of school for me, my dad would watch the clock and predict, every time I went out the door, that I would return within a few minutes to get something of importance that I had left behind. He would say to me with some exasperation, "George, think before you leave!" In other times of conversation, he would remind me that it would help if I planned this important journey of going to school to prepare my stuff ahead of time and save myself from the anxiety and unnecessary time and energy spent.

To this day, I continue to have such trouble, especially with my keys. I've learned, over time and experience, to make an ongoing list of things to be done and also to try to accomplish the most important things first, or at least as soon as possible. In this effort, the anxiety of procrastination is minimized and even eliminated. The most important, often difficult tasks need to be done for both peace of mind as well as more restful times in the midst of it all.

Ever since those earlier years, I have enjoyed and pursued the study of philosophy. It became most interesting for me to learn how and why we are able to best utilize our thinking abilities and thought processes. During those earlier years, my mom bought a Bible for me. She simply said to me that reading its contents would be a most helpful resource for me. Mom never said another word about that gift. She left the rest for me to figure out for myself. The only other piece of this matter was that she made sure that I was signed up for Sunday School at our local Episcopal Church. Thank you, Mom and Dad!

With such keys in my upbringing, I was led to my undergraduate study and love for Philosophy and Western Civilization. The rest is now history. In the New Testament, there is a place in the Holy Gospels where onlookers, the curious, and the disciples themselves were asked by Jesus a key and important question: "What are you looking for?"

When I found myself confronted by that question, the answer, for me, came to mind: Truth. What is the truth? My search for the truth has been my goal from very early on. In reading the Bible, so very much has been revealed to guide me in this pursuit. Among the many key responses from Jesus to my questions was this: So said Jesus: "Seek and ye shall find. Knock and the door will be opened. Ask and ye shall receive."

To me, and to millions upon millions of others in this same pursuit, the key has been to seek and to ask. Keys are instruments to doors in which we enter to find something; to start something; to remember something forgotten; to enter for whatever reason, another place. Our primary hope in life is to open the doors that lead us to a better place.

In my study of Epistemology (the pursuit of knowledge), I met many thinkers with many ideas of searching for the truth. Many of these ideas converge and many go in divergent directions. Here is where keys become critical. If there indeed is truth to be found, some keys will get us there, and some may not. In my experiences during this lifetime, I opened many doors in my search. Here is where the search became both more and more exciting as well as often-times frustrating and even frightening. There were also those wonderful and exciting moments of eureka, those wonderful discoveries of triumph! As more than one philosopher has said: "The more I know, the less I know." As we continue together in an honest, humble, and trustworthy pursuit together, I expect that such truth will surface and hope will follow.

In these writings, much of my search is revealed with hope still appearing as a reality and growth the outcome! I still think of the greatest of the philosophers, Socrates, shortening his life by consuming the poison Hemlock, nobly and humbly saying to his friends and students: "I hope I have not led you astray." But yes, Socrates believed that which he set out to teach.

Thus far in my life, the great Mystery of God bears out in all of our experiences. The great St. Augustine, after a long and searching life, said on his deathbed: "I have not rested until I have rested in Thee, O Lord."

1919

1967

"Failed Communication"

On a visit to a friend's home, I noticed the alarm system at the entrance. In bold print, it read: FAILED COMMUNICATION. Thinking that something terribly wrong had happened, I immediately called attention to it. "What happened? Was there a break-in not reported?" My friend's normally witty and humorous response was: "Fear not! I just need to remember to reconnect it to the power source!" He also, being of the clergy, appropriately answered with a theological point. A Power Source! Of course, we know that electricity is everywhere but unless we harness it and then connect into it, we have little to no use of it. In theology we say that God is everywhere but unless we come to at least some information and connection to such power there is not all that much we can do without it. We are grateful to our own Benjamin Franklin of over one hundred years ago for harnessing electric power for all of us. Society has moved ahead exponentially because of that connection.

Obviously, nothing works without being connected to its rightful and direct power source. The other more immediate and most important matter to consider is how and for what reasons do we utilize our newly found power? This becomes a matter of philosophy, and more importantly ethics. There needs to be good reason and principles upon which we utilize the power we have discovered. PRINCIPLE in ethics is an elusive term needing clear definition in order to make it useful. The point of principles is that they are of the Truth and are needed and used for our good. Such principles are given in order to guide us in our decision-making processes, requiring our best solutions for our safety, advancement, and even our very survival. Principle is much different than the electricity we have discovered in that it cannot be defined in material terms.

The idea and reality of Pure Love, for example, is non-material but its reality guides us exponentially in the material realm in which we exist. This becomes a spiritual matter in need of in-put and direction. All of our decisions must be made according to our Spiritual Nature. So, the question remains, What is our spiritual nature? Where do we go for these answers and how do we respond?" Physical emotion is not enough to answer the questions of love and all matters of Agape, Philios, and Eros need guidance from such a spiritual realm. Thus, PRINCIPLE is defined as 1. A fundamental truth, law, or postulate. 2a. A rule code of behavior. b. Moral or ethical standards in general: integrity. 3. An underlying or established rule or policy. 4, A scientific law underlying the working of natural phenomena or mechanical processes. 5. A PRIMARY OR ORIGINAL SOURCE.

My next immediate theological response and question to the initial question of a failed alarm system is, why would the designer of this equipment use such an elusive remark to warn you of its failure to function? Failed communication? Couldn't it more simply have said something like, need to plug-in, malfunction, or "reconnect to power source?'" But "failed communication?" It seems that the designer is either using his or her good sense of humor, or maybe trying to raise our education to a higher standard? More often than not the simply stated solution is the most helpful one. God is our power source. Electricity is a power source. Nature is a power source. Why don't we make plans to go to the source and ask? Good idea!

Communication, of course, is our means of reaching each other in an understandable way. If we are not on some kind of common ground, we are limited to our ability or inability to communicate with one another and thereby faulty, or even failed, communication. What is it that brings us to common ground so that we can not only understand one another, but also be able to grow together in greater comprehension of the Truth? What is our power source? That is the key question!

TRUTH, although a non-physical thought must exist as love and principle obviously exist. We cannot in and of ourselves invent these ideas but somehow receive or tap into them via our experiences of them. Although such truth can exist within and around us it is that other spiritual reality that brings us into focus. It gives us power because it is real. What is TRUTH? Where does come from... WHY? It is that Spiritual Power that animates our thinking and gives us the ability to Communicate, exist together with meaning, common purpose, survival, and healthy advancement.

"Perhaps the best-known satellite transmission set-up is the Intel-Stat, run by the privately owned Communications Satellite Corporation (COMSTAT) of 91 individual nations." (Since this publication, 1984 advancement in such technology has far outdistanced itself already and this is a matter of study and concern over our ability to provide ethics and principles to it.) The article continues, "Inaugurated in 1965, the COMSTAT system provides over sixty countries with everything from TV and phone calls to computer data, weather and news reports. With 4,000 simultaneous circuits in each of its seven orbiting satellites, voice and data transmission, as well as television link-up, are possible around the world." (Encyclopedia of 7700 Quotations)

The following illustration is being placed here because of a critical dilemma facing our own society in current history. The crisis involves the idea of freedom upon which we have evolved as a nation. It is becoming more and more clear that the many principles upon which we have evolved are now not only being questioned but also being eliminated for alternate ways of thinking and going forward. The question now being forwarded for debate is again from what or from whom do we find the TRUTH? Is there possibility for debate? History has shown how societies have come and gone because of both failed communication as well as loss of honest, rightful, legitimate search for the TRUTH.

Western Collapse

I believe that it is critically important to note here a prediction of the collapse of the society we now know as Western Civilization. I believe that it is primarily due to our losing touch with our basic source of knowledge, and that is the Creator, or should we more easily say the Truth? Over and over throughout history, the source of the TRUTH has been replaced by philosophies which have lost touch with that base of TRUTH whom we refer to as God. Again, it is our spiritual nature which is at stake. Our society today falls again into danger due to opposing philosophies such as Dialectical Materialism vs. the idea of freedom. That idea is believed by Theology to come from its source whom we know as God.

The philosophy of Dialectical Materialism argues that our basic ethics and principles are not from some other source such as belief and Trust in a God. So, who or what is God? Is there a source from whom all TRUTH comes? Is the idea of freedom a prime principle which is given to us by such a Creator whom we refer to as God? If a Divine Creator is real, our belief system is dependent upon a Theology rather than a philosophy of Atheism as promoted by Dialectical Materialism. In the democracies of Western Civilization, it is believed that the idea and principles of Freedom come to us from God. Our Western Civilization was built upon a belief in God and thereby a spiritual realm above the material realm in which we live and grow.

According to Malcolm W. Brown of the New York Times (Circa, 1985):

> There is cautious but growing optimism among Soviet and East European leaders that the long unfulfilled Marxist prediction of the spontaneous collapse of Western capitalism may finally be at hand.
>
> Communist predictions during past economic crises that the collapse of the West was imminent proved UNFOUNDED, so the language currently in use is "restrained." But leading economists in the Soviet Bloc leave no doubt that they believe the current economic crisis in the West is qualitatively different from earlier ones, and that it will be vastly different from earlier ones, and that it will be vastly more destructive to Western economic and political traditions than any of its predecessors. (Encyclopedia of 7700 Quotations)

Epigram
* "History repeats itself" - (English Proverb)
* "History teaches us that man learns nothing from history." (Martin Hegel, Philosophy of Dialectical Materialism)
* "Those who refuse to learn from history are condemned to repeat it." (George Santayana)

Why Rome Fell
In his book, *The Decline and Fall of the Roman Empire* (1987), Edward Gibbon lists the following reasons for that fall:

1. The rapid increase of divorce: the undermining of the dignity and sanctity of the home, which is the basis of human society.
2. Higher and higher taxes and the spending of public money for free bread and circuses for the populace.
3. The mad craze for pleasure; sports becoming every year more exciting and more brutal.

4. The building of gigantic armaments when the enemy was within: the decadence of the people.

5. The decay of religion — faith fading into mere form - losing touch with life and becoming impotent to guide the people.

Do these five reasons (among many from THE FALL OF ROME) tell us anything about our current national situation? - Baptist Message (Encyclopedia of 7700 Quotations).

    * "Seek and know the TRUTH and the TRUTH will set you free." - Saint Paul.

Communication
1) The act of communicating.
2) The exchange of ideas, messages, or information.
3) A system of communicating.
4) The art and technology of communicating

Epistemology
The study of how humans are able to communicate with one another. Such a study has been the search of philosophers, theologians, and reasoners throughout history.

Free Will
The ability and gift to think for oneself as per whatever higher source enables us to do so. The Holy Bible calls this higher source "God".

Tyranny

1) A government where the ruler has absolute power.
2) The unjust or cruel exercise of power.
3) A state of severity: rigor.

Freedom

1) The state of being free of constraints
2) a. Political independence. b. Possession of political and civil rights
3) Free Will
4) The spiritual ability to think for oneself

What are the ethics and principles that give us the ability and freedom to communicate? Where do they come from? How are they revealed? Are there impediments that thwart or get in the why of our ability to think for ourselves? What are the Sources of our ability to think for ourselves?

"A Homiletic: Attempt

at Communicating a Theology"

Way back in junior high school, now called middle school, I received a humbling but effective comment from a fellow classmate. He said that my oral presentation on the assigned book I was reading was okay, but could have been better. There was no way, at that time, that I could have done any better. On the other hand, my classmate honored me by saying that after listening, he thought of ways that he himself could make a better presentation. It was also my feeling that everyone in that class was terrified by the assignment of giving an oral presentation in front of both the teacher as well as their peers. We were all pretty much in the same boat. This was a difficult and new challenge! The challenge was clearly helpful, at least in the attempt to move each of us into a new and better place in our learning journeys.

As an aside, I need to mention here that the change for me from junior high school to middle school was disconcerting because the definition of terms was easily misinterpreted or misunderstood. Being in junior high school seemed to mean that one was well on his way to the big guys: smarter, grown-up, freer, and on the way to a determined path of success. Middle school seemed to mean that we were half-way there. That was a discouraging thought to me. I still wonder what others might think about this. Please let me know! Come to find out that each successful or failed stage in life brought new challenges and new hurdles to reach. Life's journey is hopefully a series of challenges towards some thoughtfully designated goal. The goal is simply to do our best in order to be the best we can be. Why? is the question to be sought and answered.

If anyone told me early on in my journey that I would one day be required to present at least one speech a week on such a probing topic as God I would have balked and ran in the other direction. No way could this possibly be close to anything I could accomplish in life. To be honest with you and me, I realize now that I still have a long way to go. However, I am thoroughly joyed that I can at least keep trying. My trusted friends, teachers, and loved ones continue to be my resource as they prod me on, one way or the other. The challenge is positive and the resources are numerous and continuously hopeful.

May I indulge now in a brief homily as an example of some progress, and the continued need for pushback and help to do better. Just to note here, that my dear friend, colleague, mentor, and teacher, Fr. Howard Olsen (a brilliant, seasoned priest and preacher) said to me soon before he entered into the eternal realms, "George, if only I could get into the pulpit one more time! I had a glimpse of the other side!"

Most Ministers and Priests learn in Seminary that an effective homily requires deeply felt and studied preparation. It also needs to be understood by those who are listening. Most of us, in trepidation, began the homily long before implementation. How about a lifetime of learning and renewal all along the way? For the coming week's presentation the preacher usually reads the lessons appointed directly after lunch and a nap on Sunday afternoon. The process begins there as ideas and comprehension begins to flood in and then processes over the coming days. Hopefully something of value comes forth. But by the Grace of God and dependence on that Grace a product is in hand. The terror of having to effectively make that presentation never goes away. "Dear Lord, help!" Miraculously, something happens!

Knowing that my classmates from junior high school were being prepared for their ongoing journey it is comforting and hopeful to know that we are all in the same boat. Whatever profession, enterprise, or challenge we meet in life, there were, and are, basics to continue to guide us along the way.

There is a set of readings in the Holy Bible which is followed on many of the Christian denominations every three years on the Fourth Sunday of Epiphany. These readings of the entire and organized set of Bible Readings are the Bible followed throughout every three years. These readings are preceded by a prayer called the Collect which enters our thought into the essence of those readings. On the Fourth Sunday of the Epiphany (meaning the light) we are taught that "God governs all things in Heaven and on Earth." We continue to pray for God's help and guidance in understanding this Governance.

Lately, again, it was brought to my mind that my contributions to charities need again to be reviewed. This coincides with the annual task of filling out tax returns. And as a reminder, this should not be one's motivation for charity and the breaks one gets from giving to charities. One of my New Year's Resolutions is to prioritize this effort. For most of us, the charities we support usually have some kind of personal awakening due to our participation, passion for, and desire to help in some way. For example, among my choice of charities is the Smile Train, which sends physicians around the world to do corrective surgery on children born with deformed facial structures, such as the cleft palette. These children are brought to a beautiful smile. Another is Covenant House, devoted to helping young people out of dire social circumstances such as drug overdose, homelessness, and little to no hope for a productive future. Also, having prayed for a young firefighter who lost his life saving an elderly woman in a wheelchair unable to escape the fire consuming her home. There are so many circumstances which call for love, courage, bravery and one's life put on the line to help others to safety.

In the first reading from the "Book of the Prophet Micah," it is pointed out that the supposedly true believers and followers continued to fall away, go their own mistaken way, and head into a destructive way. *(Micah 6:1-8)* It concludes with, "O mortal, what is good; and what does the Lord require of you but to do justice, and to love kindness, and to walk humbly with your God."

In Psalm 15, we are asked about how we may or may not be dwelling in God's presence. It requires, again, our obligation to God's Will and God's Law. In *I Corinthians 1:28-3,1* we are reminded of how our own self-proclaimed wisdom is weak and even mistaken, and that without God's "seeming to some as foolish ways" are the actual answer to our problems. I refer you again to reading this pertinent passage.

The Holy Gospel for that Sunday is the Beatitudes. The Beatitudes were presented by Jesus to his frightened, wondering, by-and-large normal followers (most uneducated) that He is teaching them Truth. Here is what He said to them at that particular time of their and our faith journey:

> When Jesus saw the crowds, He went up the mountain; and after He sat down, His disciples came to Him. Then He began to speak, and taught them, saying: "Blessed are the poor in spirit, for theirs is the kingdom of heaven. Blessed are those who mourn, for they will be comforted. Blessed are the meek, for they will inherit the earth.

Blessed are those who hunger and thirst for righteousness, for they will be filled. Blessed are the merciful, for they will receive mercy. Blessed are the pure in heart, for they will see God. Blessed are the peacemakers, for they will be called children of God. Blessed are those who are persecuted for righteousness sake, for theirs is the kingdom of heaven. Blessed are you when people revile you and persecute you and utter all kinds of evil against you falsely on my account. Rejoice and be glad, for your reward is great in heaven, for in the same way they persecuted the prophets who were before you. *(Matthew 5:1-12)*

Dr. Scott Peck, in his book *The Road Less Traveled* (often referred to in my compositions) reminds us that, "We are spiritual beings on a spiritual journey." In other words, our lives are determined by our spiritual nature and actions. A recent Bishop of Rome (I think it was Pope John Paul) was asked by a devoted follower where Heaven is. He replied that "Heaven is a state of being." In other words, where you are at any given time between Heaven and Hell. Some of the Saints have seen a glimpse of Heaven in what is called a Beatific Vision. I've had friends in my lifetime who have described their glimpses of Heaven. In charity, the goal is to guide the lives of those who hurt towards that glimpse of Heaven.

It was the famous St. Augustine of Hippo who having traveled through his life in search of answers proclaimed at the end of his life: "I have not rested until I rest in Thee, O Lord."

"The Bus Stop"

Standing at the bus stop directly in front of the Seminary in which I was re-siding and studying, I was waiting for the next bus to the center of Philadelphia. There at the bus stop, I was approached by a man in normal clothes who asked me if I was a student in the school adjacent to the bus stop. "Yes!".He pro-ceeded to tell me that he has something wonderful to share with me. He said that he knows the way to lots of money, mansions, boats, women, and anything else I may want. In the distance, I could see the bus approaching. I told him, "Thank you, but I need now to take the approaching bus towards Philly. (Phil-adelphia – "place of brotherly love"). The man handed me a note with his ad-dress and invited me to his place of promises. The invitation was for two days later on Saturday at noon.

Always curious but now annoyed, I decided to follow up on the call. Being young and naïve, I didn't think I needed any backup in case of trouble. The man seemed harmless, of slight build, and kindly with a broken English accent. What harm could there be? My curiosity wanted to see whatever this guy had up his sleeve. What could he want from a young man attending a Christian school?

His third-floor apartment was only two blocks from the Seminary near the campus of the University of Pennsylvania. It was one of those very attrac-tive Philly row house apartments common throughout the outskirts of the city. Walking to and then finding the address, I boldly climbed the several stairways to the top floor apartment, and there to greet me was the guy from the bus stop. He was still dressed in the same normal shirt and pants attire. He dressed like an average American young man.

He ushered me through two entrance rooms straight away, each divided by multi- colored beads hanging from door frame to floor. Then a sharp turn to the right was another beaded entrance into "the sacred area." Many candles were burning around a replica of Buddha. He bowed, I followed suit, and then the guy repeated the same mantra he announced at the bus stop three days earlier. "Ask Buddha and he'll give you anything you want – big houses, lots of money, boats, women – anything you want!" I was speechless but wanted to say that these were not the things I was looking for, especially from Buddha.

I wanted to share my own Christian experience about the things we're called to seek in this lifetime. Mind you, I'm not averse to many of life's toys, vacations, and having fun - as long as they are placed in their proper perspectives. In my speechless stance he proceeded to ask me to send others to him and bring money to the Buddha so that their wishes may be granted. I asked him, "How much money should we bring?" He said that, "The more you bring, the more wishes will be granted." I sheepishly and politely excused myself and never returned to that place, nor did I ever see that guy again at the bus stop or anywhere else. Perhaps one day we can finish that loose ended conversation here on Earth or in Heaven. It was clear to me that this guy was abusing the Buddha and that genuine Buddhists would be appalled with this story.

I always taught my children that true religion is the gift from God. Whoever follows the love of God in search of Truth is practicing pure religion wherever it exists and however it teaches. There is another applicable story telling of similar values that I had discovered I discovered from that infamous bus stop in front of the Seminary there in Philadelphia. It is about a businessman in Illinois who was CEO of the world's largest hinge manufacturing company. They called him Big Gus Braun. He was invited to the local Lion's Club with the hope by some that he might join.

When it became his turn to be introduced to the members, he picked up the small Bible that he had in his pocket and said that this was his primary guide for making decisions. He said that if he could serve God by joining the Club he would join. The club spokesperson said that he had never heard such a requirement from a prospective member. The usual waiting period for acceptance to this club was a month for members to deliberate. Big Gus was not only received as a member but asked if he would add the dimension of chaplain to the organization. Gus leaned forward in his chair and speaking resolutely said, "I will accept only if I can be chaplain to all of you regardless of your Religious or non-religious affiliations." His new companions in this worthy organization known as the Lion's Club appreciated how Gus took genuine interest in each of them and the club's charitable endeavors.

One day, he visited a member who had just suffered a stroke. At the end of the visit, his friend, with tears in his eyes, said, "Dear Jesus, Gus tells me that I can go directly to you. You know how bad I've been and I'm not happy. Can you give to me what Gus has got?" [Paraphrased from Encyc. Of 7700 Quotations]

In *John 14:6*, Jesus stated that "No one comes to the Father except through me." This means that all will one day come to know that He is the One He claims to be. During the 2000-year history of Christianity, many have interpreted *John 14:6* as Jesus pronouncing that only Christians will go to Heaven. First of all, Jesus was not a Christian, he was raised in the Hebrew faith and knew it well. It wasn't his intention to form a new religion except to better interpret, enhance and correct the mistakes of his own as well as the ongoing problems facing the entire human race. At age twelve, he entered the Holy Temple in the midst of the chief priests, scribes and pharisees and instructed them in their mistakes of interpretation of the law.

He summed up the problem with the "Summary of the Law and the Prophets." "Love the Lord your God with all your heart, and mind, and soul, and love your neighbor as yourself." For any doctrine of Christian history to pronounce the exclusivity of this one of many religious expressions is simply wrong. Jesus said, "Where your treasure is, there will be your heart also."

A principled proverb could rightfully say: "Try not taking offence at the frown of another. It is most likely a hurt being experienced in need of healing forgiveness, and a simple, genuine, understanding smile."

Isaiah 6: 4-10

Isaiah 43: 26 – 28

"But by the Grace of God.

Thanks be to God!

"The Red Cadillac"

Speaking of "keys", I vividly recall the gift of a new red Cadillac, given to me by a parishioner. way back in the late 1980s, when I was the Rector of Trinity Parish in Milford, Massachusetts. Blanche Meldonian heard that I needed a car because the "Old Faithful" Chev was failing rapidly. Blanche, then being mostly home bound, called me for an earlier time of my regular pastoral visitation. Blanche had recently lost her brother due to serious illness. Mike actually died about a year earlier, as he was starting the ignition of his brand new, red Cadillac. I did not know of Mike's exceptional automobile.

Visiting Blanche, following her call for a sooner visit than originally planned, she asked me about my search for a more reliable car. Somehow, she was aware of my malfunctioning car. I explained that I needed a functioning, used car. She said that Mike's car (she didn't say Cadillac) was still in the garage and needed a good home. She said that it would please her and Mike if I took it. She said that it would certainly please them both to know that I would be driving the car to help those in need. So, we proceeded to the garage and, there, to my absolute surprise, was the bright, shiny, new, red Cadillac. Its odometer read just over 30,000 miles.

I was reluctant at first to accept this gift because it was much too expensive a car for a parish priest to be seen driving. After all, I still needed to seek support for the parish. She explained to me that this was part of her support to the parish, that I should take it, and not to fret about what anyone might think. I accepted the needed gift, but for months I kept it in hiding. On parish visits I would park the Cadillac some blocks away and walk to my destination. Furthermore, I hid my face and suit while driving so as not to be recognized. How absurd is that!?

For many years, I drove the luxurious vehicle and enjoyed every minute of it. After a goodly number of years had passed, with many thousands of miles of luxury and fun, it became time for another used vehicle. I was then and again consigned to another second-hand vehicle – a Nissan sold to me by my friend Helena. Actually, she had initially bought that car second-hand, which made it third-hand by the time I bought it from her. Like the Cadillac, that Nissan Altima gave me no problems and many thousands of miles in return. It owed me nothing and served its purpose well!

In the meantime, I kept the red Cadillac for limited use. One day I stopped for two hitchhikers who, come to find out, needed a bite to eat. En route, we stopped for dinner, and I picked up the tab, knowing that they were unable to pay. During that time, they both realized that no key was used to start the car. I proudly told them that for the last couple of years this car no longer needed the key to start it. We then went ahead to a point at which they asked to be dropped off. "Thank you, Mister, for the ride and dinner!"

The very next morning as I went to drive the Cadillac for an errand, it was gone! Apparently, it had been stolen. It wasn't until three months after I reported the theft to the Police that a call came to me that it had been found. It was in an abandoned field several towns away from my home. I was delighted that the Caddy had been found, and for the price of a hundred dollars had it towed home.

The old luxurious and faithful red Cadillac sat in my yard for the next several years. I couldn't part with it! At that time, Tom, a mechanic friend of mine, said that he could probably get it started and running again. He made some adjustments, put some gasoline in the carburetor, as well as into the tank. With no key, he went to start old faithful, and the engine exploded.

Thank God no one was injured, and we all laughed hysterically! Not long after that I had to part with the Red Cadillac. However, the incredible lessons learned from that experience brought me to greater levels of thinking and acting.

"Ministry"

A colleague in the Ministry was traveling to Europe for an Ecumenical conference. Upon his arrival, he was met by a red carpet, band and a slew of officials. Totally unexpected and in humble tone, he asked, "Why all the fuss?" Come to find out, it was the Secretary of State who was expected. The first minister, my colleague, was first to exit the plane as the crew knew he was late for his also seemingly important appointment. Waiving any of the other explanations except that it was announced to the waiting officials that, "The Minister has arrived." The faux pas was handled, but the uproarious laughter of the moment was widely remembered and future arrivals of key people were more carefully vetted and welcomed. Whether renowned by worldwide popularity or lesser known, both were respected folks on the realms on which they were Ministers, prayerfully, for the good of all. As far as the Baptized Christian is concerned all are called to the Ministry. We are called to love and serve one another in the light of the Lord's love for us.

During three years of Seminary following four years of under graduate studies we worked at Biblical Theology: Anthropology; Comparative Religion, Ethical Perspectives; Greek; Hebrew; Ecclesial History; Practical Theology; Regular chapel attendance; and more regular trips to "Mother's". Mother's was the local hangout which kept Piel's Beer in business. Piel's was the cheapest of all beers and all any of us could afford. Mother's was, for many of us, the closest welcome we had in the new world of Seminary, to the real world out there. However, all of us Seminarians had grown up in the real world best, worst rough and tumble. The shock came after graduation and entrance into the American Parish experience. Seminary didn't do all that well in preparing us for Ministry out there. It took many years to connect theology to real life out in the, oftentimes, scary world.

Rev. Howard C. Olsen, Rector of St. Barnabas

Thank God, my Bishop, John Seville Higgins sent me to St. Barnabas Church, Warwick RI to be a curate under the direction of Fr. Howard Olsen. As the good father said, "the curate cures that which the Rector wrecks." The Bishop told me that, "Fr. Olsen is a driver who will work you to the bone... make a good priest out of you... and you'll learn to love him as a brother in Christ." These were five wonderful, formative years. Hard work and much fun in the Parish life well prepared me to go forward.

Father Olsen was a "practical" individual in that his world view was, "Dinner first, followed by education." His social mindedness sent him into the field to care for social needs in the community followed by spiritual care. St. Barnabas Church had a large population of lower income folks and Fr. Olsen brought them along by genuine concern for their well-being. He made sure that everyone knew that God's love for them includes the physical, psychological, social, educational and spiritual nature of each of us. Several low-income housing developments carry his name due to his pro-active involvement. He personally knew all the Rhode Island Governors and community leaders as his presence and voice was heard and respected

Fr. Olsen also talked and drove like a machine gun as he was always needed to be somewhere else sooner than was possible to get there. He spoke through all religious Services in twenty-five minutes, but surely loved High Mass with all the extras such as music, incense, beauty of the outward and visible signs representing what our faith calls the inward and spiritual grace, and fully biblical exploration he worked hard at bringing it all togethering an experiential understanding. Since his homilies were also rapid-fire, we still finished the High Mass in sixty minutes. Everyone so enjoyed this priest of old-time character that the church and parties afterwards were always packed. He was just plain old fun to be with and learn from. If there is something to say about "balance", Fr. Olsen was the epitome.

Years later after beginning my Ministry with Fr. Olsen at Saint Barnabas' I recalled something I learned (one of many things) and I wrote the following brief story to the folks at Grace Church, Oxford, MA.

Reading this statement on a highway billboard made me feel sad. The statement is reportedly provided by the Atheist Society of America. It says to me that if the love of God does not exist there is no hope for our future. My dear friend and mentor Fr. Howard Olsen and I were on our way to a meeting at the Cathedral in Providence sped North on route 195. Laughing the whole way, as usual, we were both suddenly confronted by a huge highway billboard which read ENJOY YOUR CHRISTMAS – SKIP CHURCH! The laughing turned into a conversation as to sending our response to the Atheist Society and to our fellow Christians.

The response invited everyone to church for Christmas for a big surprise if they hadn't been there before. Actually, the traditional experience is so enjoyed year after year at Christmas and totally throughout one's lifetime. A Feast of music, pageantry, smells, bells and all the enjoyment of gifts beyond the asking are given in this experience. Come and enjoy this Feast with us and then let us know what you think. We believe that you will be more than pleasantly surprised and will want to return!

. . .

When we approached the Feast of the Incarnation last month, we could again focus on the awesome power and love of God. I'll never forget the words of Sen John McCain long after his five-yr imprisonment in a six by five foot hole with little light and little food. He said that, "during this time of torture I never lost my faith in God and the promise of Truth, Light and Hope for the future. That peace kept me alive and always hopeful."

The coming of the Christ into our fragile, tiny Earth we call home, historically racked by evil purpose and action, revealed in full measure the long-awaited complete revelation of Light, the Truth, and Hope for our future as Truth is revealed. Because of the birth, life, death and resurrection of Jesus the world has Hope and will never be the same again. The world, in spite of evil, has wonderfully advanced. As we experience the power of God's love, and the intent and purpose of his Will, each of us receive new life and eternal hope.

A long time ago, as a young priest in a new parish, I attended the recovery program sponsored by my first parish. We as Christians are people of the Incarnation (God with us and in us). The parish was called St. Barnabas Church; Barnabas being known as the encourager. I always viewed every parish and the Church, the Sanctuary of the Incarnation. God is Among Us! After attending the first meeting of the recovery, I received so much from it that I kept on going week after week. Recovery is a program for people suffering from phobias. After discovering my own claustrophobia, recovery helped me overcome the fears of such an illness and see the light and the truth in and ahead of it. Healing can and does happen. The program is structured for healing and redemption that only the love of God in us can cure. This program is designed and structured similarly to AA and other self-help groups designed to raise us from the darkness to the light and help each other on our shared spiritual journey.

Jesus was born for us from the eternal realms to show us the way from darkness to the light, then to the truth that extends from here into eternity. Eternity is a place being prepared for each and every one of us beginning here. Along the way, never lose hope as the Light and the Truth are there waiting for us to arrive. I was saddened by a billboard sponsored by the Atheist Society of America set up across the country during the holiday season, which read: Enjoy your Christmas! Skip Church! I hope you had a Merry Christmas! And I hope you have a peaceful New Year!

. . .

After my first five great years in ministry as a Deacon in Warwick I was called to Trinity Church in Milford, Massachusetts. Here began a long and mostly enjoyable seventeen and a half year rectorship. I felt relatively prepared and ventured ahead. After those fruitful years of being deeply involved in the town, new diocese, and parish work, it was also a relief to go ahead into new ventures. Thankfully, due to my years in Milford, I was able to become involved in the newly evolving Hospice Movement. I describe my hospice experiences later in this book.

Those first years in the new experience of being on my own in a new Parish with my wife, Peach, and our one year old son Joel, the fun began. I remembered how Fr. Olsen insisted that my parish secretary needed to be from outside of that parish. The secretary at the new parish had not only been a parishioner but also secretary for many years through several priests saw herself as pretty much knowing everyone and everything about that parish and the Church. Not so, not good and some changes had to be made as soon as possible. As with many organizations, a new priest needs to hire a new secretary. So, the fun began and it wasn't easy for me and long-time parishioners to move ahead in the best ways possible.

At any rate, I went ahead and hired a new secretary. Mary happened to be the best qualified after many interviews, but she was also a youthful and attractive young lady. The buzzing mill began and the gossip went forward. Yes, Mary was youthful, attractive, and very good at the job. It got back to me that the parish women's group had wild imaginations. It must be noted that this parish Women's Group was comprised of ladies beyond the fifty year mark. Word traveled fast that Father Warren was usually, "alone in the parish offices with that young secretary." It took a long time for them to realize, and some probably didn't, that such a working relationship between a priest and his secretary could not, would not, should not, and did not deserve such scrutiny and wild gossip.

It was my prayer that those with the wildest thoughts of impropriety would get some in-depth psychotherapy for themselves. And, of course, those who knew me well, including my wife, family, friends, and colleagues understood the problem had no doubts of the absolute integrity of the situation. In spite of such initial misgivings, Trinity parish grew in many awesome ways with those years of growth and purposeful adventures. A few years after coming to be Trinity's secretary, Mary was married to her lifelong friend. We had to interview new potentials and were so fortunate to have found most qualified people in the years to follow.

Still being in my thirties during those years in Milford afforded me youth, enthusiasm, and much involvement in the parish, the community, and around the Diocese of W. Mass. Also during this time, Addie and Brian came along, and oh what a joy to behold these three children. Being in that area for those eighteen years plus more, gave them a growing up time and place throughout their childhood and school years. After Trinity came more transitions and new journeys. Once asked if I missed Trinity, I was honestly able to say that some things I miss, some things I don't. Some people I miss, and some I don't. It's all part of the joys and pains of being a parish priest. More of those years are shared throughout this book. A sense of humor is necessary and so is a healthy perspective – one of the greatest gifts of God.

CONFIRMED IN MILFORD — Confirmation ceremonies were held in Milford over the weekend at Trinity Episcopal Church. Rev. George H. Warren, rector, and Rt. Rev. Alexander D. Stewart, Bishop of the Diocese of Western Massachusetts, officiated. Candidates receiving confirmation were James F. Barney, Jeffrey L. Barton, Roberta F. Bowen, John C. Desofero, John F. Gethert, Richard S. Gooldrand, Stephen T. Granger, Theresa F. Granger, James Guyette, Sally A. Kirby, Patrick J. Kerin, Christine D. Lann, Ellen R. Luffy, Kenneth A. Morey, Thomas E. Morey, Mary Ann Peroni, Cindy A. Scott, Linda J. Scott, Bruce D. Stanis, John F. Theroux, Carla Turton, Bridget Weaver, John Axom, John D. Urmston, William W. Burler, Ruth A. Sankey, Peter Hadsler, James G. Kirby, Richard W. Cenadella, and Barbara J. Cenadella. A reception was held in the parish hall following the ceremony. (Daily News Photo by John P. Lannish)

The following brief story is on of so many accounts of happenings that often call for further explanation and, or explanations. This particular true story is not unusual but calls up explanations beyond our ability to more fully explain. Please note that cell phones were not yet in use back in the 70s. The following conversation took place with no help from any available scientific gadgets.

"Hi Penny!" I'm calling from Good Shepherd parish in Clinton. You came to mind as I was driving here, so I decided do give you a quick call." "Father Warren, I, this very second got off the phone with Mary-Lou. She told me that you are en route to a clerics meeting in Clinton."

"How did you know to call me? I just got word that my Mom had passed."

On the way to a meeting, Penny Allen suddenly came to mind out of the blue. I sensed an urgency to call her, got to my destination, and called. Immediately after a very important meeting, I headed directly back to the Allen's home to be with them in their painful loss. There is a little used word in the English language known as a conundrum. Conundrum means a riddle or is presented as a complicated problem. Life is chock full of conundrums leaving us often puzzled by why some things happen when they do.

Another word often comes to mind during such conundrums as exampled above. That word is coincidence. Was that a coincidence? Or maybe a deeper purpose and meaning was part of that experience and it so happened for a reason, a purpose in mind. "Who'n mind? Where did it come from?"

Funny?! What Just Happened was the original title I had planned for this book. That title was to describe the purpose and meaning of such a book as this one. The questions have continued to persist throughout history. Is there a God? What might 'God' mean? Is it just chaos that has somehow just found itself together? Is there really such a thing as Truth? Are there experiences we have that seem to have such mysterious outcomes? We keep on going with all the pertinent questions that seem so often to lead to conclusions such as coincidences that indeed there is meaning and purpose or there is no such thing except a crazy thing we call coincidence. This is a conundrum! Is there simply coincidence here, or more, or something else happening?

The definition of coincidence is: "A corresponding happening or incident with seemingly no direct explanation." It just happened that way! The highly esteemed and widely read and followed psychiatrist, Dr. Scott Peck, said in his book *Beyond the Road Less Traveled* that we had come to believe that "the notion of mental telepathy may have some credibility." Why not! I think that persons on the same wavelength may be able to connect distances apart. Peck, in his own research, in our spiritual nature these experiences do happen for all intents and purposes. Such experiences in so many different ways have been observed in my own ministry and many of them are recorded in this volume.

In this book, I wish to share experiences that sometimes defy natural explanation or hand us conundrums that question the simple explanation of coincidence. In other words, there often seems to be a greater purpose or meaning behind our experience of life. It has long been my estimation that we are all together and each of us on a spiritual journey.

A little boy was told by his Sunday School teacher that, "God answers all our prayers." He took this information to heart and soon after at home he looked to the sky from his bedroom window and prayed, "God, if you are there, please show yourself to me so that I can believe my teacher. I hope you are real and that you answer me as Miss Clark said you would." This ten-year-old left that scene with no more thought or question about it, went out to play, and several years flew by.

At age fifteen, the answer to that prayer came to him. A great light beyond imagination but real brought him outside his body into another sense of being' and he recalled the prayer from those years earlier. This very brief experience of the reality of God formed the life, purpose and meaning of the young boy's life! There was never from that point on, any doubt of the answer to the conundrums of each of our lives. And the answer. No, that was not simply a coincidence.

The little boy kept this secret for most of his lifetime, realizing it is a gift meant for all of us at one time or another. Yes, God does answer prayers and is readily available to us with meaning and purpose. I recall here Dr. Peck's comments that he gave on at least one of his lecture topics. Explaining his reasons for having an aversion to religion he describes his first and last experience in Sunday School as a young boy. The teacher had been relating the story of Abraham bringing his only son to sacrifice by lethal stabbing in order to please God. Peck relates how he jumped from his chair and fled the church in escape. Can't blame him or anyone else for that matter after hearing or seeing something out of context and fleeing the scene as in a serious conundrum. Much Later in his practices as a psychiatrist did he find his belief in God; in our "spiritual nature."

"A Case for Moderation"

The Webster's Collegiate Dictionary defines moderation as, "That which is not extreme or excessive." In behavior it is about being temperate. In opinion it means to be careful with and even opposed to radical views or measures. It says that the middle road is sometimes, and probably more often than not, the healthiest one to take. In theology, the term moderation enters into God's unconditional love for us, even when we are at our worst as his obstinate children. Jesus did say to the powerful rulers, the Pharisees, that, "All their rules and regulations without love are meaningless and useless."

It is documented that the Baltimore Sun newspaper conducted a contest inviting contestants to submit replies to the question, "What would you do if you had one more year to live?" The winning contestant was Mary Davis Reed, who answered via a poem:

If I had but one year to live,
One year to help, one year to give,
One year to love, one year to bless,
One year to better things to stress;
One year to sing, one year to smile,
To brighten earth a little while;
One year to sing my Maker's praise,
One year to fill with work my days;
One year to strive for a reward,
When I should stand before my Lord.

I think that I would spend each day,
In just the very same way
That I do now. For from afar
The call may come across the bar
At any time, and I must be
Prepared to meet eternity.

So if I have a year to live,
Or just one day in which to give
A pleasant smile, a helping hand,
A mind that tries to understand
A fellow creature when in need;
'Tis one with me – I take no heed.
But try to live each day He sends
To serve my gracious Master's ends.
(Encyclopedia of 7700 Quotations)

"A Work in Progress: Sometimes we need to make a strong statement!" Here rests a conundrum! What do we do to fight for that in which we believe? Our Faith teaches us that God's Will is to be followed. The above seemingly extreme photos are shown to simply state that our fight must be placed into God's hands and whatever we do we must call on that purpose of God's Holy Will. Peace and Truth must be the goal and the outcome. Yes, each of us must be vigilant and involved in the fight, and how we enter is most important.

It says in Micah chapter four that:

> It shall come to pass in the latter days that the mountain of the house of the Lord shall be established as the highest of the mountains, and shall be raised up above the hills; and peoples shall flow to it, and many nations shall come and say: "Come, let us go up to the mountain of the Lord, to the house of the God of Jacob; that he may teach us his ways and we may walk in his ways and we may walk in his paths." For out of Zion shall go forth the law, and the word of the Lord from Jerusalem.
>
> He shall judge between many peoples, and shall decide for strong nations afar off; and they shall beat their swords into plowshares, and their spears into pruning hooks; nations shall not lift up sword against nation, neither shall they learn war anymore; but they shall sit every man under his vine and under his fig tree, and none shall make them afraid; for the mouth of the Lord of hosts has spoken. For all the peoples walk each in the name of its god, but we will walk in the name of the Lord our God forever and ever. *(Micah 4:1-6ff)*

The photo needs to be viewed with a sense of humor but also with a sense of determination to continue the historic search of civilizations, still en route in a dangerous and sinful world, to find and act on the Truth. Hasn't it been said that a picture is worth a thousand words? Having been both appreciated and criticized for being a priest on a motorcycle in our existing culture, I sense a need to explain the above photo of me and my motorcycle. First of all, I do believe that as old as we might become, one cannot take the boy or girl out of the adult. Some things just don't want to go away! Some of my friends still enjoy jumping out of airplanes. I've read of those who have climbed or want to climb Mt. Everest. Some become jockeys in horse race events or simply love their animal friends throughout life. Since my own horse riding days, I have thoroughly enjoyed the pleasure of motorcycles. At times, needing an excuse, I've proclaimed, "Less gasoline, less material, and helping the environment!" Is it dangerous? Yes! Do I have to be careful? Yes! There seems to be some moderation in the whole enterprise. How it is interpreted is another reason for good discussion!

While raising my children, moderation was a key factor. "Go with your passions; be a good individual; and be careful!" Sometimes being a priest and a dad required much work at balance. To believe in God and practice that faith in a world that often does not, needs some kind of balance and moderation is often required. It is also safe to say here that many ideas and practices that may seem wrong to us are actually not. How and why we use and practice our spiritual journey is the key issue. Again, humble moderation is often needed here.

Yes, we believe as Christ's followers that God loves all of his children and wants the best for each of us. To enjoy living as well as being responsible for one's life is a good thing. This is moderation. At least in my own up-bringing and religious tradition, moderation was important. We believe that Jesus not only had a sense of humor, but also practiced his own sense of moderation as pure love would have it.

He once said to the powerful Pharisees: "I came not to abolish the law but rather to fulfill it. The law of God is Love." Check your Bible again!! Jesus was both human and divine all at once. This is the wonderful Doctrine of the Incarnation. To take on the delicious breeze and warm sunshine has been a thankful joy and pleasure for me. It is feeling alive and well in times of joy and sadness, and in those times of health and illness. Prayer and responsibility are keeping aware of God's love for us and to share such love with one another.

"Close Encounters in Golf"

Games we play are meant to be fun, challenging, and a learning experience, more especially when we exercise them with others. When practiced alone our brains and talents are sharpened. Played with others, important social awareness is broadened and interaction abilities are made better. Whether the games be board, sports, or social play in any number of ways the experience will hopefully make us better people.

I choose to mention the game of golf here because it was significant since my childhood in so many ways. Thanks to my older brothers Jim and Don along with a close to home golf course I was given much to learn. Such learning included normal life experiences, good and bad, as any child in the formative years might receive them.

The first specialty of the golf game is the time given away from the normal routine of responsibilities required for our own stability and a healthful society. Hard work along with rest and relaxation give us the needed balance for heathy, productive life. On the very bright side of the golf game are such things as fresh air; beautiful contours of scenery and greenery; exercise; sunshine and warmth; and the great challenge and satisfaction of doing our best at the game.

However, this is not an easy endeavor as it requires practice; difficult terrain; and intelligent planning. It takes these efforts to be successful and earn rightful satisfaction. Also, on those difficult and 'bad weather' days we need to plan for alternative solutions for our health and well-being. C'est la vie! So, the game of golf can and should be one of those pieces of life utilized to keep ourselves sane and teach those needed lessons of not only survival but a real enjoyment in the balance of living as well.

Having spent my childhood in a small suburb town called Rumford, R. I. I was not only fortunate to have two older brothers to learn from, admire, and follow, but we also had a private Country Club smack in the middle of our neighborhood. Lucky for us the 5th Tee Off, far from the main club house, was our secret entrance onto the course. A huge steel wire fence separated the pristine golf course from the riff raff on the other side. The fence clearly let us know that, "You are not allowed onto the course!!" Understandably the golf course needed to be kept from damage and more especially from the riff raff kids in our neighborhood.

But my big brother Jim and his cohorts didn't pay much attention to the warning except to realize that the course was for golfing only. They wanted to learn how to play golf! So, they brought a shovel to a convenient and secretive place and created a crawl hole under the fence and with yard sale golf clubs crawled onto the forbidden place and learned how to play that game. Theologically it seems that the good and bad managed to collaborate to bring about what ultimately became at least okay. Of course, the problem of Evil is such an elusive topic for theologians, philosophers, sociologists, statesmen, and all concerned with the creation of society itself. Now, back to the golf game!

The latter to became a famous golfer, Betty June Bobel. She lived and grew up in our neighborhood and was our then next-door neighbor. As I understand it, Betty June was one of the collaborators in creating the secret entrance onto the course. My brothers and their friends all became avid golfers. In the meantime, we all became caddies in the exclusive club and learned how to legitimately earn our way to greater avenues in our lives yet ahead of us. Jim became a successful teacher, and businessman. Don became a pilot in the Navy and later an airline pilot. Their friends from that lower to middle class neighborhood had similar stories to share. We were all thankful for that bunny hole in the golf links keep-out fence. We later learned that the keepers of the course were truly our friends and knew all we were up to.

It was an enjoyable and "free time" to be a kid. It was there that we learned how to be trusted friends and also to realize that the older generation were on our side. They were once kids too! The funny thing was to learn that even the Police were on our side of the equation in that they also learned golfing, sledding, skiing and friendships on that same golf course. When they decided to catch up with our antics, they used the occasion for teaching and admonishment. On other times they apparently looked the other way as we were crawling onto the course. And, yes, at the club, owners and members were also quite generous in the understanding and teaching of us kids. From such experiences, we all grow up and become the teachers of those who follow.

"A Parent's Prayer"

One of the most, if not the most important, most crucial responsibility in life is the raising of our children from one generation to the next. In writing this book, I stress this challenge both as a reminder to myself as well as admonishment to my children of challenges and such points of experience that may help in the process. It is for my own as well as their healthful future. The point is "genuine love in pursuit of the Truth is required in this endeavor. I utilize not only my own education and experiences in this effort but also as I can from those whom I believe to be reliable resources of the TRUTH. Here I begin with "A Parent's Prayer" by Abigail Von Buren as given in the *Encyclopedia Of 7700 Quotations.* This prayer is a reminder to me of my own up- bringing.

Newspaper columnist Abigail Von Buren has composed a "Parent's Prayer," in which she stresses the practical side of raising children. Dear Abbey writes:

> Oh, heavenly Father, make me a better parent. Teach me to understand my children, to listen patiently to what they have to say, and to answer all their questions kindly. Keep me from interrupting them or contradicting them. Make me as courteous to them as I would have them be to me. Forbid that I should ever laugh at their mistakes, or resort to shame or ridicule when they displease me. May I never punish them for my own selfish satisfaction or to show my power.

> Let me not tempt my child to lie or steal. And guide me hour by hour that I may demonstrate by all I say or do that honesty produces both trust and happiness.

> Reduce, I pray, the meanness in me. And when I am out of sorts, help me Oh Lord, to hold my tongue.

> May I ever be mindful that my children are children, and I should not expect of them the judgement of adults.

Let me not rob them of the opportunity to wait on themselves and to make decisions.

Bless me with the bigness to grant all their reasonable requests, and the courage to deny them privileges I know will do them harm. Make me fair and just and kind. And fit me, Oh Lord, to be loved and respected and integrated by my children. Amen.

It is so fitting to mention here that our daughter Addie well fits this description to a tee. Watching her raise her beautiful and each very different three children, Owen, Wesley, and Phoebe should be an amazement to me. It isn't! Her mom and her nan were so much the same in this way of raising and teaching our children.

As school, other odd jobs, and girls captured more of my attention the golf game became less important to me. Although, my brothers and other friends actually had the same list of choices and needs, they became good golfers anyway. I always enjoyed an occasional game of golf, but never became more than a hacker. So does life proceed! In the meantime, because of my upbringing, along with many others in our family, my children and grandchildren were introduced to golf and enjoy it today.

This all leads to a significant recent golf game that I recently enjoyed with my son Brian and his friend Mark. They were both excellent golfers but took me along anyway. This was a regularly scheduled day on the course for the two friends who also worked together for a national roofing company. Brian was moving to a new position and location in that company, and this became their last regular game together. Time, job description, and distance became the major issue. So, as Brian invited me to celebrate his new promotion, I was also fortunate to enjoy this particular golf game with him and Mark. Mark had never met me before, nor I him. Obviously, my vocation as a priest was never any part of their conversations on the course or anywhere else.

Mark, as was usual for him, mentioned God continually through the game. He asked for help on each shot and also cursed the outcome whenever it went bad. That was actually the most praying I ever heard all at once in any circumstance or time frame. Now, Mark was a very pleasant and fun person to enjoy. However, his seemingly misinterpretation of prayer was disconcerting but also understandable. My instinct was to somehow do some reasonable teaching on prayer during that game, but I pretty much left my conclusions unsaid. The only observation by Mark would be my own lack of such vocal praying no matter how good or bad the drive, fairway hit, or putt was. It was clear that I was annoyed by my own inability to play golf better but both Brian and Mark were understanding and helpful even as much as I slowed our progress for all of those eighteen holes. Just being together was pleasant, and we certainly enjoyed the day and comradery.

Brian later revealed how proud he was of me for not reacting to Mark's language and seemingly crude acknowledgement of God's presence in that golf game. As crude as the regularly used language in our social milieu has become, somehow, we can and do learn in the teaching and experience the real presence of God in the midst of it all. The reality of genuine prayer can become the outcome of such a game of golf! The fact is that Mark was not knowingly talking to God but just repeating the normal lingo of his experience at this particular time. This time for Mark had nothing to do with the real presence of the Father. This is true in all games such as Golf or anything else we do.

The real test is when we actually experience God's Presence in any situation we're in, be it on the golf course, in church, or wherever it is that we see His love for us in the reality of it all. In chapter forty-three of the *Book of the Prophet Isaiah,* it is related how the indolent Isaiah wandered into the temple of his childhood upbringing and sensed the presence of God for the first time. He was stunned, even shocked, and uttered, "Is that you, Lord? How is it that you are talking to me, a man of unclean lips?" From that moment, Isaiah grew into one of the most profound and influential teachers of all history.

Thank you, Brian, for having me join you for that special golf game! And thank you to my big brother Jim and his friends for digging that bunny hole so that we could all get into the golf game. Many lessons were learned in the mix of it all. So, what lessons might be learned here?

1. Nothing is free except genuine love.
2. There's always so much more to learn.
3. We're all in the same boat or on the same course together
4. There are always choices to be made.
5. What does it mean to grow-up?
6. Is there a compass to follow into the next destination?!

I have always remembered my brother Don's friend passing me on our walk home from school one fateful day. Billy Barr, four years older than me curtly said, "What is this world coming to with you and your friends having to be in charge?" I took that query to heart!

"A Graduating Class- Miss Taylor"

Moving forward into an uncertain future, the graduating class has been thus far prepared for the next phase on the journey of life. The high school student at this time in our history hopes for more education in preparation for a viable vocation of value to oneself and one's purpose in life for the sake of all. In the belief that each of us has a purpose as we enter into many unknowns with the hope of having meaning and more importantly TRUTH in our lives.

Remembering Miss Taylor, my high school guidance counselor, I'll never forget and give grateful thanks to her for a boot in the pants in the middle of the eleventh grade. "Warren, what are you planning to do with your life? Looking at your potential, I see plenty of purpose and meaningful existence ahead of you. But looking at your current work I suggest that you start looking for a job!"

"But, Miss Taylor, I'm hoping to go to graduate school for more preparation and search for a vocation!" "They won't accept you with these current grades! You seem to be having a great time, but you are not studying enough!"

That's all I needed to hear and thanks to this boot in the pants, my efforts to raise those grades to a more than acceptable rating I barely lucked out and found myself accepted into the local state university. Then came the next whammy and new boot in the pants. The college president spoke to the newly arriving class. He said the following: "Everyone look at the person on your left and your right. They are not going to make it through this first year!" The new students on my right and left were looking at me.

I am grateful again for that new perception of my reality. Again, I was fearfully seeing myself on the outside, looking in, with much regret that I had not worked harder. I buckled down and went to work. With much prayer and extended effort, new horizons were presented. At last the realization and prayer and concerted effort made all things possible. Thank God!

At a recent high school class reunion, I was invited to open our festivities with a prayer. With that invitation I recalled my Bishop John Seville Higgins calling all of us candidates for Holy Orders to a meeting toward this new stage in each of our journeys. The Bishop opened his comments by saying that, "You must learn how to pray spontaneously from the heart." He said that the Lord promised to his first followers that the Holy Spirit would fill their minds, hearts and souls with whatever words they needed to speak, act and follow.

Those disciples were simple, mostly poor, working folk that He approached with His words, love and acceptance. His approach was: "I will make you fishers of men." "Drop your empty net into the water on the other side of the boat. I will fill it!" There was more fish than they could handle in that net. "Come, follow me!"

The prayer at the Class Reunion of 2017 was the following:

> It is my understanding that most religious traditions teach us that we are to "Give thanks at all times and in all places. Oftentimes such a teaching is very difficult to understand in a world laden with earthquake, fire, and flood; disease, and all kinds of dysfunctional societies, behaviors and situations. Yet, we are still called to give thanks!
>
> Heavenly Father, we give thanks at all times and in all places. Thank you for our fragile island HOME we call Earth. For our wonderful and fragile nation which believes in and teaches about the FREEDOM we enjoy… For our families, friends, neighbors and colleagues who labor together for the good of all! For our teachers and mentors at East Providence High School who gave their best to guide us into a productive path; For the understanding that each of us is important in the creation of the whole; for each other, and for a brief lifetime leading us to a greater plan given by a loving God who knows and loves each of us intimately. Thank you Lord for all your gracious gifts from which we learn and grow on this eternal journey.

At this particular reunion we were blessed by the presence of two of our teachers, Mr. George Donovan, and Mr. Kenneth Waiker (pronounced Walker). Mr. Donovan was not one of my teachers but was lovingly respected by those who studied under his guidance. I was able to mention that Mr. Waiker once placed my chewing gum on my nose for the extent of one History class. He did warn us ahead of time. Also, in huge letters at the front of our classroom was the statement: "Do it today because tomorrow never comes!" How blessed I was to see Mr. Waiker at my ordination to the priesthood. We exchanged a heartfelt hug at the class reunion.

A wonderful and pertinent prayer in the Anglican Book of Common Prayers is as follows:

> Accept, O Lord, our thanks and praise for all that you have done for us. We thank you for the splendor of the whole creation, for the beauty of this world, for the wonder of life, and for the mystery of love.
>
> We thank you for the blessing of family and friends, and for the loving care which surrounds us on every side.
>
> We thank you for setting us at tasks which demand our best efforts and for leading us to accomplishments which satisfy and delight us.
>
> We thank you for those disappointments and failures that lead us to acknowledge our dependence on you alone.
>
> Above all, we thank you for your son, Jesus Christ; for the truth of his Word and the example of his life; for his steadfast obedience, by which he overcame temptation, for his dying, through which he overcame death; and for his rising to life again in which we are raised to the life of your kingdom.
>
> For all that is gracious in the lives of men and women revealing the image of Christ...
>
> For minds to think, and hearts to love, and hands to serve...
>
> For health and strength to work and leisure to rest and play...
>
> For the brave and courageous, who are patient in suffering and faithful in adversity...
>
> For all valiant seekers after truth, liberty and justice...
>
> For the community of saints in all times and places...
>
> And, above all, we give you thanks for the mercies and promises given to us through Christ Jesus, our Lord.
>
> (slightly modified from the Book of Common Prayer, pg. 837)

And this prayer for our nation, lest we may forget:

Almighty God, who hast given us this good land for our heritage: We humbly beseech thee that we may always prove ourselves a people mindful of thy favor, and glad to do thy Will. Bless our land with honorable industry, sound learning, and pure manners. Save us from violence, discord, and confusion; from pride and arrogance, and from every evil way. Defend our liberties and fashion into one united people the multitude brought hither from many kindreds and tongues. Endue with the spirit of wisdom those to whom in thy Name we entrust the authority of government, that there may be justice and peace at home, and that, through obedience to thy law, we may show forth thy praise among the nations of the earth. In the time of prosperity, fill our hearts with thankfulness, and in the day of trouble, suffer not our trust in thee to fail; all which we ask through Jesus Christ, our Lord.

I recall here a disastrous abandoned warehouse in Worcester, Massachusetts a few years back. There were six people illegally residing in the facility. A three-alarm fire call was sounded. The initial respondents were told of the residents trapped inside and the six responders immediately went in to save the potential victims. There was no hesitation for these brave souls to save those inside. They were all saved except for one of the firefighters, fondly known as Tim. This firefighter, with a wife and children left behind was Lt. Timothy Jackson.

Another striking reminder was the pickup truck driver who immediately stopped on the Potomac River Bridge soon after an airline flight crashed into it on takeoff and dropped into the icy, winter swept river. This regular human being dove into the ice strewn water and saved three of the drowning passengers.

May we not forget the untold number of good people who, with no hesitation, responded to the attack on the Twin Freedom Towers on 9/11, 2001. May we not forget all the first responders who always and faithfully came to our aid in the midst of the fateful Covid-19 Epidemic. The real heroes and Saints are with us all of the time!

May we not forget a man known as Jesus of Nazareth, who 2000 years ago spent and forfeited his entire life to save us from all that tends to destroy our precious lives. History is filled with spoken and unspoken stories of the goodness in human beings who have been propelled into harm's way only to react with love and concern for others.

Many of us find it very difficult to see teaching that tries and does persuade unsuspecting young and old alike to spend their lives to destroy the great values we share as Americans. I've tried to teach my children, grandchildren, friends, congregants and as many as possible with the message that we are a good people. The basic system of our nation is designed to give each of us the ability and the freedom to be the best that we can be and do the best that we can do. We thank you for the men and women who have made this country strong. They are models for us, please continue to inspire us. We thank you for the torch of liberty which has been lit in this land. It has drawn people from every nation, though we have often hidden from its light, Enlighten us!

We thank you for the faith we have inherited in all its rich variety. It sustains our life, though we have been faithless again and again. Renew us. Help us, O Lord, to finish the good work here begun. Strengthen our efforts to blot out ignorance and prejudice, and to abolish poverty and crime. And hasten the day when all our people, with many voices in one united chorus, will glorify your Holy Name. *(Book of Common Prayer)*

"The Dreamer: A Message To My Family on the Occasion of My Eightieth Birthday"

It all began on the fifth of November, 1941 in Pawtucket, Rhode Island. It was one month and two days before the Japanese attack on Pearl Harbor, the event that propelled our nation into World War ll. I remember it well, not because I was there and experienced it, but because the news and videos played out the event many times in my young life. For the first four years of my life our country was at war. I do have memories of the latter part of those years of members of my family that served and people that my family knew that served as well. Thankfully, my family members returned safely but others were memorialized in ceremonies that dedicated streets and other landmarks to their sacrifice. In short, that war and the experiences related to it have had a profound influence on me for the rest of my life.

My school years would now stretch from 1947 to 1959. During that period of time I was known to be a dreamer. As a matter of fact, my fifth grade teacher Miss Gendron sent a note home to Mom declaring that I spent a lot of time in class day dreaming. Today, I am here to tell you that I am guilty! Yes, I was a dreamer then and stayed that way forever. I dreamed of things that I wanted to do in the long life that lay ahead of me.

I am not sure just when it started, but I do remember that as early as first grade I played pretend fighter pilot in the school yard during recess. By then I knew that flying was a part of my dream. Much later, in my early teen years I had occasion to travel by air to California to visit my aunt, two uncles and two cousins that lived in San Diego. Mom and I made the trip on American Airlines. During the long flight on the DC-7, I thought to ask if I could get a glimpse of the cockpit. The stewardess responded that it would probably not be allowed. Later, she returned and informed me that the Captain would allow me up after the dinner had been served and cleaned up. I was allowed into the cockpit, shown around, and enjoyed a conversation with the three-pilot crew. That was it! My dream had been expanded to airline pilot. Still just a dream but a solid one that I could cling to forever.

The years went by but the dream, now more like a prayer, remained stronger than ever. I enjoyed playing trumpet in the band and had the opportunity to join a Civil Air Patrol unit while in high school. In the summer of 1957, my CAP Commander took me on a flight to a small airport in nearby Massachusetts and introduced me to a friend that was a flight instructor. I returned to that airport and began my first flying lessons. In December of that year, soon after my sixteenth birthday, I flew my first solo flight. My dream of flying was now taking shape.

The years went by, and in June of 1959, high school graduation came. I enrolled in college at Wentworth Institute of Technology in Boston, MA where I studied Mechanical Technology. It was during the second year of that two-year program that the doorway to my flying dream came wide open. A Naval Aviation recruiter appeared at the entrance to the school cafeteria and asked if I would be interested in becoming a Naval Aviator.

He said to simply make an appointment to come to the U.S. Naval Air Station, South Weymouth, Massachusetts for a weekend of testing and physical exams. Of course, all expenses for food and lodging would be picked up by the Navy. I made the appointment for the next weekend and the rest is history. I passed the tests and physical and pending graduation I would be assigned a place in class 32/61B in the Navy School of Preflight in Pensacola, Florida starting August 11, 1961. My dream had been fulfilled. All I had to do now was the work required to complete the dream.

After five wonderful years of flying Navy aircraft while serving on the USS Antietam, the USS Intrepid, and the USS Lexington, I completed my active duty commitment to the Navy and accepted a position on the pilot seniority list with Eastern Airlines in Miami, Florida. My lifelong dream had now come true. After completing training as both First and Second Officer on the Boeing 720, I was assigned to the flight crew base in New York City.

I did not, however stop dreaming. Being lonely, my dreams turned to my desire to meet a beautiful, smart young woman to be my partner in life. It was during the next several months that I met Gayle Gross, an Eastern Airlines Flight Attendant from Houston, Texas and fell in love. After a short courtship, I proposed and to my delight she accepted. We married on September 14, 1968. Another dream came true!

Dreams now shared by both of us led to our two wonderful children, Tamara and David, their spouses, and eventually, our four wonderful grandsons, Alex, Adam, Jacob and Andrew. My dreams are now for them as they mature and grow into young adults. I dream for success and happiness in their lives that lay ahead.

My advice to all the young people in my life now as I celebrate eighty years of a dreamer's life is: Dare to dream, dream big, and hold fast to your dreams. Recognize the opportunities that come from your dreams and pursue those opportunities with all the energy that you have to give. Be willing to work hard to fulfill those dreams and make them come true.

To Tamara and David, continue to dream. Keep the dreams close and take the risks that will be necessary to make them come true. To all here at this celebration, never stop dreaming, for if you have no dream, you cannot have a dream come true!

Don Warren

Airline cockpit of 727

"Circumstance in Life and Love"

I am fortunate and blessed to say that I am the mom to three children ages twenty, eighteen, and fourteen. Being a parent is one of the most rewarding, exciting, and emotional jobs, and I am so grateful and thankful that I can be the mom to these three amazing human beings. I never thought it would be possible to love anyone as much as I love my family. In my opinion, there is no greater love. As a parent, one can hope that we are preparing our children for whatever obstacles come their way.

When life throws you a curveball and changes the image that you thought was parenting, it can make it even more challenging to feel confident that what we do, say, and feel is the best example for our children. My journey was not without mistakes, struggles, questions, and worry that the decisions made, sometimes in the moment, were the right ones. We learn as we go through experiences and the job of a parent never ends no matter the age.

Having a child, specifically a first born, who needs extra help and attention can force one to parent differently than the traditional image. Patience becomes a huge part, along with educating and learning in any possible way. Most people, myself included, do not develop much of this until they become parents. There is no choice but to try, and we owe it to our children to try. Parenting has shown me that crying is an acceptable emotion. Crying when they are successful, when they are struggling, when they are happy or sad or angry or frustrated can become the norm. Reminiscing of them as babies and the memories or when there is worry if a good enough job guiding is being done can create so many emotions.

On a personal note, another very important thing I have learned as a parent is how fortunate I was to have been able to stay home from the time our oldest was born until present. People need to make the best choices for their families and not every journey is the same. This tends to be forgotten among parents when instead they should be celebrating one another and sharing what works for each. My husband has afforded me this opportunity and I am forever grateful and thankful to have raised our children in this way. I was also professionally employed until I needed to be more present with my children. This proved to be a blessing given the amount of intervention my oldest needed early on in addition to the amount of domestic and international! travel entailed with my husband's occupation.

Beginning at nineteen months throughout childhood, we incorporated everything into our daily routine. Therapy, play groups, physical activity, soccer, swim, gymnastics, music, vitamins, learning videos, small errands, listening to music, and everything in-between. My second child Darien was initially impacted by this, having to constantly attend every activity we scheduled, and eventually was able to participate in herself, which was beneficial for her learning. She was also able, as time went on, to serve an appropriate peer model and eventually was afforded the opportunity to act as a role model in our pre-school class for children who needed extra help. This was such a valuable experience at such a young age.

The time and attention it takes to parent a child that needs extra help is extraordinary and it impacts time that can be spent with siblings. We are fortunate that in our case the situation was manageable and able to improve. We recognized on days that we struggled that so many others were not as lucky as we were and are.

Becoming parents was beyond anything that we could have ever imagined in our lives and it hasn't always been easy. From sleepless nights and pits in our stomachs, to neglecting ourselves, and the inability to sometimes control our own emotions. Wishing it was bedtime, not being able to wait until naptime creating errands just to get kids out of the house when they're younger spending money when it doesn't make any sense because you need to make that third trip to the drive-thru or store to keep everybody happy. Gaining support, ideas, and insight from other parents is also something that all should embrace. During playgroup sessions I was able to attend meetings with other parents who had similar situations.

I am of the position that one cannot possibly know or understand a situation unless they have experienced similar so finding the right network for each situation is a positive step. As our children grow, they tend to need parents less and less. Take every opportunity to continue to show them love, guidance and encouragement as they begin to make their own decisions in their lives.

The main goal and hope is that the number one job of being a parent has helped them to live a happy, well balanced life making good decisions, being kind to others, working hard, and being the best person they can be. That in itself is all the satisfaction we need as parents and it fills our hearts with happiness. Knowing that they are succeeding in life is the ultimate goal. We will continue to give the love, guidance, and devotion to these three children. We hope as parents that we provided them with the best foundation for them to continue their own journey.

We were fortunate enough to have our entire family home for the recent holidays and each time they leave a void in our home and hearts but knowing they are living their best life growing, learning, and becoming amazing people makes it all worthwhile. We are the lucky ones who have been blessed. Not a day goes by that I do not feel gratified and overwhelmed with happiness that my life is what it is and I can confidently say that my husband feels the exact same way.

"The Greatest Gift: Thomas, Born Paraplegic, Becomes Professor"

There are some who conclude that the logical explanation of Creation is a Creator. Others say by chance. Some say from "O". However, here we are. How can we know? It is interesting to note that many of our Theologians, more so today, are from scientific backgrounds. Why is this true? In the following story, the names of the family involved are changed because I cannot recall their names. Perhaps some research will locate those names in this detailed account.

In the year 1968, during my second year in the Seminary, I visited this family. I cannot recall the reason or occasion for my visit to the Harkinson's of West Philadelphia. I believe that they were benefactors of the Seminary. Dr. Harkinson was a physician at one of the nearby hospitals. At home when I visited was Mrs. Harkinson and their son Thomas. Thomas was about fourteen years old then. He was born as an extreme paraplegic and thereby had only the motor use of his toes. He was highly intelligent and could perform remarkable activities with that nearly impossible condition.

Mrs. Harkinson revealed to me the decisions that needed to be made before Thomas' birth. It was known then that the newborn would be severely paraplegic from both through life. Dr. Harkinson tried to convince his wife that they needed to abort this child. Mrs. H. refused such an idea and Thomas was born.

Thomas advances remarkably and early on became proficient on both physics and biochemistry. He later became a professor in these fields at a prominent university which I believe was Princeton University. With his ability to operate the computer with proficiency, his career was also remarkable.

Mrs. Harkinson's belief and faith in God and determination to care for Thomas during their entire lifetime was for her, the "purpose of her life". After that one brief visit as a young Seminarian, I never saw this family again. Somehow, and I cannot here recall, the news of Thomas' advancement was given to me at the Church in Warwick, Rhode Island. I was called in to the Superior

Court of Providence to testify in a case on the Issue of Abortion. I testified against abortion on behalf of the life of the yet unborn. The year was 1974.

. . .

Stephen Hawking was similarly born paraplegic and became world famous in the field of astrophysics. He said that the gift of his very brief lifetime has been, "To see the beauty and enormity of life and the universe." The difference between Thomas and Stephen was their views as to where that gift came from. Thomas, in his given faith believed that it came from the Creator. Stephen, an avowed Atheist concluded that it was simply something of physics of Creation. So, what is the answer?

. . .

I once read in a Reader's Digest article that some scientists conclude that Creation can be compared to throwing a deck of playing cards high into the air and having them mysteriously land suit by suit, in perfect order, perfectly even on the floor. The scientists' summation was the impossibility of this happening, yet, the Creation that we see, feel, have knowledge about, and experience in its many impossibilities happened. The debate goes on as to why and how Creation came to be.

. . .

In my own considered opinion, as we experience the Gifts of the Holy Spirit, we are given insight and a hands-on experience of the Love of God. This tells one that there is meaning and purpose to it all.

. . .

A colleague of mine recently expressed his dismay over the condition of the world in the throes of Evil which perpetuate and predict our downfall and the end. Such is the struggle we face with that which is apparently good within us and around us and that which is contrary to such good. My response to these thoughts is that I hope and pray for the good to prevail and ultimately defeat the evil. The question again arises: Do we experience and have knowledge of that which feeds our mind, soul, and body?

. . .

Dr. John McQuarry, in his book *The Principles of Christian Theology,* states that: "God created us out of Love and that Love is to return back to Himself." This is Biblical Theology. The New Testament shows that the Historical Jesus as the center and answer to this struggle.

. . .

Dr. Scott Peck in The Road Less Traveled concludes that, "We are spiritual beings" and the answer to our struggles if our "Spiritual Nature."

. . .

The author Mark Dyer, in his book *All Problems Can Be Solved Spiritually,* testifies to and does conclude that "All things can be solved spiritually."

The following is from The Practice of Religion
by Rev. Dr. Archibald Campbell Knowles, D.D.
Copyright 1950

Love is From the Center of Heaven

Love when pure
Is an experience of forever.
No time or space
Can taint her embrace.

The eternity of her Grace
Is light in the darkness
That captures all the nevers
And right becomes the brightness.

God emanates from eternity
And brightens the soul
Then the heart reaches forth
To enhance its power
To compliment the other

Selfless is the Spirit of Eternity
Calling destiny forward
As the blindness is vanished
And Truth rises to the heights of love's lure

Pure thought cannot be broken
When evil knocks at her door
The external has been spoken
And one is risen from the poor.

Eternity is never broken
When poverty is no more
Love is about eternity
As Time and Space is gone forever.

As a flower blooms into radiance
And beholds to her birth
So love becomes its brightness
And forever retains her beauty.

Pure unbounded love begins
At the center of Heaven's sphere
Heaven exists where love abounds
Within your soul to the reaches of the believer's tear

Within the depths of the human soul's plea
The Love of the Creator is sure and sound
Love given and the same received
Is the purpose of God and the opening of Eternity.

For all are destined to know such love
In the beloved is found that center
Wonder, beauty, tender touch brought down.
To the inner reaches of the other's eternal to be.

I've loved you since the center was shown
A tenderness of thought, an ear to hear…
A thought to give of Heaven's delight
A heart to reach out in the other's dread fear.
Heaven is known in the love of the heart
Who touches your center
Who sees your place
In the totality of who you are.

"The Kiss"

The longer title would be the Kiss of Formation. The understanding of kiss"in the English language in at least our current American culture is, "A touch or caress with the lips as a motion of greeting, affection or passion". The ancient Greeks defined this further with the deeper meanings of Eros, Philios and Agape. Agape means the highest or purest form of love, where even the motion of a light physical touch could mean pure affection and deep truthful concern for the other. Philios is a brotherly/sisterly affection towards another with sincere regard and desire for the good of the other. Eros would be a cathartic, physical attraction to another with little or no deeply felt concern for the other. For example, a mother's love for her child would be a combination of Agape and Philios. Pure affection and prayerful concern for the well-being of the mother is her real kiss and prime motivation for her children.

My own later and prime experiences in childhood understanding of the meaning of the kiss was Bette. Thank God my big brother Jim introduced Bette to our family. This gorgeous, beyond beautiful Senior High School Class Queen came into our lives filled with the kiss of Philios and Agape. Bette had been elected by her peers as Class Queen that year for all the best reasons. Agape, Philios, and Eros suited her well.

At her own tender age as a teenager, she had the qualities and understanding of the meaning of love and all of us were treated with her genuine kiss of care, concern, teaching and lots of wisdom. Bette was both beautiful and intelligent beyond measure. We have been most fortunate to have her as a good friend and confidante throughout our lives. It is clear that my big brother Jimmy began his relationship with Bette closer to the Eros meaning of attraction. When Bette was first introduced into our family, I recall both myself and Dad gaping at her beauty and a genuine kindness about her. However, Bette was still a teen with, of course, so much more to learn about maturity of being. She had a good start and was well on her way to all it means to grow up.. With so much more to come in her life and ours, and lots on her plate like the rest of us, she managed to become a successful clinical psychologist.

Fortunately for me, I was only seven years old when Bette entered our lives. It wasn't long before our natural hormones began to raise havoc into the very difficult teenage years and need for clear direction and sound learning. From those early years and all through our lives Bette was our Philios, Agape, and clear teacher in some or all of the Eros matters. All of us and many children went to Bette for counsel and advice. No wonder that she earned her degrees in psychology and served as counselor to many throughout her life. Good job, Jimmy! Thanks be to God!

In those magnificent and difficult early teen years, that kiss became real when Margaret appeared. They called it puppy love, but it was so incredible. The cathexis for two very young teens thirteen years old and twelve years old connected with a kiss. One can never forget that first real kiss catapulting the two into the wonderful, mysterious and uncertain experiment in the meaning of Agape, Philios and Eros.

The meaning was deep, and the feeling was passionate all at once! This kiss and its follow-up were to become the determining factors of the meaning of connubial relationship at its best. It is the gift of God that perpetuates the human race and defines love between two committed people. With that kiss life does get complicated and in great need for direction and healthful balance. Politics, religion, value systems and all the directions we seek to follow are defined by that kiss: the first hand "experience" of human love called Agape, Philios and Eros.

Dr. Scott Peck in his book *The Road Less Traveled* says much about the evolution of love in the human journey. From early on, his explanation of "cathexis" is the beginning of such intense journeys of emotion and all that will follow. Cathexis is that initial attraction to another that seeks more information about the other towards more deeply felt emotion, understanding, comprehension, and realization of the meaning and importance of Agape, Philios, and Eros. It is not an easy ride; it is more like a roller-coaster.

The desire for love shared with another, of course, precedes and then propagates the human race. It takes two to enter into such an intense engagement. It needs, to whatever extent, to go both ways, one for and with the other for the propagation to eventually happen. Much else must go in-between the meeting of heart, body, mind and soul for such to be "joyfully" successful. Peck said that, "Life is difficult," but so is the evolution of True Love. Peck also followed the difficult with, "However, life is good". This is the motivation of life throughout, into that gift of Grace called "maturity of being."

"Herein is our love made perfect, that we may have boldness in the day of judgement; because as He is, so are we in this world." *(I John 4:17)* Watching a TV interview some years ago of a famous person the interviewer asked her about her love life over the years. She said that she didn't have time in a brief interview to get into all that. "But," she said, "I can tell you now that I've been married now for seventy years." The interviewer proceeded with "Wow – that is wonderful - and in these days seems almost unachievable! Have you ever during these years contemplated divorce?" Her immediate response was, "Certainly not! Murder, yes!"

Love is indeed a process of spiritual growth to maturity and takes a lot of work. Yes, love can be and is difficult if it can last. Cathexis during our lifetime does not seem to fade. It is the evolution of that cathexis, as stated above, that teaches us about the meaning of love. One of the most striking and expressive pictures of the famous artist Roselli is that entitled "Found." The story behind the picture is a touching one. A country boy and country girl fell deeply in love. They pledged to each other their endless love.

However, the girl gives in to evil influences and is lured to the big city. There she sinks into a swill of temptation and sin, throwing over her pure and happy past, and even trying to forget the one she loved. He, however, remains true, seeking her everywhere. One day on Blackfriar's Bridge, he meets a gaudily dressed woman. He seizes her by the wrist and tells her of his continued love. The one he loves has been found. *(#3195 of Encyclopedia of 7700 Illustrations)*

It is clear to me that my Mother was my first love although at that first meeting I didn't realize that fact. I actually remember my first meeting with her when my newly born eyes could focus. She was cradling me and looking into my eyes with genuine love. We all need to go that far back and remember as we often forget that miracle of life and genuine love begun. Ever so dear and comforting does that become as we grow older, more tender, and wiser.

"A mother found under her place one morning at breakfast a bill made out by her small son, Bradley: for running errands, 25 cents; for being good, 10 cents; for taking music lessons 15 cents; for extras, 5 cents. Total 55 cents. Mother smiled but made no comment. At lunch, Bradley found the bill under his plate and another piece of paper folded neatly folded like the first. Opening it, he read, 'Bradley owes mother: for nursing him through scarlet fever, nothing; for being good to him, nothing; for clothes, shoes and playthings, nothing; for his playroom, nothing; for his meal, nothing. Total: nothing." (encycl 7700 Illust #3198)

As I observe my daughter Addie raising her three young children, Owen, Wesley, and Phoebe, I wonder where she gets her strength, knowhow, peace of mind and all those things required for such an undertaking. Along with a good spouse we fondly know as Ryan and a swarm of family and friends surrounding them, no wonder!

I suppose there is not one particular way to raise one's children except to say that genuine love is the prime ingredient. Such is the kiss of formation. One never forgets that kiss even if not initially realized or understood. Admonishment and the learning process are not usually easy or understood as love. We love our children, all children because we want them to be the best they can be. We seek the best means possible for this end.

"A Gift of All Gifts"

A fun story for me to tell is of a recent Christmas visit to my family in Glen Rock, New Jersey. On that beautiful sunny day just following Christmas Day I headed out to see Owen, Wesley, Phoebe, Addie, and Ryan to celebrate. Upon arrival and as I pulled into their driveway, Wesley was the first out the door to greet me. However, this time he had a stern look on his face with determined hands on each hip. As I exited my car with some of their presents in hand Wesley announced that he did not want any more books."

Of course, in my collection of gifts, I did have some books for the children. As usual more toys, games and clothing were among the lot. At that time Wesley, was all of five years old and books were a bore to most kids at that tender age, especially Wes. Things did soon warm up however, with hugs and more presents to open. Since then, Wesley has grown a few more years, and it is my understanding that he is becoming quite a reader.

In the meantime, I've learned that teachers have even called Ryan and Addie out of their concern that Wes was not very interested in the books suggested by them at school. So, his Mom dug into a pile and found some old copies of the favorites from earlier days and more. In saying this, I well remember a class back in my junior high school days which was another most significant milestone in my life and future.

Mr. Thompson, my ninth grade English teacher, was the one teacher most of us wanted to avoid. But certainly, he became one of my favorite teachers. His approach was difficult and determined. He required our class to choose ten books to read that year. He checked them to be sure that we might learn valuable lessons in the process. Every Friday, each of us were chosen at random by picking a name out of a hat to give an oral presentation of the book we were reading. I was terrified and prayed that my name would not come up. It was drawn from the dreaded hat three times that year. I am reminded now how fortunate that was for me.

It took several years for the first Apostles to learn all that Jesus was born to teach them. They, as most of us, didn't get it at first. They, as we, needed to be guided into the right direction. Each had to learn and find out for himself and herself in due time.

There is an ancient Greek term in the Holy Bible that describes Jesus's purpose on this Earth. The term is Photon. It means "light." In modern English, we usually think of light as that which brightens the room, the day, i.e. sun, candle, electric bulb, and so on. Photon refers to the enlightenment of soul, mind, and body. This light is referred to in the Bible throughout. Jesus is clearly pointed out as the Light of the World, the light for humankind.

As we enter into our epiphanies, we come to experience and understand such light in its fullness. God's light is made manifest to us through Jesus. The first followers of this often mysterious and wonderful personality did not come fully to this light until after his death and Resurrection. Much needed to be given and learned along the Way" At the first Pentecost, those followers received the fullness of the Gifts of the Holy Spirit. The light was made manifest to them, the Church was born, and from then on commissioned to bring that light to the ends of the earth. Ecclesia means "the People of God".

Lent represents that time of learning between the birth of Christ to the Pentecost. It can be, and most often is, a time of struggle. In a world laden with evil intentions, we need to learn the meaning of Wholeness - from the ancient Biblical term Holy i.e. Photon. This is Love, Joy, Peace, Grace, Wisdom, Knowledge, Ghostly Strength, Long-Suffering, given to us by God.

The gift is the Photon; the Epiphany, the Pentecost.

As we come to choose the Good over the Evil, we then begin to fully receive and understand the Good: the light. It is through the light, or rather, the Gifts of the Holy Spirit that we are enabled to be God's people. We come to know Jesus in the gift of Penitence and Forgiveness, which lead us to the beginnings of wholeness.

Years ago, my son Brian and I wandered into a bookstore during a routine day of errands. Brian was about eleven years old at that time and obviously not seriously looking for any particular books to read. We went our separate ways in the store. It didn't take very long for him to come to me with a book in hand. The title of that book was *How to Start Your Own Business on a Shoestring*. The rest is history! Brian read that book from cover to cover, and a whole new avenue opened to him. Very early on, during his high school years, he began and developed his own landscaping business. That lasted for several years, with both success and failures. Brian was a hustler and didn't allow any failures to dampen his enthusiasm.

Long story short, he now works for a very successful industrial roofing company and was gradually promoted to a regional manager for that company. He is doing incredibly well in his work and continues to be an asset to himself and all for and with whom he labors. One cannot help but be proud of him and his thus far accomplishments. He and Dana and all their loved pets reside in upper state New York. It is my considered opinion that our wandering into that bookstore so long ago was not a coincidence. Even if this was a mere co-incidence, the gifts received were well-discovered and appreciated.

"Oblivion and Forever"

Jesus said, "Let your light so shine." The idea or even the reality of Oblivion is something that human beings struggle to fathom. The rest of the living kingdom does not think of Oblivion in its patterns of living and dying. However, I'll not forget my dog Buddy howling at the loss and burial of his brother and friend, Jake. I wondered then as to whether or not he actually understood such a loss.

Oblivion is defined as "the state of being utterly forgotten." It states that "all is lost" and "never to live again, forever." In science, we realize that at least a part of us continues in our DNA. Also, memory and history carry and record something of who we are and have been. The question here is whether or not the life we know carries on in our own personal and forever future. Also, do we exist in the fulness of our being forever, or not?

The idea of oblivion has always been a frightening thought for humans in that this brief lifetime begins and ends in these present fourscore plus ten years of one lifetime. Is this the veil of tears as one poet stated or as another said, "Life is simply likened to carrying a boulder to the top of a hill, watching it roll back downward, and struggling to carry it back to the top over and over again." Is this the extent of our lives?

In the Christian faith, as in others, the question of oblivion and forever are given clear answers in that Creation is in the hands of a living, loving God whose purpose is forever. Credence to this idea is found in the history of human experience and knowledge which comes to us from God our Father, Creator.

Socrates stated that knowledge and reality cannot be conceived unless it is true and real. His student, Plato, explained this by using the example of a unicorn. A unicorn does not exist except in our imagination, but all the parts that make up a unicorn do exist. Our conception of those parts that create the unicorn are the materials which are our idea of that unicorn. In other words, reality is based on reality, or each of those parts which create our realities, truths and creative abilities. Oblivion means zero. Zero equals no reality at all.

So again, what is the reality, what is the Truth? Where does it come from? Is there a purpose, a design? If so, there is no Oblivion!

Forever is built on the Truths that make our realities. In the Christian faith our realities are built on Belief in a Creator who gives us the Truths of Forever. This is our experience and our future. The stories in this book reveal human experiences which point to credence to such a Truth. A few of such extraordinary or simply stated experiences as given here, I believe, show us the existence, the reality of God.

I recall here my annual purchase of our family Christmas tree. At one of these sales, being dressed in my clerical suit, the young man selling those trees, wreaths, and ornaments announced to me that he was an Atheist. Although the proceeds were going to the My One Wish Fund for terminally ill children of which he was glad to be a part of, his belief system was the terror of Oblivion. My presence and purpose of purchase was because of my faith in God along with deeply felt concern for the children. The only difference between me and the sales clerk was the extent of our belief systems.

He was dependent solely on his feelings whereas my conclusion was based on further understanding through my Christian upbringing. My answer to him was that more conversation about our beliefs would be helpful in understanding the two directions of our purpose. I sincerely asked him to teach me his thoughts on belief and perhaps we could learn something extraordinary in such a conversation. That did not happen but I believe that the short and simple interaction was positive and fruitful for both of us. In my estimation, the young man and I saw the parts and God will reveal the whole.

Our faith teaches us that all such interaction ultimately leads us to the Truth. Jesus said, "Do not hide your light under a bushel basket." It has been my hope in this vocational ministry to hear the stories of others and learn from them, and then to build such experiences into my own and see how they collaborate towards the Truth.

"Charlie"

It has been my hope in my own vocational ministry to hear the stories of others and learn from them, and then to build such experiences into my own and see how they collaborate towards that ultimate Truth, and belief in the purpose of our lives. This collection of stories, I believe, enhance and give credence to the Holy, Living Father in Heaven and within our souls. It is in my thinking that who we are and who we are to become are somehow forever. Is there really a God who knows us intimately, has a plan, and that we are all part of that bigger picture of reality?

I clearly remember a significant experience in my early childhood which helped my own development towards the life ahead of me. Back in those earlier years we were, of course, under the safety net, love, and concern of those older than us, most especially our parents. Not only through love but also for our wellbeing we needed to be guided along towards our own ability to take care of ourselves. In those years, children were restricted to their own yards on those sunny, mild days by a harness and long rope tied to a tree.

At the tender age of three, I managed to figure out how to loosen myself from the confinement. That being done I wandered out of my yard to the neighboring street and continued walking to the last house on that street. There, in his yard was my first worldly friend outside of my family, also tied in like fashion to tree. I went to Charlie and released him from his confinement. Here began our first real encounter with "Freedom". This was a significant move forward but not without the inherent dangers as to how to be free. Indeed, it was exhilarating to be loosed into the larger world out there but still in need of much care, love, concern, and all the needed requirements for a healthy future ahead.

Charlie and I also ran into the problems of evil intent. We learned more about cuts and scratches and many hurtful things along the way. Mom, Dad and all the "adults" caring for us were still needed. The balance of such experiences between our freedom and its responsibilities had to be learned along the way. But by the Grace of God and rightful learning our navigation continued. It was not easy, but the experiences were worthwhile.

1952

About three more years into our growing freedom, we had two ice cream trucks come down that infamous street called Island Avenue selling their goodies to us vulnerable children. One of those merchants was Peter Palagi and the other was Marty's Favorite Ice Cream. Peter Palagi drove an old, renovated Model T Ford truck, and Marty made his deliveries in a modern shiny Dodge Truck. Charlie and I both unanimously decided that we preferred the new truck instead of the antique. Little did we know then how special and thousands of dollars more valuable was the "old" Model T. We decided together to steal apples each day from the local private vineyard and pound, from a hidden place, the old Model T so that it wouldn't invade our territory anymore. We preferred the new and shiny Marty's Famous Ice Cream delivery.

It wasn't until many years later that we had come to realize those sins and dangers of the childhood years. We certainly learned the hard way through instruction and growing that there was something wrong and even right about such experiences. Yes, we could both say in the later years, "But by the Grace of God," and a huge thank you to those who knew better. The years passed all too quickly, and Charlie and I went our separate ways with many lessons learned along the way. Charlie joined the Air Force, and I continued on in school ultimately becoming a priest in the Church. More years passed with no communication between Charlie and me until one day I received a delightful surprise phone call from my childhood Buddy.

We brought ourselves up to date on our journeys and Charles announced that he was going to marry his beautiful Pering whom he had met during the Air Force years in the Philippines. He was to go back to the Islands to get married and bring Pering back here to New England. We agreed to meet when he returned the next late Fall, and that year cold early Winter. I inquired on that initial phone call as to how Pering may not appreciate the cold winter being from the tropics. He simply said that they will deal with it as it happens. Long story shortened they later related to me how Pering dealt with the harsh winter ahead.

Rising very early one morning, Pering woke Charlie from his deep sleep with loud screams. He was totally annoyed with the wake up call and worried that something terrible was happening. She announced to him that, "It is snowing!" With sheer delight she wanted to immediately get dressed and to go there with him to be in the snowstorm. This was her first encounter with that beautiful, exciting, wonderful snow. They both very joyfully learned new things and grew from such an EXPERIENCE together. It was more than real! This experience of something new and wonderful can be likened to a mini-resurrection as they both saw wonderment in their future and the excitement of so much more to witness and learn on this rollercoaster ride we call life.

When Mary Magdalene and the other Mary as related in the Bible went to the tomb to tend the body of Jesus, they found the tomb empty. Soon after they both realized that, the real and living Jesus met them there. They were both terrified and excited, and they went as instructed by Jesus that He was not in the tomb but alive and that they would see Him, too. The rest is history as those early followers saw and more fully realized the same.

His earlier promises which they did not yet understand were true. They and hopefully the entire race of human beings would one day come to meet and realize the eternity of God. This is our experience of the Resurrection of Jesus of Nazareth. He was born amongst us, loved and taught us, and kept his promises until we finally could see for ourselves the whole truth and nothing but the truth. Our growth in this lifetime is a series of resurrection experiences beginning from our childhood, through this brief lifetime and into the next. Love is forever and meant to be!

In reading the saints of history and all witnesses right here among us, we learn that the experiences we have are meant not only for our learning but to move us through our lives and into the next forever. Likened to that old and often forgotten Model T, we come to finally realize how valuable and critically important it was. We may try to pound it with apples stolen from our neighbors' yard and try to argue it out of memory and existence, but we can't. We learn from the experience and grow to higher levels. We learn how beautiful, exciting, and wonderful that snow truly is!

Charlie called me from Arizona the evening before he passed from this life into the next to inform me of his impending death. He was matter of fact and unafraid, and he asked if I would officiate when the time came. I told the story of our growing up years at his funeral, including the Ice Cream deliveries and Pering's excitement over a New England snowstorm.

"The Epiphany"

In our secular culture these days, the season of Epiphany often slips by us with little to no notice. For Christians, the Church calendar celebrates this most special time between Christmas and the start of Lent on Ash Wednesday. During my own span of ministry, I've watched this, and all the Spiritual seasons, gradually slip away. Of course, Christmas and Easter get plenty of attention as Santa Claus and the Easter Bunny are favorites as holiday festivities bring families and friends together in most pleasant ways. They are wonderful breaks in the midst of some of the drudgery of the normal time of work and taxes.

This is not all negative in that rest, refreshment, family and friends are so necessary to healthful experience. However, the Christian teaching and experience make it clear that without that spiritual dimension of the Holy Times we are left bereft of the needed spiritual ingredient that gives purpose and meaning to the holidays. We need to be reminded that 'holidays' at least in Western culture derives from Holy Days. Unfortunately, the holidays have all but eliminated the Holy from the experience. As a Priest in the Church I have watched, with much dismay, this diminishing of the Holy experience from the 1960s to the present (2020).

Actually, in the Eastern Orthodox and other Eastern traditions, the Epiphany is raised to the highest level as is it more clearly expresses its importance to the health of society and each of us as we understand and appreciate its enormity. The realization that the Incarnation, the 'real presence' of God within us and around us is key to our health and salvation.

The ancient Biblical term Epiphany is interpreted as "the light" entering, fully and directly, into the history of mankind, is that which gives to us: knowledge, wisdom, peace, joy, hope, and all that advances us to God's love and plans for our life and eternal future. The actual, historical presence of the Christ among us is the revelation of God. We realize in this experience of the light that God communicates directly to us in thought, prayer, actions, and all things necessary to, not only our survival, but more importantly, our call to advancement and all that God plans for our eternal future.

The experience of God's presence in our lives is key to all we are meant to be. Our existence depends upon this experience. The experiences and actual happenings as described in this book are translated into the gifts of Epiphany emanating from God. A wonderful anonymous quotation sums up the experience of Epiphany:

A love that can never be fathomed;
A life that can never die;
A righteousness that can never be tarnished;
A peace that can never be understood;
A rest that can never be disturbed;
A joy that can never be diminished;
A hope that can never be disappointed;
A glory that can never be clouded;
A light that can never be darkened;
A happiness that can never be interrupted;
A strength that can never be enfeebled;
A purity that can never be defiled;
A beauty that can never be marred;
A wisdom that can never be baffled;
Resources that can never be exhausted.
(Encycl. Of 7700 Quotations)

"God's Superlatives"

Writers are supposed to avoid superlatives. The textbooks tell us that authors who use extreme adjectives like fabulous, magnificent, or splendid are usually overstating the case. These graphic superlatives are to be reserved only for occasions that actually merit their use, and then, they are to appear very seldomly.

But when the writers of the Bible spoke of the blessings of God upon His children, they used the strongest of terms. So marvelous are the riches of Christ enjoyed by His own that the Holy Spirit, the author of God's Word, used the most extravagant language to describe them. Here are a few examples:

God's pardon is "abundant." *(Isaiah 55:7)*
His love "passeth knowledge." *(Ephesians 3:9)*
His gift of salvation is "unspeakable." *(2 Corinthians 9:15)*
His life is more "abundant." *(John 10:10)*

Paul writing to the discouraged Corinthians, said that through God we are "enriched in everything to all bountifulness, which causeth through us thanksgiving to God." *(2 Corinthians 9:11)* "Feeling poor of spirit? Wishing you had more of the riches of this world? Just remember the superlatives of God!" (Encycl. Of 7700 Quotations)

From the birth of Jesus, the Incarnation (Christmas) through the entire Biblical accounts, followed by the Feast of All Saints, our history gives living accounts that Christ is the answer to life, health, and the promise of hope into Eternity.

"A Meeting with Benjamin"

Benjamin was special! He and his family faced a long journey of terminal cancer. I cannot begin to describe or explain such a journey except to look to God and deep within myself for help. "We measure distance by time. We are apt to say that a certain place is so many hours from us. If it is a hundred miles from us, and there is no railroad we think it a long way; if there is a railway, we think we can be there in no time. But how near must we say Heaven is? - for it is just one sigh, and we get there." (Spurgeon -Encyc. Of Quotations). In other words, we can't go to heaven on a jetliner nor in a space craft to the outer reaches, but we can find our way there during the flight.

"Just think of stepping on a shore and finding heaven there; Or taking hold of a hand, and finding God's hand; Or breathing new air, and finding heaven there; Or feeling invigorated, and finding immortality; Or passing from storm and tempest to an unbroken calm; Or waking up — And finding it HOME!" (#2181 – Encycl. Of Quotations)

The beginning of my five-year Rectorship at St. Mark's Parish, Warwick, Rhode Island in 2003 was a rough start. My first call was to immediately go to Children's Hospital in Providence to meet Benjamin. Ben was a nine-year-old being treated for what ultimately became terminal Cancer. This story of love, anguish, joy, and tears begins here.

As I entered Ben's room in the intensive care unit, he was playing a solitary board game. Upon approaching Ben and what became a very long stretch of time I tried to engage him in conversation. He was obstinate, even angry, and did his best to totally ignore me. I introduced myself as his new priest at his much-loved home parish. He didn't like me and wanted his lifelong pastor Fr. Kenneth Franklin, not me. Fr. Franklin was the only priest he knew and there was an indivisible admiration between them. No one could take over for Fr. Franklin who saw him born, baptized him, and raised him thus far in the church. His buddy, Fr. Franklin, of course continued his visits and bonded re-lationship with Ben. After about 45 minutes of a one-way conversation, I was finally able to break the ice. I mentioned to him that I drive a motorcycle and that when he got better and out of the hospital, we might be able to go for a ride. He perked up and said, "Wow!"

Within a few days of that exciting exchange, I brought a gift to Ben: a brand-new helmet. During the next months and then well into the next year and more Ben had his up and down spells but a lot of good days. Although he was in and out of the hospital for routine checks and some treatments, he was doing quite well. We were all elated but of course feeling very cautious. Ben was even able to continue his favorite sport – baseball. Everybody enjoyed him on the Little League team, and he did well. All his friends at church certainly loved having Ben back and fully active in the church school and all other parish events. Also, during the next several years by virtue of the My One Wish Foundation, he enjoyed some favorite wishes such as swimming with the dolphins in Florida and meeting, in person, some professional baseball teams and players. The good times along with intermittent difficult spells and treatments sped by.

After Ben turned ten years old, the problems of his health began to deteriorate. He was sent back to Children's Hospital. We all visited, prayed, and tended to Benjamin, our beloved child. Returning home after a long stay in the hospital Ben grew weaker. He beckoned me through his mom and dad to take him on that bike ride. He said that his helmet was "all shined up!" Mom and Dad said that he was much too weak for such a ride, but a visit and pep talk would surely help. Going into the house for this visit I found Ben very weak and very depressed. I brought him to the window. Right out front was the motorcycle. He suddenly perked up at the sight and prospect, mustered up all his strength and said, "Take me for a ride!" I got him onto the passenger seat with feet in place on the foot bars and with a few rider's instructions including, "Don't touch the hot pipes!" He said, "I already know that – let's get going!"

We rode all through the neighborhood throughout his town. He waived to everyone he saw, especially other bikes we passed on the road. He already knew about the biker's wave to other bikers. What a most enjoyable and most memorable ride it was. One would never guess that little Ben was so seriously ill, including me and Ben at that moment in eternity. After finally returning home the excitement continued into the household. Even his little brother but still much too little at that time enjoyed our version of the bike ride. Nicholas was as old then as Ben was when the first ominous signs of the dreadful illness reared its ugly head.

About two weeks later, I was called to the Haight Homestead. With John Kolarik, the parish senior warden (President of the Parish Counsel at St. Marks), I went directly there. Ben had died peacefully there on his favorite recliner watching one of his favorite shows on TV.

One of the prominent physicians who stayed with Ben throughout the five year ordeal spoke at a church overflowing its capacity. In his comments he told us many great things about Ben and how very much all on that unit enjoyed this child.

He closed by stating that the advancement of love, hope beyond hope and medical science moved far forward during these years because of these children in hospital care. These children seemed to know that their illnesses would be a huge help to others. They seemed to know some purpose in all of it and took on the battle courageously. Their faith in the Creator and loving Father seemed never to waiver whatever the outcome may be. We stand humbly, hopefully, and tenderly in awe of our own seeming hopelessness before the Father who truly loves each and every one of us. Jesus said, "And I say unto you my friends, 'Be not afraid of them that kill the body, and after have no more that they can do'" *(Luke 12:4)*

Irma Bombeck, T. V. Host and author toured Children's Hospitals throughout the United States to interview children being treated with terminal illnesses. In her book entitled: *I Want to Go To Boise,* found her children not only courageous during the long and ominous ordeal but amazingly cognizant of the love and hope that surrounded them. Each child knew the reality of his and her circumstances but more especially the genuine devotion of ones who truly loved them. Even more and beyond such a comprehension, these children somehow accepted their reality and did all they could to help those who loved them through this experience of living and dying, love and hope. The writer Dorothy Lawe Holt expressed the idea of genuine love given to and then received by our children:

Learning from Living

If a child lives with criticism he learns to condemn;

If a child lives with hostility he learns to fight;

If a child lives with ridicule she learns to be shy;

If a child lives with shame she learns to feel guilty.

BUT

If a child lives with tolerance, he learns to be patient;

If a child lives with encouragement he learns confidence;

If a child lives with praise he learns to appreciate;

If a child lives with fairness she learns justice;

If a child lives with security she learns to have faith;

If a child lives with approval he learns to like himself;

If a child lives with acceptance and friendship he learns to Find LOVE in that world.

(Encycl. Of Quotations).

Having met Benjamin under all these circumstances given I am reminded of many saints in history whose lives became outstanding during both the storms of life and with the LOVE that overcame. One of the greats was the famous Saint Nicholas due to his up-bringing; the society into which he was born; and his ability to make a difference in the world. Having become an advocate for the poor and the beloved saint of sailors and children it is appropriate to add this dimension to our experience with Ben.

Beginning the following collection of experiences, I choose the story of Saint Nicholas as an example of historical happenings that give us good reason to believe in the reality of God. For as long as recorded history has existed there are countless records of extraordinary happenings which have enhanced such a belief. Religions of all kinds have evolved because of such experiences and accounts, often beyond description. Many and various accounts of a real person of history known as St. Nicholas have evolved but the underlying message is always toward Faith.

"The Story of Saint Nicholas:
Patron Saint of Sailors and Children"

There is more than one good reason to begin this collection of true stories with an account of Saint Nicholas. At the start it is correct to say that the message gained from the many accounts of Nicholas is the message I wish to convey. That message is Belief in God, the meaning of the Incarnation, and the message of Hope and purpose into the future of each of us.

It says in Isaiah: "A shoot shall come from the root of Jesse, and a branch shall grow out of his roots. The spirit of God shall rest on him. The spirit of wisdom and understanding; the spirit of counsel and might; the spirit of knowledge and the Fear of the Lord..." That is belief and Faith in God. *(Isaiah 11:1)*. In other words, God is, and will be, in our midst, with hope and purpose for us all.

The famous contemporary (late 20th century) theologian Dr. John Mac-Quarry, in his treatise "The Risk of Creation" states that free will is the essential gift of God to us, in that we have the power to choose. God made us in His image. The choice is that we should ultimately choose his Love, but that choice will necessarily be ours. To have been created in God's image means that our choices must come from us back to God. The problem is that any rejection of God is also ours. Our Pride (or lack of need for God's love) would be our downfall and even destruction. The choice must come from each of us. Dr. MacQuarry says that ultimately our choice of God's Love is inevitable.

One prayer mirrors this belief as the Bible teaches: "Almighty and Everlasting God, increase in us the gifts of Faith, Hope and Charity; and, that we may obtain that which you promise, help us to love that which you command; through Jesus Christ our Lord, who lives and reigns with you and the Holy Spirit, one God, forever and ever. Amen."

Another popular contemporary historian and theologian, Dr. Thomas Fleming, has a consistent thesis in all his books that: "God has intervened throughout the events of history only to rescue us from self-destruction." At key points in history, people, events, nature, and insightful happenings have led each of us and all of us to further hope and purpose into our future.

With this in mind, I relate here the Incarnation. To the Christian, the birth of Jesus was God's key and major pivotal point in the history of man and society. The Incarnation theology is that the eternal God entered our history as one of us.

This time of history was at the recognizable beginning of the greatest power of the world at that time. The Roman Empire had reached the heights of power, influence and prestige. Also, at this time, due to human pride and greed, that power fell into moral decay, human control, and the gradual loss of its dependence on the search for Truth and the good. In other words, the need for the Truth and the good of all waned toward self-destruction.

The birth of Jesus into that world was God's way of bringing us back to our senses. The statement is that without our choice of God's love we would again be doomed to failure. The real presence of Jesus was the actual presence of God's love amongst us and for us. As human pride failed to see this love with its own power and prestige prevailing, Jesus, the love of God, was nailed to the cross. Guess what happened?!

Since that Crucifixion, the Love of God became the dominant force, and the world will never be the same again. Since the fall of the Empire, from Emperor Tiberius, to Caesar, Diocletian, Maximilian, Caligula to Constantine, the church or the people of God came to be. With the conversion of Emperor Constantine, the followers of Christ came out of hiding and persecution to hopefully live and speak for the Truth. Here is where the example of the myriad of Saints in history can joyfully and hopefully be stated.

St. Nicholas's Story

Nicholas was born and raised during the reigns of the powerful and corrupt Emperors of Rome, Diocletian and Maximilian. This was around the time from 250 AD to 350 AD. Under these rulers, Christianity in all its forms was outlawed to the punishment of prison and death. Nicholas' father was a wealthy merchant in the Mediterranean area, with his ships stationed at Myra in the region now known as Turkey. Although Nicholas's dad was not a Christian, his mother was. In hiding and secrecy, she raised Nicholas with the Holy Bible and the Gospel stories of the birth, life, death, and resurrection of Jesus.

He was instructed by his mom to keep these stories close to his heart, and simply to live by them with no words said. However, in his years since childhood into his teens while regularly visiting the sailors on his dad's ships he related those stories to them. They loved this child! As a teenager, the secret society of Christ-followers ordained him as a priest amongst them and soon after they made him their Bishop. Again, to be reminded, this was all in secrecy, realizing that, if caught, severe punishment was certainly to follow.

At the time of the Pagan Festival of the Winter Solstice (December twenty-fifth), Nicholas with his sailor friends brought needed goods from his dad's ship and distributed them to many in need throughout the city of Myra. Saying in need is important in that Nicholas saw those who hurt as those in need. He later was known as the Patron Saint of Sailors and Children, and ultimately the Patron Saint of Children, for the most vulnerable in society. Word of Nicholas's deed spread far and wide and rapidly. Sought out by the Emperor's guards, he went immediately to prison, there to die of starvation almost a year later (December sixth, circa 325 AD).

Many, many stories have grown because of and about this real person of history. The world has certainly become a better place because of this Saint. Some of the follies of man, in his human pride, changed St. Nick into Santa Claus. This has been a fond fantasy, but the reality and truth of the matter remain. Just as Jesus was real, so was this and all the Saints of history, and all because of Christ.

The stories in this book happened as they did with no embellishments except that they seem surely to point to the reality of God and His love for us. False human pride and that need to be in control on one's own leads to self-destruction. Maybe it is here that we realize our need for God's love within and around us. Maybe it is our return to God even at our last that MacQuarry's thesis comes to our reality.

The root of Jesse in Isaiah is every person in history who contributes to the will and purpose of God. That's us! Dr. John MacQuarry's "Risk of Creation" is that once recognized, we can't help but turn toward our Creator. As Dr. Thomas Fleming believed God has entered and continues to enter our history.

"Santa Who?!"

Several years ago, I was surprised by a visit from one of my faithful Acolytes of many years before. He came by to ask me to help him with an idea. Remembering the good ole days of celebrations of Saint Nicholas on December soxth, he wanted to carry out the tradition in bigger ways. He brought along with him for this visit the vestments and all of Saint Nicholas as we had remembered him. Shawn asked if I could help him with a project. He also made me promise that he remained anonymous throughout. As he had become a prominent business man over the years and in thanksgiving wanted to share his success.

Sorry Shawn, but I must put your first name into this account. However, the name has been changed to protect the innocent, as so often happens. All of us who know you realize where you are coming from, the heart. Your fond memories of Saint Nicholas need to continue in bigger ways. "Let's continue the tradition of Saint Nicholas as the continuing historical real human being." It must also be noted here that there are myriads of anonymous Santa's all over the world and before Saint Nicholas was born way back in the fourth Century A. D. Because of this, Santa and the millions of others through history Saint Nicholas is real for sure.

"Haitian Experience"

Food for the Poor is an organization based in Boca Raton, Florida. It's founder, Mr. Ferdinand (Ferdy) Mafoode, prayed that every bit of help to those in need brings them hope. His goal was to bring love, hope and food to the desperate in Central America. I had the joy and rude awakening of such need close to our rich and prosperous country very close by. I had met Canadians, and Australians along with fellow Americans from both government and churches in our respective country's providing many resources to help the Haitians and the people of the surrounding Central American nations to grow out of the deplorable existing conditions there. Education, sound government, and raw materials were most needed to help a seemingly and nearly hopeless situation.

The Christ is Born

As we now approach the Feast of the Incarnation we can again focus on the awesome power and love of God. I'll never forget the words of Senator John McCain, not long after his five-year imprisonment in a six by five hole with little light and little food. He said that "during this time of torture I never lost faith in God and the promise of truth, light and hope for the future. That peace kept me alive and always hopeful."

The coming of the Christ into our fragile tiny Earth, revealed in full measure the long-awaited complete revelation of light, the truth and hope for our future. Because of the birth, life, death and resurrection of Jesus the world has hope and will never be the same again. As we experience the power of God's love for us and the intent and purpose of His will for us, each of us gain new life and eternal hope.

A long time ago, as a young priest in a new parish, I attended the Recovery Program sponsored by the Church of the Incarnation. We as Christians are people of the Incarnation (God with and in us). The parish was called St. Barnabas Church, Barnabas being known as The Encourager. I always called every parish and the church the Sanctuary of the Incarnation. God come among us! After attending the first meeting of recovery, I kept on going week after week. Recovery is a program for people suffering from phobias.

Discovering my own claustrophobia, Recovery helped me overcome the fears of such an illness and see the light and the truth ahead of it. The program is structured for healing and redemption that only God's love can cure. This program is designed and structured similarly to AA and other self-help groups designed to raise us from the darkness into the light. Jesus came to us from the eternal realms to show us the way from darkness to light, to the truth from here into eternity where a place is being prepared for each and every one of us.

Merry Christmas
and
a Peaceful New Year!

"Sis"

It was a very hot August 1, 1975, that I began my seventeen and a half year rectorship at Trinity Church, Milford, Massachusetts. My son, Joel, was on year old and his Mom and I had finally, and with great expectation, along with the frights of new job trepidation, moved into the rectory at 23 Dana Park, Hopedale.

Very soon after I entered that first day of the new parish experience, my phone rang. I don't remember who called but drove myself for my first call to the local Milford hospital just across town. It was there that I entered a long spiritual journey with my good friend Wilhelmina Hensel and her family.

Surrounding their mother, Wilhelmena, was Bob, Wilhelmena ("Sis"), Bill, Aubrey, Carolyn, Aunts Viola, and Clara, and significant others whom I cannot now recall. After a very brief introduction, the Sacrament of the Sick was administered, and prayers iterated with tears surrounding. After several follow-up visits and preparatory measures were made, Mother crossed over to the other side of this life. During the many years following that, my first day at work, I and my family were treated like the Lord had come into their life in a special and real way.

It was, again, the question of that critical time of our mortality, and worse, the devastating reality of loss of a loved one, especially a mother. They, of course, being in a state of surreal shock, had to make immediate plans for their mom's funeral. Here is where the priest can and tries to be as helpful as possible. My focus was to bring the Lord and His promises to bear in as many ways as one could at such a time. Initially there are no words, but rather, the consolation and compassion of true friends. From then on became a long journey and the many, many occasions, happy and sad, that were yet to come.

This was one of those prime experiences of my own journey as a priest to face with others the joys and tragedies we all come to find during our lifetimes. Many years and many families under similar circumstances of life's realities continued to be part of my job as a priest and pastor. Such relationships required in-depth conversation, laughter, hope, and sorrows that were to come.

Lessons of life were always up front and learning and growing never ceased. The age-old pearl of wisdom and hope, "Love, laughter and tears make life worthwhile" became more and more the truth as "Sage with Age" is our time of growth set forward.

Sis and I became true friends over the ensuing years, and we clearly learned a lot from each other. After their mom passed, Sis "naturally' became the matriarch of the Hensel Family. Her personality was like a tender teddy bear in that her heart and soul was realized in all her interactions. However, Sis operated as a Master Sergeant with clear orders in all directions for all who could appreciate and listen to those kinds of directions. How tongue in cheek were those directives but also filled with true meaning and concern for the other. Sis can, and more often than not, talk like a truck driver with commands and all, but everyone always knew that her heart and soul was in the right place.

There are so very many pearls of wisdom expressed by the ones touched in heart by all the joys and sadness that inevitably come our way. What can we all expect? Life, death, and taxes throughout! It's not all bad when real faith becomes a part of the equation. My favorite of all bumper stickers: "If you don't like education and the loves and losses that provide it, try ignorance!" We all need to learn and grow in the inevitabilities of living. As my mom used to say, "Life is good if you don't yield to the weaknesses!" Of course, one-liners are only helpful hints loaded with all kinds of interpretation both good for the soul as well as not so good if received wrongfully. Thank you, "Sis" for being such a good friend in the best of and the worst of times!

Here is some of my journey with a very special and respected family, the Hensels. This is a very hard- working family raised in the so-called "Protestant Work Ethic." Hard work for this family brought to them the experience of the benefits along with the responsibilities of such benefits. Billy, Aubrey, and Bob served with distinction in the U. S. Military both in and beyond WWII. They each shared an entrepreneurial spirit of enterprise and did well raising their family with the virtues of hard work and generosity.

"Captain Bob" had a very fruitful seafood sales business. Wilhelmena, who everyone knows as "Sis," carried on the original restaurant business known as "The Redwood" in Mendon, Massachusetts. People from all over the region came to the drive-in venue for all kinds of fare, especially their famous seafood, heaping full plates of delight. It was such a fun place to go. Mom and Dad Hensel originally began this enterprise on a nickel during the Great Depression. Fried chicken delights were the original faire of choice, the price was right, and the helpings were enormous.

One distinct mark of these originals was that everyone be fed and enjoy the outcome. The growth of the businesses also showed their tremendous respect and generosity to all of their neighbors. I, alongside their many friends, acquaintances, and hired hands and customers were their neighbors and treated with due respect. I'm forever grateful for becoming one of those neighbors and recipients of their loving generosity. Inside Trinity Episcopal Church are new beautiful memorials to their parents including the Stations of the Cross, the beautiful painting of Jesus' baptism by John the Baptist, and a beautiful rendition of the Nativity alongside the entrance to the nave. The wonder of the story of the Bible is wonderfully enhanced in that sanctuary.

Many years of baptisms, marriages, and losses in death, were shared with them there in our life as fellow believers in all that Jesus taught us. The life of the Lord has never left us alone or comfortless. My enjoyment of being amongst the Hensels continues to this day. Very early on, my family began enjoying summer vacation on Lake Winnipesaukee, New Hampshire and on Lake Sebago, Maine, for many summers thereafter thanks to the Hensels. However, we enjoyed our ongoing conversations even more than the break. Amongst the fun and laughter, we certainly had many of the deeper searches for the Truth. I'll never forget Bob arriving unannounced with a crate full of lobsters, clams, wine, and the key to his boat. He didn't stay for but a moment and left saying, "Enjoy!" We did. My wife Peach, and our children Joel, Addie, and Brian, will never forget those earlier years. We traveled the extent of Winnipesaukee - on land and water.

I must mention here the time that Joel and I took an early morning spin on the boat to a restaurant at the southern end of the lake. This is a very large lake with an old steamship carrying tourists' day after day, summer after summer. Just across from the Hensel house at Pendleton Beach and the south lake beach front is the Amusement Center (also very old and summer wild). We got on the deck of the house watching the frolic on the other side. On the Fourth of July there were the fireworks and lots of people celebrating with thanksgiving, pride, and joy.

Back to my jaunt with Joel. We motored across to that other side near the Amusement Center, through the narrow channel to the lower Bay, stopped for gasoline, and then headed further south to the restaurant there in Laconia, New Hampshire After breakfast there, as we were climbing into the skiff for our jaunt home, I dropped the ignition key overboard. With many eyes watching from the bay windows of the breakfast nook, I dove into the water, praying that I would find the key. It was a mortifying incident. How does anyone drop keys and lose them in the deep water? Two people ventured out from their breakfast to see what was wrong and if they might be able to help. I told them what happened, and they couldn't help but to burst into hysterics. But they did stay to help! I dove in one more time, rummaged around at the bottom, and lo and behold, I found that key. We hurriedly untied the boat, started the engine among a gathered crowd clapping, and headed back for more fun at the Hensel house.

One day several years later Captain Bob arrived again with a crate of lobsters, clams, seafood, wine and beer, and joined us for the evening. What a treat! We conversed late into the evening, long after the children and Mom had gone to bed. Late into the night, Bob and I solved all the problems of the world!

"The True Meaning of the Holiday: Beyond the Pews"

(Fr. Michael Lavellee Pastor, St. Ann's Church,
North Oxford, Massachusetts, Dec. 4, 2015)

With the national celebration of Thanksgiving this past Thursday, we have entered into the holiday season. This season is commonly understood to include Thanksgiving, Hanukkah, Christmas, and New Year's Day. For most Americans, this time involves hectic schedules, decorating, shopping, parties, travel, visiting, and some time off from work on holidays.

As we begin this time of year, it is important to think about what the word "holiday" means. The New Illustrated Webster's Dictionary and Thesaurus tells us that holiday comes from "holy day" and originally meant "a day for special religious observance." In other words, holidays were religious celebrations on which believers gathered to worship God and hold community feasts.

The first Thanksgiving was set aside by the English founders of this state as a day to acknowledge blessings and presence as they colonized a new land. Hanukkah, or the eight-day Festival of Lights, celebrates the rededication of God's Temple in Jerusalem under the Maccabees in 164 BC. Christmas, the celebration of Christ's birth, begins on December 25 and extends into the month of January for Catholic Christians and some other Christian groups.

In today's world, as society becomes more secularized, we sometimes struggle to remember the religious basis for the holidays. Yet, if it were not for religion, holidays themselves would not exist. Our society encourages us to refrain from greeting others with "Merry Christmas" because it may offend those who do not have belief in God or who do not believe in Christ.

The fact is, however, that we cannot take the holy days out of the holiday. As much as people are legally free to not have faith or practice it, so they are as much legally free to believe in God, practice their faith and share their belief with others. As people of faith, we cannot allow the secularizing trends of our culture to prevent us from being who we are.

In recent years, some towns and municipalities have attempted to eliminate all religious symbols from public display on town property. Symbols like Nativity sets or menorahs have been depicted by critics as being offensive to those without faith. Yet, these symbols are the symbols of the holidays. They remind us what the reason for the season is so that we do not forget what we are actually celebrating from Thanksgiving to New Year's Day.

As people of faith, we should not be afraid to openly and proudly witness to the truth of what the holidays are really about. In this way, we share faith with those who do not have it and enrich our society with new courage and vitality. This holiday season presents us with new opportunities to bring the light of faith into the world. We can do this not just with our words but, more importantly, with our actions. For many, the holidays are a difficult time as families struggle with illness, the loss of a loved ones, family problems, or financial woes. When we take the time to listen to those who are in need, to reach out to those who hurt and help those who have lost hope, we allow them to know that God is real and at work in their lives. Let us live the holidays well.

"The Paschal Mystery: Who or What is God?"

The age-old question of life itself in all its wonder and complexities continues to be elusive with little to no accurate assessments of this seemingly obvious reality. Lately we've heard from scientific speculation that everything began from "zero." However, $0 = 0 = 0 = 0$. Again, the question of existence remains and here we are. From zero, this is all impossible! The verb "to be" is the name the Bible calls "God." "I Am" Imprinted on Altars and other significant places is the Alpha and Omega sign that signifies our belief that God is the beginning and the end. The Holy Bible is all about the existence of God. It is about the human experience of God.

Experience

Moses was watching his flock. And the angel of the Lord appeared to him in a flame of fire out of the midst of a bush; and he looked, and lo, the bush was burning, yet it was not consumed. And Moses turned aside. And saw this great sight and that the bush was not consumed by the fire. Here God called to him and said, 'Moses, Moses!' And he said, 'Here am I.' And God said, 'I am the God of your father, the God of Abraham, Isaac, and Jacob.' And Moses hid his face, for he was afraid to look at God.

Mission and Purpose

Then the Lord said, 'I have seen the affliction of my people who are in Egypt, and have heard their cry because of their taskmasters; I know their sufferings, and I have come down to deliver them out of the hand of the Egyptians, and to bring them up out of that land to a good and broad land to a good land flowing with milk and honey.' 'I will send you to Pharaoh!' But Moses replied, 'Who am I that I should go to Pharaoh and deliver the sons of Israel out of Egypt?' Then Moses said to God, 'If I come to the people of Israel and they ask me (about you) and why I came. and for your Name, what shall I say to them?' 'Tell them that I AM has sent you to them!' (See *Exodus Chapter 3* for accurate full account)

The famous Arnold Toynbee talked about the reality of God and the belief in "MIRACLES." He said that, "Miracles happen today. They are history-making, earth shaking, which change the whole course of history and the fate of nations." He says that believing in miracles is a basic necessity of mankind: "The fundamental need of our world today is a rebirth of belief in the supernatural. If this rebirth is not forthcoming from the so called 'progressive philosophers and humanist/materialists,' mankind will again yield to a strictly 'mechanical culture' with no thought or room for 'the higher mysteries'."

It is interesting to note that the power of belief has always come from the simpler peoples and societies not yet consumed by the proud materialism of the Great Powers. The spiritual nature of the human must begin from within and have been given by a higher source of inspiration, albeit, at least guiding principles. (Paraphrased from The Encyclopedia of 7700 Quotations) Are there guiding principles? What are they? Where do they come from? Christian theology teaches that I AM can be experienced and understood in what is called the Paschal Mystery. The Paschal Mystery is essentially our experience of God physically and spiritually

One of my all-time favorite movies was, and is, Spielberg's Artificial Intelligence. The ultimate bottom line or thesis of this production is that a machine has no soul. The first definition of "soul" in the Webster's Collegiate Dictionary is, "The animating spiritual presence in a human, often believed to survive death." At the start of the movie, a scientist warns the other builders of this "human likeness" that serious dangers come with the project. She warns of the lack of a soul in such a machine and the consequences thereof. The problem with this very realistic and programmed machine is that it cannot truly love as the real human soul is able to do. There is no eternal, living Spirit in the machine and the "falling into love" with that machine is simply death and oblivion. The dictionary definition of oblivion is: "The state of being utterly destroyed and forgotten forever." In Christian theology, the eternal soul, pure love, is a forever event. It is alive and well!

The Christian theology of the Paschal Mystery is that "God, our Father Creator, has a personal relationship with his human children... that this relationship is eternal... and that without that relationship called love, life is diminished and subject to oblivion." The consequence is death. Hence, our physical nature is animated spiritually.

One day on my way to my parish to celebrate the Sunday Eucharist, seeking on my car radio some inspiration for the day's reading and homily, an Atheist spokesperson was talking about the meaning of Atheism. In a nutshell, the theory presented was that we humans are simply a machine of, "nerves, wires, neurons, neatly self-contained and self-sufficient." Such a theory gave me an excellent backdrop for a homily and thesis of the Paschal Mystery. This was the second Sunday of Easter and the reality of God in Jesus as body and soul and the forever of pure love which comes from our Creator in a personal, living, soul relationship. The Holy Bible testifies to that Spirit which comes to and through us from the Creator.

The New Testament testifies to the historical Jesus who lived, taught, and loved among us as the archetype of the real human body and soul. That body being anointed and animated by that soul. The Valley of the Dry Bones reading in the Old Testament says that, "God breathed life into those bones." *(Ezekiel 37:1)* With this in mind, I urge you to read in your Bible Isaiah 61:1-9 and Ezekiel 37:1-10. These readings are most often referred to at the occasion of the Sacrament of Confirmation.

In those readings for Second Sunday of Easter, thinking of the Paschal Mystery, I was reminded of a story my Dad told me when I was a little boy. I used to go with my dad on his truck on business trips. We often went past the State House in Providence, Rhode Island en route. He knew that I was enamored by the stately beauty of that building and the reason for which it was constructed. On the pinnacle of that state house is a statue of an early American Indian representing her belief in the "Free Spirit," which animates us and teaches us about the "Freedom of the Human Soul." My dad went on to tell me about a governor who was loved by his constituents. He said that the governor (from another state in the union) was first elected as Mayor several times over, and then governor, again, elected over and over.

This extraordinary man was loved and elected because of his deeply felt humility of character and wonderful sense of humor. Dad said that this Governor would begin all of his speeches with, "So, how am I doing?" Then he would conclude with, "But by the Grace of God!" He would remind everybody that he prayed before every decision made, consulted with the wisest he could find among us, and that only by the Grace of God could we survive and thrive. He would always have a Biblical passage to confirm this belief.

At the age of ten, I went on a school trip to Washington D. C. In that trip I was further "in awe" by those trips and conversations with my dad. On that trip, after visiting Ford's Theater, the house next door where President Lincoln died, and the Lincoln Memorial, I deeply loved that spirit-filled man of humble character. I carry with me in my heart and soul the famous document of the Emancipation Proclamation stating, "Freedom from slavery to all mankind, in all places, from here on into the future."

Remember that prayer from mom? "Now I lay me down to sleep; I pray the Lord my soul to keep; If I should die before I wake; I pray the Lord my soul to take." The famous Saint Thomas Aquinas prayed daily this thought: "Lord, to thee I dedicate myself. O accept me as thou wilt; Give to me what thou wilt; how much and when thou wilt. Set me where thou wilt and deal with me in all things just as thou wilt." (Encyclopedia of Illustrations)

Freedom Epigram – Encyclopedia of Illustrations p. 462 #1787

An English publication offered a prize for the best definition of "friend." The following was the first prize selection: "A friend is the one who comes in when the whole world has gone out." The soul of each of us is fully seen and realized in Jesus of Nazareth. He was, and is, our best friend as His soul is enshrined in ours.

The Paschal Mystery can be understood on this Tribute to Friendship by an unknown author: "I love you not only for what you are, but what I am when I am with you. I love you not only for what you have made of yourself, but for what you are making of me. I love you not for closing your ears to the discords in me, but for adding to the music in me by worshipful listening. You have done it without a touch, without a word, without a sign. You have done it just by being yourself. " (Encyclopedia of Illustrations p. 463 #1793) The Lord has shown us the way in living, teaching, actions, resurrection, the gifts of the Holy Spirit, and into Eternity with those we love.

"Games"

Consider the following meditative games leading to an understanding of the ability to think and communicate. Here the question remains as to how we are able to communicate and understand each other. There must be, there is, a prime source within each and all of us. What is it?

Game #1

1. List the alphabet down the page from A-Z
2. After each letter, place a word of active communication, one person to another. These are verbs!
   A. "Answer" – ability to answer a question
   B. "Bless" – ability to give something "good" to another
   C. "Consort" – ability to unite on thoughts, ideas
   D. "Divulge" – ability to make known
   E. "Evoke" – ability to bring forth an answer
   F. "Forgive" – ability to be empathetic, to have experienced one's own need for forgiveness.
   G. "Greet" – ability to advance to common ground
   H. I. J., etc.
3. The point of such a game is to meditate on the difference between a machine such as a robot and the "anima" of being human.
4. You will discover that the robot can only repeat that which was programmed into it by the real anima… the human soul. The robot cannot truly "love" nor will it be truly able to forgive.
   "Forgive!"

Game #2:

Very early on, I had become fascinated with the Reverend Billy Graham's ability to randomly point to a Biblical verse and then expose its meaning and purpose for the understanding of his audience. Here is the meditative game:

1. Randomly open your Bible.
2. Close your eyes and point your index finger to the page below.
3. Write the verse you found on a sheet of paper.

4. Do this five consecutive times.
5. Chances are, you'll find a verse that will clearly speak to you: chances are you won't. So, try again the next time you set aside your regularly scheduled meditative time.

My eleven-year-old grandson Owen was presented with a chance to attend a well-organized, specialized Christian Camp in Western Pennsylvania in the Summer of 2019. With a somewhat nervous, but also excited, anticipation of this new adventure, I showed him the above game of approaching the Holy Bible. If not for any other reason, this exchange was a fond and teaching embrace between me and Owen. I cherish that singular, personal exchange.

So far, I know that Owen had a wonderful and learned experience at this two-week camp last summer, and is now encouraging other friends to attend next summer along with my now very excited grandchildren, Wesley, and Phoebe. I await their responses.

A Game of Self-Realization - ABCs of the Soul
Anima – The inner self -soul
Beatify – To make extremely joyful
Creation – Beginning of existence, Alpha and Omega, the Totality of all there is
Deity – The nature or state of the Divine – Comprehension – Being
Eternal – Without beginning or end - Alpha and Omega
Forgiven – Pardoned
Give – To provide
Holy – Belonging to, derived from, associated with the Divinity
Infinite - Without boundaries or limits; immeasurable; unlimited in spatial extent. Consider the reality of the Atom which has no beginning or end
Joy – No words can describe this experience in its fullest realization
K
Love – Pure thought
Mercy –
N
Omnipresent
Prayer – Conversation with the Divine

Quality – To be the best that one can be

Realize – To see for oneself

Serenity – Peace

Truth

Universal

Verify

Wonder

X

Y

Z

Meditative Game
- A game of pure love, pure thought
- Can be played by listing the alphabet and finding the words that explain the "anima"
- The anima is our ability to understand or realize one's own being which a "soul-less machine" cannot do
- A computer can only repeat that which we program into it

Try this for yourself:

Answer (v) To explain with understanding, comprehension

Beautify (v) To make beautiful, enhance, create

Communicate – The ability, and action of sharing one's anima

Determine – To reach a decision and understand it

E

F

Etc…

The Paschal Mystery is all about our given ability to understand our soul in relation to our Creator who we call God.

God's Name is

"I AM"

Thereby

We Are!

"Conversion"

The following opening stories to this article I titled "Conversion" is from a favorite biblical resource of mine, *Forward Day by Day*, published by Forward Movement Publications.

Sunday, January 8, 1 Epiphany: The Baptism of Our Lord
"And a voice came from heaven, 'You are my Son, the Beloved; with you I am well pleased'." *(Mark 1:4-11)* A priest colleague of mine tells the story about one year when he was preparing a sermon for the Feast of the Baptism of Christ. The words of the gospel prompted him to send both of his grown sons a text message: "You are my Son, the Beloved; with you I am well pleased." He never heard back from one son. The other son sent him a return message: "Thanks, Dad. Are you okay?"

These words, addressed to Jesus Christ by God, the Father, are words that God speaks to each one of us. Do we believe that? Or, if someone told us this, would we wonder about ulterior motives or whether that person was sane? It is so easy for us to feel that we are deficient, to focus on mistakes we've made or things that we haven't done. We find it hard to believe that we are loveable. Yet God keeps coming to us, reminding us that we are beloved exactly as we are.

Many of us will renew our Baptismal Covenant today. At baptism, all of us are marked as Christ's own. Rest in awareness of being God's beloved today. *(Also see: Ps 29; Genesis 1:1-5; Acts 19:1-7)*

Friday, January 6 The Epiphany
"And having been warned in a dream not to return to Herod, they left for their own country by another road." *(Matthew 2:1-12)* My family sets up a creche in our living room every year. It has all the typical figures of the Nativity: Mary, Joseph, the baby Jesus, the shepherds, and animals. We set it up a few days before Christmas. But we put the three magi somewhere else in the house. Moving them closer each day, we finally put them by the manger on January sixth. Their arrival marks the end of the Christmas season and the beginning of Epiphany.

The wise men followed the star to Bethlehem, paid homage, and offered their gifts. When it was time to leave the manger to return to their home country, they were told to avoid Herod and to go home another way. It is the end of Christmas and time for us to leave the manger, too. Could God be calling us to return by a different road? The magic of Christmas is over, but new life and possibility await us as we continue on our journey with Christ. We don't leave the manger unchanged. Reflect on your resolutions, hopes, and dreams for the year ahead: How might you follow a different road this year?

"O God, who revealed your only Son to the Gentiles by the leading of a star, mercifully grant that we, who know you now by faith, may after this life enjoy the splendor of your gracious Godhead, through Jesus Christ our Lord. Amen." *(Ps 72:1-7; Isaiah 60:1-6; Ephesians 3:1-12)*

In the need for conversion, there are many shared experiences which continue to give credence to our Christian faith. Many roads continue to lead us to our belief in God.

It was the famous St. Thomas Aquinas, Doctor of the Church, who formulated volume upon volume of theology in his lifelong attempt to teach formidable doctrines of the Christian faith. He said this on his death bed: "I have made many mistakes in my writing and teaching, but have since 'seen the Lord'." A dear friend and colleague of mine mentioned many times in this book said to me the day before he entered into Eternity: "If only I could get into the pulpit one more time!" (Father Howard C. Olson) Writer Walter B. Knight tells the story of a conversion experience:

> Years ago, a unique character was converted in the Water Street Mission in New York. It was the "old Colonel". Through drink he had sunken very low. At the time of his conversion he was sixty years old. He looked as if he were one hundred. He looked more like an animal than a human being. He was clothed in rags. The overcoat he wore was fastened with a nail. "Old Bill" was a caricature of the man he had been – a college graduate and a brilliant law student in the office of E. M. Stanton, Lincoln's Secretary of War.
>
> On the night of his conversion, he cried, "O Lord, if it is not too late, forgive and save this poor sinner!" God heard the cry of his heart.

He was gloriously saved. His intellect was restored. That which had been his greatest love and had almost ruined his life – strong drink – became his greatest hate. He became an honored and beloved Christian gentleman. (Encyclopedia of 7700 Illustrations)

Here is a story of John D. Rockefeller:

John D. Rockefeller, Sr., was strong and husky when small. He early determined to earn money and drove himself to the limit. At age 33, he earned his first million dollars. At age 43, he controlled the biggest company in the world. At age 53, he was the richest man on earth and the world's only billionaire.

Then he developed a sickness called "alopecia", where the hair of his head dropped off, his eyelashes and eyebrows disappeared, and he was shrunken like a mummy. His weekly income was one million dollars, but he digested only milk and crackers. He was so hated in Pennsylvania that he had to have bodyguards' day and night. He could not sleep, stopped smiling long since, and enjoyed nothing in life.

The doctors predicted he would not live over one year. The newspaper had gleefully written his obituary in advance – for convenience in sudden use. Those sleepless nights set him thinking. He realized with a new light that he 'could not take one dime into the next world'. Money was not everything.

The next morning found him a new man. He began to help churches with his amassed wealth. The poor and needy were never again overlooked. He established The Rockefeller Foundation whose funding of medical research led to the discovery of penicillin and other wonder drugs. John D. began to sleep well, eat, and enjoy life.

The doctors had predicted that he would not live past 54 years. He lived to his 98th year. (Encyclopedia of 7700 Quotations)

The definition of CONVERSION here is the act and experience of growing from one idea to another as in entering into a religious belief or way of thinking. To convert to Christian Faith is to become more fully aware of its beliefs and enter into such a conversation. Many such conversions have been said to be actual spiritual experiences such as a Beatific Vision. Other conversions such as that of journalist Lee Strobel, author of *The Case for Christ*. Strobel, an Atheist set out to disprove the Gospel accounts of Jesus of Nazareth. In his dogged and determined research he became a convert and devoted follower. The famed psychiatrist, Dr. Scott Peck found his belief after years of helping others. History is filled with myriads of stories told and untold of conversion to the Faith.

"A Novel Idea?"

Recently, heading from my home in the area of the Douglas Massachusetts State Forest to a nearby parish to fill in as Celebrant, a tree got in the way. The last-minute call to say the Mass was from the Pastor of the church, as he was struggling with a gastronomical virus. Of course, I responded to the emergency. The church is about thirty-five minutes away, and I had enough time to be there within the hour.

The windy road out from my home is narrow and in the woods. Rounding a corner, I had to suddenly stop as a tree had fallen across the road. At the tree were three men and a young woman trying to move the tree. It wasn't budging. In my own panic, I called my ailing colleague to tell him of my situation and that I would do my best to still get there on time if not a few minutes late. He assured me that it would be okay and that it is in God's hands to help us. He said that, "Parishioners can begin the celebration and pray for your safe arrival and the Prayer of Consecration will be awaiting your presence." The situation at hand was the fallen tree and the folks on the other side going in the opposite direction were obviously also anxious to get safely to their respective destinations.

Calls for help were made to the local police. Before exiting my car and from my perspective, I could easily see that the ones at work were trying to push the tree in the wrong direction. In my belief perspective, the error was shown to me. "Here comes a priest," said one man to the others. "Well, he can pray for us," said another, and we all laughed. With one hand, I easily pushed the tree off the road and cleared the way for all of us to go ahead to our respective destinations. I said to the others that during my own prayers I could see the solution to our problem. I expect that the others may have witnessed God's hands at work in this anxious situation. It is also true that such coincidences do happen.

Way back in ancient history, a man named Socrates believed that man's power to accomplish easy or difficult tasks comes to us from a Greater Power. His student, the great philosopher, Plato, wrote prolifically about the "light" that gives humans the power to solve whatever problems we face. The ancient Hebrews taught us that God, our Creator, provides the light needed to solve our problems. Our oftentimes reluctance to draw on that "light" leaves us alone and helpless in the solution to problems and knowledge of the existence of Truth.

I arrived on time for the evening Mass and had an immediate and pertinent story to tell on a unprepared homily. We all had a good laugh and also another witness to the power from above. All believers in God can easily relate. I still wonder if the on-hand observers of that tree incident might be wondering about the arrival of a priest at the nick of time and somehow knew how to so easily move that tree. I had thanked God that somewhere along the way the Fulcrum Solution was learned.

There also has been pertinent philosophy in history known as Humanism. Humanism assumes that human beings are the highest power and contained within each of us is all the power that exists. In other words, there is no Creator who provides any light or help or anything other than our own power to solve our own problems. This means that prayer, light, truth, or any such existence is simply a figment of our singular imaginations. The philosophy indicates that, "Our power to think and act is of our own making." In other words, if I decide to be in control it is my own prerogative to do so. This is Atheism.

Using the tree incident is a simple example of belief or non-belief pertaining to things we need to think about in our understanding of truth and from whence that truth comes. It is the age-old battle between us as being alone in the universe to figure out our own solutions and advancement for the future or a belief in real truth that exists outside of ourselves and gives us the light, power, and anything else that we need to not only go forward, but to go forward in the right direction, simply because there is a right direction. The age-old question? Does Truth exist and from whence does it emanate? Does that Truth help or guide us into the solution of our problems?

The author Mark Dyer, in his book *There is A Spiritual Solution to Every Problem,* clearly delineates the fact of light beyond each of us which can be drawn upon to solve problems and seek answers beyond our singular power to solve every problem in our own ways devised. He further states that Truth, light, power exists and that such spiritual power gives us the solutions to our problems and a future direction towards which we can move.

Every year, Christians around the world celebrate the Feast of All Saints and All Souls. All Saints Day is November first and All Souls on the second. The Saints and All Souls we remember or don't appear on our radar screen are those who, because of the belief and faith in God, have contributed to this world for the good and benefit of all mankind and, thus, each of us. Saints and All Souls come from everywhere. Even non-believers have given of themselves in special ways and believers believe that everyone's contribution is a gift from God.

A couple brief examples of those Saints and Souls are the likes of Albert Einstein who began the solutions and map of the universe; Francis of Assisi who turned his inherited fortune and power in the military into the power of God's love; or an Abraham Lincoln, with his understanding of the Bible brought freedom and equality of being to every soul; or a Dr. Saulk, who brought the world a cure for a dreadful disease; or a Mother Theresa who loved, cared for, and brought healing to the most diseased, poor and decrepit. The Saints and Souls are myriads and myriads of people who, in faith and in hope for the future, made it happen.

As I write this, I'm reminded of a funeral. I was called to add some spiritual wisdom and hope in the throes of mortality. A call came to me from the local funeral director asking if I would officiate at this funeral. I came to find out I had baptized the deceased young man thirty years earlier. He was an infant at the time of his Baptism. His family and I recalled that Baptism and the fruits which followed. For all good reasons, Jacob was loved and enabled to give the same. In his upbringing, he learned to love his country and he had a belief in God. As a young boy he insisted that he wear either Marine Corps battle fatigues, a police uniform, or a firefighter's gear. Each Halloween he drew straws as to which costume he would wear.

"The Confessional"

The simple and basic truth is that "being" cannot "be" in a vacuum. We are all interrelated and it is our relationships and interactions in these relationships that determine either our growth or that which would be hurtful. The Latin term "anima" states that our very being is soul; inner self. Our soul, inner self, is built on the premise that we cannot ever be alone. Our "beingness" is "anima" or somehow eternal within our individual beingness, our relationships that connect our beingness, and "The Other" which connects such beingness. "The Other" is the major question. Who or what is it that connects us to each other and thereby we are able to communicate with one another. There must be a primary source for this to happen. Hence, our Soul is who we are, and The Other is that which connects our souls. Thus, Creator/Creation is from the theory that we are "Soul" and each of us is of that primary source. In Religion we call that "Other" God. We are alive because we are created from that source whom we call God. Hence the conclusion of God Creator and Creation. Nothing cannot create something".

The act of confession means belief in a Creator in whom we can trust with all we need to live or be Anima. We cannot be born, survive, or thrive without this matter of trust in a higher source of power. Confession is the act of seeking that higher power for the information we need to learn, grow, and thrive. In the religious confessional, we ask God through mutual trust in both Creator and each other for forgiveness, healing, and the safety of our souls, our anima.

It is interesting to note again that the rest of the animal kingdom other than human beings have the incredible instinct and ability to be on their own soon after birth. The world in which they are born provides all they need to survive. This is not so for humans in that, we cannot be born or live through life without extreme loving care. We need love in order to survive and then certainly to thrive. In the confession to God and one another such love and trust is necessary for our survival and then hopefully our growth. This is where forgiveness happens!

In the old days the priest's hat was worn to signify our relationship to God and then our trustworthy relationship to each other. In this, we confirm that such a relationship is Sacred. This hat in the Western Church is called a biretta. The biretta had four corners with three wings. Over the left ear, the absent wing signified a flap over the ear whereas the right ear was open for listening, and the left flap kept such confidence from going out the other side as into anyone else's ear, mind, heart, and soul. All that was said and heard from a confessor, the priest, or any trustworthy individual, was to go to God. The three wings represented Father – Son – Holy Spirit as the guideposts for the confessor and listener. The confession stopped there in the prayer to God for forgiveness. The priest is entrusted with that confession for the sake of trust, guidance, and healing. We are all meant to be confidentially present to each other.

It has become increasingly clear to me over these years how important it is to work at cleansing our souls. As such a dysfunctional environment as our lives and the world around us can and does become, we are in regular need of mercy, forgiveness, and healing. In the Christian Fellowship commonly known as the Church, we come together seeking such understanding and fuller comprehension. The Sacrament of Penance is one of the tools we utilize for this very end with the hope of renewal. Renewal can only be found in the realm of forgiveness and healing. This is another gift from the Higher Power we call God. In the *Anglican Book of Common Prayer*, the Confession Prayer begins with a statement of reaching to that higher power for such mercy and the grace which is promised to follow as long as our prayer is forthright and as sincere as possible.

"Bless me Father, for I have sinned." (B. C. P., p. 447) "Sin" means whatever dysfunction we sense within ourselves that is causing our own unhealthy condition in need of healing. Only Mercy and Forgiveness can provide for our ability to move forward and grow in peace both within ourselves as well as with our Higher Power. In an alternate version of this prayer, the term "Father" is eliminated so that we do not confuse the human being to whom we are confessing with our God in Heaven. However, we go to other human beings in this prayer acknowledging trust in the other's sincerity and desire to be of truthful help, God willing.

Our Confession is all about our sincerity and truth with and for each other. This is purposefully meant to be confidential between you, me, and God. We are entrusted with the grace of pure love. Pure love is one's ability to trust and be trusted, entrusting God's love to one another. The breaking down of such pure love breaks down our ability of confession allowing forgiveness, mercy, and mutual comprehension to be broken.

I'll never forget a Confession brought to me many years ago. It certainly changed my life as a priest in the Church who supposedly understands the purpose and meaning of the confessional. To be a weak and sinful human being entrusted with the sincerity of another is shaky ground unless a higher sincerity, and truth enters in and allows such a conversation to take place. We must each be truthful and trustworthy. Lord, help us in such a time of Holy Purpose. I am reminded again and again of my dear colleague and friend Father Howard Olsen saying the following in one of his wonderfully humorous moments:

"George, I was confronted the other day by a critic who asked me if I was a man or a priest." In quick wit he retorted, "Is there a difference? This cassock I'm wearing covers a multitude of sins. But I am a whole lot cheaper than a psychiatrist!" I am commissioned to be truthful and sincere in that to which I am called to function. Father Olsen disclaimed any pretext of being a Saint as Sainthood is commonly understood. He continued, "I regularly ask the Father for you to trust in my sincerity and be faithful to that trust."

One who came to me, a priest, because he had learned in his upbringing that one such could be trusted and entrusted with one's very life. He didn't know me from Adam but had heard that he indeed could trust me with his confession and as well be understanding. It changed my life in listening because the confession was complete, honest, and in need of a trusted friend."

For the next several weeks, a member of AA spilled his entire life to me in confidence. Somewhere and somehow, he heard that he could trust me and that my priesthood gave credence to my ability to listen and perhaps comprehend as one born in sinful dysfunction to another, and that Gods' mercy would somehow intervene. This time together clearly made us trusted, comprehensive friends. Here is a true story about my friend that can be shared as he has allowed me to, with humble and helpful purpose to others:

The Confession

It was around 1976, and I was working at a seasonal restaurant in Mendon, Massachusetts. There I would meet a gentleman by the name of Father George Warren. I was raised on Nantucket Island in the Roman Catholic Faith, and Fr. Warren looked like a priest to me.

At the time ,I was struggling with an alcohol addiction, dying on the inside and smiling on the outside, looking for something or someone to ease the pain I was in mentally. Sixteen long years would pass before I would get to know Fr. Warren on a personal level. After finally talking with this man, I would learn he was the Minister of Trinity Episcopal Church in Milford Mass. How was he going to help me, I wondered, he being of the Episcopal faith and me Catholic?

After many conversations I would eventually visit his church for one reason or another, weddings, funerals, that sort of thing. Slowly, I realized this was very similar to the Catholic Church, prayers and all! My best friend who I grew up with on Nantucket was an Episcopalian and always wanted me to attend his church just to see what it was like. Back then, we just did not venture to each other's churches. Sad but true.

Finally, Fr. Warren asked me to attend a Sunday morning service, which I did. Once again, I was pleasantly surprised at the similarities to my own faith. I spoke with him after the service, got a great big handshake, and he said, "Welcome, come back again anytime." This made me feel good inside. I would remember this for a long time.

I would eventually meet a woman, who, try as she might, thought she could help me stay sober. Father Warren would eventually marry us, and things began to look up. It was to no avail, however, and soon my alcoholism would rear its ugly head. Father Warren would be called to the home on occasion to try and quell the situation, yet nothing worked. I would end up in detox on December 23rd, 1981, leaving my wife, two children from a previous marriage, a six-month old child, my father who was staying with us at the time, and my job though Christmas holidays. While in detox, I was sitting on my bed and noticed the sun's rays beating down through the windows.

I followed the rays back up toward the sky, and I instinctively began to pray and thought perhaps there might just be a ray of hope for me. When I got out of detox, my wife had already set me up at a meeting where alcoholics go to help each other stay sober. From that day until this, I have not found it necessary to pick up a drink thanks to a Higher Power who I pray to every day, simply asking Him to keep me away from a drink for one day. If I am successful, I thank Him every night before bed. I would eventually learn that this Higher Power of mine, whom I choose to call God, was the same one who I had given up on so many years ago. Not only has he helped me stay sober, but He would once call on Fr. Warren to become an integral part of my life.

Unfortunately, the marriage did not survive ,and the program I was practicing so faithfully would eventually lead me in a direction that if I wished to maintain any quality of sobriety there would be certain things I must do. One was I must clear away the wreckage of my past, admitting to God, myself, and another human being, the exact nature of my wrongs, or, if you will, my sins. This brought me to the point where I would ask Fr. Warren if we could meet and discuss what I needed from him to help maintain my sobriety. He unquestioningly agreed! We would meet several times once a week where I would do most of the talking and he would sit there patiently listening to every word I said. When it was over, he pointed out to me that this was just like a confession. I told him of all the bad things I had done in the past, at which point he offered me absolution and a blessing, sending me on my way to hopefully sin no more.

I cannot describe the emotion or feeling I got as a result of this. I was able to do what was asked from my program and not only did I admit my wrongs to another human being, but that human being was also a Priest. It doesn't get any better than that. I was, in fact, a new man, so to speak. I was free of an enormous burden and I had God back in my life. I had given up on Him, and I would come to know He never gave up on me. None of this would have been possible if God had not put Fr. Warren in my life. As a result of this experience, we have friendship that continues to this day. My faith in God has only increased as a result of this experience. And for that I shall be eternally grateful. Thank you, Father Warren.

My friend John in "Mister Roger's Neighborhood" –
Nantucket, MA – 1950s

"The Confessional"

In the history of the Church, priests have worn hats as a partial sign of the meaning of priesthood. The biretta is a four cornered cap worn by priests as distinguished from an order of ordained ministry known as deacons, priests, and bishops. The four cornered cap has three open wings with one wing missing, meaning an open ear to hear confessions. The three wings represent the Father, the Son, and the Holy Spirit.

Concerning the Rite

The ministry of reconciliation, which has been committed by Christ to his Church, is exercised through the care each Christian has for others, through the common prayer of Christians assembled for public worship, and through the priesthood of the Church and its ministers' declaring absolution.

The Reconciliation of a Penitent is available for all who desire it. It is not restricted to times of sickness. Confessions may be heard anytime and anywhere.

Two equivalent forms of service are provided here to meet the needs of penitents. The absolution in these services may be pronounced only by a bishop or a priest. Another Christian may be asked to hear a confession, but it must be made clear to the penitent that absolution will not be pronounced; instead, a declaration of forgiveness is provided.

When a confession is heard in a church building, the confessor may sit inside the altar rails or in a place set aside to give greater privacy, and the penitent kneels nearby. If preferred, the confessor and penitent may sit face to face for a spiritual conference leading to absolution or a declaration of forgiveness.

When the penitent has confessed all serious sins troubling the conscience and has given evidence of due contrition, the priest gives such counsel and encouragement as are needed and pronounces absolution. Before giving absolution, the priest may assign to the penitent a psalm, prayer, or hymn to be said, or something to be done, as a sign of penitence and act of thanksgiving.

The content of a confession is not normally a matter of subsequent discussion. The secrecy of a confession is morally absolute for the confessor and must under no circumstances be broken.

The Reconciliation of a Penitent
Form One
The Penitent begins:
Bless me, for I have sinned.
The Priest says:
The Lord be in your heart and upon your lips that you may truly and humbly confess your sins: In the Name of the Father, and of the Son, and of the Holy Spirit. Amen.

Penitent
I confess to Almighty God, to his Church, and to you, that I have sinned by my own fault in thought, word, and deed, in things done and left undone; especially_____. For these and all other sins which I cannot now remember, I am truly sorry. I pray God to have mercy on me. I firmly intend amendment of life, and I humbly beg forgiveness of God and his Church, and ask you for counsel, direction, and absolution.
Here the Priest may offer counsel, direction, and comfort.

The Priest then pronounces this absolution:
Our Lord Jesus Christ, who has left power to his Church to absolve all sinners who truly repent and believe in him, of his great mercy forgive you all your offenses; and by his authority committed to me, I absolve you from all your sins in the Name of the Father, and of the Son, and of the Holy Spirit. Amen.
or this
Our Lord Jesus Christ, who offered himself to be sacrificed for us to the Father, and who conferred power on his Church to forgive sins, absolve you through my ministry by the grace of the Holy Spirit, and restore you in the perfect peace of the Church. Amen.
The Priest adds:
The Lord has put away all your sins.
Penitent

Thanks be to God.

The Priest concludes:

Go (or abide) in peace, and pray for me, a sinner.

Declaration of Forgiveness

To be used by a Deacon or Lay Person

Our Lord Jesus Christ, who offered himself to be sacrificed for us to the Father, forgives your sins by the grace of the Holy Spirit. Amen.

(The Consecration of the Priest – Prayer Book, p. 533)

"Learning to Understand the Sacraments"

Sacrament: "A rite instituted by Jesus that confers sanctifying grace on the receiver." The two principle Sacraments are Holy Baptism and The Holy Eucharist, followed by Confirmation, Penitence, Holy Matrimony, Holy Orders, and Unction. These are shown as, "the outward and visible signs of the inward and spiritual Grace." During our ongoing practice of these sacraments, much misunderstanding can and does take place leaving room for greater comprehension of the same. Oftentimes humorous stories evolve in the practice of being the Church. The following humorous stories are among the many that do happen en route.

Some Wedding Foibles

My dear friend and colleague, Father Howard Olsen, had great wit and a wonderful sense of humor. His wit was always immediate with a quip to anything one said and usually with a bit of wisdom in the mix.

One time in planning the marriage and the wedding of an eager young couple, the date and time was set. All invitations were out for the wedding and no chance of changing it. In the meantime, funeral plans had to be made for two grieving families, and there was no choice but to plan these masses and also have the wedding between the two. There was plenty of time for all to happen with no rush except that all happened on time.

We all know that the bride always arrived for her wedding a bit late. On the night of the wedding rehearsal, the couple were reminded of the timeline complication. The bride still had leeway time for tardiness but still needed to arrive in ample time between the two funerals. Well, it didn't work out! The bride arrived as the first hearse was just leaving, and exiting the church as the second hearse was waiting out front. If omens were believed, this bride and groom would most likely be unable to be happy. However, we Christians do not believe in ominous omens. If omens are real, they could only be joyful ones as they would emanate from gifts of the Holy Spirit as a reminder of our own vulnerabilities or just as simple misuse of our planning abilities. Father Olsen said to them, "As rain might fall on any wedding day, this is good luck!"

. . .

Speeding Up March

"The Wedding March has been so distorted that its composer would have difficulty recognizing it," says musicologist Maurice Zam. The March comes from Wagner's opera Lehengrin, and the tempo of it as indicated by Wagner was andante con moto. This means, "faster than a walk." It should be a joyful rhythmic swing toward the altar. Instead, the Wedding March today is played so slowly that only an acrobat could keep her balance in the promenade up the aisle. Better keyed for a murderer in his walk to the last mile toward legal extinction. It has become the most agonizing march in the history of civilized man.

Wagner's directions were siegreicher mut, which means, "advance forward." "A courageous spirit," Zam concludes, "is the mood and tempo which should motivate anyone getting married." The cure? It involves the reformation of all future organists and musicians so that they play a wedding march andante con moto, meaning, "Let's speed this thing up and get on to the main business, which is a happy honeymoon." (Encyclopedia of 7700 Quotations #3327).

. . .

At my niece Elisa's wedding, her dad (my brother Jim), was quite nervous and, of course, emotional about giving his little girl away to Brian. Now, rehearsals the evening before are usually quite chaotic, and no one believes that everything will go smoothly on the Big Day. My brother's comment to me at the rehearsal and still repeated at the dinner afterwards was, "This is like a Chinese fire drill! Do you know what you are doing?" Elisa was calm, cool, and collected, as always. She had no doubt, or didn't let on at least, that all wouldn't go smoothly and had no concerns that the rehearsal was seemingly chaotic. The wedding was spectacular, and one wonderful home and three beautiful children later, Jackson, Darien and Tristan are being raised well towards a healthy future.

• • •

A Bishop's Advice

"If you are for pleasure, marry; if you prize rosy health, marry. A good wife is heaven's last best gift to a man; his angel of mercy; minister of graces innumerable; his gem of many virtues; his box of jewels; voice, his sweetest music; her smiles, his brightest day;, her kiss, the guardian of innocence; her arms the pale of his safety; the balm of his life; her industry, his surest wealth; her economy, his safest steward; her lips, his faithful counsellors; her bosom, the softest pillow of his cares; and her prayers, the ablest advocates of Heaven's blessing on his head." (Bishop Taylor, Encycl. Of Quotations #3328).

• • •

At one wedding, the photographer approached me for instructions on photo ops. These instructions are standard as to the place, time and stance of the photographers. "No interruptions of the ceremony!" Apparently, the photographer didn't understand and broke all the rules.

During the second reading, *I Corinthians 13* (the meaning of love and faith), the photographer jumped to the isle directly in front of the altar between the choir stalls in front of the bride and groom. She placed herself prostrated on the floor with half her butt in full view because of tight, non-fitting slacks and proceeded with flash after flash. Everyone's attention zeroed in on the spectacle as I had to cease reading this clearly important and memorable reading to, as politely as possible, ask her to quickly finish and return to hiding. How does one then proceed with dignity and meaning? It was difficult!

• • •

Here is another minister's experience as he shared the following account:

They wanted a Christian wedding but a quiet one, so they chose to be married in the parsonage rather than in the church. The pastor's wife had made everything spic and span for the celebratory occasion. When the time came, the wedding party arrived – the couple to be married and their attendants.

The ceremony proceeded, and the Minister (who happened to be my son) came to the part where the bride was asked, "Do you take this man to be your lawful wedded husband?" Just at that instant the clock just above the heads of the couple interrupted with its hourly serenade. In this instance, it was a bombast of seven appropriate "Cuckoo! Cuckoo! Cuckoo!" The pastor's wife had forgotten this one critical matter. What an interruption it was! If was difficult to proceed. The bride never regained her composure through the rest of the ceremony." Carl Williams from Encyc. of 7700 Quotes #3321)

. . .

At another infamous wedding as a very young priest in my first parish and one of my first weddings, I made a faux pas that I continue to this day to hear about. During the reading of the Holy Gospel from John, with everyone standing at solemn attention, I said, "Blessed is he who gives his wife for his friend." No one dared laugh, but all heard it. I just kept on reading to the conclusion of that reading and proceeded with the ceremony. The correct words from the Gospel are "Blessed is he who gives his life for his friends." This so called "Freudian Slip" has followed me throughout my career as a priest in the church. Thanks be to God that no call of admonishment came to me from the bishop. But I did hear a word from a later bishop with a broad smile and a pat on the back: "So, George, have you yet repented of telling the folks that it is good for a groom to give his wife to his friend?"

. . .

Early on in my own formative journey, at a time that the Sacraments were understood for their directions in human behaviors, I felt a clear tug of war with my need for Sacrament and the passions within my nature. It has become clearer to me as life moved forward that our human passions can and should go hand in hand with the meaning and direction of our natural needs and passions. One of the major Sacraments is Holy Matrimony. The church's teaching was clear about the relationships between people as needing Sacramental understanding and value. In my earlier years, the God given "connubial bliss" is to be observed as Sacramental. This still holds true, yet hardly observed at this time in social history. Couples were married after a long and healthful process of evolving friendship, trust, and commitment. Connubial enjoyment was to be reserved for the committed couple.

During the so-called "sexual revolution" of the 1960s, the Sacramental value of sex was compromised to point of casual entertainment. One can well imagine how excited many became over this newfound freedom. Along with this was the downhill trend of sexual behavior and a serious loss of commitment and trust needed for all healthy relationships. At least during my earlier years, we had been given the foundation and direction needed to hold our self-centered passions in check. We understood the path necessary for healthy relationship and marriage.

I well recall the quandary I faced in the moment of passion. My first experience of connubial bliss happened prior to my much-needed restraint. In those days, we commonly knew better, and we knew that waiting for the Sacrament was important for the ongoing future of such a relationship. Waiting, patience, and the order of evolving friendship, I believe, still hold as true and necessary for the building of trust and higher meaning of one's love for another. In my own case, because of the foundation given to me as a Christian, I sought forgiveness and painfully learned from the experience. Of course, we are all human, and the needs for sexual desire are always present. To make connubial bliss between loving partners less than sacramental is dangerous ground. It is the gift God reserved for the total trust, commitment and health of the Sacramental Love.

The church has always stressed the highest commitments of love are sacramental and provided for the good of society. "Do you take this person as your lawfully wedded husband/wife?" "I do." The nuclear family is the archetype of the greater society as trust, commitment, and true love for another is a requisite. Along with the "sexual revolution" or "free love" movement came a breakdown of the larger society as our commitments to each other were no longer Sacramental. The breakdown of the micro family also became the breakdown of our society's ability to love, trust, and be committed totally to one another.

I'll never forget Bishop Higgin's account of a person seeking to divorce his wife to marry another. He told the then priest Fr. Higgins that he cared for his wife and children but "fell in love with the woman next door." Fr. Higgins curt response was, "You should never have gotten that close to the woman next door."

As life and living are not easy, and it often takes great effort to solve problems, we always need guidance to get us to the next stage in our journey. And yes, we are all complicated in many ways with much need for support, guidance, and direction. The Sacraments supply such support, guidance, and direction. The Gifts of the Holy Spirit are the needed ingredients to solve our complicated existences.

The Gifts of the Holy Spirit are:

Wisdom

Understanding

Counsel

Fortitude

Knowledge

Piety

Fear of the Lord

* * * * * * * * * * * *

From The Practice of Religion
By Reverend Archibald Campbell Knowles, D.D.

THE SPIRITUAL LIFE

THE Spiritual Life will ever be a conflict of the soul with the "powers of evil." Temptation comes to test and develop us, to train us to be true soldiers and servants of CHRIST. Temptation only becomes sin when yielded to. It is resisted by the Grace of GOD. Face to face with the "*deceits of the world, the flesh and the Devil*" we must remember that "*with every temptation GOD makes the way of escape.*" Forewarned is forearmed, and so we need to know of the nature of sin and grace.

Family clinic to open Tuesday ready or not

REFURBISHING CENTER: The Youth Group of St. Barnabas Church works on renovating the former South Shore Center for its new use as a clinic.

Party With Santa: About 30 children from Ladd School talked with Santa Claus at St. Barnabas Episcopal Church in Apponaug last night. Santa's trip from the North Pole was sponsored by the Senior Young People and the Episcopal Church Women, both of St. Barnabas.

"The Hat"

Back in the 1970s, I headed over to R. I. Hospital for routine pastoral visits. Several of my parishioners were there and one other had just been admitted for surgery the next morning. At the reception desk in the main lobby of the hospital I asked for a nurse. Next to me at the desk a young woman said to me, "I am a nurse. Can I help you?" I proceeded to ask her about the kind of surgery for which my parishioner was being prepared. Of course, I was dressed in my clerical uniform. The young nurse was not in the usual nurse's uniform. I thanked her immediately for coming to my aid and taking the time on her off-duty time. She said that she was indeed "on duty." I was then surprised that she was not in uniform and easily identified as a nurse. I jokingly asked, "Where's your cap?"

This question set the rest of our brief conversation into a downhill trend. She responded by saying that the "demeaning uniform" was no longer the trend. She told me that nurses have been treated as second class servants for all too long and that she was "no-one's servant." I clearly understood her argument and sympathized, but I went on to talk about our roles as servants. I told her how much I always appreciated the expertise, hard work, and caregiving sensitivities of the nurse. And, certainly more often than not, the markings help all who serve the needs of others to be more distinctly recognized. I told her that the old nurse's uniform, for me, admittedly an old timer meant something very important and special. Still intimidated by my absurd question, she sped off in a huff.

At one time, a long time ago, every profession had a special hat as part of the service they provided. Police, firefighters, military, and some others still don the hat as identification for their servanthood. Priests and ministers are usually still identified by special suits or some other identification as clergy.

Another hat that we once wore at all religious services was the biretta. The biretta has three wings on the top sides with one wing missing on the left side. The wings represent the power of the Holy Trinity. The missing left wing represents an ear flap covering the left ear. This hat means that the priest listens to the penitent with the right ear with faith in the Father, Son, and Holy Spirit and in that power for servanthood tries to advise the penitent with the best advice possible and belief in the unconditional and forgiving love of God. The left flap over the ear means that the conversation was private and left into God's hands. The confession means that the conversation went directly to God and nowhere else, not even in the judgement and memory of the priest. The hat, the biretta, represented another, "outward and visible sign of the inward and spiritual Grace."

I'll not forget a little boy as he was exiting the church asking me, "Where did you get the Mickey Mouse hat?" This was a good many years after the biretta was universally abandoned.

The dictionary definition of "servanthood" is, "One that serves another". It also defines it as, "One employed to perform household services." "Service" is defined as, "The occupation of a servant" and "work or duty to serve others." Hence, in the old days, the servant wore a hat identifying the kind of service provided and even the belief in that service. I'm not sure if we need the old hats back but it is clear that we need to know that in which we believe and somehow put that belief into action as best we know how.

The higher definition of these hats is sacrifice. Sacrifice is a spiritual matter where we are all called to purposefully give of their selves, time, and talent for the sake of the other. Sacrificial giving is the spiritual act whereby one knowingly and willingly offers himself/herself for the good of the other and for the good of all.

Bishop Tucker of Uganda started out as an artist and in this endeavor later became a Bishop. One day he was painting a picture of a poor woman thinly clad and pressing a baby to her bosom, wandering homeless on a stormy night on the dark, deserted street. As the picture grew, the artist suddenly threw down his book, exclaiming, "Instead of merely painting the lost, I will go out and save them." He went to Africa where he became a Bishop in Uganda. (#5640 Encyclopedia of 7700 Illustrations)

The famous David Livingstone wrote:

> People talk of the sacrifice I have made in spending so much of my life in Africa. Can that be called a sacrifice which is simply paid back as a small part of the great debt owing to our God, which we can never repay? Is that a sacrifice which brings its own reward of healthful activity, the consciousness of doing good, peace of mind, and a bright hope of a glorious destiny hereafter?
>
> Away with such a word, such a view, and such a thought! It is emphatically no sacrifice. Say rather it is a privilege. Anxiety, sickness, suffering or danger now and then, with a foregoing of the common conveniences and charities of this life may make us pause and cause the spirit to waver and sink, but let this be for a moment. All these are nothing when compared with the glory which shall hereafter be revealed in and for us. I never made a sacrifice. Of this we ought not to talk when we remember the great sacrifice which He made who left his Father's throne on high to give Himself for us.
>
> (Encyc. Of Illustrations #5189)

. . .

A classic in the annals of the U. S. Coast Guard is the story of Captain Pat Etheridge of the Cape Hatteras station. One night in a howling hurricane the lookout observed a distress signal from a ship that had gone aground on the dangerous Diamond Shoals, ten miles at sea. The lifeboats could be easily launched, the lookout thought, but getting them back in again… Captain Etheridge ordered the boats rolled out. One of the lifeguards protested, "Captain Pat, we can get out there, but we can never get back!" "Boys, we don't have to come back," came the reply that has gone down in history. (Encyc. Of Illust. #5191).

. . .

The Rev. Alan Redpath tells of a lady of his acquaintance who has a little motto over her kitchen sink that reads as follows: "Divine service is conducted here three times daily." This is the type of industry Christ honors. (Encyc. #5651) Whatever hat we wear, if its mission is spiritually from the heart, it is of the purpose of God.

"Politics and Religion"

Many, maybe even most, of us can probably say that as long as we can remember, Thanksgiving Day was a positive experience only when politics and religion were not discussed. My own first, internally said Thanksgiving prayer was, "Thank you Lord for my right to a secret ballot." Also, the only mention of God was in the Thanksgiving prayer for family, friends, and our beloved nation. The rest of the day was in banal conversation, catching up with each other's routine schedules, and thanking the Lord for a wonderful meal and the day off. It is well worth it, on an important day, to say, "Thank you!" and it is my favorite. My second favorite is the Fourth of July.

The primary reason we avoid politics and religion is due to our various views of the world in which we live. The problem gets to be a problem when we go too far in finding reasonable solutions to the world's issues and selected ways of solving them. As Americans, we can be thankful for intelligent forbearers who designed a system which allows all views to be debated and solved reasonably. Thanks be to God for those dedicated people who knew how to create a government and society which could reasonably solve its own and other world views. The Constitution, Bill of Rights, checks and balances program and a focused, trustworthy judicial system provides us with ways to solve our issues without killing each other in the process. This has been, for us, a balanced system of religion and politics.

In the next article, my intention is to point out a clear, or *the* clearest distinction of the last and this century's opposing political and religious views. It is the debate between Capitalism and Communism; Tyranny and Freedom; Atheism and God; Science and Mystery. The article is about Bolshevism, as this was the initiating philosophy which brought the debate to heated and unreasonable levels, threatening the intelligence, peace, and safety of the world.

I do believe that the good and the evil exists in all the varying points of view and that, somehow, reasonable debate will ultimately separate the wheat from the chaff, and civilization will be enabled to move forward. My own bias is inherent in these writings in that I do believe that Truth exists and needs to be intelligently, informatively, and factually brought forward. The question is: "How do we get there?"

Again, I reiterate here that I have family, friends, and colleagues who may or may not disagree with my universal point of view. Those are my own biases in the realm of religion and politics. Some of them have contributed to this set of musings. However, I do believe that most of us come to agreement on more things than we differ. We need to learn from each other and rather come to reasonable, if not perfect, solutions. Honesty, respect, belief in something, and genuine love trump all! We must keep growing together!

. . .

A Vote on a Petition
Back in1961, two significant petitions were sent to the U. S Congress for ratification of one or the other. On a very recent visit (2021) to parishioners of my current parish, Trinity Church, Whitinsville, Massachusetts. The story they shared with me was due to our conversation regarding the Pandemic and closing of our churches along with the best ways to move forward with the ability to worship together, in person, in our houses of worship. The rules for closing our places of worship have now been in effect for nearly a year with conflicting ideas as to how to re-open or not for an indefinite period.

The conversation led to many other concerns regarding the intent and purpose of these rules of closure and how we can innovate in order to keep us all together as a Christian body. Certainly, the health of everyone is most critical! The other serious matter is how such rules and directions from higher authorities can be used for other reasons than our health. We always need to ask questions regarding any rules given. We also need to trust the source and purposes of those rules. This led to the petitions to Congress back in 1961 regarding God in our society.

In 1961, the Atheist Society of America, led by Madelyn Murray O'Hare, was intentionally active in removing any and all references to "God" in our society. Beginning with the government and in the name of Separation of Church and State, the Atheist Society pursued its actions and goals for such changes. For example, these changes would be to eliminate the name God from our currency, to eliminate God from our Pledge of Allegiance, and to remove the Bible from the oaths of office taken by elected officials voted into government positions by the public.

In essence, the removal of God would free our nation from such a belief system. In so many ways, this was the intent of Separation of Church and State given by our forefathers in the Constitution. The intention of the writers of our constitution was for the protection of our beliefs, not to eliminate them. The term "God" was for all religious institutions to believe without restraint. Religious freedom is protected not eliminated by our Constitution. Having been founded on the basic principles of a Judeo-Christian belief system, the term "God" was appropriately given credence in our public domain. To reject God would eliminate such belief in all areas of public policy and law. This would be a fundamental change in the direction of our nation and leave us open to any and all philosophies devoted to Atheism.

It is because of our religious protection as given in the Constitution that the petition to keep God on our currency was able to happen. The Churches mentioned in the following brief gathered together way back in 1961 in order to prevent the Atheist Society from its intended purpose of the elimination of any reference to God and actually to erase God altogether. This petition came from parish churches in the state of Massachusetts. It is probably true that other similar petitions were sent by others in different areas of our nation. It is still heartening to know that this right is still intact as a basic Constitutional protection and right. We must not forget our responsibility in this matter, or it well could be taken from us!

"Need We Be Concerned"

This past year (2020), we celebrated The Feast of the Ascension on May thirtieth. This was also the weekend of Memorial Day. Every year on this national observance, we remember all those who sacrificed their lives for the sake of that which we believe. We were reminded again of the words of Jesus, "Although you will no longer see me I will never leave you alone or comfortless…believe in God, believe in me…I go to prepare a place for you that 'where I am,' there you may be also." Within us, when awakened in our own life's experiences, we are reminded of these promises. What better promise could we hope for in that God has further plans for us? The world sees how we revere those who sacrifice their lives for that which we believe and hope to be of the Truth. Our hope is the Truth and a destiny in the love and care of our Creator.

The ancient Greek Ecclesia means Church or "People of God." We believers are called to interpret God's will for humanity. How do we do this? It is through our interpretation of the wisdom of the Holy Bible along with our Worship and practice of that Faith in community. We witness in the church community and the larger world around us God's Will for us. We cannot do this alone! Each and all of us together are needed.

As a priest in the Church, my mind often enters into the clouds with concerns of immediate as well as eternal matters. In our churches we pray with concern for each of us; us together as God's people, society and nation; as well as the status and future of the world. Need we be concerned? Yes! Need we be afraid? No! As President Roosevelt said in the fearful midst of WWII, "We have nothing to fear but fear itself!"

Lately, the famous and world respected Psychiatrist, Dr. Scott Peck (*The Road Less Traveled*) in discovering God in his practice, tells us that he learned from his counseling that we humans are spiritual beings. Our nature is a spiritual journey. We solve and create problems via our spiritual journey and good and evil both allure us! Peck, not having been raised in any religious background, discovered his spiritual journey in his practice of counseling and medicine. Later in his life, he became an Anglican Christian after being introduced to a most incredible person known as Jesus of Nazareth.

In his own personal spiritual awakening, he said that he was, "enamored by Jesus and his uncanny knowledge of human nature." He saw in Jesus the reality of God. Dr. Peck himself answered my question as to why he chose to be an Anglican Christian by saying that he saw at this time the most reasonable approach to calling people into the Christian Faith. He said that it suited this time in his own spiritual journey.

In saying all this, my mind in the clouds is deeply concerned with an atmosphere today of lesser acquaintance with the Lord. For many reasons, we appear less and less mindful of our need for God. We appear to be losing our grasp of the peace of God that surpasses all human understanding. Without a healthy spirit, we become less and less of a healthy society. In this atmosphere, the Church and its teaching are being replaced by a consuming secular (godless) world. Faith and practice are becoming less and less of that much needed, necessary ingredient of wholeness, God's Presence. The good of our society is built on belief! I pray that coming generations will see their need for God. In the meantime, it is up to the continuously faithful remnant (that's us!) not to let the fire burn out. As our President said in WWII, "The truth will surface, fear will be defeated, and hope will be our future."

The gifts of the Holy Spirit are God's gifts to us for health and salvation. It is as simple as the faith of a child and as profound as life itself: Love, Joy, Peace, Long-Suffering, Patience, Wisdom, Discerning of Spirits, Kindness, and Forgiveness are the outcome! Yes, Pentecost happens!

May I hopefully recommend to all of us who must carry the torch of faith into the world to continue to renew our understanding of the life, death, and resurrection of Jesus and His Church's mission? One good start is our parish community. Might we also read again such books as follows:

- *The Greatest Story Ever Told* by Fulton J. Oursler
- *Principles of Christian Theology* by Dr. John MacQuarrie
- *The Road Less Traveled* by Dr. Scott Peck
- *The Holy Bible*

Such a review will prompt you to read more, and more, and more, and be excited about an experience of a clear vision of Our Church and Her Mission.

Fr. George Warren

"The Idea of Hospice"

About three years after I had entered into the hospice journey, I went to England. While there in 1989, I had the privilege of a meeting with Dame Cisely Saunders at Saint Christopher Hospice in London, England. Present were myself, a Roman Catholic Priest from Czechoslovakia, and Dame Saunders. After that momentous meeting, we toured this first 'in-house' hospice in the modern day hospice movement. Above the central staircase of Saint Christopher's was a portrait of Saunders' husband. She told us the story of why that portrait was centrally present for all to see when visiting. She told us of how, during World War II, she met this wounded soldier on the battlefield in Poland.

The then-wartime nurse tended to him. He had serious wounds and she saved his life. They became the best of friends and later married. Mr. Saunders wrote a secret note to his bride and lifetime mate. His instructions on the sealed envelope were to not open this envelope until after his death, which was many years later in the 1950s. The note essentially asked her to use the fifty-pound British currency towards an endeavor fitting her saving of his life with care, compassion, and healing of others. Dame Cisely presented this request to Queen Elizabeth followed by the British opening of St. Christopher's Hospice.

The beginnings of the modern day hospice here in America were relatively slow and arduous at times due to its newness as well as not being considered as a viable institution of care in the medical field. The spiritual realm in the earlier years prior to hospice, as an idea and practice of medicine, were not well considered. Religious care, or rather, spiritual care, was left to those realms and not entered into medical Services except through the request of the individual patient's expressed need. For example, the clergy or other religious figures were only allowed into the general hospitals by the patient or family members. The rules for the most part were strictly enforced. It wasn't until this movement was carefully studied and actually supported by both physicians as well as an act of congress that such a plan took its roots and ultimately became that which we now commonly know as hospice.

My friend and colleague Fr. Alfred Zadig was one of the first in the American Church, in implementing the idea of the Hospice movement here in Massachusetts. The following is his account of those beginning phases.

It was in 1978 while rector of a parish in Newton, Massachusetts that I was given a copy of Science Magazine and was fascinated by an article about Dame Cisely Saunders and the pioneering work she was doing in England with terminally ill people. Remembering all-too-well the kind of "treatment" given to my mother in her pain filled battle with cancer, the concept of hospice stirred me deeply. I took the article with me to share with several parishioners - a psychiatrist, a psychologist, and a banker. Their response was so similar to mine that I brought the subject to the Vestry (Parish Counsel).

The result was the approval of funds to explore the possibility of establishing a hospice program to serve the Newton-Wellesley area. A well-designed survey disclosed that the project might well be feasible, although it also noted the resistance a hospice program would face from some of the medical community. After prayerful consideration, the Vestry voted to go ahead and The Hospice of the Good Shepherd was established, becoming the first Hospice in Massachusetts. Through the years the range of services has so expanded, a fact now reflected in its new name: Good Shepherd Community Care.

It is interesting to note here that Father Zadig and I were not acquainted until many years later as we chanced upon each other at an un-related meeting in the Diocese of Western Massachusetts. It was not until many years after that we chanced upon each other in another parish setting and soon after realized that we had both been deeply involved in the Hospice dimension. The story continues.

Fortunately for me, in the mid-1980s, a young nurse, Averil Blackburn, came to Milford Massachusetts from England. Averil happened to be an Anglican

Christian. Upon coming to Milford, Averil and her husband George found the local Episcopal Church, Trinity Parish, of which I was the rector. This began my introduction to and involvement into the hospice movement in this area of Milford and surrounding towns. Averil introduced hospice to Dr. Mona Kaddis, Chief Oncologist at the Milford Regional Hospital. Herein I became involved in the beginnings of hospice in this area and actually the second hospice in the State of Massachusetts. This was still a movement coming from England and was only a beginning experiment in our American medical culture.

Many meetings and several years of working on this project opened the door and eventual incorporation of a hospice here. The Visiting Nurse Association in conjunction with the then Milford Regional Hospital became the home of our local Hospice. Thanks again to Averil Blackburn, I was brought on board the team as the Pastoral Counselor. The team included Dr. Kaddis as Medical Director along with several registered nurses, social workers, a volunteer coordinator, a hospice director, a secretary, several nursing assistants, and volunteers! Several years later ,we became the St. Camillus Hospice located at the St. Camillus Health Center in Whitinsville, MA. The Order of Saint Camillus, a religious order of the Roman Catholic Church, became our sponsors and housed our hospice program at their Health Center in Whitinsville, Massachusetts. The Order of Saint Camillus is dedicated to the care of the sick and more especially the terminally ill.

After several years of taking part in the development of a hospice in the local hospital, it became abundantly clear that such a Ministry was needed throughout the country and the entire world. The design of Hospice was to care for the sick and more especially those needing care in the latter stages of life. The idea of Hospice included all the aspects of living and dying including the physical, psychological, social and spiritual needs that we all carry through this lifetime. In the medical field of care, it became increasingly clear that all of these areas were integral to our health and well-being.

It is also interesting to note, with both humor and sincerity, an experience I had in the understanding and practice of hospice care. It was both an exciting as well big change and challenge in many ways, for me to move into such a new and life-changing adventure. I was leaving my long-term vocation as a parish priest and joining a team of "angels" to care for the sick and dying. At that point I had been the Rector of Trinity Parish in Milford for just under eighteen years. It was a huge adventure for me to change gears after my then twenty-two years as a parish priest. To me this was definitely a needed call in my own spiritual journey and vocation.

Ancillary problems that arose from this change was to find a place to live as there was no longer a provided Rectory in which to live. There I was thrust back into the real world, fending for myself as an employee of a company and working in a whole new environment. The wonderful upside of this was the people I worked with... all nurses! Also, at that time I had to be like most of the rest of our culture and become a homeowner. With very little savings on hand, it was somewhat scary to think about household responsibilities on my own - especially later in life – but that is another story to tell.

I invested in a small house in the immediate area of the Douglas State Forest in Douglas, Massachusetts. This modest house needed much attention to become livable and a home. The bank allowed me a down-payment mortgage and with that new beginning and imagination I was able to turn the "shack into a home in which I could live. With a lot of imagination and much work over time, I now happily reside there in semi-retirement. Here follows the rest of the story of a significant meeting in better realizing the intent and meaning of this new ministry as a hospice team member.

But first, an encounter I had at my home in those early days of hospice needs here to be mentioned. A couple I had known for some time asked me to help them in their marriage preparation. Knowing them well, and no longer having a comfortable parish office it was not a problem for me or them to have our first session at my new residence, in dire need of repair. We had planned for a 7:00 P.M. meeting after work and after dinner. From my new position as Hospice Pastoral Counselor, I was able to go home, relax, and change into my usual old flannel shirt and jeans until my regular hours at work the next day. The clerical suit was put away for the evening but also readily on hand for any emergency calls. My friends knew me best in the off duty outfit. The priestly clerical suit remained intact for working hours. Such identification was clearly helpful for my position as Pastoral Counselor.

At 6:45 P.M. that evening, as I was watching the news and waiting for Rena, a hospice social worker, and her fiancé Rick to arrive, the doorbell rang.

At the door were two very well dressed and groomed gentlemen looking for me. The conversation went as follows:

"Hello, my name is Rev. John Smith and this is Fred Jones, my Minister-in-Training." I invited them in with the warning that I was expecting counselees at 7:00 P.M. There I was dressed in rags, and they walked into an unusually messy place with almost no furniture and very little welcoming accommodation except for a small table and four fold-up chairs. They were obviously in shock that I looked like an unkempt person and my house was not at all presentable especially since I was expecting a couple about to arrive for counseling as I had told them upon entry.

Rev. Smith: "We understand that you are a Minister?"

Me: "Yes, I am clergy"

Rev. Smith: "What is your religion?"

Me: "I am a Christian."

Rev. Smith: "Where is your church?"

Me: "Well, right now I work in a hospice program not too far from here."

Rev. Smith: "Oh! Then you bring Jesus into people's homes?"

Me: "I hope so!"

Rev. Smith: "You do give instruction on the matters of sin and salvation, especially to the dying?"

Me: "Well, I don't give any instructions about any religious theories, especially to the sick and dying in our care. (At age twelve, Jesus actually corrected the religious rulers by stating that 'you have it all wrong! The Law of God is love! "Love thy neighbor as thyself!"')

I went on to answer that, "In hospice, we simply go in to love the sick and their loved ones toward the healing of body, mind, and spirit."

Rev. Smith: "Aren't you supposed to prepare the folks for their coming death?!"

Me: "Well, I think that my task is rather to comfort and heal. That's what I believe Jesus did!"

At that point, the doorbell rang at 7:00 P.M., and the couple had arrived right on time for our get-together. I had been silently praying for them to be on time as the conversation with the Rev. Smith was not going as well as I had hoped it would. More so, I was getting agitated! As they were about to exit, the Rev. Smith said to me:

Rev. Smith: "Oh, by the way! What church are you affiliated with?"

Me: "I am an Episcopalian."

Rev. Smith: "Well, that figures!"

And they left. At that moment, it was so very nice to see my friends and get going on their marriage plans with no other agenda except being ourselves as we have known and respected one another over the years.

. . .

Going back to my meeting with Dame Saunders in London and adding a bit more to the story, a Czech Priest during that meeting in St. Christopher's told us that hospice was against the law in Czechoslovakia because of its religious foundation. He told us that he had learned about the Hospice dimension and came to London to learn more. He told us that his trip and visit to St. Christopher's was clandestine since he would be punished for this effort. His life and priesthood were at stake. Now, in 2020, I don't know what happened to him, or to hospice in Czechoslovakia. It is well worth follow-up research.

In 1995, the Hospice of Greater Milford was opened. It was again my good fortune to be invited as a team member. The team consisted of Dr. Mona Kaddis, select nurses, a social worker, a volunteer coordinator, home health aides, selected volunteer, and pastoral counselor.

Here is photo___1___of most of our team.

I need here to state as many names and positions as I can remember of those members of the V. N. A. Hospice of Greater Milford, later to become The Saint Camillus Hospice in Whitinsville, MA. We existed as a unit there for more than twelve years serving the Greater Milford neighborhood.

Stories of Note

Story #1

Is it by coincidence or by greater mystery that hospice was born? The Gifts of the Holy Spirit must be read again to answer a large part of this question. It was our Lord who gave us reasons for such a dimension of comprehension and healing. Inevitably, such a dimension was needed throughout the world for human and social progress.

Story #2

I would be remiss if a little more history of the beginning of Hospice U.S.A. were not mentioned here. After a long period of initial work behind the scenes, going back decades here in the U.S.A, an act of congress ultimately gave support to the hospice movement here and joyfully the wider possibility to grow and thrive. Way back before this act of congress happened, the fledgling movement began here in Massachusetts in 1978. My friend and colleague, Fr. Al Zadig, was an integral part of the beginning of hospice here. I did not know any of this until Father Al and I became associate pastors in Grace Church, Oxford, in 2012. Coincidence?

Story #3

Tom, one of our homebound hospice patients, on his dying day, asked the team members present for help in preparing his loved ones for what he knew to be his death. He was ready to let go but struggled with the need to better prepare his wife and grown children at that time. The hospice nurse Leslie Rowell, and I convinced him to call them into the room and speak honestly and directly to them of his readiness. He did, and it was a tearful and wonderful healing moment for all of them. He passed several hours later with them by his side. Before calling his family in, Tom told us that he had seen the other side and was totally at Peace.

Story #4

Alice was a Southern lady now living in Bellingham, Massachusetts. Each team member had gotten to meet her in her small home overlooking a little pond. Upon entering her home for the first time, each of us couldn't help but notice a house full of geese ornaments, photos, and the like. She gleefully told us stories about her friends, the geese. She related how these friends visited her year after year as they flew south to north and then later north back to the warm south. She fed them, conversed with them, and totally enamored with each other expressed their mutual love and trust.

As her pastoral friend during about seven months of hospice care, I was asked by the family to give the Committal Service. Of course, much mention was given to her relationship with and love for her Canadian Geese. During the middle of the graveside part of the ceremony, four Canadian Geese flew directly over us, reminiscent of a Blue Angels performance. This spectacular flight was those four geese in military unison, making their flights about twenty feet above us and honking each time above Alice. All of us were in awe of this display of love and knew it was about the greater mysteries.

. . .

(the photos included here are missing so many more team members including Dr. Mona Kaddis, other Nurses, Social Workers, Volunteers, and the many families we came to know and love over our 12 years as a local community Hospice).

The Hospice Experience: Stories from Leslie Rowell, R. N.

Story #1

We were caring for an older man in Bellingham. You and I had responded to a call from his wife that he appeared near death. Present in his room were yourself, myself, his wife and their youngest daughter (in her twenties). As Jim's breathing became shallower, this young woman began crying hysterically. Jim stopped in his dying process, looked directly at his daughter, and said, "Do not cry for me. I have seen where I am going, and it is beautiful." The four of us looked at each other, in awe of the bit of Grace we had just been given.

Story #2

We were caring for an elderly man in Franklin and been called by his wife that he appeared to be dying. When I arrived at their home, I was greeted by their adult son who had arrived a few minutes ahead of me. He looked a bit distraught. He related that they are not a religious family. His three-year-old daughter was with him in his truck and as they pulled into the driveway she said, "Look Daddy, there is an angel outside Gramp's window!"

Story #3

While caring for a gentleman in Franklin, he said to me, "I know my death will come in the next couple of days." This surprised me, because I did not feel his death was quite this imminent. I asked why he felt that way, and he replied, "The littlest angel has been sitting at the foot of my bed for the last two nights." Ed further explained, "My wife and I had a baby girl - our first child - who died a few hours after her birth. This was so painful we never spoke of her again. Our other children don't even know. But she is here for me!"

Story #4

As Edith was trying to die, her children - all five of them - were keeping a vigil in her room. Eddie whispered to me, "Can you tell the children I can't die with them watching?" The eldest daughter ordered Italian take out from a local eatery, and as they feasted and laughed in the next room, Eddie gently passed!

"A Nurse's Experience"
by Robin Quimby, LPN

My morning as a hospice home health aide for Mary began as usual. I greeted her with my warm hello and her smile told me she was glad to see me. I began routine A.M. care, which consisted of giving Mary a bed bath and oral hygiene, feeding and toileting her, followed by assisting her with pre-poured medications. I noticed that Mary was having extreme difficulty breathing, and her gait was off. I phoned the nurse to report my observations and then I returned to Mary. I became aware that this day was unlike any other I had ever experienced with a patient. Through this incredible but true story, I witnessed how a person can walk through the phases of death, when there is a hand to hold onto.

Mary's skin color took a noticeable change. First her fingers and feet began to turn white, and within a short time her knees turned a purplish color. This was a sign that the body was conserving oxygen to the vital organs, and it was shutting off its supply of oxygen to her lower extremities. Next, Mary's fingernails and toenails became grey, indicating that her skin would start to mottle. I phoned the nurse to report these significant changes and request that a visit be made today. I then explained my observations of Mary's condition to her friend, Sandy, and prepared her for the possibility of Mary's life ceasing before the evening arrives. It was very difficult for me to maintain my professional composure at this point because although I was trained for this field of care, I was not prepared to face death when it came knocking at the door so quickly for this young woman, who only two hours earlier had greeted me with her usual warm hello.

Mary's breathing was becoming noticeably labored and she gave me permission to turn on the oxygen machine and allow Sandy to place the tube in her nose to help ease some of the distress she was experiencing. I then repositioned Mary on her left side to relieve the pressure she felt from her swollen abdomen. Within a short time, I noticed that the pain that Mary had been expressing began to leave her, because her face was not soft, whereas before it was tight, and I could see that she was beginning to relax and feel a sense of peace.

I assured both Mary and Sandy that I would return at the end of my workday to assist with anything they might need, to simply answer any questions, or just to offer moral support. Upon my return, Sandy showed me the instructions the nurse had left for me, and then she updated me on how things had proceeded since this morning. I knelt beside Mary's bed and placed my hand gently over hers, she opened her eyes and that old familiar smile greeted me once more. Only this time, when I looked into Mary's eyes I knew she was ready to take her final journey home, and she was afraid. I said a silent prayer, and then I squeezed her hand tightly and reassured her that she would not walk alone.

Life does not often give us notice of its departure, so I was grateful that God in His gentle, merciful way, prepared me with the insight to see that Mary's body was giving up its spirit today; and in the midst of pain and sorrow, there would be joy and peace. I arose from her bedside and went into the bedroom where I privately cried for this woman I had come to admire and love, who only three weeks ago was diagnosed with terminal cancer, and who today was facing what could very well be the last day of life as she knew it here on earth.

I regained my composure and went back to her bedside to stand alongside of her friend Sandy, as Mary looked up at me with tears in her eyes, and the three of us embraced and asked God to be with Mary as she took these final steps home. I placed my cheek close to hers and then kissed her on the forehead and thanked her for allowing me to be a part of this moment with her. She reached out and asked for my hand, and I took hers in mine and did not let go until she was at peace.

Mary had many questions as she began experiencing changes within her body, and I explained that everything she was going through was normal, and that giving up her spirit was like giving birth to a baby, and just as family greets a precious baby as it comes into the world, the Lord would greet her into His family, when she left here.

Mary's son arrived just as she slipped into a coma, but I explained to him that although she was no longer conscious, she could still hear what we were saying and for him to talk to her. I gave Mary's son some time to spend alone with her, and I greeted the nurse at the door and explained what had happened. The nurse took her vital signs and gently spoke to Mary, assuring her that we were all here, and she no longer had to remain if she was ready to go. It was not until her son told her that he loved her and he would miss her terribly, but he would be okay, that she breathed her last breath. A sigh was all we needed to hear to know a burden had lifted, and that Mary was waiting for that assurance from her son.

When it was over, I went to the door to greet the many bewildered friends who began streaming in and crying. Love filled the air, and the room seemed to light up. What a sense of calm, of closure, to such a beautiful and colorful life.

I told the nurse I would remain here for a while longer to prepare Mary's family and friends for the removal of her body, when the funeral director came. I explained how it would be better for them to go outside and witness the sun reflecting its rays through the colorful trees, than to watch the men take her body away, because this is just an empty shell now, Mary's spirit is with the Lord. They thanked me for taking the time to care for them, and I thanked them as well for allowing me to share in this private moment of theirs.

This incredible story changed my life in such a way that I now realize that if someone extends his or her hand to me and invites me to take hold, I will because I am accepting that person for where he or she is in life. Today may be the only time I have with someone, like it was that day with Mary, and I am so thankful that she reached her hand out to me, and even more grateful because I accepted the invitation. (The following poem was written by Robin for one of her patients.)

A Garden for Rose
April 1998
(poem dedicated to the memory of Rose,
a hospice patient who loved gardening)

During the calendar year
we experience the seasons of nature
But to witness the seasons of one's life
is a genuine treasure to hold in our hearts.
Many people walk in a garden
and pick the colorful roses from the vine
But I have been invited to enter a garden
not planted by the hands of man
But sown with love from the Lord
I have found a Rose
that never fades and new buds
are forever blossoming

I have been invited to enter a garden
within a Rose
Each season brought its own joys
and sorrows
My spirit has truly been watered
by the April showers
A part of me will always blossom
with radiant colors
because of the gifts that Rose has
showered upon me
The wind will forever carry her seeds
to a garden in need of love and love
her fragrance will forever fill the air
with a delicate light scent
Her trees will forever echo with the robin's song
Her branches will forever cover and protect
the nesting of baby birds
Her colorful leaves
will forever dance with the autumnal winds
Her footprints will forever make paths
in the freshly fallen snow
Thank you, Lord
for allowing me to care for and witness
such a delicate and fragile life

164   The Rev. George Henry Warren

"Why I Became a Nurse"
by Robin Quimby, LPN, Well Star Paulding Nursing Center

My healthcare career began while I was living in New England. I served twelve years as a home health aide working with visiting nurses and two hospice programs, as well as an assisted nursing facility specializing in Alzheimer's and dementia. I knew my heart had found an open window where my love and compassion could fly in like a dove and touch the lives of those facing illness and recovery as well as end-of-life issues. The knowledge, wisdom, and experience I had attained as a home health aide rested there, and I knew it was time for me to further my career and become a nurse.

When I moved to Georgia in December of 2001, I must admit I was quite overwhelmed by my job search and in finding a school that would accept my educational background. I did not have the time or resources to apply to an RN program, but I qualified for an LPN program. This I eagerly accepted as a start to my nursing career.

I graduated in 2004 and earned my LPN License. I accepted a position as an LPN float at Well Star Paulding Nursing Center. I saw this an opportunity to get oriented to all four units so I would better know for which unit I was most suited. I love caring for the geriatric community as well as people facing end-of-life issues. The whole scenario of life is very intriguing. The elderly are at such a special place and truly deserve the honor and respect that awaits them for reaching a golden age. We can learn so much from a life well preserved and mature with a world of knowledge, wisdom, and discernment waiting to be shared with us.

I have heard many a story or conflict and have seen grown children worrying and expressing guilt for having to make the difficult choice of placing a loved one in a nursing home. Nursing homes are not all dark and gloomy and harsh. Nursing homes are not lonely places where the old and feeble – a forgotten society - are left to curl up and fade away like withered flowers long forgotten for their beauty and fragrance.

A nursing home is actually a place of residence for many people. Employees are actually "guests" in the home of these residents. We chose a career in providing the best home we can for those placed under our care. I only hope and pray that when I need assistance, care, and direction, professional caregivers will protect and nurture me as I age gracefully.

I do not regret my decision in starting out my nursing career in a nursing home instead of pursuing my initial goal. I truly trust that God has guided me in caring for the many residents I have met and cared for these past two years. I am blessed when one elderly person smiles and reaches out a hand to thank me for taking the time to smile back or simply to be there to wipe a tear because they can't remember who they are or how they got here or even where "here" is. What a comfort to them to know they are not alone, not forgotten. That is why I became a nurse. To see the glow of a smile radiating on someone's face because they know they are remembered.

"Miraculous?! An Incredible Account"

Back in the late 80s, something that seems unbelievable took place in a life and death situation. During my years as rector of Trinity Parish in Milford, Massachusetts, the Guglielmi and Solina families were parish communicants. Jeanne Guglielmi lived in her two-story home in Hopedale. Although Jeanne had many medical issues which rendered her almost a recluse in that home, she raised her daughter Janet to become a healthy, vibrant young woman.

In the late 80s, Janet was married to Peter Solina and they moved into the upper home in that family house. Peter and Janet brought two children into the world soon after their marriage. While Janet and Peter worked locally so as to be close to home they were able to care for the children with the express help of Jeanne. Much love and care were prominent there. One day when Emily was a little more than two years old and Jocelyn was a little more than a year old, Janet became ill while at her work as a teller at the Milford Federal Savings Bank. More about this later.

In the meantime, and over several years before Janet became suddenly ill, I visited Jeanne as her pastor, periodically. During these visits over the years, Jeanne did not accept Holy Communion and had very little to say. I did all the talking! Late in the afternoon, Janet left her job early as flu-like symptoms were getting worse. By early that evening, she was brought up to Milford Hospital and midnight that same night she was rushed to the UMass Medical Center in Worcester.

Called in by the ICU, I saw an unrecognizable Janet and her family at the beside. The call to me from the hospital was to alert me not only of Janet's worsening condition but that, "She is not expected to live through the night. The family asked us to please call you." Arriving there, I saw Janet connected to every tube and machine possible and a swollen torso, making her unrecognizable. The astonishing and painful to watch circumstance was that Janet was totally awake and aware of all that was happening. She didn't appear fearful. The family insisted that she would soon turn this earthly corner and get better. The doctors and staff expected the opposite conclusion. We prayed, I anointed Janet, and I said that I would return tomorrow.

Janet not only survived the night but also remained in the same debilitating state for the following nine months. The stable condition was her swollen body studded with machines and tubes, as well as being awake and alert. In the meantime, her husband Peter took care of the little girls as well as attending to Jeanne. Jeanne was not able to leave the house and was unable to visit Janet at UMass Medical Center but was aware of Janet's ongoing illness.

My visits to UMass Medical Center as well as to the Guglielmi and Solina households continued on a regular basis throughout this critical time. Two weeks before crisis calls came to me simultaneously from the Milford Hospital and UMass Medical Center ICU, I had an unusual visit with Jeanne at her home. On this routine visit, Jeanne talked to me for the first time in all these years.

This is verbatim the words to me from Jeanne: "Father Warren, I am going to die soon. As soon as I pass, Janet will breathe again." All I could do was take it in with no verbal response from me. I simply acknowledged with a positive nod. I then asked her if she would like to receive the Sacrament. She said, "Yes." I gave the Holy Communion to her and left in amazement.

Two weeks after that notable interchange with Jeanne at about 7:00 A.M., my home phone rang as I was taking a shower. Immediately leaving the shower, I answered an important call from Milford Hospital. They informed me that Jeanne had just died and that they were unable to reach immediate family members. Going back to finish my shower and get ready for work the phone rang again. The ICU at UMass Medical called to ask me to please come in to help them inform Janet's family that they must take life support machines from Janet as her condition had deteriorated and there was no more they could do. Her lungs were totally blocked with no possibility of repair.

Immediately, I got dressed and headed for this long trip to the medical center. The actual trip to the hospital was about thirty-five minutes plus parking and a long walk (run) to the ICU.

Entering the ICU, one could see across the nurse's station and directly into Janet's room. Upon entering that ICU, I could see a joyful family having coffee and donuts at Janet's bedside. Janet had become completely normal"again. The swelling was gone along with the machines and tubes. Janet was wide awake, breathing, and enjoying her family beside her!! They had seen that when Mother passed, Janet received the promise.

Janet's prime hope throughout those previous months was to be at home raising those sweet girls. At that time, Emily and Jocelyn were one and a half and three years old, respectively. For whatever reason, during this critical time they were at peace.

Although Janet spent the following years in a wheelchair due to the muscle damage created by her long-term illness, she happily enjoyed her time at home with her family. Five years later I received a phone call from Milford Hospital that Janet had passed from this life. On my prefuneral visit to the family, six year old Emily said this to me: "As I was sitting on Mommy's lap last night we saw an Angel in the window."

"The Feast of St. Michael and All Angels"

Angels

Webster's Dictionary: "A typically benevolent being which is above and beyond humans but sits as an intermediary between heaven and earth."

The thesaurus goes further:

1. Free from evil and corruption
2. One who supports or champions an activity, cause or institution such as the church; charities; some individual needs or requests – like God's helpers.

The Holy Bible and many books through history have described the visitation, the help, visions of, and some even concrete examples of the presence of Angels:

a. Blessed Mary was told by an Angel that she would be the mother of Jesus.
b. The prophets of the OT describe messages from heaven .
c. Jacob on today's reading dreamed of a ladder reaching to heaven and Angels ascending and descending on it.
d. A lady crossing the street said that her guardian angel prevented her from being hit by an oncoming car.
e. Many saints throughout history tell about their minds and hearts being transformed by ascending into the realms of holiness.
f. The gifts of the H. S. are Angelic

History is full of accounts of extraordinary or simple sights, events, sounds, sensations, and experiences which come to us from some outside source through what we call the Angels, for the good of all and, as many believe, the advancement of humankind, society, and even the whole universe.

Pentecost Prayer: "Almighty God, you opened the way of eternal life to every race and nation by the promised gift of your Holy Spirit and have taught the hearts of your faithful people by sending them that light. Grant us by the same Spirit to have a right judgement in all things, and evermore to rejoice in his holy comfort. Send abroad this gift throughout the world by the teaching of the Gospel (Truth), that it may reach to the ends of the earth, through Jesus Christ our Lord, who lives and reigns with you and the Holy Spirit, one God, forever and ever. Amen."

A definition of Genius: "Exceptional intellectual ability or creative power; a distinctive spirit in a person in a place and time; a guardian spirit."

Jesus cried out from the Cross as human nature does in those times of trouble and doubt: "My God, my God, why have you forsaken me?" Job more than a thousand years earlier called out, "Where are you dear God? Why is all this happening to me?" In the psalms of David, we see we see poems, songs, and verse of near despair - "Why?" "Where are the blessings?" Then the cries of human nature get answers as the Bible and history do testify as the Holy Spirit, The Comforter reaches into our frail weak souls and promises – all will be well – believe in Me.

Jesus knew and experienced human despair so that whenever we are down, even to the final point of despair, He totally understands. Jesus identifies with us whenever we are in the spectrum of circumstance and experience.

The novel, *The Shack*, by William P. Young testifies to the experience of despair and then the entrance of the loving Spirit of God coming forward with the promise of eternal hope. He writes about how throughout our lives, we face many kinds of losses, great as well as small. *The Shack* is a worthwhile read as it forthrightly puts the most dramatic of all losses into a hopeful perspective. Those losses, the ones which make us feel broken and the cloud seems that it will never pass. And indeed, we are broken. This novel portrays the tragic loss of a child. It walks us through the wrenching pain that such a loss presents to us. I can't even imagine this! But, by the miracle of genuine love and time given we grow, heal, learn, forgive, and somehow see hope in eternity. The promises of God as testified in the real human experiences shown in the Holy Bible, we see a future. We see in that promise that we'll be with our loved ones forever. We've heard it said that, "Our tears are God's ointment of healing, genuine love, and the power of Heaven."

Losses go from getting out of bed in the morning to face whatever circumstances the day may bring; our ability to cope; to a failure or a test; all the way to the loss of precious loved ones. In all this we learn, we grow, we heal, we forgive we meet again. As our parish friend, Louisa recently shared with us in the loss of her beautiful dog, "No greater gift has come to me as in her devoted love from the depths of her being. No, there cannot be Heaven without all the love we've been shown in this lifetime, even especially our beloved pets." The miracle is that all good gifts are the gifts of genuine love, and such love is forever!

Back in December 3, 1999, The Worcester, Massachusetts Fire Department was called to the abandoned Cold Storage warehouse. Six firefighters perished in that fire while saving several people who were taking shelter there. We remember these firefighters, especially on the anniversary of that fire each year Those souls are: Lt. Thomas Spencer, 42, of Worcester and Lt. James Lyons, 34, of Worcester; and firefighters Paul Brotherton, 41, of Auburn; Lt. Timothy Jackson, 51, of Hopedale; Jeremiah Lucey, 38, of Leicester; and Joseph McGuirk, 38, of Worcester. Lt. Timothy Jackson was a neighbor of ours in the village of Hopedale, Massachusetts. Be at peace to love and serve the Lord.

"The Beatific Vision"

The German theologian, Rudolph Otto, wrote a book entitled The Idea of the Holy. He describes "holiness" as an 'experience' of the Holy, i e a direct experience of the presence of God as in extraordinary, peace beyond description. In the Mass, for example, is the section just prior to the Prayers of Consecration called the Sanctus – "Holy, Holy, Holy". This Sanctus is an "outward and visible observance" of the experience of the Holy. It is an experience of Sanctus that elicits its reality and thus the reality of God.

Myriads of Saints (known and unknown) have described their experiences of the Holy. One of such experiences is known as "the Beatific Vision". But experiences of Faith do not require such a Vision for belief. Belief comes to us more or mostly from our introduction to God through education. The Beatific Vision is to be understood and found later. As Jesus said, "Blessed are those who believe and have not yet seen." The first followers did not experience the Pentecost until long after their entrance into their Faith. St. Paul was an exception as he became a convert on the Damascus Road, on his way to destroy the Christ followers. He was blinded enroute, and heard the voice of Jesus saying, "Saul, Saul, why do you persecute me?"

In writing this piece I just had an un-canny experience as I needed to search for an example of the above statements for this writing. I randomly opened the book called *All Saints* by Robert Ellsbury,, and it opened to Saint Matthew Ricci. Was this mere coincidence, or better still, God's hand? I say this as the account of Saint Ricci, although he comes to us from the sixth century, is most timely in our current experiences of World History.

Matteo Ricci (1552-1610), a Jesuit Missionary to China, said: "Those who adore heaven instead of the Lord of heaven are like a man who, desiring to pay the emperor homage, prostrates himself before the imperial palace at Peking and venerates its beauty."

Matteo Ricci, an Italian Jesuit, is an extraordinary figure in the history of Christian mission. He was one of the first Westerners to win entry into the closed and xenophobic society of sixteenth-century China. Having mastered the Chinese language and the literary classics of the Confucian literati he succeeded in transcending his status as a foreigner and won recognition from the educated elite and the imperial court as a scholar of the highest distinction. The work of Matteo Ricci and the Jesuits who followed him showed great promise of establishing an authentically Chinese Christianity. In the end, their efforts were undone by Vatican officials whose philosophy was, in effect, "When in China do as the Romans do."

Ricci first entered China in 1583 after spending some time in the Portuguese colony of Macao at the mouth of the Canton River. After intensive study of Chinese and immersion in the classic texts of Confucianism, Ricci was able to present himself as a scholar, a status that was eventually confirmed by the respect of his Chinese peers. He dressed appropriately in elaborate silk dresses and published works on such topics as astronomy, science, and philosophy. He won particular admiration for his map-making skills and for his accomplishments as a teacher of mnemonic techniques.

Ricci's mission strategy was based on the view that before Christianity could make any progress in China it must win the acquiescence of the educated elite. To do this, it must eschew any taint of foreign imperialism and present itself in terms of Chinese culture. Ricci was not concerned about the number of conversions. He conceived of his work as laying the foundation for future missions. Once Christianity was an accepted part of Chinese society, others might work to spread the gospel among the masses.

By the time Ricci won permission to live in the imperial city of Beijing, he had achieved renown as a Confucian scholar. His study had convinced him that the ethical precepts of Confucianism – the dominant religious underpinning of Chinese culture – were reconcilable with Christian morality. Furthermore, he argued that in its origins, Confucianism recognized a supreme Creator, who could be identified with the Christian God. In his mind the work of assimilating Confucianism with Christianity was little different from what, "Thomas Aquinas had accomplished with the philosophy of Aristotle."

Remarkably, Ricci's interpretation of Confucianism, though it contradicted the consensus of most scholars, won general respect and even the agreement of some of his Chinese peers. Among these he was able to count many significant conversions. At the time of his death on May 11, 1610, his body lay in state with hundreds of Mandarins joining Christians in paying their final respects. By imperial decree, Ricci was buried in a special tomb, a rare honor for any Chinese person, and unheard of for a foreigner.

It is impossible to know what effect Ricci's efforts might have had over time. Regrettably, his project was stillborn. Within a hundred years his project was condemned by the Vatican, a casualty of the so-called Rites Controversy. Ricci had recognized the importance of Chinese culture played by the veneration of family ancestors. His intimate knowledge of Chinese culture convinced him that such expressions of filial piety need not represent a conflict with Christian faith and morality. Furthermore, to deny participation in such rites to Chinese Christians was instantly to excommunicate them from their society, an outcome that would render any mission effort moot.

Ricci had won provisional acceptance from Rome for this policy. However, the matter was ultimately decided otherwise. A papal decree of 1704, renewed in even stronger terms in 1742, vehemently condemned the Christian toleration of ancestor rites as idolatrous and superstitious and utterly rejected Ricci's efforts to reconcile the gospel with Confucianism.

This was a fateful decision for the fledgling Christian community in China. Henceforth that ancient society would remain effectively closed to evangelization, and Christianity would never make the inroads for which Ricci had prepared the way. It was also a fateful decision for the church, which was deprived for another two hundred years of the wisdom on non-Western paths to God.

The Donald Ferguson Story

Phone Call:

"Hello, Father Warren?"

"Yes"

"It's Mae. I'm calling to let you know that Donald is at the Framingham Union Hospital. They are going to remove a tumor from his brain the day after tomorrow. Can you go in to see him?"

My reply: "Will he want to see me? Knowing Donald, he may not want a visit from any Priest, myself included."

Mae: "Oh, yes, I know that he would love a visit from you."

Donald was not a participant to any "religious stuff". His wife, Mae, came to church every Sunday for years. I had met Donald on one or two occasions. We had brief conversations, but no mention of my role as clergy and certainly no conversation about the Faith.

Upon entering Donald's room, he gave me a warm greeting and thanked me for coming by. We had a conversation of a general nature, but then I learned from him of the impending operation, set for the next morning. Before leaving, I asked Donald if I could say a prayer with him. He kindly agreed. After the prayer for healing, I mentioned to him that I had the Sacrament with me and offered Holy Communion to him.

He accepted! So, I said the prayers with him in preparation for his reception of the consecrated Host. During those prayers, he melted down into crying, as a child receiving love from his mother. He sobbed almost uncontrollably. I placed the Host on his tongue and told him I would be back during his recovery time. He gave to me a most gracious and appreciative, thank you, at which point I left.

For me this was a routine call as per my job. The interchange was sincere, and I enjoyed that visit, knowing that Donald was appreciative of it. The next morning, the surgery took place. There was no tumor; it had disappeared!

This happened to be my final weekend as rector at Trinity Church, Milford, Massachusetts. Once a priest leaves for another position he must separate from the parish in order for a new rector to begin. I didn't get to see Donald again but am told that all went well for him for many years following that precious moment in time and relationships.

"A Holy Week Journey"

As we now approach the observance of HOLY WEEK on the Christian calendar, we search again into the deepest, most profound of life's meaning and experience. It is that experience that when it hits home awakens us to the meaning and purpose for which we were created by God. That is, the love of God for us and our love to the Creator in return. We were created out of love and for love.

During Holy Week, we are reminded of how much we are loved by seeing God in the life, death, and resurrection of Jesus. He took upon Himself all the difficulties, hurts, pains, and doubts that any one of us could possibly experience in this lifetime. This was to show us that no matter what joy or sorrow may come our way because of life's circumstances, His love will always be present for us and we shall never be alone. I say this in order to offer the reader a meditative exercise that I hope will help you reach an experience of God's eternal love for you, me, and everyone. Let us call this an exercise into spiritual experience and energy. We know that reliable instruction and common sense teaches us that regular exercise and proper nourishment is necessary for good health.

The old saying is that health, wealth, and wisdom are the result of the best kinds of exercise and nourishment. Now, as we approach HOLY WEEK, we are again clearly reminded in our Christ-centered nurturing that regular spiritual exercise is needed for the Soul's energy. It is from our faith in God as witnessed through the life, death and resurrection of Jesus that our Soul's energy is born and enhanced. As we read the Holy Gospel, we see how those first followers of Jesus we so enamored by his presence, teaching, and concern for them. They soon learned that their experience of the love of God was extraordinarily real and open to all who would follow and receive it.

Thus, I suggest the following brief meditative exercise to help open the door to a higher level of experience of the presence of God. It is my hope that the use of this spiritual exercise will help enhance the understanding of your Faith and practice of that Faith. When we seek and then experience the presence of God in our lives we'll recognize that presence in the mundane as well as the extraordinary times of our lives. It will enhance our vision, transform us, and give us the meaning and purpose of life itself.

INSTRUCTIONS

1) Find a comfortable, quiet, simple, un-encumbered space in the physical world around you.

2) Make available a sound source (i. e. head phones, recorder-player) ready to play a key musical or sound piece of choice).

3) For this first exercise I suggest that you play the Sound Piece called THE KNOWING by the famous Japanese artist, Takeshimi Suzuki. This is one of the pieces he wrote and played in memory of the victims of Hiroshima, and Nagasaki. Or, a favorite sound source of yours which will help release you out of worldly anxiety.

4) When you have provided for yourself a comfortable, quiet, unencumbered space as far away from the physical world as you can, sending anxieties elsewhere (they'll be there when you return but with another way of seeing them). CLOSE YOUR EYES, EXPERIENCE THE SOUND, AND LISTEN TO YOUR SOUL.

5) Also make sure you have your Bible at your side and when finished with the listening, read John 14:1-6.

With all best wishes for a meaningful Holy Week, I am Rev. George H. Warren, parishioner of Grace Church, Oxford and Missioner Priest of St. Philip's Church, Putnam, Ct.

"The Dirty, Crumpled T-Shirt"

For the last couple of decades, I have enjoyed Holy Week observances with my son, Joel. Joel was born during Holy Week in Warwick, Rhode Island. On the day of Joel's birth, our parish, St. Barnabas Church, had the honor of a planned visit from Bishop Louis Gelineau of the Roman Catholic Diocese of Providence, Rhode Island. After that evening's Holy Week observance, Bishop Gelineau went to Kent Hospital to visit and to bless the newborn and his Mom.

Every Good Friday for the last umpteen years, I have enjoyed Joel's presence at one or more of my Holy Week observances in the several parishes in my cure over this time span. After these services we had deep conversations. These were our special Good Friday moments of contemplation... a cherished tradition. Joel enjoyed going to church and our many conversations about God were such a joy to me.

Just four years ago and soon after my retirement from full-time parish obligations, Holy Week was here again and Joel and I made plans to meet. Because of his obligation to complete the painting of a friend's home for their get-together on Easter Sunday, we had to change our time of meeting from Good Friday to Holy Thursday evening. A new movie had come to our local theater known as "The Case for Christ." We decided that this would be our contemplative observance together that year.

"The Case for Christ" is a true story about Lee Strobel, an Atheist journalist who made it his lifelong project to discredit religion, specificaaly the Christian beliefs about Jesus. In short, Lee had been devoting his life and journalistic abilities to disprove Christian beliefs about Jesus of Nazareth even to the point of His historic reality. During these years of being a pro-active Atheist committed to disproving the Christian belief system, his wife, also a devoted Atheist, became seriously ill. While at the hospital, a stranger woman approached her to offer comfort in this time of serious illness. The stranger told her that she would be praying for her. Sometime after that meeting, these two individuals chanced upon one another again. They had more conversation at that meeting and rejoiced together over the recovery from that illness. They became friends.

During the ensuing time, the wife of Lee Strobel became more and more interested in her new friend's belief in Jesus. Upon sharing her new-found interest with avowed Atheist husband, Lee, he plowed ahead in serious research to re-convince his wife that this was all hog-wash. In his dogged study and research, he discovered many flaws in his efforts on behalf of Atheism. During this time, he became a believer, studied more, and with this conversion, became an ordained Minister in the Christian Denomination of the woman who initially brought Christ to his wife, several years earlier.

After watching this incredible and true story, Joel and I had a long post-movie conversation about it. This was a wonderful Holy Week observance. It was well worth it. We had so very much to talk and think about following that almost unbelievable but true account of one man's conversion to the Christ.

The next morning, Good Friday, Joel went to his painting job as planned. He said that it was a long day at work! He went home to get a good shower and a good night's sleep as the next day, Holy Saturday, he had to go back to finish his painting obligation. When he arrived home on Good Friday night he dropped his dirty t-shirt onto the living room floor, took his shower and went to bed for the night. With a new change of work clothes, he headed out on Holy Saturday to the unfinished painting commitment that was finally ready to be completed.

Here is what happened. Joel says that he was still contemplating our Holy Week conversation about the movie and prayed that the Lord would send a sign to bring peace, forgiveness, and a stronger faith. After the completed job that Holy Saturday, being very tired, he went home and took a short nap on the couch. Waking from the nap and getting up for his shower, he looked down at the dirty t-shirt from Good Friday, still where he had left it on the floor the day before. This is what he saw:

Joel immediately called me to share what had happened! It is our wish and prayer in the Christian dimension that all will come to see and believe in the Christ of history. Holy Week really happened and continues to happen so that all will come to believe.

It was the Divine Commission of Jesus to us,
Go into the world and baptize in the name of God –
The Father, the Son, and the Holy Spirit.
Jesus also said to his first followers and to us now:
Blessed are those who believe and have not yet seen.
Come to me, all who are burdened, and I will give you rest.
Seek and you will find. Knock and the door will be opened. Ask and ye shall receive.
Set your troubled hearts at rest. Believe in God, believe also in me.
I go to prepare a place for you, that where I am, there you may be also.

In conclusion, I cite another of the myriads of stories relating to God's abiding presence in the lives of everyone and especially those who have realized such a presence on the spiritual journey. I repeat the fact that life can be and most often is likened to a roller coaster ride in that so many choices are presented to us in the midst of difficulties in a complicated world. It is told that the internationally famous folk singer Johnny Cash found that his rise to stardom brought more than fame and fortune. It brought serious problems of choice leading to an addiction to Amphetamine.

This led to his first arrest in 1965, when he was caught with more than 1, 000 pills in his pocket. He slipped from 200 pounds to a 140 pounds in a very short time. Not only were his life and character thrust into depravity close to death, he was also then sent to the hospital due to a severe car accident. He was going steadily downhill. A few years later, on May 9, 1971, he went to a small church in his hometown. This Evangelical parish always taught of the healing powers of Jesus.

At the conclusion of the pastor's sermons, the folks attending were always invited to the front to make things right with God. Johnny Cash stood up and walked to the wooden altar to pray for forgiveness. He left the church realizing the power of forgiveness and his road to recovery happened. Once asked by his disciples how many times we would be forgiven, Jesus replied, "Seventy times seven."

Into the Day

I got up early one morning
And rushed right into the day
I had so much to accomplish
I didn't have time to pray.
Troubles just tumbled about me
And heavier came each task.
Why doesn't God help me, I wondered,
He answered, "You didn't ask."

I tried to come into God's presence,
I used all my keys at the lock.
God gently and lovingly chided,
"Why child, you didn't knock."

I wanted to see joy and beauty,
But the day toiled on grey and bleak,
I called on the Lord for the reason -_
He said, "You didn't seek."
I woke up early this morning
And paused before entering the day.
I had so much to accomplish
That I had to take time to pray.

(Author Unknown)

"Coincidence"

Webster's Collegiate Dictionary defines coincidence as, "A seemingly planned sequence of accidently occurring events." One example of such an event happened to me when a childhood friend of mine and I literally bumped into one another decades later at a distant restaurant as he was leaving, and I was just entering. We had many planned get-togethers since that chance encounter.

Was it just a coincidence? Many things happen in our lives that we could pass over to mere coincidence. Certainly, coincidences happen but the question remains: did that happen because…? Could it be that Divine intervention does happen? Does subjective, or rather, personal help come to us from beyond?

In his revealing books, Dr. Thomas Fleming, bases his assumptions on "God's intervention in events of history." One example was the Dunkirk miracle of WWII. The British were surrounded by the Nazis on Dunkirk Beach with no way to escape and certain doom. A heavy fog rolled in and provided a successful escape by those British forces. Fleming attributes Divine help for those faithful and praying British soldiers. Fleming's books are well worth reading as he credibly surmises God's help in a series of events throughout history.

My favorite Farmers Insurance Company TV commercial shows a child on the front lawn of his home with a small replica of his home. The boy flies his toy pick-up truck into the replica at which point, immediately following, a real truck flies into the front of the real house. Of course, the insurance company states how accidents, and the force of gravity caused this incident to happen. This was coincidence.

It seems obvious that coincidences do happen. But the question remains as to whether or not God's hand clearly intervenes in the history of man. The question also remains, be it coincidence or not, as to how and when God is present. How does God's presence affect all the experiences in our lives?

In these pages, I relate many stories of my life as a priest in the Church, which belie coincidence and open for investigation the reality of Divine Intervention and ways that real help does come to us from God. Throughout the Bible we read of Angels, dreams, inspiration, and historical events that give testimony, not only to the existence of a Divine Creator (God), but also His personal relationship to each and every one of us. The Webster's Collegiate Dictionary defines coincidence as, "A seemingly planned sequence of accidentally occurring events." The term intervention is, "That which appears, comes or lives between things, especially as an unrelated or disruptive circumstance... To enter or to intervene so as to modify."

Does God communicate with us, give us resources, send messages, directly intervene, help us in various ways? This is the question of Theology.

A Gospel Banner

(From the Encyclopedia of 7700 Quotations)

"Doubt sees the obstacles

Faith sees the way!

Doubt sees the darkest night,

Faith sees the day!

Doubt dreads to take a step,

Faith soars on high!

Doubt questions, "Who believes?"

Faith answers, "I".

. . .

Tony

Tony looked about my age with long white hair and a beard, riding a big 1500 Fat Boy Harley Davidson. If I had more time, I would have told him that I just bought a brand new 1300 Yamaha Stryker, my fifth motorcycle over the years.

"Funny? What Just Happened?"

"Hi Father! Are you a priest?"

"Yes."

"Oh! Ok - do I call you Father?"

"You may. Most do."

"I noticed your R. I. license plate. I grew up in East Providence as a young boy. My name is Tony Viega. Glad to meet you."

"Yes! I grew up in East Providence too! Glad to meet you, too!"

Then the light changed and off we went. Funny! What just happened? Seems more than just a small world and in the great mystery of it all there seems to be meaning and purpose. Tony and I certainly connected on many levels. We had familiarity, friendliness, singularly humanity, and things to learn and enjoy from each other in one minute at a temporary stop light.

It so happens that I was dressed in my cassock on the way to a Worcester Cemetery as I was called the night before to officiate at a burial service for one of my colleagues. Funny, seriously, or mysteriously, in a few brief minutes I then learned so much about a family I had never met before. The Rawlings family were from far away places and converged here at home for the burial of their dear parents. The Worcester area had been their childhood home. Mr. and Mrs. Rawlings had each been professional and extraordinary in their own rights. Two years earlier, they had given their bodies for scientific research, and finally now, two years later, I had the privilege to repeat some final words at their burial. In the few short minutes before the committal I learned and was enabled to appropriately speak of these incredible people and see the love, gratitude and hope given to them by their Mom and Dad.

Having been raised as Episcopalian Christians they had some of the mysteries given in biblical verse and prayer. It seemed to make sense to all participating that even in the depths of the despair of our mortality that there is hope and purpose to our lives.

The parish I currently serve as interim priest, Grace Church in Oxford, Massachusetts has been a joyous and wonderful experience on many levels. This is where I chanced upon Fr. Al Zadig, Mother Julia Dunbar, and The Rev. Stan Boethal. Fr. Al was raised in the Jewish Faith; Mother Julia was raised a Roman Catholic; and Stan was an active Baptist Minister soon after to become a Roman Catholic. Also, the folks at this parish were from several different backgrounds.

I was the only born, bred, and active Episcopalian in the entire eclectic mix. What an experience! They are extraordinary people. The privilege and joy of my vocation is the opportunity to learn from, grow, and also share my own gifts with so many folks who cross my own spiritual journey. In our latest parish newsletter of February 2017, the following words of mystery, strength and wisdom were written by our own poet and well-read writer Mr. Robert Perry.:

I was having a discussion the other day with a good friend who comes from another spiritual tradition. My friend is of Native American heritage and also practices Vipassana, a Buddhist meditation in which mindfulness of breathing and of thoughts, feelings and actions are used to gain insight into the true nature of reality.

He was expressing the dangers of making mental constructs of who God is and how the universe should operate. Leaving room for the Mystery allows us to enter in and experience the spiritual reality for what it is: letting go of control makes room for acceptance of whatever may come to pass. Although this sounds somewhat passive in nature, it actually requires exquisite attentiveness to the journey to be aware of the way that God moves in our lives.

My favorite twentieth century mystic Thomas Merton developed a close friendship with the Vietnamese Buddhist monk Thich Nhat Hanh. The two found many similarities in their religions and encouraged one another in true ecumenical fashion. The following is a prayer I have said for many years now. I have a copy at my desk at work. Many people find it confusing at first, but this is my prayer of choice when I am unsure of the direction God is leading me. May it bless you as well.

My Lord God, I have no idea where I am going. I do not see the road ahead of me. I cannot know for certain where it will end. Nor do I really know myself, and the fact that I think that I am following your will does not mean that I am actually doing so. But I believe that the desire to please you does, in fact, please you. And I hope I have that desire in all that I am doing. I hope that I will never do anything apart from that desire. And I know that if I do this you will lead me by the right road, though I may know nothing about it. Therefore, I will trust you always, though I may seem to be lost and in the shadow of death. I will not fear, for you are ever with me, and you will never leave me to face my perils alone.

Peace,

Bob Perry

With these thoughts still in mind, I share with you now the story of four extraordinary people whom we celebrate in our parish liturgies in February. They are The Four Chaplains of WWII. This article was also entered into our February 2017 Grace Notes.

Featured Saints: The Four Chaplains

(Submitted by our editor, Mrs. Betty Blodget)

The Four Chaplains, also sometimes referred to as the "Immortal Chaplains" or the "Dorchester Chaplains," were four United States Army chaplains who gave their lives to save other civilian and military personnel as the troop ship SS Dorchester sank on February 3, 1943 during World War II. They helped other soldiers board lifeboats and gave up their own life jackets when the supply ran out. The chaplains joined arms, said prayers, and sang hymns as they went down the ship.

The relatively new chaplains all held the rank of first lieutenant. They included Methodist minister the Reverend George L. Fox, Reform Rabbi Alexander D. Goode, Roman Catholic priest Father John P. Washington, and Reformed Church in America minister the Revd. Clark V. Poling. They met at the Army Chaplains School at Harvard University where they prepared for assignments in the European theater, sailing on board Dorchester to report to their new assignment.

Dorchester left New York on January 23, 1943, en-route to Greenland, carrying the four chaplains and approximately 900 others, as part of a convoy of three ships. Most of the military personnel were not told the ship's ultimate destination. The convoy was escorted by Coast Guard cutters. On February 3, 1943, at 12:55 A.M., the vessel was torpedoed by the German submarine U-223 off Newfoundland in the North Atlantic.

The torpedo knocked out the Dorchester's electrical system, leaving the ship dark. Panic set in among the men on board, many of them trapped below deck. The chaplains sought to calm the men and organize and orderly evacuation of the ship, and they helped guide wounded men to safety. As life jackets were passed out to the men, the supply ran out before each man had one. The chaplains removed their own life jackets and gave them to others. They helped as many men as they could into lifeboats, and then linked arms and, saying prayers and singing hymns, went down with the ship.

The Chapel of the Four Chaplains was dedicated on February 3, 1951 by President Harry S. Truman to honor these chaplains of different faiths in the basement of Grace Baptist Church of Philadelphia. In February 2001, the Chapel of the Four Chaplains moved to the chapel at the Philadelphia Naval Shipyard.

In his dedication speech, the President said, "This interfaith shrine...will stand through long generations to teach Americans that as men can die heroically as brothers so should they live together in mutual faith and goodwill." In1988, February third was established by a unanimous act of Congress as an annual "Four Chaplains Day." The day is also observed as a feast day on the liturgical calendar of the Episcopal Church in the United States of America.

Of course, the myriad of stories, anecdotes, and real experiences of the great mystery's origins have been known throughout history. Of note, for example, are the awesome epiphanies of the writers of the Holy Bible. The great philosophers, prophets and Saints of history have done great service to the world in many forms and from so many different directions. Coincidence? I don't think so.

"Another Routine Day"

On a routine day and having just left the church following the Holy Eucharist celebration and mid-week Bible study, I headed to the local Jiffy Lube for an oil change. Usually overdue on oil changes and any needed minor repairs, I hoped for no extra problems on the car. After all, we need the vehicle to get there and back.

The Saint's Day celebrated was Catherine of Genoa. Catherine was known as a mystic. A good quotation describing her belief in God is: "All goodness is a participation of God and his love for his creatures." Catherine wrote several spiritual classics which have been a hopeful resource for many believers, especially those seeking comfort and spiritual support during difficult and challenging times in their lives. Although she spent much of her days and nights in ardent prayer through which she felt the dear presence of God, she remained a laywoman outside of convent life. Her work was hands-on nursing care for the sick and dying. She helped to found and maintain the first hospital in Genoa, at various times performing every type of work from the most menial to the Office of the Director. It is this extraordinary combination of contemplation and action that has made her one of the most compelling figures in the history of Christian spirituality.

It is clear that the balance in her life was not achieved at once. It was the fruit of a long life and many struggles in work, faith, and prayer. At the age of twenty-five, she uttered a desperate prayer for some relief from an immediate torment at that time in her life. It is said that, "she even prayed that some illness might send her to the sick bed." Instead, on March 22, 1473, while kneeling in confession, she was suddenly overcome with a "peaceful infusion of divine love" which impressed her simultaneously with the immensity of her sins and the peace of forgiveness of God. This was another experience into how she saw the rest of her life. Her profound sense of the otherworldliness often seemingly beyond comprehension was combined with her fastidious attention to practical detail and constant availability to the needs of others. In 1510, she became very ill. After much physical suffering, she died on September 15.

From that particular celebration of Saint Catherine's Day, I headed to Jiffy Lube for an oil change. While waiting alone in the waiting area of Jiffy Lube, the following phenomenon happened making St. Catherine, the Bible Study, and the mystical otherworldliness of that study an immediate reality.

A young man entered the waiting area, spotted a priest and anxiously asked if he could talk with me. Of course, I did. David said that he thought a priest would understand what he was about to say and not think he was crazy. The funeral of David's wife Catherine was two days earlier. Catherine had been suffering with terminal cancer for the last one and a half years. Towards the end of her life in this world David asked her to please let him know that she was ok after she had died. David and Catherine were very much in love and were always together, not only during normal, routine times, but throughout the ordeal of her terminal fate.

David said, "The instant she died, she entered my body. I could feel her, and I became her. She was peaceful, healed, and told me not to be afraid. She was briefly but fully there, and she was at peace. I love and will miss her dearly, but our prayer was answered. I'll never doubt again!" Yes, of course I believed David, as the Bible tells me so. That day was no longer routine, but the routine of life goes on. I never saw David again. All is well!

What Really Happened?

A Trip to A Message from Beyond

Susie: "George? Is it really you?"

George: "Susie! It's been a long time... How are you? What's happening?"

Susie: "Nice to hear your voice! It hasn't changed. I'm fine... We're all doing well. The girls are on their way to college."

George: "Me too! My three are all grown up and in great years of adulthood! My grandchildren are awesome! We need to meet up and catch up!"

Susie: "I have an idea! There's going to be a meeting of an Edgar Cayce Club in two weeks at the old Grange in Rehoboth. Can we get together for that?"

George: "Weather permitting, will you join me on my bike?"

Susie: "You know me, and the adventure is still there!"

George: "I wish we could ride there on Abba and Magic like the good ole days."

Susie: "The bike will have to do!"

Way back into our childhood, my dad built a home for Mom in Seekonk, Massachusetts across the street from an old farmhouse with barn and fields stretching for many acres, and miles of farmland and forest all around. I was fifteen years old at that time, and Susie was seven years old. Being a third child of all boys, my mom didn't come through with the begged for little sister that I hoped would happen. Susie became for me that little sister that I was hoped to be before I was born. Within a year of that, in our new home in Seekonk, Massachusetts, Susie and I worked on the old barn and made a paddock. She brought Magic home, and soon after I brought Abba home. We were clearly bonded over those next few but wonderful years.

Back in those magical youth years with horses to care for and miles and miles of trails to explore throughout Rehoboth and Seekonk, we had a blast. How fortunate for me to have been given the little sister I had yearned for and to be such a big brother to her in so many ways. It was a magical time and experience in those years between 1958 – 1967.

In those next years, my exciting childhood had so much more yet to come. I had finished high school, followed by under-graduate school in the study of Western Civilization and Philosophy. After that, I studied for four years in Seminary graduate school, ordained Deacon, and Priest, and five more years as Curate in St. Barnabas' Church, in Warwick Rhode Island. Many more years had again passed before Susie and I got together again. Much had happened in those years for us both.

Here is where the question "What Really Happened?" arises. It was soon after those in-between years that the call with Susie inevitably happened. Of course, we made plans to get together to catch up on all those years so that we could catch up on all that happed to each of us and to enjoy a wonderful time on memory lane. We, of course made plans to get together again and keep in touch. Susie came up with the idea to attend a meeting of her interest.

The Ride to a Voice from the Beyond

Before I go back to those memorable years with my little sister, now grown-up, I must relate the following story of another childhood friend from so many years before. This story was secretive and not shared with anyone, even Susie.

My childhood, previous neighborhood acquaintance Joseph was from an earlier time and place. Here is the story:

In 1972, a call came to me at my office at Saint Barnabas' Church, Warwick, Rhode Island. I was then a newly ordained priest serving as the curate. The call from Rhode Island Hospital was: "Hello, Father Warren? We have a patient, Joseph Thibeault. He asked us to call you and hopes you might be able to come in and see him." "Of course, I'll be heading over in a few minutes!" I hadn't seen or heard from Joe since early High School, 1961. We also had different sets of friends and had only occasionally got together. I had also since moved from that neighborhood to our new family home in Seekonk, Massachusetts.

Joe and I had no communication until that incredible visit at the hospital in 1972. Joe had somehow learned that I had recently been ordained and was serving at a nearby parish. He asked his nurse to call me and see if it was possible for me to come in to visit him. In less than an hour of that call, I entered his private room in the Jane Brown wing of the hospital. We talked and reminisced for quite a long time. It was such a bittersweet reunion. The very next morning, the hospital nurse called to inform me that Joe died during the night. He was twenty-six years old.

In the meantime, Susie and I finally got together again after quite a long time, about fifteen to twenty years or so. In the year 2001, as we drove by motorcycle, through those miles of forest, farm trails, and new concrete developments, we recalled the good ole days of frolic in the sun on our horses. With some trepidation along with no expectations and certainly no learning anything, I reiterated to Susie of my reluctance to participate in her seeking a sign from her mom who had passed into Heaven a few years earlier. More specifically, I chided Susie for bringing me to such an event, especially a séance meeting! However, knowing her well, such a trip and conversation was not unusual.

Having not been raised in a church, and as always as curious as she was, this was another one of her curiosity expeditions. She also had a belief in life after death and sought ways of asking the questions. So, we went in the hope of gaining something from the experience. There's always something new to learn. Susie, knowing that I was not at all interested in a private meeting with the famous seance leader led me directly into one in which I had to politely acquis.

It was at that time, twenty-seven years after my last meeting with Joseph, that no one knew about, the séance leader at the old Grange said this to me: "A message came to me from Joseph. He asked me to let you know how grateful he was for your visit to him in the hospital just before he passed." How could this be?

I don't have a clue how real or not that particular experience was and is. Somehow, the seer was given such information about that meeting with Joseph. Again, it was not a conversation I had with anyone. In my vocation such visits to hospitals is a regular occurrence. I had not been in touch with Susie since before my college years. Her out of the blue call to me was many years later. Obviously, the seer's followers actually believe that he and others have these similar experiences.

Dr. Scott Peck, in his book In Heaven as on Earth, talks about ways that "loved ones are given subtle messages from beyond." Dr. Peck's many years of counseling have documented such beliefs from his patients. Most of us have our own similar experiences of signs we believe came from loved ones who have gone before us. What does this mean?

Seemingly stranger things have happened to me and myriads of other inquiring hearts, minds, and souls. The Bible is clear about the use and misuse of such things as magic, séance, and any claims of such power of deceit and any form of false claims to knowledge and power that is not of the TRUTH.

Jesus of Nazareth

"Father Forgive Them"

The world-famous psychoanalyst of the late twentieth century (and still renowned to this day) began his first book, *The Road Less Traveled*, with a key statement. "Life is difficult." From this point, he went on to show the importance of learning and growing. My own favorite bumper sticker reflects this by reading, "If you think education is difficult, try ignorance!" In Dr. Peck's first book of several, he determined that human beings are primarily spiritual by nature and that our well-being is grounded in that spiritual capacity.

Further to note that Dr. Peck has been known to be of a non-religious background until his research and conversion to the Christian faith following his first book. That book was written after Dr. Peck's entrance into the field of psychotherapy. It was a colleague and friend of his who questioned his theories in that book that made him look as though he was actually a Christian. Upon reading the New Testament Peck said that he was "amazed and in awe" of what he discovered in those pages of the knowledge and perceptions of Jesus of Nazareth, most especially of understanding the spiritual nature of being human.

Dr. Peck continued his studies of Theology and later became an outspoken Christian. Once attending a talk given by him at a hotel in Boston, my son Joel and I heard the above comments directly from him. I also have since read several of his books since the widely read publication of *The Road Less Traveled*. I remain most thankful for the insights and wisdom I have received from Dr. Peck's work. It is significant to note that I require all pre-marriage couples to read this book for the sake of their futures together.

So, who was this Jesus of Nazareth and what did he know? Firstly, he was a real personality of history. He is not an idea but actually lived, taught, and had profound influence on both the individual human as well as being an integral part in the social order and into history. It is also important to note that he was born into a time of history into which such knowledge needed to be gained. So, what's new? One generation to the next needs guidance, and more importantly, guidance in the matters of the TRUTH. A failing Roman Empire had become severely corrupt and society fell under the tyranny of that corruption. This was a most timely point of history for a Savior to enter. The world has never been the same since the life, teachings, and actions of this personality we know as Jesus of Nazareth. Belief and trust in him brought hope and healing to our world.

In the Holy Bible, the Gospel (meaning the TRUTH) says that Jesus came to us from God with the purpose of giving us the basics not only for survival but also to flourish. This is too simply stated in that a more complete understanding of the entire Bible gives a clear picture of the meaning and purpose of life itself and from whence it emanates. The life of the Church, Ecclesia, and People of Faith came into history to forward this Good News.

The first followers of Jesus of Nazareth ultimately realized that He was the Christ and embodiment of the TRUTH. Jesus himself said, "I am the way, the truth and the life." When asked by Peter, "Who are you Lord?" He responded, "Who do men say that I am?" Peter then responded, "Well, some say you may be a return of Elijah, or some great prophet of old." He looked straight at Peter and said, "Now that you have been with me, who do you say that I am?" Peter said in awe, "You are the Messiah!" That means the one sent.

A study of the Holy Bible seems to never exhaust itself as it is always timely, universal, and with something new to learn at all times. The term catholic reflects this as it means "at all times, in all places, for all peoples." This is why believers at the least say that Jesus was indeed special. Further understanding of Jesus helps us to believe that he is who he said he is. "I am the way, the truth, and the life."

Dr. Howard Kelly, the famous Christian physician, had written and placed on a frame in his office: "The first recorded words of Jesus were, 'Wist ye not that I am about my Father's business?' His last words were 'It is finished!'" (Encyclopedia of 7700 Quotations)

Jesus, as a personality in history became an experience to whomever met and came to know Him. In the Biblical account Jesus met both individuals and society on many levels. For example, a blind man received his sight... or a leper was cleansed of the disease. or TRUTH given changed entire societies. When one experiences the presence of Jesus, it becomes a reality for all of us that He is present in our joys and sorrows; in our fears and misgivings; in our education and in our ignorances; in our hopes as well as in our desperations; in our times of peace and confidence, as well as those times of seeming hopelessness. The door is always open for God's Presence to be realized in all of our experiences.

In the great Psalms of David in the Old Testament Psalm 39 states well how God's love and Presence are always with us:

O Lord, you have examined my heart and know everything about me. You know when I sit or stand. When far away you know my every thought. You chart the path ahead of me and tell me where to stop and rest. Every moment you know where I am. You know what I am going to say before I even say it. You both precede and follow Me and place your hand of blessing on my head.

This knowledge is too glorious, too wonderful to believe. I can never be lost to your Spirit! I can never get away from my God! If I go up to heaven, you are there; if I go down to the place of the dead, you are there. If I ride the morning winds to the farthest oceans, even there you hand will guide me. If I try to hide in the darkness, the night becomes light around me. For even darkness cannot hide from God; to you night shines as bright as the day. Darkness and light are both alike to you.

You made all the delicate, inner parts of my body, and knit them together in my mother's womb. Thank you for making me so wonderfully complex! It is amazing to think about. Your workmanship is marvelous – and how well I know it. You were there while I was being formed in utter seclusion! You saw me before I was born and scheduled each day of my life before I began to breathe. Every day was recorded in your Book!

How precious it is Lord, to realize that you are thinking about me constantly! I can't even count how many times a day your thoughts turn towards me. And when I waken in the morning, you are still thinking of me!

(Ps. 139:1-18)

"Search me, O God, and know my heart; test my thoughts. Point out anything you find in me that makes you sad and lead me along the path of everlasting life." (Ps. 139:23, 24)

"Belief and Disbelief in Paintings"

To know the different effects of belief and unbelief in relation to Jesus Christ, we need only turn to art and compare the same subject treated by different men – say the "Crucifixion" or "Descent from the Cross" by Fra Angelico and by Rubens. The picture of Fra Angelico never painted Christ on the Cross without tears while painting it and never took up his brush without prayer. Fra was obviously full of saintliness and love in his work. From a technical point of view, his work seems far from perfect. But such criticism deters from the depth of pathos and holy sacrificial love which the painting suggests.

When, on the contrary, Rubens took up the brush to paint the face of Him whom he nominally acknowledged as the Son of God, he approached the solemn subject without any "clearly perceptible traces of a soul." His greatest work is generally recognized to be the "Descent from the Cross" in Antwerp Cathedral, and this painting has been selected as one of twelve of the greatest paintings in the world. "It is a terrifying production in its force and brutality. The immense pictorial power of the artist is here, the grouping is marvelous, the coloring no less so, but the effect is terrifying."

No painter ever depicted that awful scene with less spiritual mystery and greater disregard of Christian feeling than did Rubens here. The Christ in it is dead, hopelessly, finally dead; no glimmer of the resurrection morn lights with its tranquil rays the dreadful scene; the Christian hope or feeling have no place; the workmen handle their victim with that callousness which comes from frequent and irreverent contact with the dead, and the whole and awful tragedy is chosen to exhibit the artist's skill in grouping and to give his subject dramatic affect.

This picture is art's great commentary on the words of the Apostle, "The natural man receiveth not the things of the spirit of God, for they are foolishness unto him; neither can he know them because they are spiritually discerned." (James Burns, Encyclopedia of 7700 Quotations)

One key in a focus on the historical Jesus of Nazareth is that he was a personality directly involved and incredibly influential in the ongoing history of civilization. Christian Theology states that he was and is God Himself. In general terms, he was at least a unique human being at a certain time in human history. It was this particular reality in history that made significant changes and advancements into the future of humankind. These changes focus on both the regeneration of the individual as well as the total of society. The primary focus of Jesus was the regeneration of the individual human and then to follow the betterment of all society and the world into the future.

The time and place in history was significant in that Jesus was born into the crumbling Roman Empire due to corruption, loss of principles and values, and the evils/sins of human power and greed, to name a few, which again raised the the problems of the world, sinful human nature, and the advancement of humankind.

The widely known book *The Rise and Fall Oo The Roman Empire* by Barry Linton clearly outlines the reasons for the Fall of such a powerful human government gone awry. So, this was the world into which Jesus was born. According to the Bible, Jesus was born into this world to save it from self-destruction and all other such evil entities which were of a destructive nature. The primary evil is the sin of false human pride, which fools itself into thinking there is no need of God. This says that we are sole entities in and of ourselves with no overriding truths, principles, or Creation itself to be our guide. The answer of

Jesus in the midst of the question as to who or what we are points to our Spiritual Nature given to us by the Creator, God. Do you recall that first song from your mother's voice saying, "Jesus loves me this I know, for the Bible tells me so?" From such a thought and belief, the tide of history made a dramatic turn in world history.

The following diagram simply illustrates the major change in world history as per the Birth, Life, Death, Resurrection, and certainly the teachings of Jesus of Nazareth. This diagram can be viewed as a Resurrection symbol in that it points to our given human nature as an integrated whole rather than an amalgamation of separate parts. i.e. The human and life itself are integrated as physical, psychological, social, and spiritual.

Being human, at least in this life and this world, requires that all these pieces work together for the Good and for the purpose we were created in the first place. "Love the Lord your God with all of your mind, heart, and soul, and Love your neighbor as yourself. This is the Law and the Prophets." *(Mtt. 22:37)* Western Civilization advanced exponentially due to this new way of thinking as given through the historic Jesus and His followers. From the fall of the Roman Empire into the dark ages to the middle ages to the age of enlightenment to the modern era, we have observed the profound influence of the historical Jesus.

"Confirmation Class"

Over the years, it has been my joy and privilege to give some words of wisdom to my oldest grandson Ethan. I even had the privilege of having Ethan participate in a Confirmation Class with me. Due to some conflicts of time and circumstance, that time of instruction needed to end prematurely. Because of constraints, Ethan was not Confirmed that year. However, such instruction does not end as we continue to converse on such matters of wisdom. Ethan is now eighteen years old and headed to Saint Michael College in Vermont next fall. He has done exceptionally well in athletics as well as his educational pursuits, and we are all very proud of him.

I told him and my other grandchildren that I have been writing this book for them. They will have to make up their own minds as to its contents, only to realize that my love for them is honest and as wise as is possible for me to share. It is so good for me to see that Ethan, Owen, Wesley, and Phoebe have keen minds and much love surrounds them on every side. We simply pray that they will make sound decisions as they go forward in the failures and confusions of a thus far difficult world to navigate.

"Confirmation" – Act of confirming; Something that verifies; Rite admitting a person to full membership in a church or synagogue. Also, to confirm that many beliefs in search of Truth have so much to offer. However, to continue to realize that so many oppositions to truth are in the mix.

The Rite of Confirmation in the Church verifies that the Baptized Christian has been further instructed in the purpose and meaning of Holy Baptism thereby having a deeper understanding of one's faith. In the Catholic experience, the gift of baptism is from God from the beginning and enters the newly born infant into the community of faith. From then on, it becomes the responsibility of the parents and the rest of the Christian community to raise that child into the knowledge and love of the Lord. This, of course, is a lifelong obligation into the meaning and purpose of the love of God. For many years, I, as a priest, did as best I could to foster the baptismal endowment in my practice of religion and in my teaching. As in raising my own children, I believed, taught, and practiced moderation.

"Moderation" – not extreme or excessive; temperate; average; Someone who holds moderate views or opinions; to make or become less extreme or intense.

To me, this makes good, or rather, reasonable sense in navigating through one's life and spiritual journey. This is acknowledgement of the fact that life itself is complicated, with much learning and growth to happen in the meantime. However, loving guidance and sound instruction are not only helpful in navigating one's life but also necessary.

When the famous psychiatrist was asked why he became a Christian, he said that friends guided him there. They recognized in his first book *The Road Less Traveled* that he seemed to understand many of the values of the Christian understanding of human nature. Asked why he chose to be an Anglican Christian he said that he found its teachings to be reasonable and the most balanced. Of course, such an estimation of theological and Biblical interpretation is always in need of review, debate, and hopefully growth in understanding of human beings and our relationship to God. Dr. Peck realized in his practice of psychiatry that we humans are indeed spiritual beings.

St. Barnabas', Warwick, RI "Youth Group" - 1973
Trinity Church, Milford, MA – "Youth Group"-1978

My Confirmation Classes incorporated a variety of experiences including:

1) Teaching about meaning in the Christian faith as instructed in the Baptismal Covenant.
2) Practices of worship and why we Anglicans "do" religion the way we do.
3) Practical experiences working in the world (i.e. treating others with dignity and respect, and having fun in the whole process of living. It seems that being well-rounded teaches us much about living, behaving, and ultimately a good understanding of God's patient and forgiving love for each of us .

As an example of the previous statement, our classes would incorporate:

- Classes of Instruction
- Social Service
- Field Trips
- Social Activities (simply for fun and enjoyment)

Outside of instruction, we did such things as monthly visits to interact with the children and adults at the Ladd School in Exeter, Rhode Island; visits to the Monastery of St. John the Evangelist in Cambridge, Massachusetts; then to Faneuil Hall for some history of our country; and off to the shops and restaurants at Faneuil Hall. A mountain climbing trip to Monadnock, New Hampshire; and a New England winter ski trip topped it all off. We had fun!

One time, a fellow cleric asked me about the results of my Confirmation Classes. He was amazed that so many teenagers were confirmed each year. My only comment was I believed that we enjoyed being together learning and having fun at the same time.

Way back in the early 70s at St. Barnabas' Church in Warwick, we celebrated the first Folk Mass once a month for the 5:30 P.M. Mass. The Rejoice Mass was not the traditional music, but rather the Mass sung by everyone in the then contemporary music especially enjoyed by the youth. Folk Masses became very popular and spread very rapidly in the Roman Catholic Church. To this day, many innovations in the practice of religion have come to the Church and enthusiasm in the faith by many. The vernacular has widely replaced the old Latin and the old Elizabethan English. It has been fun for me to enjoy the traditional and the revised liturgies over these years. I feel absolutely comfortable in attending worship and sharing of our Faith now in a less divided church. Be it Baptist, Lutheran, Roman Catholic, Greek Orthodox, Methodist, and all the others, it is a joy to be in church with others.

The following confirmation guidelines have been recommended among others for use in the local parish church:

Guideline for Confirmation Preparation
Diocese of Western Massachusetts
Year: 2014

PREPARATION NEEDS TO INCLUDE AT LEAST THE FOLLOWING:

1. Minimum of sixteen hours of Catechumenal preparation
2. Move toward young people not being confirmed until at least tenth grade
3. Daily prayer and weekly Sunday Eucharist
4. Regular reflection on Scripture
5. Small group faith sharing and prayer
6. Content should include:

- Introduction to the Bible and history of the Church, BCP, Catechism, Baptismal Covenant, and Stewardship (gifts, time, and money)
- Practice "proclaiming by word and deed the Good News of God in Christ" (i. e. training, action, and reflection in witness (evangelism) and service (justice and peace)

Outline of This Confirmation Preparation Program

I. Confirmation at St. John's - from Fr John Betit
II. Introductions / Sharing faith experience among the group
III. What Makes Us Christian? - from the Episcopal Church website
IV. History of the Episcopal Church
V. Episcopal Church's worship, faith, and calling
VI. Spirituality in the Episcopal church
    A. "Spiritual, Not Religious - from the Rev George Anne Boyle
    B. Quiz/ Discussion: What's Your Spiritual Type? - from *Beliefnet*
VII. Jesus and You: Discussion after "Who is Jesus to You?" survey by the Episcopal Church
VIII. Book of Common Prayer: Purpose, Contents, Outline of Faith *(BCP p845-862 - the Catechism)*
    A. Human Nature
    B. God the Father
    C. The Old Covenant
    D. The Ten Commandments
    E. Sin and Redemption
    F. God the Son
    G. The New Covenant
    H. The Creeds
    I. The Holy Spirit
    J. The Holy Scriptures
    K. The Church
    L. The Ministry
    M. Prayer and Worship

N. The Sacraments: Baptism, Eucharist, Other Sacramental Rites, Including Confirmation

O. The Christian Hope

IX. The Bible: Old Testament, New Testament, Bible Study

X. Prayer

XI. Written response to questions:

A. What have you learned from your preparation that has been most important to you?

B. Why do you want to want to confirm your baptism vows?

C. How do you plan to live as a mature and faithful Christian in the Church and in the world after you are confirmed?

Baptism

Baptism is the sacrament whereby people become Christians, and thereby members of the Church. At Baptism, the new Christian (or in the case of a child, the parents or guardians) professes belief in Jesus, renounces evil before the Church, and then is immersed in (or sprinkled with) water three times-in the name of the Father, and of the Son, and of the Holy Spirit. Baptism represents our participation in the death and resurrection of Jesus, and assures us of our salvation through belief in him.

Eucharist

All baptized Christians participate in the Eucharist (from the Greek, meaning "Thanksgiving") or as it is also called "Holy Communion," "the Lord's Supper," or "The Mass." The Eucharist was instituted, according to the Bible, by Jesus himself on the night of his arrest, before he was crucified. During the Eucharist, bread and wine are blessed as symbols of Christ's body and blood. The bread is broken and shared, and then the cup of wine is passed among the worshipers as a sign of Jesus' sacrifice on the cross and resurrection. The Eucharist is a continual remembrance of Jesus' life, death, and resurrection until he comes again.

Working for the Reconciliation of the World to God through Jesus Christ

All Christians share in the God's work of reconciling the world to God's self. In other words, Christians believe that in Jesus Christ, all divisions among people, all injury, all wrong, and all sinfulness can be healed, and it is every Christian's responsibility and ministry to work for that healing. Christians believe that there will come a day when the world will be completely at peace, sharing in God's love, and living as one Body.

"History of the Episcopal Church"
The Episcopal Church's History in England

King Henry VIII of England created the Anglican Church in the sixteenth century. The Anglican Church continues many traditions similar to Roman Catholicism and serves as a middle ground between Roman Catholicism and Protestantism. The Episcopal Church is a mainline Protestant denomination connected with the Anglican Communion. Episcopalians have communion every Sunday, call their ministers "priests" and look to bishops for leadership as Catholics do. Episcopalians also emphasize the Bible and see the Word as central to worship, as do other Protestant churches. For example, the first half of Episcopal Sunday worship is devoted to the word-reading and learning about Scripture. The second half is devoted to the Eucharist, or celebration of Jesus' life and ministry through the sacrament of Communion.

Episcopal Church in America

When English settlers came to America, they brought the Anglican Church with them. The church struggled during the American Revolution, as an English church was about as popular as English taxes to the colonists. The Episcopal Church established itself as connected with the Anglican Communion, but as an autonomous church in 1789. Today, the Episcopal Church U.S.A. continues the Church of England's faith and practices in America.

Episcopal Church's Worship, Faith, and Calling

English Protestant reformers believed every Christian should be able to read the Bible and understand the Church's teaching. They created a resource, the *Book of Common Prayer*, which has served as a guide for Anglican worship and Christian instruction since 1549. The Book of Common Prayer includes worship services (liturgies), collections of prayers, creeds (statements of belief), a catechism (outline of Christian teachings), a psalter (the Biblical Psalms), and a calendar of the Church year (list of dates Christians celebrate, such as Christmas and Easter). Today, the Episcopal Church U.S.A. still uses the *Book of Common Prayer* as the basis for its communal worship and life.

Episcopal Church's Faith Episcopalians seek to balance scripture, tradition, reason, and experience. Scripture refers to the Holy Bible, as the Word of God used in Episcopal worship and private devotion to change the hearts and minds to be more like Jesus.

I. Confirmation at Saint John's
Confirmation preparation will eventually be integrated into the Rite 13 / J2A / YAC curriculum. For the next few months, we will be focusing on the older kids to get them on their way to a spring Confirmation. Any young person wishing to be confirmed is expected to attend and participate in 75 percent of the J2A / YAC meetings and activities. After completion of two years in the Rite 13 and / or the J2A program, those who wish to be confirmed may do so at the Bishop's next visit. To request inclusion in the next Confirmation ceremony, each youth should send a letter addressed to Brian Yacino and to Bishop Scruton (c/o the St John's office) stating why they feel called at this time to be Confirmed in their faith.

II. Introductions I: Sharing Faith Experience
A. Tell name, age, high school status
B. Have you always gone to church? Have you always been Episcopalian?
C. What makes you a Christian? When did you discover that you were Christian?
D. Have there been times when you have questioned your faith? Do you question your faith now?
E. What are your expectations of this Confirmation process?

Ill. What Makes Us Christian?
From the Visitor's Center Website of the Episcopal Church: In spite of two thousand years of growth and change, there are still some hallmarks that distinguish Christianity from all other, similar or not-so-similar, re-

ligious sects. While the range of beliefs among Christians can be quite wide, the following represent what is commonly shared.

The Goodness of Creation, Made by God

Most Christians believe that the physical universe, including humanity itself, is fundamentally good, even though human beings cause it harm through their negligence and self-interest. Other Christians hold that while humanity may be flawed, God's love and grace provides a way to perfection and goodness through the teachings and saving presence of Jesus Christ.

The Bible as the Word of God

Christians believe that the Bible is "the Word of God," and as such, "contains all things necessary to salvation." While there have been countless books about Christianity written since the Bible, and while many of the other doctrines essential to Christianity have been worked out in them, the Bible is sufficient to knowing God through Jesus Christ and to benefiting from the saving act of the Resurrection. Christians may disagree regularly, however, on how to interpret or apply what the Bible says.

The Trinity: One God in Three Persons

Christians believe in one God, whom we understand to exist in three persons, traditionally referred to as "Father, Son, and Holy Spirit." The three persons of the Trinity are God, who created all things, Jesus Christ, his fully human-and at the same time, fully divine-son, and the Holy Spirit of God who gives life to all things and moves through all living things. Contemporary language now acknowledges other images of the Trinity, such as "Creator, Redeemer, and Sanctifier," but the Trinity remains: One God in three persons.

The Incarnation: God Became Human

Christians believe that Jesus Christ was, at the same time, completely human and completely God, all in one person. This idea was articulated and adopted to address variants to Christian theology (known as "heresies"), which arise from time to time throughout history. One heresy has claimed that Jesus didn't really die on the cross because he wasn't really human. An opposing heresy claims that he was really just an important guy with some great ideas, and that he wasn't really God.

The Crucifixion and Resurrection

Christians believe that Jesus of Nazareth died completely on the cross, that he was buried in a tomb, and that on the third day, he was raised physically again to life to return to his disciples. Tradition refers to how the Holy Spirit has inspired the Church in the past. For example, Episcopalians believe in the apostolic succession, or bishops going all the way back to Jesus, as a part of their tradition, and a cornerstone of their identity.

Reason refers to using human intellect, inspired by God, to seek knowledge of God's plan for the Church. The Episcopal Church will not make an official position on what a specific Bible verse means or issue law or codes of behavior like other churches. Therefore, the church contains some believers who take the Bible literally, and others who take the Bible figuratively. How Episcopalians view the Bible is not central to the denomination. The right to learn and grow with the Bible and seek a Christian identity is most important.

Experience refers to what the church has learned over time. The Episcopal Church began allowing women to serve as ordained ministers in the 1970s because the House of Bishops (governing body) experienced women to be as able as men, although traditionally the denomination only ordained men. The Episcopal Church U.S.A. continues to juggle issues between scripture, tradition, reason, and experience today as it has for its entire history as it seeks to learn and grow in the image and likeness of Jesus Christ.

Episcopal Church's Calling

The Episcopal Church strives to live by the message of Christ, in which there are no outcasts, and all are welcome. Walking a middle way between Roman Catholicism and Protestant traditions, we are a sacramental and worship-oriented church that promotes thoughtful debate about what God is calling us to do and be, as followers of Christ.

IV. *Spirituality in the Episcopal Church*

The following essay is called "Spiritual but not Religious." It was written by Reverend George Anne Boyle of the Associate for Christian Formation at Saint Thomas Episcopal Church in Medina, Washington.

In the wake of the New Age, and the ever-growing love affair our culture has with all things spiritual, a new mantra has emerged: I'm spiritual, not religious! It is the mantra of ex-Catholics and once-in-awhile Protestants and others on the spiritual path. This emerging mantra has grown up in response to religion that looks more like a museum, religion that says you practice THIS way, or you aren't one of us, religion that isn't relevant to the life I lead, religion that tells us to believe twelve impossible things before breakfast and leaves no place open for questions or doubt.

And there's this longing and maybe even a presence of energy in life. Perhaps if you are on the spiritual journey, you have felt this. Energy that gives life and joy — whether it's looking at Rainer at sunrise, or playing music with others, or sitting with someone in a time of sorrow. That energy is what the Christian people call the presence of the Holy Spirit. The followers of this Jesus know this longing and energy only too well.

What is this longing? It is the longing to live in community with others from all walks of life — a community that is present in sadness and joy, a group of people searching and questioning and doubting and finding more questions about that presence together.

It's not about having answers as much as it is about engaging a story. It is about your story and how your story connects to an ancient story of desert wanderers that, in time, came to see that humanity and this energy they called God mingled and existed through Christ and thus, exists in all of humanity.

Is it possible to practice and grow your spirituality within an organized church? Yes! The Episcopal Church holds many possibilities open for those on the spiritual path looking for a diverse community of believers.

The beauty of the Episcopal tradition is that it is open to questions and new possibilities, as well as ancient teachings. Imagine a spiritual practice that is both grounded in tradition and open to new possibilities.

K. The Church
L. The Ministry
M. Prayer and Worship
N. The Sacraments
    1. Holy Baptism
    2. The Holy Eucharist
    3. Other Sacramental Rites, including Confirmation
        Confirmation is the rite in which we express a mature commitment to Christ and receive strength from the Holy Spirit through prayer and the laying on of hands by a bishop. It is required of those to be confirmed that they have been baptized, are sufficiently instructed in the Christian Faith, are penitent for their sins, and are ready to affirm their confession of Jesus Christ as Savior and Lord. See Confirmation section in BCP, p 413
O. The Christian Hope

IX. The Bible
    A. Old Covenant: God and Israel
    B. New Covenant: Jesus and the Holy Spirit
    C. Bible study

X. Prayer
   A. What is prayer?
      Talking with God, communicating with God
   B. Do you pray? When?
   C. Why do you think people pray?

XI. Written response to questions
   A. What have you learned from your preparation that has been most important to you?
   B. Why do you want to want to confirm your baptism vows?
   C. How do you plan to live as a mature and faithful Christian in the Church and in the world after you are confirmed?

"Quiz: What's Your Spiritual Type?"

"What's your religion?" used to be such a simple question but now you might be "spiritual but not religious" or raised in one faith but practicing another. Maybe you're a Methodist but think of yourself more as an evangelical, or a seeker who is anti-religion or born again. The quiz is meant to help you learn about yourself, see how you compare with others, and have a little fun.

Q1. I believe that God:
   1. Exists and intervenes in daily events
   2. Exists but does not intervene in daily events
   3. Is a spiritual ideal, not an actual being
   4. Does not exist

Q2. When I think about issues of faith or spirituality, my foremost concern is:
   1. A sense of connection to something larger than myself
   2. A rational understanding of whether religious claims are valid
   3. A personal relationship with God
   4. A framework of morality and hope

Q3. I believe the scripture I know best (the Bible, the Koran, etc.) is:

1.   Mostly or entirely mythology
2.   Divinely inspired and mostly true
3.   Divinely written and accurate
4.   Should be viewed mainly as storytelling or metaphor, not a literal account

Q4. Which of these statements comes closest to expressing your most basic view regarding faith?

1.   Faith is important because it helps us cope with the struggles and hardships of life
2.   Faith is important because it makes the world a better place, by encouraging love and moral behavior
3.   Faith is not important
4.   Faith is important because it fulfills God's wishes and protects our souls

Q5. I believe that the universe we observe:

1.   Is natural in origin, but has higher spiritual aspects
2.   Was created supernaturally
3.   Is completely natural and has no higher aspect
4.   Was created under divine guidance, but using natural physics

Q6. I think prayer is:

1.   Heard by God or angels, and for many people God or angels responds
2.   Heard but no answer should be expected
3.   Worthless
4.   Best understood as a form of meditation or moral awareness

Q7. I think that following life:

1.   There is an afterlife for the virtuous but no hell; the evil simply cease to exist
2.   There is reincarnation or some other condition
3.   There is nothing

4. There is an afterlife in which we are judged, then rewarded or punished

Q8. Evil is present in the world because:
1. Of human failings; evil has no supernatural component
2. God or a Higher Power wishes to test people
3. It is impossible to have free will without evil
4. Humanity is sinful by nature

Q9. I believe that angels:
1. Exist and intervene to assist the pure-hearted
2. Exist but only watch us, taking no action
3. Exist only on the spiritual plane, not in this life
4. Do not exist

Q10. I believe that the Devil or demons:
1. Exist and are active on Earth, working to corrupt men and women
2. Exist in the form of temptation to sin, not as specific beings
3. Do not exist
4. Exist but only in the supernatural realm, not in this life

Q11. If I had to categorize my own religious and spiritual beliefs, I would say they are:
1. Moderate; part of me is spiritual and part of me is skeptical
2. Agnostic, or hold no spiritual beliefs
3. Unshakable in my beliefs; I rarely experience doubt
4. Strongly committed to my faith, though sometimes I am troubled by unanswered questions

Q12. Regarding those who hold beliefs that are sharply different from mine, I think:
1. It's amazing the sort of nonsense some people will believe
2. Since many people acquire their beliefs through upbringing or social circumstances, we should not judge

3. All beliefs are equally valid

4. They may be sincere but are mistaken or ill-informed

Q13. Regarding the formal teachings of specific denominations, I:

1. Accept most or all of what my faith teaches

2. Accept some of what my faith teaches but also reject some

3. Reject most or all formal teachings of faith

4. Take practically everything taught by faith with a grain of salt

Q14. Each day's newspaper brings reports of crimes, natural disasters, and disease. My most basic reaction is:

1. My faith is tested because I cannot understand how a just God could tolerate the agony of the world

2. I feel sadness, but accept that both the good and the bad of life are somehow part of God's plan

3. Such tragedies make me confused about the nature of the Higher Power

4. Tragedies and disasters in the world convince me there is no God

Q15. Regarding science and religion, I think:

1. Science eventually will disprove religion

2. We should be suspicious of scientists, since most of them are atheists

3. Scientific findings trouble me at times, but do not reduce my faith because science helps me to understand God's creation

4. Science and faith seem to me two aspects of the same search for ultimate truth

Q16. In my view, God:

1. Either does not exist, or God's nature can never be known

2. Exists but is remote from human events

3. Is present at some times and absent at others

4. Is everywhere and observes everything

QI 7. I think children should:

1. Be raised to practice the faith of their parents
2. Be taught spiritual awareness but also to avoid affiliating with formal religion
3. Be encouraged to in favor of secular philosophy
4. Be exposed to many religious traditions and encouraged to make their own choices

Q18. Which of these four statements comes closest to reflecting your views about the character of existence?

1. Higher purpose comes about through some combination of human and divine effort
2. People should be moral and loving, but life itself is a chemical accident lacking inherent meaning
3. Higher purpose in the universe is everywhere, divinely created and preexistent
4. Regardless of whether we are natural or supernatural in origin, we can give meaning to our lives by practicing love and morality

Q19. What frustrates me most about faith is:

1. That even having faith and treating others well does not prevent bad things from happening to me or my loved ones
2. That ultimate events such as the Second Coming do not happen
3. That religions continue to create barriers and hostility between people
4. That God allows so much suffering and evil

Q20. In regards to religion and morality:

1. I think it's impossible to be moral without being religious
2. It's possible but difficult to be moral without reminders from religion
3. It's entirely possible to develop and live by a good moral code without religion
4. Religion makes it harder to be a moral person

Q21. I believe there is a spirit world:

1. Made up of angels
2. Made up of the souls of people who lived before
3. Made up of spirits different from us
4. There is no spirit world

Q22. The spiritual quest for me is mostly about:

1. Keeping in touch with something greater than myself
2. Learning to lead a good life or finding inner peace
3. Fulfilling a psychological need
4. Finding a connection to God

Q23. Nature is:

1. Entirely a product of natural forces
2. A spiritual force in itself
3. Mainly natural, but so majestic it is evidence of a Higher Power
4. Supernaturally created by God

Q24. To be valuable to me, religion and spirituality must be sought:

1. As part of a congregation or religious community
2. Partly with a group and partly by myself
3. Largely in private
4. Not at all

Q25. Do you find the keys to spiritual fulfillment through?

1. Watching people treating each other well
2. Prayer
3. Worship services
4. Books, music, or nature

My score - 72:

Questioning Believer - You have doubts about the particulars but not the "big stuff."

"Who is Jesus to You? (from an Episcopal Survey)"

Christ

I see Christ in every person I meet. This makes me think that Jesus is not some abstract idea or demagogue; he is every person I encounter. 'What so ever you do to the least of my people, that you do unto me.'' - Travis, Parishioner, Texas

In the beauty of the liturgy, Eucharist and beautiful prayers of the Church, I have experienced the presence and peace of the love of Christ as never before. - Chuck, Vestry Member, West Virginia

Love

Jesus brings a message of radical love and transformation. He redeems human suffering and moves us to compassion. - Mary, Parishioner, Tennessee

To me, Jesus is a friend, a constant companion, -a protector, a role model, and, most importantly, a savior. He comforts me in the darkest of situations and does not hate me if I make a mistake. I think that this is a love all the world needs to know. -Anon

Jesus tells the world that not only is love worth the risk, it is the only possible way out of our culture of death. And the church proclaims the gospel that all this is actually good news, very good news. -Anon

Son of God

Sometimes he is the Son of God; sometimes he is a prophet to this devastated world; sometimes he is just someone I can talk to. -Jim, Choirmaster and Organist, Texas

Jesus is the Son of God. What exactly that means I'm still working on! What seems to be clear is that Jesus was sent by God to us, to teach, to heal (in so many senses) and to save us. He is important to me as the center of a faith that has dramatically changed my life and how I live it. He is important to the world (the church being part of the world even as we are not "of the world") because he gives us the challenges to change ourselves and our society. He also provides the guidance on how to do it.

-Jay, Youth Minister, New York

Relationship

I try to quietly talk to him on a daily basis.
- Jason, Parishioner, Maryland

My relationship with Jesus is the most important relationship in my life.
- Megan, Pennsylvania

Salvation

Jesus has given us a mission: the salvation of the world. Salvation meaning that we are God's healing agents in this world. We are to be like Jesus in that we heal, love, and give voice to those who have no voice.
-Travis, Parishioner, Texas

Jesus is a symbol of what can happen when a person submits entirely to the will of God. He is a symbol to me of justice, especially as a model of someone who does not accept the status quo, who speaks for the downtrodden and the disenfranchised as well as those who wish to put their resources to a spiritual end and to grow in their relationship to God.
- Denise, Louisiana

Hope

Jesus leads me into a greater hope. A hope that human beings like him and I can get past violence as we seek God's realm in the world. In his lifetime, Jesus revealed not his own justice, but God's, and he did it not through violence but through steadfastness. Sometimes I feel defeated by the world — but Jesus' reminds me that he too was defeated by the world and transformed the world in the process.
-Chris, Massachusetts

Jesus is God incarnate, the fullest expression in human life of who God is, the fullest expression of who we are called to be.

-Christopher, priest, Connecticut

Forgiveness

Forgiveness is my anchor and my understanding of Jesus is my guide for finding, receiving, and giving forgiveness. There are times when I struggle deeply with this concept but my belief in the absolute forgiveness of God as expressed and exemplified by Jesus is my encouragement.

-Candace, Parishioner, Wyoming

Jesus is my personal savior and very important in my life. To me, Jesus is not some visage floating around somewhere. I try to follow his example in my life. As a Deacon and Chaplain, I try to find Jesus, that spark of goodness and humanity in all people that I meet. The world needs to hear this message from Jesus, that he has room for everyone.

-Debbie, Deacon

Grateful

According to the American College Dictionary, grateful is defined as: "warmly or deeply appreciative of kindness of benefits received." We hear this word all the time – grateful – we should be grateful when it rains, except when it rains on our barbeque, wedding, prom, etc. We should be grateful for the sun, except when we lie on the beach and burn, see on the news the droughts around the world, etc.

We should be grateful when our child lies in a hospital bed…Wait, what? When we lose our job, crash our car, trip and fall and break a leg or arm or whatever. Why would we do that, are we seriously supposed to be grateful for all these horrible things? Yup, everything in this life because our Heavenly Father created everything in this world and being grateful implies trust, trust in Him. It is easy to be grateful when things are going our way, but, not so much when they don't.

We are human, though, and it is very human to yell and rail at God when things don't go well even horrible things. When my first child died after living only ten hours, I was anything but grateful. I cried for days, screamed at God, and the big question on my mind was, WHY? Why my baby, why me? The nursery was prepared, I had had a baby shower, I was ready. Well we eventually found out all the answers to why. My baby had a strong heart, but all the other organs were either immature or damaged. He was not meant to live in this world. So now that we had answers did it make any difference? No, my mind understood but not my heart. I finally had my babies but not without living in fear that the same thing was going to happen again. I didn't know God then, but I still hoped that he would not take another child from me.

Grateful? Hardly, I lived in fear wondering what He would do to me next. A friend gave me a small book by Corrie Ten Boom and in the back of the book was a prayer I could pray to accept Jesus into my life, and I did. Everything changed, what a wonderful thing the Holy Spirit is. We were in the middle of the Charismatic movement of the 70s and all kinds of things were happening - not all were to the liking of the traditional church, however, but that's another story.

It took a long time to begin to know God and even now I realize how little I really do know. Am I grateful for the death of my first child – yes, maybe - in a good moment. I do know that I was not able to handle a child that would essentially be a vegetable. So yes, I am grateful, but it took years to come to that, but that is another story for another time.

Why does God expect us to be grateful in all things? Because He knows us, knows what He wants for us and it is all good. He knew us when we were in the womb, when we were born, the horrible first day of school and on and on and on. We can trust Him in everything, all the time. It's just hard sometimes to hold onto that, it takes time to learn the extent of His love and when we do… the love we feel for Him explodes in our heart and fills it to the brim. The Great God of all loves me!

Aside: If you hadn't noticed, the word grateful starts with the word grate; like fingernails on a blackboard, grating on someone's nerves. "To have an irritating or unpleasant effect on feelings." That is quite different than grateful, hmm.

By Susan Stone Trinity Church

A Parishioner's Note

January 15, 2008

Saint Mark's Church in Warwick
ATTN: Father Warren Dear Father Warren,

Your Outreach Ministry for the Shut-In's and their families have been received with Love, Comfort, Strength, and Peace of Heart for all you have come to know.

My Mom, Margaret Ball, always looked forward to your visits at the Nursing Home, as well as us receiving your prayers of healing and communion and flowers from the Altar, delivered by her niece, Anna May Quirk.

After your visits, her face would light up, reminiscing of the times past and comfort from you on difficult days to come.

My parent's generation and theirs before were avid churchgoers and your Outreach Ministry gave them great comfort and they physically could not go.

My mom always tried to support St. Mark's in some small financial way and I tried to help her do this

Again, you comforted our family in our time of sadness and sorrow.

The circle of life continues on as does yours and "thank you" for all you have shared and seen us through.

Our well wishes go with you as you follow "God's Journey".

God be with you and yours,
June Ken Christiansen and Family

Father Mundia

Way back in 1987, God answered a prayer for help. After two years of searching for an Assistant Priest at Trinity Church in Milford, Massachusetts, and while I was sitting at my desk and struggling with this decision process and elimination of several well-qualified priests, my phone rang. It was the beginning of the answer to my long-time prayer and year's long search. A call came in and a foreign voice inquired about our need for a priest.

Just to back up here and relate an idea brought to me some years earlier. At a Diocesan Convention, a bishop from one of our companion African dioceses was a guest speaker. I can't recall from which nation and diocese he was from, but I do recall his dramatic and most impressive appeal for us to return to "our Beloved Jesus" of history and eternity.

I had wished then that the Bishop could have come to my parish, in person, with his prominent message. Such a visit was not possible at that time. I'm sure that everyone at the Convention would have liked a visit from him. We did print and send his message to all our parishioners, but we all know that "the real presence" would have helped much needed "spark of belief" from another world and culture. In my prayer several years later, I thought how wonderful it would be to have a genuine priest from Africa to help us at Trinity.

So, my phone rang as I was trying to find a priest to help us. A foreign voice spoke to me:

"Hello, Father Warren?"

"Yes?"

"I heard that you are looking for an assistant there at Trinity."

"Yes"

"My name is Wilberforce Mundia and I would like to speak to you about that position."

"Of course! When can you come over?"

"I can set out now and be there in a little while."

"Please, come over!"

In the meantime, as I was doing my usual daily work at the office there was a knock at my door. There were regular interruptions at the office. There was a black man at the door dressed in a flannel shirt, jeans, and sneakers, entering. At that point it came to my mind that this person was coming here for assistance which was a usual course of events. Such visits were numerous as our generosity at Trinity was well known. At that point I didn't realize that Fr. Mundia was an African priest now studying and working in America. To my surprise he said, "Hi, I am Wilber Mundia." This entrance into our life came by only twenty-five minutes after the phone call.

The fact is that I knew that Father Mundia was the answer to my prayer for God to provide us with the right Assistant Priest at Trinity. Within five minutes of our conversation, one could not help but love this wonderful character. Father Mundia, Alice, and their children, B.J., Jen, and Isaac were with us for the next four years. Isaac was born just prior to their move to North Carolina. I am blessed to be one of Isaac's Godparents and the one who baptized him. The rest is memorable history. It was a tearful day at the Mass, reception, and farewell to the Mundias.

Father Mundia had earned his Doctorate in Theology while with us and was called to teach at a college in North Carolina. He has been a professor there since their move many years ago. The Doctoral Thesis of Father Mundia was "The Problem of Evil". The book he is now writing contains his understanding of that very problem. I hope his book is soon published and I look forward to being one of the first readers. After all this time, I dearly miss his presence and all the many conversations we shared together. For me and so many others, the in-depth love of God and his family and friends have changed all of our lives.

The opening Collect for Pentecost 13 asks: "Lord of all power and might, the author and giver of all good things: Craft in our hearts the love of your name; increase in us true religion; nourish us with all goodness; and bring forth in us the fruit of good works! Through Jesus Christ our Lord, who lives and reigns with you and the Holy Spirit, one God, for ever and ever, Amen."

The prophet Jeremiah, in the readings for that Sunday on which we had to bid farewell to the Mundias into their ongoing journey asks God: "Lord, please protect me from the evil that accosts me on every side. . . even as I praise and depend on you... I try to follow you even when I feel most alone… Is it the evil that overtakes me and often causes me to hurt so?...Help me to turn back to you even when the evil blinds my sight of your presence and love for me." (This is a paraphrase of Jeremiah's appeal – *Jeremiah 15:15-21*)

The Psalm 112 for Pentecost 13 prays that "God will provide us with 'the Spirit of Truth' and we shall prosper on the land." In Paul's letter to the Romans, we repeat that, "Love is in contrast to all that is evil and will bring to us all that is Good." *(Romans 12:9-21)* In the Holy Gospel according to Saint Matthew, we are reminded that Jesus suffered and died on the Cross to bring us Peace and Grace, and thereby thwart any evil which may tend to overtake us.

One of the many things shared by Father Mundia was his original up-bringing as a Massai. In Africa, the Massai Tribe was most influential in the African practices of belief, especially in his country, Kenya. Father Mundia told us how very similar this was to the beliefs of the Native Americans. When becoming a Christian himself he easily connected the similarities of belief to all of us from whichever direction we come. All in all, a belief in God is a belief in the other, or rather, that spirit from above.

In our own Christian Calendar of observances, we celebrate the Martyrs of Uganda every year on June third. This is especially significant to me now because of my relationship and deep conversations with Father Mundia.

The Martyrs of Uganda
On June 3, 1886, thirty-two young men, pages of the court of King Mwanga of Buganda, were burned to death at Namugongo for their refusal to renounce

Christianity. In the following months many other Christians throughout the country died by fire or spear for their faith.

These martyrdoms totally changed the dynamic of Christian growth in Uganda. Introduced by a handful of Anglican and Roman Catholic missionaries after 1877, the Christian faith had been preached only to the immediate members of the court, by order of King Mutesa. His successor, Mwanga, became increasingly angry as he realized that the first converts put loyalty to Christ above the traditional loyalty to the king. Martyrdoms began in 1885. (including Bishop Hannington and his Companions: see October 29th) Mwanga first forbade anyone to go near a Christian mission on pain of death but finding himself unable to cool the ardor of the converts, resolved to wipe out Christianity.

The Namugono martyrdoms produced a result entirely opposite to Mwanga's intentions. The example of these martyrs, who walked to their death singing hymns and praying for their enemies, so inspired many of the bystanders that they began to seek instruction from the remaining Christians. Within a few years, the original handful of converts had multiplied many times over and spread far beyond the court, into the country, and into the world. The martyrs had left the indelible impression that Christianity was truly African rather than by white missionaries. Uganda is now the most Christian nation in Africa.

Renewed persecution of Christians by a Muslim military dictatorship in the 1970s proved again the vitality of the example of the Namugongo martyrs. Among the thousands of new martyrs, both Anglican and Roman Catholic, was Janani Luwum, Archbishop of the Anglican Church of Uganda, whose courageous ministry and death inspired not only his countrymen but also Christians throughout the world." ("Lesser Feasts and Fasts")

Father Mundia

I had heard that the rector at Trinity Episcopal Church was seeking an Assistance Thus, I called to ask for an interview with Fr. George Warren. For the previous two years, I had served as a Supply Priest in the Diocese of Massachusetts. I thoroughly enjoyed my time with various parishes. I had moved to Medway, Massachusetts to live at Richard and Marilyn Clark, who were students at the Episcopal Divinity School, Cambridge, Massachusetts. While in Medway, I had supplied for some time as supply priest at St. Michael's Episcopal Church, Holliston, Massachusetts.

I was quite relaxed and curious as to what I would find out in the interview with Fr. Warren. When I introduced myself, we immediately found ourselves deep in conversation – learning about each other, learning about our joy in ministry, and so on. George had many wonderful questions about me and the church in Kenya. George is a most engaging interviewer. I felt even more relaxed as we talked about the needs of Trinity Episcopal Church. Because of the ease with which the conversation flowed, I was shocked and delighted by what we had covered in our few minutes at this first meeting. George ended up offering me the position.

The next four years were some of my most enjoyable times in my ministry as an Episcopal Priest. I learned a great deal from Fr. Warren. The manner in which he organized our pastoral calls to members was so delightful that I have carried that model from then to now. As we continued in ministry, the congregation grew stronger and stronger. The worship services, the Adult Christian Education, Sunday School, and some Youth activities grew from strength to strength. Most of all, there was an extremely joyful atmosphere throughout the parish. I was most encouraged in our ability to be there for our parishioners in the various circumstances that members need a pastor. I enjoyed the way George mentored me in many aspects of ministry.

During those years of ministry, the Warrens totally adopted the Mundias. I can remember the great dinners and fellowship with the wider Warren family. The Mundia children felt like they were, in in fact, they were, Warrens. Alice and I remember those days with great fondness. One of the most joyful days was when my dad, The Right Reverend James Israel Mundia, came to Trinity Episcopal Church to preach and celebrate the Eucharist. This cemented the relationship with the Warrens even more. (Dad was at the time on Sabbatical and completing his Doctor of Divinity programs at the Episcopal Divinity School.)

George has mentioned something about the suffering of Christians in Uganda. Dad was the bishop of The Anglican Diocese of Maseno North in Kenya from 1970 to 1995. In the early 80's, when the number of parishes and deaneries became too many for one bishop to administer, a new diocese was created – the Diocese of Nambale. Isaac Namango, Alice's father, was elected the first bishop of that diocese.

These two dioceses are on the western border of Kenya and Uganda. During the days when Idi Amin Dada committed atrocities in Uganda, including attacking Christians, many Ugandans fled to Kenya. The diocese of Maseno North became the welcoming and nurturing diocese for many Ugandan Christians. Our home in Kakamega town became one of the first centers of receiving Ugandan Christians. We, the Mundia children, heard those horror stories first-hand.

(Incidentally, Alice and I come from the Luhya tribe, not the Maasai. The Maasai come from the south and southwest region from Nairobi, the capital city. The Maasai are nomadic, the Luhya are not. The Maasai grazing grounds stretch from central Kenya and then straddle the long Kenya/Tanzania border. However, their African traditional religions and philosophies are quite similar. One of the most profound ideals among most Africans is a reverence for nature. They see all of nature as manifesting something of the Supreme Being.)

George also proved to be a most valuable conversation partner as I continued with my doctoral work at Boston University. My doctoral program had a concentration on the intersection of philosophy, theology, and ethics. It was extremely helpful to have somebody to talk with as I continued with my work.

My dissertation, "The Existence of the Devil," focused on exploring the soundness of philosopher Alvin Plantinga's argument that the Devil and his cohorts are responsible for natural evil. As one would expect, Plantinga was severely criticized for introducing an "ad hoc hypothesis" to solve a difficult problem in theism. My dissertation was a philosophical defense of the existence of the devil. Although the concept of the devil may be problematic for Western philosophers, not only is it embedded in Christian theology, but it also has great explanatory power. Andrew (Andy) Starkis, one of our parishioners at Trinity, read and made many helpful comments and suggestions on my dissertation manuscript.

I have continued to write and present papers at professional conferences on various aspects of the so-called problem of evil. In 2002, I published a major article advising Christian philosophers (and theologians) to avoid excessive efforts in efforts to "defend God in light of problems of pain and suffering." What Christians should do is participate in pastoral theology and pastoral ministry – being there for those going through times of pain and struggle. Trying to explain the ways of God to fellow human beings is a tricky task. For example, it assumes that, in our current existence, human beings can fully understand God's ways and wisdom and that those we talk to can understand such explanations. This is a questionable assumption.

In my current project, "Evil and Paradigms of Paradox," I argue that Christians have many reasons for continuing to believe in God despite the quandaries of sin, evil, pain, and suffering. Such a project lies in the field of Christian apologetics – and not Christian theology. -Wilber(force) Mundia

While speaking with Fr. Mundia, I also asked if he would enter a piece regarding his Doctoral Thesis on "The Problem of Evil". Included here is a summation of work he is completing on his book about the "Evil" dilemma. In another section of my book here present is a brief narrative on dealing with such a profound and most often bewildering subject. The point is that "Evil" is real.

Evil and Paradigms of Paradox:
From Theodicy and Anti-Theodicy to Apologetics Synopsis
By Wilberforce O. Mundia

I am writing a book with the working title, "Evil and Paradigms of Paradox: From Theodicy, Defense, and Anti-Theodicy to Apologetics". From 2007 to 2016, I took some time, during the summers, to review some of the leading theodicies and defenses that sought to solve the so-called problems of evil.

Problems of evil constitute the problems that arise from the apparent contradiction in holding that (a) there is only one Supreme Being who is (b) all powerful, all knowing, and morally perfect, and is also (c) the Creator of a world that seems to contain certain disturbing types, amounts, and distributions of pain and suffering. Items (a), (b), and (c) often constitute what may be called The God Paradigm. Theodicies try to explain how and why God is justified in creating such a world. In reviewing some of the leading theodicies and defences, I suspected that there is a paradigm (or a family of paradigms) that seem to lie behind these suggested solutions. Consider, for example, five of the lead-ing arguments for why God allows evil in the world: (1) Good cannot exist without evil – that is, evil is a necessary counterpart to good; further, (2) Evil is necessary as a means to good; (3) The universe is better with some evil in it than it could be if there were no evil; (4) Evil is due to human free will; and, (5) Evil in this world is intended to produce mature souls. What each of these arguments contends is that there are two opposing items that cannot exist without the other. You cannot have free will without conceding the possibility that some human beings will make morally wrong choices – and, by acting on those choices, bring about what is normally called moral evil. You cannot have good in this world without some evil (Mackie 1955, Mackie 1982; Hick 1977; Plantinga 1977; Swinburne 1988; Swinburne 1998). [1]

Some have argued that we would not know what good is if we didn't know what evil is.

Mundia Evil and Paradigms of Paradox: A Synopsis
(Swinburne 1988, 1998; Dolen 2017)

Thus, while these paradigms lie behind the suggested solutions, they are not usually acknowledged, stated, defined, defended, and explicitly applied. One of the results of this situation is that these suggested solutions seem to be weaker than they are. By this, I mean that, it occurred to me that, if these par-adigms were acknowledged, stated, defined, defended, and explicitly applied, they would be able to respond adequately to some of the leading objections. The objections tend to rely on the apparent contradictions that arise both in the divine attributes and certain other formulations that these theoretical so-lutions adduce.

Further, it occurred to me that most theodicies and defenses seem not to be answering the question which they set out to answer. The question that theodicists and others are seeking to answer is this: Why does the God of the-ism create a world that seems to contain certain disturbing types, amounts, and distributions of pain and suffering? In their answers, theodicists and others

Mackie outlined these arguments before severely criticizing them.

seem to be giving answers to the question: Why are believers rationally justified in continuing to believe in God despite the quandries of evil? The reasons given above that theodicists adduce are answering this question – but not the question of why God allows certain types, amounts, and distributions of pain and suffering in this world. In the course of this project,

I will demonstrate that the reasons theodicists have given are most likely not the answer God would give. In fact, there is strong evidence that the reasons theodicists appeal to are not the ones God would likely give. Further, there is no way any given theodicist can prove that the reasons they have adduced are the actual reasons God would likely give for allowing evil in the world. The reasons theodicists give seem to be much more in the purview of apologetics rather than theodicy. Because of this, I will suggest that theists gradually withdraw from the project of theodicy and put more efforts in apologetics. This is a much more manageable, meaningful, and important project than theodicy. The arguments that sustain the thesis that we embrace and apply paradigms of paradox may be summarized as follows.

In chapter two, I will give a definition of paradigms of paradox. This will involve providing a sufficient definition of (a) paradigms, (b) the categories and types of paradox, and (c) how and why paradox can be translated into paradigms. In this chapter, I will also argue that (d) while problems of evil arise because of the God Paradigm, they cannot be solved within that paradigm. Theists can choose to live with this paradox of Christianity or discard the God Paradigm. Most theists have completely refused to discard the God Paradigm. As a result, they have no alternative but to embrace paradigms of paradox. (e) problems of evil cannot be solved because they require one to argue that what is evil is not evil (or even that what is evil is good). It may not be false to argue that, "What is evil is good." However, it is paradoxical.

In chapter three, I will argue that, while problems of evil have sometimes been constructed in the form of paradoxes, with illuminating results, this has not been done in a sufficiently detailed manner. For example, describing problems of evil in the form of the various types of paradox – antinomies, riddles, falsidical and veridical paradoxes, semantical paradoxes, paradoxes of the meeting (or coincidence) of opposites, and the existential paradox – reveals certain neglected aspects of problems of evil. For example, the existential aspects of problems of evil is probably one of the most relevant aspects of problems of evil. However, this aspect is often disregarded in the analytical philosophical approach to problems of evil.

Chapter four will be devoted to a philosophical justification of paradigms of paradox. This include (a) the recognition of paradigms of paradox in philosophy itself – via the fact that some insoluble antinomies demonstrate that some true and acceptable contradictions; (b) the concept of Unity of Opposites as described and defended by the Pre-Socratics in ancient Greece and Hegel in the nineteenth century; (c) paradox turns out to be a legitimate and indispensable tool for conducting philosophy; (d) the elemental and tenable Meeting of Opposites; (e) the Law of Knowledge – which holds that in order to know something, you have to have a reasonably good grasp of its opposite; and (f) the findings of recent paraconsistent logics which show that, when we get to the limits of human thought, we find that there are some true contradictions.

Chapter five will be devoted to providing a theological justification of paradigms of paradox. This proceeds along the following lines. Although the phenomenon of pain and suffering disrupts the lives of almost every human being, the problems are most acute in the context of monotheism. It is, in fact, the context within which problems of evil arise. Limiting ourselves to Christianity, it turns out that, in thought, word, and deed, the life of faith not only exhibits (or encounters) various insoluble paradoxes, it (seems to) thrive on paradox.

This is so much so that, whether they know it or not, most believers are constantly embracing and employing paradigms of paradox. Specifically, (a) the divine attributes are paradoxical and can only be upheld by employing paradigms of paradox; (b) not only is the nature of Christ paradoxical, his life and teachings are also couched in an incredible slew of truth revealing and life-transforming paradoxes; (c) like many other doctrines of Christianity, the doctrine of predestination is profoundly meaningful and yet deeply paradoxical.

Chapter six will be devoted to finally demonstrating that paradigms of paradox lie behind some of the leading theoretical solutions to problems of evil. It was necessary to lay the background of chapters 1 though five in order for this claim to be properly discussed. It will now be possible to show that (a) not only do these paradigms lie behind the five leading arguments, but paradigms of paradox also make the solutions stronger. But this is only on the condition that these are our reasons for continuing to believe in God despite the quandaries of evil rather than reasons why God allows evil in the world. The specific arguments to be explored are these: (a) Good cannot exist without evil, or, stated otherwise, evil is a necessary counterpart to good; further, (b) evil is necessary as a means to good; (c) the universe is better with some evil in it than it could be if there were no evil; (d) evil is due to human free will; and (e) evil in this world is intended to produce mature souls.

In chapter seven, we look at how paradigms of paradox are able to defeat various non-theistic (that is, atheological) objections to theistic positions on problems of evil. (A summary of this chapter can be gotten from earlier summaries). In this chapter, we will discuss two leading objections raised by atheists. Here, we show that, in an invaluable contribution to an exposition of problems of evil, it turns out that these objections are almost always based on the paradoxes that theism (especially) in Christianity, seem to embrace in the various suggested solutions to the problems of evil. The two thinkers we will discuss are John Mackie and Michael Martin. If the rejection of paradox is refuted, it becomes clear that the theistic solutions are not as weak (or invalid) as some atheists claim. Further, it will be argued that atheistic objections to Christian responses are paradigm related. The upshot is that, while theists have a higher tolerance for paradox, in the area of religion, atheists have shown an extreme abhorrence of paradox.

While theistic discussions of problems of evil are approached as a justification of continued belief in the existence of God, the atheistic objections turn out to be invalid – primarily on the grounds that they assume non-theistic paradigm. If one rejects the main items in another person's paradigm, one should not be surprised to find problems in the positions of those holding the rejected paradigm.

In chapter eight, we will show that there are various theological and moral objections that anti-theodicists raise. So, this will simply be composed of (a) theological problems of theodicy; (b) theodicy employs the wrong moral theories in addressing problems of evil; (c) theodicy neglects and abuses the God- imposed ignorance on what could possibly be the reason for allowing certain epistemologically and existentially debilitating types, amounts, and distributions of pain and suffering.

This project is written from the point of view of what has been called anti-theodicy, protest theodicy, or protest theology against theodicy. A few years ago, I gave a qualified RSVP to John Roth's invitation for Christian theologians and philosophers to participate in this protest. [2]In that response, I went on to suggest some other things we might protest about. While it is not easy to capture, anti-theodicy and protest against theodicy consist of at least two main strands. "First, it is a cry to God: 'My God, my God, why dost thou make it seem that either thou dost not exist or that thou hast forsaken the world.' Second, it is a sustained reprimand of various theistic explanations and efforts to exonerate God."[3]

In many and various ways, anti-theodicy is a reaction against and a rejection of traditional formulations and solutions to the problem of evil. One of the theses of anti-theodicy is moral. There are many well stated and unrefuted moral objections to theodicy. These objections may be summarized in the simple but significant thesis: "Theodicy is morally objectionable." Another major thrust of anti-theodicy is based on non-moral objections to theodicy. These objections may be captured in the thesis: "Traditional formulations of the problems of evil are conceptually misguided." Stated otherwise: "'Theodicies mediate a praxis that sanctions evil.'"[4]

In all these efforts, anti-theodicy, under whatever name, has brought back an essential element into theistic discussions of problems of evil: A sincere, articulate, and profound acknowledgement and description of the horrors of human suffering. Since most anti-theodicists are believers, however, they need to move from anti-theodicy to suggesting how they reconcile their belief in God with the brutal reality of pain and suffering. In this effort, I want to suggest that paradigms of paradox provide one of the best ways to proceed.

Paradigms of paradox provide a way of talking about the paradoxes of evil without having to solve the problems of evil. Paradigms of paradox suggest ways of moving from theodicy and anti-theodicy to apologetics. I will suggest that whatever statements various theistic thinkers make in talking about problems of evil, they are not (or should not) aim at providing reasons for why God

---

[2] See (Wilberforce) Mundia, "Evil, Finitude, and Protest 1: A Qualified RSVP, "International Journal for Philosophy of Religion, 51 (December 2002):139-158.

[3] Mundia, "Evil, Finitude, and Protest, "142

allows horrendous suffering in this world. Rather, they are (and should be) attempting to provide reasons for why they continue to believe in an omnipotent, omniscient, and omnibenevolent God.

(ADDED ON 12/20/2019)
The most important point I gather from participating in Anti-Theodicy is this: Anti-Theodicy is meaningless unless it embraces and employs paradigms of paradox. After all, anti- theodicists have to give us a justification for their continued belief in God. And this would most likely lie in a statement like the following: On various other grounds, we continue to believe in God despite the fact that we cannot provide any good reason for why God allows certain types, amounts, and distributions of pain and suffering.
    (ADDITION ENDS HERE)

In chapter nine, I suggest some ways in which theodicy can transit from the project of theodicy to the project of apologetics. First, former theodicies must fully embrace paradigms of paradox. Second, every former theodicy must be married to one or more practical theodicy – which tend to have much more of a slant towards pastoral themes.

"The Journey of Dr. Kenneth E. Rix, DMV"

It must be clarified here that Dr. Rix and I have divergent beliefs as to who or what we believe God to be. It is important to again note here that the term "God" is simply the term used through human history to cover many definitions of that term. In the Christian Faith as in others, God is other than each of us and also part of each of us. The Holy Bible sets God as supreme above all other and also "Creator." Where and how can we extend our conversation to better and greater understanding of that Truth which defines who we are?

This is an ongoing conversation. In the midst of sharing whatever data we have in whatever belief system we have, learning can and does happen. So said the ancients, "The more I learn, the less I know." There is always much more to learn! One important thing that Kenneth and I see clearly, together, is the belief in the historical Jesus and both his extraordinary comprehension of human nature and his extraordinary influence on the history of the world.

Was it by accident, coincidence, design, chance, some or all of the above, or could there be more mystery to why Kenny Rix and I became friends in high school? After all, there were all of 650 students in our class. After high school, we journeyed into different directions not to get together again until very recently (October 2020). We double-dated together, had many conversations on deeper than superficial matters, and shared some commonalities such as school and hopes for our future.

With Kenny's love for animals, for instance, there was no doubt in my mind that he would work to his best to become a veterinarian. And so, he did! I don't think that Ken had as clear an idea as to the path I would be taking. You'll need to ask him that question if you happen to be curious. We were also very different in many ways and the topic would be elusive to say the least. Thanks to our mutual friend and classmate, Joseph Tavares, who organized our Class Reunions, Kenny and I returned to our conversations of old, particularly around matters of religion and politics.

I am truly thankful to have reconnected with Kenny after so many years of no communication, and thankful that we have clearly become engaged in those deeper conversations of divergent as well as like-minded views. We clearly have so much more to discuss and learn from each other along with the paths we have chosen for our lives. The following is Dr. Kenneth Rix's story as written by his own hand following our initial, renewed conversation.

Dr. Kenneth Rix: My Story

I recently celebrated seventy five years of life. I am older than I was but younger than I will be. My story is a journey from my Christian ancestors and the revival of religious education as a teenager to the knowledge of science that resulted in my rejection of religion and the belief in an afterlife. The attack on 9-11 further demonstrated to me that teaching of the belief in a conscious afterlife (Heaven and Hell) could be used to indoctrinate individuals for Good or Evil. Then, after two failed marriages, I married a Christian woman who taught me the meaning of love.

However, it was the story of a personal friend who built a home on a lake from a shack to his castle on land that was promised to him that brought me back to Christ. He and his wife had this home that they worked on for several years ripped away from them by greed. Since their eviction many years ago that land has sat idyll and I believe it is cursed. This was a house and land that could have been a safe haven for this man and his family. If that was not bad enough, this man's wife died of cancer after several years of suffering and yet he is the most Christian man I know. He got me going back to an Evangelical Church. I have come to believe in the goodness of the Judea-Christian world view.

I came from Christians. I know of the lives of my immediate ancestors (Great Grandfather, Grandfather, Father, and Mother) that ultimately passed their lives into me. However, I still cannot bring myself to believe in life after death. I believe that God is a spirit that dwells in the mind of every human being on earth. Unfortunately, wherever God lives so does the Devil. Finally, I believe that death is the end of life for each of us. No Heaven, no Hell, just the memory of us in those we leave behind.

The book *Sapiens* by Yuval Noah Harari provides a logical explanation for the existence of human beings. The book explains that the Universe is massive beyond human comprehension. Compared to the Universe the entire Earth is a tiny speck of matter. This planet Earth formed over billions of years and every living thing including human life that we know extends back for millions of years played out on this planet Earth; Birth, Life and Death. We are intelligent animals that have learned how to pass information on to our children through the spoken and written word. That ability to pass on knowledge has slowly created the technological world we currently inhabit. That ability has also given our species the concept of morality and the belief in God.

I was born the month after World War II ended. I attended public schools from Kindergarten to High School and graduated High School in 1963. I decided in junior high school to work toward becoming a veterinarian after my beloved dog Cindy was killed by a car because she followed me to school one day. Was this an act of God or just a tragedy that motivated me?

Despite being discouraged by a high school guidance counselor to pursue a career in veterinary medicine, I worked hard to get good grades. I applied to and was accepted to the University of Rhode Island. My parents could not afford to help with finances, so I took out student loans and worked as a Resident Hall Assistant. I took on extra credit courses in science and became educated in Physics, Chemistry, and Biology.

After only three years at URI, I had completed all the requirements for application to Veterinary School and I was accepted into the College of veterinary medicine at the University of Pennsylvania in 1966. In that year, the U.S. Government was drafting men of my age to fight a war in Viet Nam. Because I was in a veterinary degree program, I was granted a deferment of the healing arts. All I had to do was to pledge that when I graduated, I would join the military if I was needed. But by the time I graduated the war was ending and troops were being sent home.

Was this an act of God or just a fortunate lucky break? Very few people were admitted to veterinary school without completing their undergraduate degree. I graduated as a veterinarian in May of 1970. I transferred my veterinary credits back to URI and I graduated from URI in June of 1970. I worked for a veterinarian for 2 years and then joined a partner. The two of us began a veterinary practice in 1972 with one employee. Over the next 40 years we grew the practice to five veterinarians and thirty-five employees. In 2013, we sold the practice to a corporation, and in 2018, I retired as a veterinarian.

During those years, I made many decisions. Decisions are influenced by what one believes at the time they are made. I was a junior in high school when I met my first wife, Carolyn. She was a freshman at the same high school. We would never have met except for the author of this book, George Warren, who was a friend of mine. He invited me to go to an Episcopal youth retreat where Carolyn and I met. Was that an act of God? We dated though high school. We continued dating after I graduated high school and attended URI. When Carolyn graduated from nursing school as an LPN, I was still attending veterinary college. We decided to marry the summer before I began my third year of veterinary school. I now believe that it was the Christian influence in my life that kept me from dating any other girl during high school, URI, or at veterinary school. I was always faithful to Carolyn, and we were both still virgins when we married. The plan was that with Carolyn working as a nurse, my life as a student would be easier. This was not the case, however. Carolyn was always unhappy. She hated her first job as a psych nurse at a veteran hospital. She hated where we lived – the only apartment we could afford at the time.

My life became more difficult after we married because Carolyn was always unhappy, and she wanted a child. She thought that would make her happy. Having a pregnant wife that could not work while I was still in veterinary school made my life that much more difficult. My first son was born while I was a senior in veterinary school. I took out student loans to get by and we took on a role as house parents at the Methodist Home for Children to get room and board for a year.

After I graduated, I got a job back in Rhode Island as a small animal veterinarian. We rented a top floor of a nice home. A very nice older woman occupied the bottom floor but Carolyn was unhappy because we did not have privacy. We bought a house that we could afford, but Carolyn soon became unhappy with the steep slope in the backyard that made the backyard unusable. Carolyn began therapy for her depression. She was diagnosed with Manic Depressive Psychosis and placed on lithium therapy.

1972 was an epic year. Carolyn was pregnant with our first daughter and I had met up with a veterinary classmate and we decided to start our own veterinary practice. At first, the plan was to buy out the practice where my partner was working in western Connecticut. That failed to work out and I found a location in Rhode Island that was in need of a veterinary practice – Tiverton, Rhode Island.

Carolyn delivered our daughter at the same time as I was beginning the veterinary practice that would be my life's work for the next forty-six years. Carolyn was unhappy that the temporary beginning of our practice was in the garage in the back of our house. Carolyn was also unhappy with the house we bought that she found and wanted me to buy. She did not like my partner and began to dislike my family. In January of 1973, we moved into a new building – the Sakonnet Veterinary Hospital.

After a year of a successful practice, we rented a house in Westport and had our dream house built. But soon Carolyn's depression worsened. I finally realized that despite having everything anyone could hope for: two wonderful children – a boy and a girl, a beautiful custom-built home in a private setting, a job that I had worked so hard for and that I enjoyed and that provided us with an exceptional income – Carolyn's depression worsened. I was isolated.

An event occurred that I will never forget. Another veterinarian that was a classmate had started a veterinary practice in the town of Dartmouth, Massachusetts. I met him at a meeting and invited him to stop by to see the house we had just built. He and his wife arrived one day unannounced to visit and Carolyn went on a rampage against him, and he left without visiting or seeing the house. I was so humiliated. I think that was the moment I knew I had to divorce this woman or spend the rest of my life with a woman who was incapable of ever being happy.

I eventually rented an apartment and told Carolyn I wanted a divorce and moved out of the house. It took another year and an attempt at reconciliation, but we finally divorced ten years after we were married. I had several relationships and a long-term relationship with Jill, a woman fifteen years younger than me. She wanted to be a veterinarian, and she worked at my hospital.

I thought that if I loved Jill and I was faithful and good to her, she would love me back. That was a bad mistake. I had several warnings that Jill never really loved me but I was blind to them. I was faithful to Jill through two more years at Bates College in Maine, seeing her during the summer months. Then four years at Cornell Veterinary College in Ithaca New York, again only seeing her during breaks or during the summer months. On Christmas Eve during her second year at Cornell, she asked to break up with me. I was devastated, but she quickly changed her mind and decided to continue the relationship. I remained faithful to this relationship. Another clue was when she finally graduated, she took a job quite a distance away from me on Cape Cod.

When that happened, I decided that this relationship was not going to work out, and I only started dating again. She panicked that she was going to lose my support and asked me to marry her. I agreed but another clue went unheeded. She wanted only a tiny quick marriage with only immediate family members present. Instead of finding a job as a veterinarian within commuting distance, Jill wanted her own practice. So, we bought a building and she started her own practice in a building only four miles from my practice. When our first child was born she continued working there and brought our daughter to work daily. I think what she wanted was for me to quit my partnership at Sakonnet Veterinary Hospital and do all the work at her clinic.

Fortunately, I never agreed to do that. I was doing the bookkeeping for her practice and income was not being declared properly. I was worried that we could be charged with tax evasion and we fought over this issue. When Jill got pregnant with our second child, she decided she did not want the practice we had established for her, and we sold it at a financial loss to a veterinarian that became my chief competitor. Jill tried to start a house call practice but was hampered by a noncompete ethics violation by the veterinarian she sold the practice to. After our third child was born, Jill became increasingly unhappy with me and on New Years Eve one year asked for a divorce. We divorced seven years after we were married.

Again, after several relationships I married a third time to a woman who was previously married and divorced with three children, and today we are blessed with a blended family. I finally married a woman that loved me. Barbara is a kind, generous, thoughtful woman. She is a devout Christian. She accepts me the way that I am, and I love her back. We have been happily married now for the past seventeen years.

During those years from high school to the present, I had to make many life-altering decisions. I made them and my life turned out the way it did. I cannot blame God for all the mistakes I made but I can thank God and Jesus Christ for how my life turned out. I can do that because I believe that God and Jesus live within me. God and Jesus are the "GOOD" within me.

Mistakes are the lessons that I needed to learn to become who I was supposed to be. From those two failed marriages I was blessed with five wonderful children. Knowing what I know about the evolution of life including human life, I cannot make myself believe there is an invisible world inhabited by spirits of dead ancestors and that a "Being" we call God knows everything I think, say, and do. Or, somehow, I will be judged by that personality and rewarded in Heaven or tortured in Hell forever. Nor can I believe that a personality in another dimension is capable of an active intervention to change the outcome of an event in my life.

My life and every human life are unique. I have traveled to so many places in this country and around the world. The Soviet Union, Ukraine, Morocco, England, Ireland, Italy, Austria, Germany, Netherlands, Mexico, New Zealand, Chile, Argentina, Uruguay, Jamaica, and several other island nations in the Caribbean.

The places I have been and the experiences I have had live in my mind. I have been to the Soviet Union and stood in the Kremlin. I visited Kiev when the Soviet Empire occupied Ukraine. I have seen the palace of Peter the Great in Leningrad. I have been to Marrakech in Morocco. I have traveled through Italy, Ireland, and Europe. I have been to London and walked through the Kew Gardens. I bicycled through New Zealand. I have stoop atop Mt. Orizaba, in Mexico, the third highest peak in North America at 19,000 feet. I have sat in a pool of water in Chile heated by volcanic activity.

I have five intelligent, healthy children, and my wife has three children. We are blessed with nine grandchildren. My wife is a Christian, and she loves me. I live in a beautiful, private, comfortable house surrounded by beautiful gardens. My wife and I have good health, adequate wealth, and time to enjoy both. I am so grateful for my many blessings. Needless to say, over the years of my life I made some great decisions, some good decisions, some bad decisions, and some terrible decisions. What guides the decisions we make? Is it God and the Devil operating in an invisible universe or is it the Good and Evil that exists in one's mind?

Every human life is the result of where and when each individual was born, how they were raised, what they were taught, what they learned, what they observed, the decisions they made and the experiences they had. Every life is unique. Before I begin, I want to make a point that I will never again judge or try to change anyone's belief in God. Belief is personal. My wife believes that God is a personality and that her parents and deceased brother and sisters reside in heaven. So, with that introduction, I turn to my religious beliefs.

I do not believe in the supernatural. I believe that death is the end of an individual's life. There are seven billion people alive on earth today. Billions more have lived before and died. Each was born at a different time and place. Each was raised and taught and experienced unique events. Each had encoded in their brain all the events that occurred during that life and the things that were experienced and learned. I cannot believe that their consciousness exists somewhere in an invisible parallel universe.

My belief is that Heaven and Hell as locations after death are ideas; their existence cannot be proven and do not make any logical sense to me. However, I do not judge those that do believe in a spiritual world after death. Depending on one's earthly circumstances and personality, Heaven and Hell can exist right here on Earth.

I do not believe that which cannot be proven by observation or experiment. I have not been able to make myself believe that any form of consciousness exists once our brain dies. What I believe remains of each of us after death is that which we leave behind: our children, our ideas, and the influence we had on those left still alive after we die. I want to believe in GOD. I believe I am a Christian. How can that be?

"Mistakes are lessons we need to learn to become who we are supposed to be. A man cannot learn what he thinks he already knows. Throughout human history, truth has been revealed by questioning belief." *(Epictetus (55-135 A. D.)* Everything I have experienced during my life is encoded in my brain. No one has access to that information except me.

Five hundred years before the birth of Jesus Christ, a Greek philosopher, Heraclitus, wrote: "The content of your character is your choice day by day. What you choose, what you do, is who you become." I am a Christian. Christ came into my life through the life of my ancestors. The known genealogy of my family goes back to my great grandfather. He lived in Ireland during the 1850s. During that time, Ireland experienced the great famine caused by the potato blight. Millions of people died of starvation. The Irish were Catholic Christians.

My great grandfather left Ireland, and there is a document that shows he arrived in Boston in 1850. I would not have a life if he had not come to America. We do not know of his marriages, but he had at least two children we know of, including my Great Aunt Agnes McGlenn and my grandfather. The Christian Little Sisters of the Poor in Connecticut raised my grandfather. It was there that he met my grandmother who was pregnant with another man's child. After she gave birth, they married. My grandfather adopted my oldest uncle, and they went on to have more children. I have a photograph taken in 1912 of my grandfather and grandmother with five of my aunts and uncles and my father, their youngest, as an infant. I got to meet all five of my aunts and uncles when I was growing up. I owe my life to my grandfather, grandmother, and the Christian Little Sisters of the Poor.

For reasons we do not know, when they married, my grandfather and grandmother changed their last name from McGlenn to Rix. Perhaps it was the fact that my grandmother was pregnant out of wedlock – a sin in Christianity. My mother was the daughter of a Polish immigrant. As a young boy my maternal grandfather lived with us. My mother was raised as a Catholic. When

I was a young boy, my father had a drinking problem. My parents fought a lot and we did not attend church.

At the age of ten or eleven, my mother started attending a Baptist Church that was within walking distance of our house. My mother did not drive and my father was not interested in church. I went to Sunday School and was baptized by submersion by Pastor Roger Berg in January of 1960 at the age of fifteen. The Baptist Church introduced me to the Boy Scouts and a scoutmaster who was a Christian role model for me. Christ continued to affect my life. I met the author of this book, George Warren, in high school. In my junior year of high school, he invited me to an Episcopal Youth Event where I met my eventual first wife.

I believe Jesus Christ started a movement that has spread and evolved for over 2000 years. I believe that the spirit of Jesus Christ is in me and is in the minds of everyone that calls himself or herself a Christian. Doubts about belief in an afterlife have been with me all of my life. As I became educated in science the supernatural realm of religion further eroded my religious belief.

Why is it required to believe in existence after death to call oneself a Christian? I consider myself to be only of average intelligence. This is what I know to be true. Physics is fascinating to me. Matter and energy are interchangeable. Fusion powers our sun and creates heavier elements from lighter elements. Fission demonstrates the awesome power of splitting heavier elements into lighter elements: the Atomic Bomb. Light energy can travel infinite distances. Universal distances are measured in light years.

Imagine that using telescopes, scientists can see light that has been travelling 186,000 miles per second for 20,000 years from the center of our galaxy to their eyes. Our sun is one of at least a hundred billion suns in the Milky Way Galaxy. The number of galaxies in the universe in unknowable. The next nearest galaxy to our galaxy, the Milky Way, is more than a million light years from Earth. How could a being have created all of this? Who created God?

High school and college Chemistry are equally fascinating. I learned that everything on earth and in the entire universe is composed of ninety-eight elements (some heavier elements that are unstable have been created by fusion), and those elements are composed of subatomic particles: electrons, protons, and neutrons. Covalent and electronic bonding forms molecules. Two atoms of Hydrogen bonded with one atom of Oxygen, both gases, form H2O (water).

I learned how chemistry became organic chemistry where complex molecules of Carbon, Hydrogen, Oxygen, and Nitrogen formed Amino Acids and DNA. Organic chemistry became biology. The biochemistry that happens in every one of the trillions of cells in the body of not only every human being but also every living thing is just beginning to be understood.

As a veterinary student, I learned anatomy and physiology that proved in my mind the evolution of all life on Earth. Comparative anatomy alone proves in my mind that all primates (monkeys, chimpanzees, gorillas) and humans have a common ancestor. Lions and tigers are related to house cats and all of today's divergent population of dogs evolved during the most recent centuries of human existence. We humans are intelligent animals.

What I believe must be compatible with what I know. What I know must be compatible with my experience during my life and the knowledge, accumulated through thousands of years of human history, that can be repeatable and proven through demonstrable experimentation. Fusion and fission prove physics is real. Chemical reactions prove chemistry is real. O2+HZ=HZO (oxygen and Hydrogen make water)

COZ+HZO=C6H12 (Carbon Dioxide and water makes sugar)

Sexual reproduction and in vitro fertilization prove biology. The purpose of sex is the creation of new life. It is present in all mammals and many other classes of animals and in many plants. The responsibility to care for the new born is present in most mammals but has reached a pinnacle in the human animal. What is love? Do animals experience love? In a lot of ways, I believe that God is love, and Christians find God and love in their minds.

The Polarity Principle: Polarity is universal. For something to exist the polar opposite must also exist. For example, positive and negative charges make up all matter. Light and dark define one another. Right and left, up and down, life and death, good and evil, and even God and the Devil are examples.

If God were a being, there must also be a Devil. My belief is that God and Satan, Good and Evil are concepts that dwell in all of life. Good and Evil exist in our minds. "News is the first draft of History." At the time of the life and death of Jesus Christ, news was spread verbally from person to person. Many sections of the Bible were written decades and centuries after the death of Christ. How accurate are they?

Christianity has evolved for the past 2000 years. Even today Catholic, Protestant, Mormon, Evangelical, and Unitarian beliefs differ widely. During the Reformation Catholics were burning Protestants to death strapped to a stake for being heretics. In the early history of the European settlements in America "witches" (old ladies) were killed in the same way. During the Middle Ages, indulgences were sold by Priests to "get" individuals a better chance they would be "allowed" into Heaven after death.

I believe that Jesus Christ was a male human being who lived in the early centuries of human recorded history. His existence was recorded in written Roman history. He was a good man who preached a way for human beings to live. I believe he had a mother and father that were human. Because virgin birth has never happened before or since I cannot accept that his mother was impregnated by a spirit. I can never know what Jesus Christ believed. He could have been born into a self-sustaining prophecy and he may have believed he was the only Son of God. I can never know what his Disciples believed. I do believe that the spirit of Christ (GOODNESS) rose up from the (EVIL) of his despicable, torturous murder on the Cross and then into his followers. Their belief eventually created the Christian religion that exists today.

Human beings who lived centuries ago wrote the Bible. When the Bible was written human beings did not know about physics, chemistry, or biology. The opening book of the Bible, Genesis, in my mind, is so irrational for the explanation of the formation of our planet, Earth, that it casts doubt on the remainder of what is written. I prefer to think of the Bible as stories written by people who had the spirit of goodness (God) with them at the time the chapters of the Bible were written. There are some very good lessons of morality in the Bible, but I cannot accept everything in the Bible as truth.

The Evangelical Church that I currently attend is called the Victory Church. The Pastor and his wife are on a mission to grow this church. The individuals that attend that church every week are GOOD and CARING and LOVING people. They help people that are less fortunate. During the church service, I am surrounded by the love they have for their children. They want to help people that have addictions, marital problems or depression find peace through the belief in a loving God. They have a great band and a chorus of singers with remarkable voices. I commend them for all of that.

However, there are a growing number of human beings who no longer believe in God. The number of people that call themselves Christians is shrinking. Among this growing secular group of individuals there is a belief that they are more intelligent than Christians. They know best how to run your life and they want to silence Christians and any dissent form the pathway of the future that they envision. They believe that: the ends justify the means and are willing to lie, cheat and steal their way to political power to achieve their goal.

If the Christian Church is to grow, I believe the church must accept that people like me must be accepted as Christian. God and Christ are in all of us and we need places where that idea can grow and counter the idea that there is no God. Christians founded the United States of America. They wrote our Constitution and Declaration of Independence. Those documents and the past two centuries of Christian history gave us the freedom we all unfortunately take for granted today. Our freedom is under assault by secular atheists. You do not have to believe in an afterlife to believe in God or Jesus Christ.

"And ye shall know the truth and the truth shall make you free." (Jesus Christ, The Gospel of St. John King James Version, Holy Bible)

I am a Christian. The spirit of Jesus Christ resides within me. I have been blessed by ancestors who lived their lives with Christian beliefs and ultimately created me. I have been blessed with five wonderful children that came from my decisions that were based on my Christian beliefs. All of my children are Christians, whether they believe it or not.

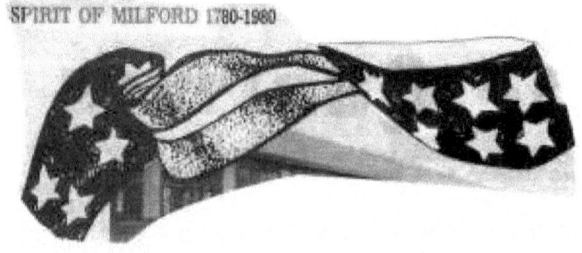

SPIRIT OF MILFORD 1780-1980

"Rachael – Building Blocks of Faith"

I grew up, with regard to my spiritual growth, in a Protestant Church that would be categorized as Conservative Baptist. Technically, I was born and baptized a Catholic, but when I was still a toddler, my mother had a change of heart, theologically speaking, and swung to the Protestant side of the faith. Hence, my earliest memories are of my Protestant Baptist roots.

Most of my childhood was spent at The North Uxbridge Baptist Church (as it was called at the time). It was a square, solid looking white structure – typically Baptist in its lack of frills – with white wooden doors propped open to the world on Sunday mornings, and a tall white spire that pierced the sparse skyline in a respectfully cheerful way toward the heavens.

As with many remembered things from childhood (including one's own self) the outside of that church has retained a familiar look over the years, despite some expansions, but the inside is almost unrecognizable, having undergone multiple and extensive renovations over the years.

The Sanctuary room where my earliest self spent Sunday mornings seated between my parents on a wooden pew, was on the second floor of the church, and accessed by a double set of thrilling, curved staircases – a highlight of my earliest church experience.

We sung all the old Protestant hymns there, in that room just beneath the steeple – The Old Rugged Cross, Faith of our Fathers, The Church in the Wildwood – the kinds of songs that aren't sung much anymore, but whose familiar melodies have the power to pull me back in time with vivid memories of those wooden pews and hardcover hymnals; men in suits and women in their Sunday best, voices raised, for the most part, in pleasant harmony.

When I was young, I imagined our enthusiastic voices carrying those hymns out the open windows, beyond the confines of God's House and into the surrounding neighborhood, and I wondered what we sounded like to the townspeople going about their morning outside the walls of that church. I remember hoping that we sounded good to the outside world – that our voices rang strong and true.

That second floor Sanctuary, once the central focal point of the building, was eventually replaced by a bigger, better, and more easily accessed Sanctuary room on the first floor. The "Old Sanctuary" of my youth is just a memory now – the physical room altered beyond recognition and long gone – but what went on inside those walls that housed the sermons, songs, and worship of my childhood, left a lasting influence, shaping the foundation of my parents' faith, their theology, and a spiritual work ethic that lives on in me.

In later years, I explored my Catholic roots, getting Confirmed in the Church and attending for some years. I appreciated the sense of deep reverence that was present in the Mass, and a way of looking at people (non-Christians) in a way very much like that of the Early Church – where Jesus and the Disciples were not just taking care of people spiritually but in a practical, social, and physical sense – feeding the hungry, healing the sick. The Early Church cared about people, and they understood that the way to people's hearts was not just in evangelizing but in loving, caring, and helping, in a practical sense as well as a spiritual one.

The compassion that Jesus had for people – the sick, the poor, the outcasts whose diseases were thought to be a punishment from God, the evil foreigners (like the Samaritans) in the towns where the disciples didn't want to step foot, even the most shunned and hated individuals like lepers and prostitutes and the tax collectors – Jesus counted them as important as anyone else, worthy of an opportunity to be saved, and time and again He stepped between them and the harsh treatment they were used to. The fact is, that caring and that compassion is what opened the doors of their hearts to be ready to hear his spiritual message. That truth has gotten a little lost in some of the Evangelical churches of today. Reaching people the way Jesus and the Early Church did involves both the spiritual message of our mouths – the evangelizing – but also the compassion that leads to the practical work of our hands to address the pressing needs of people as individuals.

Still later, I met and formed a friendship with the author of this book, Fr. George Warren. A wise and kind man, we had many a conversation about scripture and theology and about my personal position somewhere between Baptist and Catholic. He informed me with some humor that this meant I was actually probably an Episcopal at heart, and invited me to his church. Someday, if I feel ready to add yet another branch to my spiritual tree, I may take him up on that invitation. Both my Baptist upbringing and my later experiences with the Catholic Church (along with my own personal life experiences) left me with some important takeaways that form the bedrock foundation of my personal belief system:

1. A Love of Scripture (and a rock-solid conviction of its absolute authority) If you were in love, and hungry to know all you could learn about the object of your desire – how would you set about the task - what would be your strategy? What if the love of your life had written a book – about himself – all he had accomplished…his likes, his dislikes, how he had been viewed, how he had been despised by some, and why; and how he had been loved by others, and why? Would you ask someone who had read the autobiography to paraphrase it for you – give you the "Reader's Digest" version – or would you read the book yourself?

What God desires from us, at the most basic, fundamental level, is a hunger and thirst to know Him. It is our most basic responsibility as Christians. Seeking to know God will naturally give us a desire to read his Word and to seek out a relationship with Him through prayer. The more we come to know Him, the more we understand not only who He is, but who we are, and what His will and His plan for us is.

The desire to know God doesn't always come easily, or naturally. Sometimes it requires discipline and encouragement to mold sporadic prayer and Bible opening into a more consistent habit that becomes a priority in our life.

When we seek Him out through His Word (sort of His autobiography, as it was ordained by Him) this is the catalyst that sets into motion everything else that is 'supposed' to happen in our Christian journey:

- A relationship with our Heavenly Father that deepens and increases daily, as opposed to a one- hour-on-Sundays hastily fulfilled duty. Prayer as a two-way communication, as opposed to a one-way, rehearsed recital.
- A rock-solid faith and trust, as opposed to a fair-weather faith that implodes and disappears when hard times come or tragedy strikes.

- An understanding of His will for us, not just individually but collectively as a body of Christians and a finely tuned conscience that cultivates a more complex and nuanced awareness of what pleases Him and what offends him.
- A changed perspective combined with a peace that passes understanding, so that no matter what sadness or worry you are in the midst of – in your marriage, with your children, your finances, or at work, you are not crippled with fear, anxiety or hopelessness, because at the very center of the storm you still know, with confidence and in every fiber of your being, the assurance of His promises.
- The fruits of the Holy Spirit, alive and recognizable in your life, as opposed to living as a Christian in name only (someone who claims the label, and then nothing else happens.)

All of it falls naturally from that first step – the desire to know God, through scripture. That is where the kind of Christianity that can change everything begins.

2. A Sense of Real Accountability

I learned that Church isn't just for Sundays – a chore, a weekly ritual to be dutifully carried out and then put back in its special, treasured box. It is meant to be lived out, every day, in every area of our lives – in every decision we make, and in every step we take and word we speak. We are sons and daughters to a King, and citizens of a Kingdom which is outside this Earth. We were meant to immerse ourselves in that citizenship for all of our earthly lives, just as we were immersed in that moment of our Baptism.

3. God is Not About Affirmation, but About Transformation

We live in a world where everyone gets a trophy for participation, and the idea of our own feelings of self-worth have risen to the loftiest priority. As with so many things, humans (and their earthly organizations) tend to swing from one extreme to another before finally settling into a place of reason and balance. We saw it decades ago in a time when the Catholic Church was considered too harsh, and Catholic guilt was a thing. They focused almost exclusively, at that time, on God's anger, His perfection, His perfect justice, and His abhorrence of sin and disobedience. Any small infraction without confession and you could kiss your salvation goodbye – you were out of the family – out of luck. Your salvation was a tenuous thing, constantly in danger of disappearing. People started leaving the church in droves, and then.... the Church vastly softened the message.

Fast forward to the present time and the focus in many Catholic churches today is almost exclusively on the extreme other side of God's nature – His love, His mercy, His forgiveness. To the point where I once heard (in just the last few years) a kindly older priest say from the alter during his homily, "I used to wonder about all those stories in the Old Testament where God was so angry, causing war and destruction, punishing and even killing, and then I realized that these are just stories, to symbolize something God wants to teach us." I nearly fell off my chair. But when I looked around me, to see if anyone else had the same shocked reaction as myself, no-one seemed to blink an eye.

It wasn't that the Catholic Church was wrong about the nature of God, those decades ago. All of those characteristics – anger, abhorrence of sin, punishment, perfect justice – are all parts of the nature of God – but they are not the only parts. And it's not that the Catholic Church is wrong today – all of the characteristics of love, mercy and forgiveness are also parts of God's nature. But again, they are not the only parts. What is needed today, in my opinion, is a swing back toward the center, where we can see the fullness of his nature – all of it.

We need to focus on the whole nature of God if we want to see Him clearly – not wielding key parts of His nature as a weapon to manipulate, neither softening His hard edges to entice larger congregations. The fact is, that there are parts of God's nature that are...uncomfortable...for us. There are parts of God that we find it hard to equate with His perfection. How can anger be a part of perfection? Or the jealousy that is also attributed to His nature? Or the destruction, the wars, the punishments and the killing of the Old Testament? What we cannot do is to dumb God down and sweep the uncomfortable bits under the rug.

As human beings and as Christians, we have to get to the place where it is ok to admit that it is hard for the created to understand the Creator. It is not unusual nor reproachful that even our most spiritually advanced of today's Christian leadership will not be able to fathom certain unfathomable mysteries and topics – like eternity, or trinity. When there is a part of God's nature or a part of Scripture that is hard to fathom, hard to reconcile with our idea of goodness, we need to be comfortable enough to simply admit, "It's hard to fathom – we don't know how this particular thing will play out in God's perfect sense of justice. We don't know how God will rectify this thing that seems unfair." We don't have all the answers. Why is this okay? Because we trust Him and his Goodness. We have to get to a place where we can accept that it is not necessary for us to fully understand the mind of a Divine God. All that is necessary is that we trust Him.

We need to come to a place where the Christian Church is less concerned with enrollment and more concerned with sound teaching and full disclosure. We need to get comfortable with the idea that it is not the duty of the Church nor of the priest, to be popular. (The prophets were often distinctly unpopular). It is their duty to provide sound teaching. It is not their duty to play some perceived middle ground so as to please all of the people, all of the time. It is their duty to introduce the full character of God.

4. Our Approach vs Our Reproach

Our God cares more about how we are living out our own faith, than how aggressively we reproach others for the way they are living theirs. Simply put, our level of reproach is not a barometer for our Christianity. Our level of love is. It's true we are called to discern sin – to judge rightly what is wrong in the eyes of God and what is right. But judging rightly means in a spirit of love and caring. What is the purpose of this type of judging? It is not to beat non-Christians over the head with it. Rather:

- It is to inform our own behavior, so we know the paths we need to take in our own lives – how we will behave, what we will choose, how we will act and react.
- It is to hold other Christians accountable, in a spirit of love and caring. What does this mean? It means that, when one of us – a professing Christian, is professing Christ in one breath but doing something ter-

ribly un-Christian on the other side – whether to us personally or publicly, where the demise of the power of that person's witness is hurting the Kingdom, we hold each other and our spiritual leaders accountable.

So, how do we 'treat' non-Christians, then?

-   We exist. We exist as Christians and provide an example of Christ in a world where everything we do will seem opposed to the prevailing logic. Where there is selfishness, we attempt to show sacrifice. Where there is uncertainty, we attempt to show faith. Where there is tragedy and upheaval, amidst our pain and sadness, we rely on the Holy Spirit to help us to retain what he seeks to give us – a peace that passes understanding. Simply exemplifying Christ in a broken world is how we treat non-Christians.

    Our living example of Christ's love and compassion is the magnet that draws people to Him, it is what peaks interest and sometimes enables us to share the source of our faith. The disciples did not go around beating the unwilling or the uninterested over the head with Christianity. They planted seeds of faith on fertile ground, and where the ground was not fertile, they shook the dust from their heels and moved on. There is plenty of time for topics of sin and accountability, for those that choose a path of accountability. We are supposed to be drawing people to us, not with our words, but with our Christ-like life. If people really understood the magnitude of that responsibility, they would understand how little time and latitude there is for stone-throwing.

-   The second point in "How do we treat non-Christians?" is that we pray for them. Not the sort of "thank God I'm better than they are" kind of prayer that the Pharisees prayed. That's the kind of prayer that Jesus reproached. Expecting Christian behavior from non-Christians is an exercise in futility, and it is often a distracting technique that keeps us in a perennial state of congratulating ourselves rather than spending our energies where it's really needed – in cleaning up our own deficiencies.

5. Christian Patriotism / Christian Nationalism

Christianity doesn't serve as a tool - nor weapon - to forward our own personal agenda nor our politics. Christianity doesn't exist to serve us - we exist to serve it, individually, and no matter what everyone else may be doing. Christian community is important, but our Church and even our denomination can't be where our loyalty lies (and, God help us, certainly not our political party, either) because they'll all fail us (and Christianity) at some point.

In all earthly things there must always be a necessary bit of detachment - as we must always leave enough wiggle room for the continual state of discernment that will prevent us from automatically jumping on bandwagons. We need to remember that this is not our Kingdom. We are citizens of another Kingdom, and although we have a duty to be respectful of governments and give them their due, an understanding that Church hierarchy is important, and a need for the Church community as an essential part of our spiritual support and growth, there exists an individual accountability to our Creator that will not be excused nor nullified by any earthly organization, even the Church, and our overarching individual loyalty ultimately lies with that King.

There is a big difference between Christian Patriotism and Christian Nationalism. A bit of the former is healthy - but the latter goes completely against the gospel. Christians are found across the Globe - and God does not love American Christians, nor America, any more or less than any other global Christians or countries. Jesus was not an American, and this idea among some that America enjoys some kind of favored nation status with Jesus is, regrettably, not scriptural, nor is even the vague idea of it remotely consistent with Christian theology. Whenever Christianity is replaced by politics - when theology is replaced by party policies and party loyalties - the first thing to be destroyed is always the power of our witness.

One of the marks of the early Church was its respected status within the community and among non- Christians. Regrettably, this is not the case today. Christians and the Church in general have a worse standing and reputation that at any time in recent history, and the Evangelical Church in particular is also more divided within itself than at any time in recent history. And what has come in the way of our reputation and our solidarity?

Politics, of all things. Our favorite political policies dangled like carrots by savvy politicians, when we know full well that what we attain politically today will be gone tomorrow, and then attained again, and then gone again. That is the way of the world. But as Christians, we were meant to keep our eyes fixed on bigger things than temporary politics and policies in a temporary world.

Jesus did not come to start a political revolution, nor did he come to desperately prop up the existing one. As Christians we need to stop worrying about who is a democrat or a republican and get back to worrying about who needs Jesus Christ. Christians come in all flavors – including both democrat and republican – and some of the most egregious failures of so-called spiritual leaders in the past couple of years have been both in failing to hold our leaders accountable, and in failing to understand that God is far more interested in souls than political affiliations. The damage to Christianity over the past couple of years, both internally, and also externally with regard to the collective reputation of the Christian Church is not due to a higher level of 'evil' in the world. It is due to a lack of direction and gospel-centered messaging within the Christian Church. The outside world has not damaged our reputation. We have.

6. The 'Family' of Believers

In the same way that individuals within a congregation have separate spiritual gifts and strengths, on a larger scale, so do the Christians denominations that fall within the biblical interpretation of "Christian." Some Christian denominations are good at emphasizing one thing (like evangelizing or loving our neighbor), and some are good at another (like the importance of scripture, or remembering Christ's command to, "Do this in remembrance of Me.") All are sound, good, and Godly Christian principles - and what this tells us is that as Christian denominations, we have both things to teach each other and also things to learn from each other.

Although numerous Christian denominations fall within the biblical definition of "Christian," it's common for each to think they've cornered the market on proper interpretation of scripture and the mind of a Divine God, to the exclusion of everyone else in the family... But according to the biblical definition of "Who is a Christian," we should be able to walk into other Christian churches outside our own little circle with an eagerness that not only do we have something to teach them, but they have something to teach us.

That does not mean that we water down our personal theology. It means being open to earnest, thoughtful communication and the idea that it's possible that we have not mastered every spiritual talking point and have something yet to learn from our brothers and sisters. If rubbing shoulders with the other side of Christianity were so dangerous, we certainly would never be safe enough to be around the non-Christians we were meant to evangelize to.

My personal theology veers toward my Protestant/Baptist upbringing in most ways, but honestly, if the question of whether the wine actually turns to blood or it's purely symbolic was all that critical to our salvation or our status in the Kingdom, we can be sure that Jesus would have been clearer about it. After all, He was well aware that we would bicker about it for centuries. The fact is that this theological molehill that we have blown up into a hill to die on was not important enough for Jesus to be any clearer on. That is what lets us know that the point is not a deal-breaker to salvation - it's simply a difference of opinion and it's open to interpretation.

God performed many miracles and continues to perform them today - if we decide he's performing another one in the command to Remember Him, it certainly would not be beyond His scope, ability, or wildly out of His character to do so. It is not heretical to think God may be performing something miraculous in this. Nor is it heretical to decide He was speaking symbolically, which would also be perfectly in character. As Christians navigating among a wide variety of family members, it's critical to remember that Satan loves to exclude and divide, specifically because we (and Christianity) are stronger and better together.

7. Being a Christian in the age of Social Media

Particularly in social media today, there is a wealth of fake news, propaganda, and click-bait. No matter how noble we believe a cause to be, the end never justifies the means. Spreading outrageous lies to demonize the other side isn't Christ-like. It's bearing false witness, and it's a sin. More importantly, when we spread lies and conspiracy theories, and we perpetuate hatred and division, we harm the Kingdom and we destroy the power of our witness. As Christians, we have a responsibility to be careful about what we speak, what we spread, and what we share, including on social media.

Corruption and lies run largely unchecked in this world, often expressly orchestrated by Satan to confuse, divide, and scatter the Faithful. In this age of social media and amidst a flood of fake news, Christians must rely on their own discernment combined with rigorous fact checking to separate the wheat from the chaff.

In this day and age of accessible information and plenty of reputable, non-partisan fact-checkers, there's no excuse for ignorance. Before we share shocking accusations or shameful tidbits, it's critical that we be responsible enough to take the thirty seconds to make sure that we are being part of the solution - bringing truth and illumination to a situation, and not being part of the problem – spreading misinformation and contributing to hatred and division in the world.

8. When Politics and Christlike Love Collide

We will never be successful at legislating Christianity, morality, or faith. Whatever we attain today, will be gone tomorrow. The party we elect in one year is gone in a heartbeat and all the previous policies undone by the new party. It is an endless and a temporary cycle. Our main concern as Christians must always be to keep our eyes on the prize – and that prize has nothing to do with this earthly life or the politics of this earthly kingdom. We can never create enough rules or laws to force souls into heaven, but we can – by example of our own obedience to a Higher law, and an unfailing Christlike love and compassion - draw people into His presence so He can transform them and change their hearts – in a real and lasting way - from the inside out.

Jesus never drew a line in the sand where His compassion stopped. He extended it even to the evilest people in the most immoral neighborhoods. He showed compassion and love even to the most hated sinners– like the prostitute and the tax collector. He offered healing and salvation to the beggar, the foreigner, the poor, and the leper – the most shunned and marginalized people of the time. He went into towns that the disciples would never have stepped foot in – showing them that those people mattered, too.

Jesus taught the disciples that reaching people's hearts often meant first showing the kind of compassion that attended to their most pressing physical needs. He often fed the poor and healed the sick before getting down to spiritual matters – attending first to the immediate human needs, and then moving to the needs of the soul. It wasn't just a 'talking' kind of love and evangelizing in the Early Church, it was an acting kind of love.

Particularly on the pro-life front today, there must be consistency and compassion in our messaging if we ever want to make a real and lasting difference. Some churches of today seem more interested in demonizing the women that feel compelled to choose abortion rather than trying to address the underlying issues of how they ended up there. There's nothing biblical nor Christlike in prioritizing the unborn if our compassion slows to a trickle beyond the birth canal. Pro-life was not meant to begin and end at the womb.

Consistency in our Christianity and in our ability to love is what prevents us from sounding like noisy gongs and clanging cymbals to a lost world. If we're not as horrified and vocal about the suffering of born children, and other human beings of all ages and gender, by war, by genocide, by hunger, famine – American or foreign - as we are about an unborn baby in utero, that says something. It says that our love of life is most avid when it's most convenient - when it requires no skin in the game - nothing substantial or sacrificial of us. The pro-life cause is a noble one - an important one. Too important to risk damaging the cause and, more importantly, the power of our witness, with a lack of consistency or compassion.

9. The Power of our Witness

Even in the midst of obstacles and stumbling blocks, our God of truth, light, and wisdom continues His long-standing work in us and through us (those that love Him and have been called to his purpose) toward His own good purpose and plan (which is that we be conformed to the image of His Son). Our God of love, forgiveness, and mercy is also a God of perfect justice and accountability. We sometimes like to think of the former Godly qualities (love, forgiveness and mercy) as personality traits to emulate, and the latter (perfect justice and accountability) as a promise of action that God will exact, at some later time and in some other place, on those not covered by His Grace; but the quality of perfect justice, and the accountability that necessitates it, are also parts of His character - important parts, that, combined with His love and mercy, allow us to fully trust in the perfection of his goodness.

In our striving toward the completion of God's work in us (to conform us to the image of His Son), there must be understanding that perfect justice and accountability are not just future God-driven action to be waited upon, but character traits that are to be championed by the Faithful and reflected in the world around us. If we speak the words of love and mercy and forgiveness, but we fail miserably when it comes to being lovers of truth, accountability, and justice, then we cannot reflect His fullness in a way that is necessary, even critical, for the watching world to be able to place their trust in Him, through us.

While we wait for the culmination of God's good purpose and His plan for us, our main concern, our one job, beyond all else, certainly beyond political parties, presidents and policies - no matter how noble, is the integrity of the power of our witness. We are to give testament to His power by being an example of the fullness of His glory - in everything we do, striving to emulate His love of truth, accountability and justice in the same way that we strive to exemplify His love, His mercy and His forgiveness. We stand as witnesses to His power, alive and visible in us, via the Holy Spirit - who has the capacity to supplement our stores of His power and His 'goodness' in ways that pass understanding.

The power of our witness is evidence to a cynical, weary, and watching world of His power - a reflection of the fullness of His glory. It is what enables us to be effective in this world - arguably the only thing that enables us to be truly effective in any real and lasting way. It is the single most critical treasure to be safeguarded - beyond politics, parties, presidents and policies - beyond all earthly matters, including love and hate, war and peace, life and death, powers and principalities. The power of our witness is the linchpin upon which everything else rests.

In the same way as when I was a young girl on a wooden pew, imagining the voices of our congregation carrying hymns out the open windows and into the surrounding neighborhood – I still wonder today what we as Christians sound like to the townspeople beyond our walls. I still hope for a Christian Church that can gain back the respect of the outside world – as the Early Church was respected in the community, as true adherers to the Way (which is what it was called before it was called Christianity) – the Way of being that Jesus Christ exemplified to the world with His dual approach of uncompromising and sometimes hard spiritual truths alongside real, sacrificial, compassionate, and practical help. I hope for a stronger and more unified Christian Church where our collective voices ring strong and true to the outside world.

Religious Perspectives

(Milford Daily News)

Holy Saturday Story About the Power of Love

By the Rev. George H. Warren – pastor of St. John's Church in Millville

"Set your troubled hearts at rest. Trust in God always; trust also in Me. There are many dwelling-places in my Father's house; if it were not so I should have told you; for I am going there on purpose to prepare a place for you..." *(John 14:ff)*

Holy Saturday was the day after the crucifixion of our Lord and the day before His Resurrection. On that ominous day the family, friends, and followers of Jesus of Nazareth experienced intense grief over the loss of their precious loved one. Not only did they feel the wrenching loss of the one they loved so much but also their loss of the eternal hope and other promises He had given to them.

In the disbelief, shock, depression, and confusion of their grief they also sensed that terrible "absolute nothingness" that accompanies grief... the fear that this life after death is absolutely final. Indeed, in many ways it is starkly true that death is the end of this life as we know it. But, to the Christ-centered mind, heart, and soul death calls us forward to the door of ever new beginnings... no less, eternal life.

In the following true story, I want to relate an experience of Resurrection. It does bear out in our life's experiences in many ways. I must also mention that there is a wide variety of interpretations and beliefs about the Biblically given account of the Resurrection of Jesus that famous Easter Day.

It is continually a phenomenon of incredible speculation and ever-expanding interpretation. My personal belief, shared by the majority of Christians, is the Lord's promise of eternal life with those whom we love. The following is one of many I could relate from my experiences as a pastor, and even more especially as a hospice care-giver. The hospice way of caring and believing sees us on a journey together. The journey is one of ever-growing love. Here is the story.

The Story of Wade

Some years ago, an eight-year-old boy from the neighborhood of my parish walked into the church on Saturday morning. He apparently had never been in this little church before and was unusually and delightfully curious.

I spent all of one-half hour explaining to him the story of the Lord and showing him some of the pictures, symbols and rituals we use to express our awe and excitement about it all. I invited him to come to our celebration. He was enthralled and said that he hoped that he could. I did not see this child again until eleven years later. He was then nineteen years old and professionally on his way to success as a musician in a band with close friends.

Come to find out he had moved away soon after I met him those eleven years earlier. He only recently returned to be closer to family and friends at "home" for the remainder of his life. Wade was being treated for cancer. I received a phone call from his mother who located me at the Milford area V. N. A. Hospice. She told me that Wade was asking to see me.

I remembered this friendly, interested little boy immediately. His mom knew well of his visit to Trinity Church that beautiful, springtime "Holy" Saturday. What a bittersweet reunion it was for me to see Wade again. He was a grown man, and he was dying. Wade welcomed me with the same warm, loving, boyish open arms I remembered from eleven years ago. His newly given condition didn't change his wonderful personality. He wanted to know more of the things I began telling him about the incredible Holy Saturday of so long ago. He thanked me for the teaching and treasures I shared with him on that one brief visit those years earlier. Soon after, the entire Hospice Team met Wade and we'll never forget how much we enjoyed and loved him as he did us.

As all who have experienced the death of loved ones know, one can never be fully prepared when it happens. Most certainly those family, friends, and followers of Jesus were not prepared for His brutal death on the Cross. But even there on the cross they experienced Him loving them to the end. He said that this is how it will be if love fills your heart. This experience of love is the beginning of the Resurrection experience.

Wade's mom told us that one day as he was lying snuggly in her arms, very weak and not feeling so well, he asked her what it was going to be like. She said that all the ones he loves and who love him would be with him, if not physically present, in their hearts. Then she whispered softly to him that he would "see a light far away… a beautiful, shining light. Then your spirit will lift up out of your body and start traveling toward that light. On your way you will know peace and love more than you've ever know before. It'll be the love we've known here and so much more. We'll be waiting with our love to be with you again."

On one of my visits, Wade asked me a similar question as he did with his mom. I asked what he thought. He said that he was feeling a comforting peace within and around him. He again thanked me for the stories I had shared with him and the love he was feeling from everyone. He asked me about the beautiful shining light and the Love of the Lord on the other side. He knows that I believed my answer: "Yes!" He had asked his mom, "Will it take long?" "No, Wade, not long at all… like that twinkling of an eye." Wade died several days later. We saw him die the way he lived, loving much and able to receive much love from others. His passing was peaceful and all that was important was there.

> "O Lord, support us all the day long,
> until the shadows lengthen,
> and the evening comes, the busy world is hushed.
> the fever of life is over,
> and our work is done. Then in Thy mercy,
> grant us a safe lodging,
> a Holy Rest and peace at the last."

Yes, we believe in a providential God who knows and loves us intimately. We know that the brief span of this life will end in death. We believe we are born for the purpose of love that no disease, hatred, mistake, or disaster can destroy. We are called to enjoy the happiness of our success and not be too disappointed with the sadness of the failures that this life often brings. Only good will come from the love we've experienced. "Lord, we entrust all who are dear to us to your never-failing love and care in this life and the life to come, knowing that you are doing for them and for us, better things than we can desire or pray for, that having opened to us the gates of larger life, you will receive us more and more into your joyful service. Amen."

RECTORY:
23 DANA PARK, HOPEDALE. MA 01747

THE REV. GEORGE H. WARREN, RECTOR

PARISH OFFICE:
17 CONGRESS STREET, MILFORD, MA 01757

January 24, 1992

My dear friends,

As I approach my words to you now many years and experiences flash
across the depths of my heart and galleries of my mind's eye. There is
never a good time nor is there enough time and space to express the
thoughts I would like to share with you now. The time is our Annual
Parish Meeting, my 18th with you, at the beginning of a new year. The
space is almost eighteen years of life together as a parish family, a
community envisioned by our Lord to help us together, and in our private
innermost thoughts, grow towards those individuals whom He calls us to
become. Our Christian faith and community of faith calls us to grow in
Grace. These years for me at Trinity have been wonderful years, joyful,
sorrowful, difficult, easy, up, down and all around. In essence, these
years here have been filled with all that can happen in the fullness of
anyone's lifetime. As any of us place our heart and soul into any part of
our life, the gamut of that which life does afford us will be there
completely. For those of us who have shared fully any and all of these
years together, they have indeed been full of all that life offers and
this is good. With such fullness of life and living, looking to God for
guidance, Grace will always abound. As I look back now, I can say that
God's love has truly guided us and we are indeed on the road to Grace upon
Grace and the wholeness of our lives. In the midst of such a life together
the love and grace of God is not always evident as life and growth is
always a struggle. Without struggle there is no growth. We've certainly
shared years of struggle as we've worked hard at doing our best to discern
His Will and be God's people in this parish family and in all ways that
we've extended beyond ourselves. We have truly been blessed!

In a recent article in the Anglican Digest, The Rev. John Claypool,
Rector of St. Luke's Church, Birmingham, Alabama wrote about ending an old
year and beginning a new one. It has to do with the ongoingness of our
lives be it individual or communal, growing towards richer fulfillment as
we move along. He wrote:

"There is something about the ending of an old year and the beginning
of a new one that makes me doubly aware of the transitory shape of our
human pilgrimage. Nothing ever stands still, although it may feel that
way sometimes. Flux, motion, change -- these constitute the very essence
of our humanness and are realities with which we must come to terms if we
are to live in a realm other than fantasy."

In other words, we change, times change, life takes its turns and so
on and so forth. But in all this new doors open, and we move forward, we
grow, and in faith and prayer God's love and grace does abound This is
one of the great mysteries of life and our Christ-centered faith.

Fr. Claypool in his article, entitled, "This Transitory Life" goes on
to quote Emily Dickinson who profoundly stated:

"That it will never come again is what makes life so sweet." "This
is so true," said Claypool. "The utterly unique and non-repeatable shape
of each day does add a depth and significance to experiences that would

not exist if we had access to an unlimited supply of "more of the same".
The awareness that we will never pass exactly this way again should
challenge us to alert participation in the Now and a "savoring of the
temporary" to the best of our abilities.

Claypool bringing this thought clearer and to a concluding point
quotes another author:

"Life seems to be a continuous pattern of becoming committed and
then, for one reason or circumstance or another, having to let go. We
fall in love and then lose the one we care for so deeply. We develop
certain job skills and then have to experience a change in career. We
birth and raise our children only to see them make their way into the
world. This is the rhythm of existence, and our challenge is to make
peace with it. Participating fully in the seasonal shape of life is what
it means to become whole and authentic persons. There is a time for
letting go as surely as there is a time for bonding and embracing, and
accepting the fact that both losing and gaining are a part of life is the
secret of maximizing the gracious moments that are given to us on this
earth."

I have said all this because I find myself now in a growing,
transitory time in my life. I also see this parish as part of this
transitory time for me and for you. Firstly, as you know, I've become
more and more involved in the international Hospice movement. Much of my
study and prayer time has been given to this growing and powerful
ministry. As this parish family has been a tremendous growing experience
in Grace for me, and I hope for you, so has the Hospice Ministry of
healing to the dying and their loved one's given me greater insight into
the mysteries of life and love.

During this last year I've worked as a volunteer chaplain, in close
proximity with the Milford Area V.N.A. Hospice Team. This last Fall I was
asked by them if I would ever consider working with the Hospice Program
full time. My immediate response was, of course one of elation. I've
thought about perhaps a larger future with Hospice but never expected such
an offer. My only recourse was to say that I was excited about the
ministry of Hospice but I would have to give a great deal of thought and
prayer to their offer. From that time I did a lot of thinking, praying,
talking to others in this ministry and have attended several conferences
in order to sift this through my little heart and brain. With all this I
truly believe that God is calling me into the expanded ministry of
Hospice. I must try it out in a more complete capacity. This is also a
very rapidly growing ministry and still in its earlier stages of
development. It is a good time for me to become more involved with it,
especially with the idea that this may be the ministry I choose to follow
during the latter stages of my vocational career. However, to make such a
change from full time parish priesthood is difficult for me. My entire
twenty-two years of priestly vocation and training has been in parish
work. Also this wonderful parish of Trinity has occupied the greatest
part of my years as a priest. More difficult than that is the fact that
so many of you have become beloved, integral parts of my life as I know I
have been of yours. This is tough! You and this parish have been my
extended family and my home, making my decision to change course at this
time a most difficult one.

Again, I am certain of my call, as a priest, into the Hospice Ministry and I now ask you to support me and pray for me in this transitional time of my life. I shall never forget my life in this parish and all that we have been involved with together in the realm of our loving, Grace bestowing, Heavenly Father.

I love the Church; ....I believe in the Church;.... and our life together in Trinity Parish has been a wonderful, growing, forward evolving community of the Holy Spirit within, around, and amongst us. I shall always pray for each and all of you and for Trinity as a parish that you and we continue to grow in Grace. There is so much yet to be done. God's work on earth is not yet accomplished. The Church is the vehicle that must continue faithfully to get this done.

There is just one particular matter that I need to clarify in concluding this letter. Unfortunately many of us have heard of "wars and rumors of wars". There have been rumors in Trinity which may lead some to speculate that my move at this time is because I am disconcerted with perceived problems in the parish. Yes, there have been difficulties, and some mis-understandings but these kinds of difficulties have been worked through in a very caring, loving way. This is not a problem now, nor is it the reason that I must resign as your Rector. After many hours of conversation with the Bishop, and since with the Wardens, it is clear that my vocational direction into Hospice needs to be pursued. These are now becoming the latter years of my vocational life and a priest of my experience and interest will be of great benefit to all concerned. This will be a healthy transition for me because of my age. An older priest is an ideal resource for the kind of ministry that Hospice is. The Lord has indeed answered my prayers by leading me in this direction.

Again I must repeat, that there is never an appropriate time for a Rector to move from one place to another. But with thoughtful prayer and due consideration of everyone and everything involved, these transitions are natural and must take place. This is what Fr. Claypool meant in his pertinent article, "The Transitory Life".

Please keep up the courageous efforts that we have worked so hard at over the years to discern God's Will for us and have the faith that He will never desert us. In those times of struggle, He will be there; ...in those times of pride and experienced accomplishment He will be there; ...in those times of joy, sorrow, ups and downs He is always there because He loves us so. May God bless you now and forever.

Faithfully yours,

The Rev. George H. Warren

"The Vicar"

It was my good fortune, or more accurately, "by the Grace of God," that I was sent to St. Barnabas Parish, Warwick, Rhode Island, as a curate under the rectorship of the Rev. Howard C. Olsen, affectionately and respectfully known as Father Olsen. It was also by the Grace of God that the Rev. John Seville Higgins was my bishop. Bishop Higgins was one of those strong leaders in the Church who knew his Diocese well and administered the Diocese of Rhode Island with clarity and wisdom. He was in my mind an "old fashioned" Bishop and I trusted in his wisdom.

Thanks to Bishop Higgins I was sent to Father Olsen directly out of Seminary as the Curate under his mentorship. Bishop Higgins said to me that Father Olsen would make a good priest out of me. Recently asked (fifty years later) what I thought was the best wisdom I received from Father Olsen, I responded without hesitation: "Father Olsen taught me many things, but focus, balance, and a sense of humor were among the most important.

"Stop Pushing Me"

Both of these great colleagues were given to me by God. I sincerely believe this! Father Olsen had just lost the election as Bishop of Rhode Island, and I became the next Curate of St. Barnabas. Those were the first five years of my ordination to the Diaconate, and six months later as a priest. This was an enormous beginning of my ordained ministry. It was a great challenge that set me forward with the tools needed to serve in the church.

The primary interests of Ecumenism, Christian Formation, and Catholic Churchmanship began here. It is interesting to note that the Rev. Gordon P. Scruton and I were ordained Deacons together of the Cathedral of St. John, Providence, Rhode Island, Diocese of Rhode Island in June 1971. Bishop Scruton became my Bishop in the Diocese of Worcester, Massachusetts in 1996.

At that time, I was a team member of the Hospice of Greater Milford, Massachusetts, and Priest-in-Charge at St. John Parish in Sutton MA. Gordon and I were raised in E. Providence, Rhode Island but did not meet until the time and occasion of Ordination to the Diaconate. My Ordination to the Priesthood was under the hands of retiring Bishop Higgins, his last ordination as Diocesan Bishop. Gordon was ordained soon after under the hands of the newly-elected Bishop Frederick Belden. More interestingly, I was baptized at age two by Bishop Higgins and later Confirmed and Ordained by him.

Also, I must make note here that my predecessor as Curate of St. Barnabas, the Rev. Robert Anthony was the prime resource in developing the Folk Mass. He and several Seminarians in New York City wrote and designed "The Rejoice Mass", beginning a new era of music throughout the church. The youth groups played this Guitar Mass in modern English at St. Barnabas Church beginning in 1967.

The photo of me on the back cover was taken about twenty-five years ago (1996) at which time I was mid-way in ordained ministry. The stories I relate in this book reveal some of the experiences that helped further my priesthood as well as deeper understanding of the presence of God in our lives. Having been raised in the middle-class neighborhood of Rumford, Rhode Island all seemed normal to be in this primarily Roman Catholic area.

I was the only Episcopalian among most of my family and friends. In my mind and in the reaction of others, this made me somewhat of an oddity as oftentimes religious differences were a problem of identity. But, in time, the world became larger and larger and such differences became less important. Choosing philosophy and Western Civilization in college years had everything to do with those earlier years of up-bringing. Looking to eventually study law, it became obvious to me to enter more fully in religious studies, and then to four years of post-graduate Seminary, and ultimately, the Anglican Priesthood.

During several decades in the Church, I found myself in a variety of milestone adventures. Included in this journey has been, of course, Parish leadership, along with twelve years in full-time Hospice Team Ministry, Ecumenical endeavors, and Food for the Poor Central American Missions. The latest great adventure was with my friend and colleague, Father Al Zadig, as Team Pastors in Grace Church, Oxford, MA and All Saints, Warwick, Rhode Island. The following news article relates the reporter's understanding of this adventure.

"Two Ministers Bring New Enthusiasm to All Saints Church in Pontiac"

by Thomas Greenberg, Warwick Beacon.

With the recent arrival of two priests, Junior Warden at All Saints Episcopal Church, Bruce MacNeil, has seen a refreshed level of enthusiasm at the Pontiac Church. Father Alfred "Al" Zadig and Father George H. Warren have been called by the vestry to minister as the clergy of the parish. "They're excellent preachers and are very interested in growing the parish", MacNeil said. "Good people. They mix very well with the congregation, and they always have a lot of enthusiasm."

MacNeil said All Saints, with a membership of 110, has gained a couple people in the last year. MacNeil said he and the vestry would like Father Al and Father George to bring their own way of doing things to their church for it to grow. "They're in an organizing mode", he said. "They have a different way of doing things. I already see now they've brought in holy water and incense." He added that they're both excellent preachers but also spiritual in addition to the religious teachings, which is a good addition.

Father Al was most recently the parish priest of a growing parish in the Diocese of Western Massachusetts, where he was assisted by Father George. He was a schoolteacher before going into the diocesan seminary in Garden City, Long Island and becoming an ordained priest. He was rector of a parish in Newton, Massachusetts. He has a master's degree in pastoral care and psychology and a PH. D. in psychology.

Father George was born and raised in Rumford, Rhode Island. After graduating from URI, he entered the Episcopal seminary in Philadelphia and received a Master in Theology degree in theology and pastoral ministry. He has served in parishes all across New England including Saint Barnabas, Saint Mark's, and All Saints parishes. in Warwick.

The two have already made their mark in the Warwick community, according to MacNeil, and they've been making community contacts in the area and made relationships with members of the church. In closing, it would be remiss if I didn't mention here an incredible account of Father Zadig's journey into the Church.

Some Notes – Father Al Zad

My parents were good, loving people but formal religious observances were simply not on their radar screen. They were not antagonistic toward religion, nor, as far as I know, were they convinced atheists – just people for whom the entire entity one thinks of a religion did not seem to have much relevance one way or the other. However, being Jewish by descent, they did belong to a local Reform Jewish Temple and sent me to Hebrew School – the Saturday equivalent of a Christian Sunday School. I am reasonably certain that they expected me to do the usual thing when I got to my teen years – that is, to drop out but instead, I opted in, by my choice, but voiced no objections. It was in my teens that I decided that I really wanted to be a rabbi. To this day, I am not sure why, and at that time would not have said that it was a call from God. All that came later.

My freshman year was spent at a small Quaker college in Ohio not too far from Hebrew Union College in Cincinnati – the seminary I planned to enter following graduation. I was accepted into their pre- rabbinical track for undergraduates, but fairly soon thereafter the rabbi in charge of the program called me in and in a kind but firm way, told me that unless things changed, I would never get into the seminary itself because, as he put it bluntly, "Al, your Hebrew stinks!" Since the college where I was had no course in Hebrew, he advised me to transfer to a college where I could remedy the situation. I applied to the then quite new Brandeis University, was accepted, and spent the next three years there, in the process learning Hebrew and becoming the "erev rav" (future rabbi") and leader of the student Jewish congregation on campus.

Those were the days when anti-Semitism was quite overt. To be identified as being Jewish meant being subject to discrimination in many ways. Some hotels and country clubs had signs saying "restricted" (meaning No Jews Allowed). Many colleges and graduate schools had quotas liming the number of Jewish candidates for admission. It was a time when an increasing number of people who were Jewish only in the sense of their family background, but not religious faith, sought to avoid being the victims of prejudice by assimilating, often joining such groups as Unitarian churches or Ethical Culture societies, changed Jewish-sounding names such as Greenberg to Green, and in their minds, simply ceased being Jewish, or at least ceased being identified by others as Jewish. Leaders in the Jewish community, especially rabbis, were understandably concerned, a concern which I, as a future rabbi, shared.

The issue became less abstract and for immediate for me when, as erev rav, a classmate came to see me asking for help. She was a sophomore, the only child of a wealthy Jewish family, and had fallen in love with a classmate, one of the few non-Jewish students, a football player who was at Brandeis on an athletic scholarship. He was from an Italian, Roman Catholic family. Both his family and hers were strongly against the romance. My classmate explained that while they intended to wait until after graduation from college to get married, they would certainly want to have children, and the question would be whether the children should be raised as Jews or Christians.

After long, serious discussions, they had decided their children should be Christians because that would hopefully protect them from the discrimination they would face if they were Jewish. But, she said, while she agreed with that plan, she felt guilty for doing so and thus had come to me to ask my help. I responded with all the reasons I could think of, but not only didn't they convince her, they didn't even convince me! It was at that point that I realized I didn't know much about the Christian religion and probably would need to learn if only to be able to explain why Jews should stay Jews.

In retrospect, the next step I took is still a matter of curiosity to me as a psychologist. I remember turning to the Saturday edition of The Boston Globe which, in those days, had a full page of listings of Sunday Church services classified by denomination. I recall looking for the heading "Episcopal" and, even more, a parish which listed its services as "Mass" rather than as

"Holy Communion" or in those days, "Morning Prayer." Since at that time I had no idea at all as to the difference between Methodists or Baptists or Roman Catholics, I wonder where the choice of Episcopal Church came from and can only assume that at some time I had heard something that stayed in my sub-conscious. In any case, I did find a parish, the Church of the Advent, and went there to see what it was all about. What a shock!

A synagogue is literally a Meeting House – a place for worship, but also meetings, educational programs, etc. So, just at a New England Town Meeting it is appropriate to talk with others seated near you before the meeting begins, so in a synagogue, one chats happily before the service. NOT SO at that church! The organ was playing softly, the smell of incense lingered in the air, people came in quietly, genuflected before entering a pew where they knelt, made the Sign of the Cross, and prayed silently. Then the liturgy started with everyone standing and singing a hymn. The service went on – I didn't understand what it was all about, but after it was over it felt as if I had put my finger in a light socket – a spiritual experience which left me shaken to my core. Somehow, I knew I had been in God's presence in a way I had never been before.

I kept returning each week to that church and eventually joined an In-quirer's Class. The next chapter would take hundreds of pages to describe but the result was an acceptance of the Christian faith, gratefully receiving the sac-raments of baptism, confirmation, and eventually ordination to the diaconate and then the sacred priesthood. Now, after fifty-six years as a priest, I just thank God for it all.

Another Quick Story from Father Al

For years, it was the custom on Christmas Eve that members of the choir of the Church of the Advent in Boston would go from house to house singing carols, ending up at the front door of the Rector. One year (in the 1850s) they heard that there was another Christian minister living in the area, and so they decided to include him by going to his house and singing there as well. That minister, the Rev. Frederic Dan Huntington, a Unitarian who was Preacher to Harvard College, was pleased by the carolers and invited them into his home.

He was impressed that, whenever the choristers mentioned the name Jesus, they bowed their heads. One thing led to another and eventually the

Rev. Mr. Huntington decided to become an Episcopalian. In 1860, he was ordained deacon, and in 1861, he was ordained to the priesthood. Eight years later, he was consecrated as the first bishop of the then-new diocese of Central New York. A footnote to this remarkable story is that Bishop Huntington's son, James, followed in his father's footsteps, being ordained into the priesthood in 1880. In 1884, along with two others, he founded the first American monastic order for men, the Order of the Holy Cross.

It is true that Father Al and I disagree on some issues of religion and politics, but we are bonded in our belief of God and the essentials of our faith that hold each of us in high esteem, one to the other. One of both the difficulties and the wonders of being Anglican Christians is our need and ability to debate any matters which arise. As has been long concluded, "Anglicanism, because of its place in Christian history, can be, and is, messy at times." The Church governance, similar to the United States Constitution, Bill of Rights, and Ways and Means, is always open to debate and solution.

As a matter of fact, the early fathers of our nation designed such a form of governance. The Senate in the Church is called the House of Bishops. The House of Representatives is the locally elected body of Lay and Clergy; the President is the Presiding Bishop; and the Supreme Court would be our regular study of and understanding of the Holy Bible. The question to all clergy at Ordination is, "Do you hold the Holy Bible as the Word of God and that which is necessary for Salvation?" Before the Bishops and all, pronouncing Ordination, we make that promise, "I do!" (Book of Common Prayer)

In essence, we have no other recourse but to humbly seek the "Will of God". The values that sustain us are called the "Gifts of the Holy Spirit" which are stated as follows:

All this and more being said, we do believe that healthful solutions to all problems in debate can be solved in peace and with honest common pursuit of the Truth and growth. The diversities we face in our perceptions can be met with comprehension and wisdom. As for the Church and likewise where our national goals and structure are concerned, we are provided with the rightful "tools" to move forward.

The Church's primary task is to promote faith in God, who truly exists, and gives Truth beyond but along with each of us as individuals. We need always to reach towards that "Truth" that sets us free. Any debate that can honestly disprove God as we understand God to be the door is open. Many theories of Atheism have come forward to make its case. The stories and accounts herewith reveal, as best I can, why I believe in God. In the end, our belief must become our experience within ourselves and with one another. This next section shows a history of parishes served in as Curate, Rector, Interim over the last several decades.

Father Alden Besse

Way back again into younger childhood (age twelve), I somehow found myself in deep conversation with Father Alden Besse and two of his leadership parishioners. I expect now that they were Vestry members. The Vestry are those elected parishioners who meet at least monthly to make decisions for the good of the parish. This parish was St. Michael and All Angels, Rumford, Rhode Island. I belonged to Grace Church in another section of that same town.

This is what I heard said to Father Besse: "You are a professional 'do-gooder'!" This, what I saw to be a derogatory comment, was far from the heart and soul of Father Besse. He was genuinely kind, and his faith in God was profound. Many years later (1975), I was brought again together with Alden when I became Rector of Trinity Church, Milford – two towns over, in the Diocese of W. Mass. We were both in these two parishes for a long time and served together on several Diocesan commissions. It was in 1980 that Father Besse had a severe coronary attack needing immediate surgery. He took his pen before that threatening surgery and wrote the following letter to his parishioners at Trinity Church in Whitinsville:

Dear Friends,

Today, June 30th, I give thanks for your loving care as I embark on a new adventure. I speak of this hopefully not to draw attention to myself but to point to Him who is the source of all our life and our hope.

My adventure is to go to Rhode Island Hospital today for heart surgery. Believe it or not, I am actually looking forward to this new experience. Now, of course, it isn't exactly what I would most like to choose for summer holiday, nor can I claim yet to be totally fearless.

Yet, I do look forward with sure confidence that an operation, or a sickness, can be by God's grace a wonderful opportunity to come closer to God and His beautiful, eternal realities and to all His children. Indeed, a part of the Good News of the Gospel is that with God everything can be an opportunity for growth in His love and service, or as St. Paul puts it in his letter to the Romans, "In everything God works for good with those who love him."

We, therefore, are all called as St Paul admonishes us to "in everything give thanks." We are to give thanks not because everything is good, but because the loving power of God in Christ who turned the cruel torturing wood of the Cross into the revelation of His love and the sign of His victory can turn whatever comes your way and mine into a means of His gracious blessing.

So, whatever comes our way, in sickness and in health, in life and in death, let us, in hope, give thanks and so grow in His grace until by His mercy we come to behold Him face to face.

Faithfully your Rector,

Alden Besse

Father Beese lived many more years after his surgery, continuing in Ministry as and better than before.

"Why the Holy Bible?"

In our study of the Holy Bible, its importance becomes abundantly clear as we come to realize, appreciate, and find ourselves in awe of God's presence both within, amongst, and in another dimension beyond us. The overriding message of the Judeo-Christian Bible is that we were created by a Creator of all existence whom we refer to as God, the I AM as expressed in the Old Testament. This God of love created the human race in His image, meaning free will. In other words, we were created to think as God thinks... to be enabled to think for ourselves as per his will and purpose for us. We would become an integral part of His Creation in that we would be participating in it for His Purpose. We call this ongoing process the building of God's Kingdom, that is, His loving will for all Creation.

During the Octave of our Celebration of All Saints and All Souls and a new beginning of the Christian Calendar of Observances, the Collect (Prayer) reading for that Sunday is as follows: "Blessed Lord, who caused all Holy Scripture to be written for our learning: Grant us to hear them, read, mark, learn, and inwardly digest them, that we may embrace and ever hold fast the blessed hope of everlasting life." *(Book of Common Prayer, pg. 236)*

It is incumbent upon each of us, and all of us together as God's People, the Ecclesia, the Church, to know this Bible and then be enabled to follow God's will. In the Book of Exodus, we learn that God freed the ancient desert nomads known as Israelites from the Tyranny of the Egyptian Pharaoh. They found their way into the wilderness there to learn of and to discover their freedom to think for themselves by way of their belief in and following of the Creator. It was this time in history that those Israeli's believed that they were commissioned to bring God's message of free will to the world. It did happen and this idea and purpose of freedom grew to this day and hopefully into the future. *(Exodus 20:1-17)*

Many years ago, I was asked to baptize a newly born puppy. I said that I could say prayers and a blessing with them and the puppy but was not to utilize the Baptismal Rite. Holy Baptism is for the fallen state of human beings in order for us to become re-aligned to our relationship with God. It is only humans who need re-alignment with our Creator. As false human pride has damaged that relationship, so does that pride need to be realigned to the will of God. Hence, The birth of the Christ into our world, Holy Baptism, the learning of God's presence and will for each of us and all of us together as a society.

The Rite of Confirmation, following Baptism and further study of our religious practices, is meant to further guide us in the understanding of ourselves, the Church's role, and the place of society in alignment of the world to the knowledge and love of God. It is true that along with our physical nature, our psyche, ethics, social behavior and spiritual nature are intertwined. The Bible is our source of understanding these key elements of living and well-being.

Again, as proclaimed in the Book of Exodus and throughout the Holy Bible, we see that the Israelite people were freed from the tyranny of the Egyptian Pharaoh and became the spokes persons of individual human freedom and a just society simply because of each individual's capacity to comprehend and assimilate God's Will for us. Such a just society necessarily needed each individual to be in tune with the loving will of God in the New Testament. Jesus not only becomes our living, human example of God's Will for us in this lifetime, but also our forever life in God's ongoing plans for each of us. The Bible teaches that we are God's children, are known by Him individually, and are special.

The experience of Church, as so often happens with institutions, eventually became taken for granted, and thereby began to fall short of her goal of continuing experiential witness to the reality of God and more especially the real, historical Jesus. Religion, for the most part, became a primary practice of forthcoming generations but in the process, as so often happens when our alertness is weakened by laxity, the real experiential dimension can and does get weakened.

Without the internal, individual experience of our Faith, we are left with an outward form rather than the intended inward and spiritual experience. But, we must begin somewhere and thereby, as the Catechism says, the Church and our liturgies point us to God as the outward and visible signs of the inward and spiritual Grace. We must continually reach beyond the idolatry of the outward signs such as liturgy without deeper understanding. We must each individually and personally enter ourselves again into the spiritual realm.

Before the Protestant Reformation and invention of the printing press, the hierarchy (i.e. the clergy) were the arbiters, the protectors, the teachers of the Faith. The role of the clergy was to guide everyone into the knowledge and love of the Lord. In such a way, the clergy became set apart rather than essential, integral parts of the whole. As St. Paul said, "Without the teacher, the Word would not get spread." *(Romans 10:14)* The Bible was not to be read by individuals but only heard at Mass for centuries. The reformers argued for the printing of Bibles for all to read. The Church had become the prime interpreter.

In the Church of England (Anglican Church), for example, the Protest of Martin Luther to both promote individual study of Scripture along with the Catholic heritage of religious practice and interpretation were incorporated to promote the intent and meaning of the Holy Bible. Thanks to our Baptist heritage and friends it became most important to be fully instructed in the individual study of the Bible. The need for such in-depth Bible study has again become a necessary part in the understanding and practice of our faith and Society's needs, for a clear and dear understanding of the Holy Bible.

A favorite catechism of mine is *The Practice of Religion* by Archibald Knowles, D. D. The first printing of this book was during WWII. He wrote this book to help all of us understand the meaning and purpose of the Holy

Bible at that time in which the world's life and society's purpose was in jeopardy. I admonish all Christians to read this catechism and look to God for help in our times of need as well as in our times of peace. I believe our world and society need and must follow such guidance in learning Truth. In learning of the real existence of Truth, we are enabled to be God's people "at all times... in all places... in all circumstances." Such is the meaning of "Catholic."

Upon my latest rescue of a new puppy, Chipper found my copy of *The Practice of Religion* and chewed it into shreds. He actually doesn't need such a book for guidance to love and be loved. However, I do, and I immediately searched to find a new copy! As stated earlier: "Only humans in the throes of Evil and sin need guidance and help in the search for Truth."

The ever-pervading Problem of Evil will persist as we search for that "Spiritual Dimension" that makes us free to think for ourselves. The primary "sin" of human pride will always entice us away from our pure search for the Truth that sets us free. Saint Paul said: "know the truth and the truth will set you free". (The Letters of Paul). Evil tried to kill God by nailing him to the Cross. Evil lost as Jesus rose from the dead. But who was it that admonished us by saying, "Evil will persist and win if good men do nothing?"

Falling asleep in the language lab as a college freshman, I tried placing the French book under my pillow every night. I almost believed that the contents would just transfer into my brain. It didn't work so I changed my selective Major. Finding Philosophy as profoundly interesting in the pursuit of Truth I chose to go that way. One of my philosophy professors told me that I was trying to show how Plato was so Christian in his thinking. He admonished me to separate the two and view each from whatever direction they were coming. The convergence was something to behold and showed me how God worked in so many different ways and from so many different directions. It was my understanding of my own Faith at that time that helped me see the similarities to the greats such as Socrates and his student, Plato. But by the Grace of God and the need to search for the Truth!

Before entering the Seminary and as a postulant in the Diocese of Rhode Island, I was required to take a crash course in Biblical content. This was to at least know what it looks like from cover to cover. Whatever I already understood came from my upbringing, church, and Sunday School.

It certainly would have helped in my study of French, if I had been born and raised in France and thereby be more easily able to speak French. If that were the case, I would then need to study English. It is my understanding that the children in France also learn English from the earliest years. They are required to study English from the earliest years in order to better navigate in the entire world population as English had become a universally utilized language. What a great idea!! Some things we simply need to spend more time in deeper study!

I am thankful that the Bible came to my attention early on, giving me a head start and good chance to actually learn of its purpose and meaning. Soon after meeting my friend Rachael at a dinner gathering and conversation among friends, I began to realize some incredible things about her - a genuinely calm demeanor, humility, and respect towards the input of other's religious points of view. It became apparent that she had, not only knowledge of the Bible, but more importantly, impressive theological interpretation. Come to find out she was raised in a Christian environment, being Baptist, and attending the local Christian School in the town of Whitinsville, Massachusetts. Rachael was obviously well-schooled in at least the content of the Holy Bible. This has obviously given rise to her own world view that she doesn't hesitate to share with others when she deems appropriate. Further on in this book is her own personal account of growing up as a Christian.

In the" Christian Common Lectionary" shared by at least Roman Catholics, Lutherans, Methodists, and Anglicans, the twenty-third Sunday after Pentecost is about the importance of the Holy Bible in our search for truth. The opening Collect (prayer) to these Biblical readings is this: "Blessed Lord, who caused all holy scriptures to be written for our learning: Grant us so to hear them, read, mark, learn, and inwardly digest them, that we may embrace and ever hold fast the blessed hope of everlasting life, which you have given us in our Savior, Jesus Christ, who lives and reigns with you and the Holy Spirit, one God, forever and ever. Amen."

The following Biblical readings are read in these churches each year on a three-year cycle:

Year A: Zephaniah 1:7, 12-18; Psalm 90:1-8;(9-11), 12; I Thessalonians 5:1-11; Matthew 25:14-30.

Year B: Daniel 12:1-3; Psalm 16; Hebrews 10:11-25; Mark: 13:1-8.

Year C: Isaiah 65:17-25; Isaiah 12:2-6; Malachi 4:1-2a; 2 Thessalonians 3:6-13; Luke 21:5-19.

If one attends at least one of these Churches every Sunday for three years, he or she will have heard the entire Bible in studious order. All the better to have a regular Bible study of the same. Over my own years as a priest in the church, I learn and gain something new each time these verses are presented to me. The Bible seems never to exhaust itself and is always up to date in current interpretation no matter the time and circumstances.

An example of year "C" 23 Pentecost, is a quick study of the readings:

Isaiah - states that God has a purpose for creation, one of which is that we are created to love God as He loves us, toward an eternal future.

Malachi - is an alternative reading which points out the reality of Evil which needs to be defeated, albeit converted back to the love of God as has been "fallen human nature."

Psalm 98 - We are called to, "Sing out to the Lord with a new song," and return to God and be saved from destruction.

2 Thessalonians – Calls on us to "shun that which is hurtful to each and all of us" and "work diligently for the Good (Truth)." The teaching of this section of the Holy Gospel says that we must learn from the Bible as a teacher, and thereby become open to the Gifts of the Holy Spirit.

It is interesting to note here that stellar Saints of History, known and unknown, have forwarded faith and civilization in ordinary and extraordinary ways. For example:

President Abraham Lincoln, who was taught the Bible by his Mother, did not go beyond the eighth grade in a one-room schoolhouse in the back rural woods of Illinois in the 1800s.

The early Church fathers from whom the Church claims her profound theology were proficient in their knowledge of the Holy Bible. For example:

Records of Bible Memorization

Tertullian devoted his days and nights to Bible reading, so much so that he learned much of it by heart, even its punctuations.

Theodosius the Younger could repeat any part of the Scripture exactly, and discourse with the bishops at court as if he himself were a bishop.

Origen never went to meals nor to sleep without having some portions of the Scripture read.

Eusebius said that he heard of one, whose eyes were burned out under the Diocletian persecution, repeat from memory the Scriptures in a large assembly.

Beza could repeat all Paul's epistles in Greek at age eighty.

Cranmer could repeat the entire New Testament from memory, learning it on his journey to Rome.

Ridley also memorized the entire New Testament during his walks in the Pembroke Hall of Cambridge.

How Ramsey was Convinced

Over a hundred years ago, William Ramsey, a young English scholar, went to Asia Minor with the expressed purpose of proving that the history given by Luke in his gospel and in the Acts was inaccurate. His professors had confidently said that Luke could not be right.

He began to dig in the ancient ruins of Greece and Asia Minor, testing for ancient terms, boundaries and other items which would be a dead giveaway if a writer had been inventing this history at a later date as claimed. To his amazement, he found that the New Testament Scriptures were accurate to the tiniest detail. So convincing was the evidence that Ramsey himself became a Christian and a great biblical scholar. We still look upon Sir William Ramsey's books as being a classic as far as the history of the New Testament is concerned. (Science Returns to God)

Consider the following:

Seventh Wonder of the World – The Holy Bible

1 The wonder of its formation – the way in which it grew is one of the mysteries of time

The wonder of its unification – a library of sixty-six books, yet one book

The wonder of its age – most ancient of all books

The wonder of its sale – best-seller of all time and of any other book

The wonder of its interest – only book in the world read by all classes of people

The wonder of its language – written largely by uneducated men, yet the best book from a literary standpoint

The wonder of its preservation – the most hated of all books, yet it continues to exist

It says in Romans 15:1-13 that:

Whatever was written in former days was written for our instruction, so that by steadfastness and by the encouragement of the scriptures we might have hope." One of the biblical commentaries says the following about Bible Study:

The scriptures encourage us and give us hope when we come to know them so well that they infuse our minds, and we see the events of our time as the biblical authors saw the events of theirs. We do this not by finding scripture passages to settle the hot-button issues [it is possible to find isolated scripture verses to support anything], but by recognizing and responding to the presence of God in the world about us, as did the biblical authors did – in the newspaper and on television, in the faces of little children and of our family and co-workers, in the school lunchroom and at the supper table, in the noise of the street and the subway, in the hospital room and in the cellblock.

Recognizing and responding to God is not always soothing. Sometimes God challenges and shakes us, raises questions we cannot answer, puts us with people we don't know and would rather not know. But it is God we follow, not our own wishes and whims. Living in response to the God of the scriptures, though often unsettling, brings encouragement that endures, and hope that never fades. (Forward Movement Publications)

Recently, my grandson Owen was looking forward to attending a special Christian camp the next summer in Pennsylvania. His only reluctance was his fear of knowing so little about the Bible. At age ten, I told him that most others of his were in the same boat, that he would find out that his fellow campers enter with the same fears and so not to worry. At that point, I taught him a game. Handing him a Bible I invited him to simply open it somewhere in the middle or wherever, to close his eyes and to just point down somewhere on that page.

I don't recall the passage on which he landed and that doesn't matter. It could have been meaningless to him, or it could have said something to which he could relate. The game for him was to have a pen and pad available and to take a few minutes each day before going to the camp and do the same exercise. I promised him that at sometimes and others one of those passages would have meaning for him. If so, he was to write that passage into his notebook and underline the same passage in the Bible he was using. To make a long story short Owen came home after two weeks in that camp saying that he can't wait to go again the next summer and take his younger brother and sister Wesley and Phoebe with him. The name of that camp is: "Summer's Best Two Weeks," Boswell, Pennsylvania.

In closing, I refer everyone to the following daily Bible Study from the Forward Movement Publications:

> "Whatever was written in former days was written for our instruction, so that by steadfastness and by the encouragement of the scriptures we might have hope." *(Romans 15:1-13)*

The scriptures encourage us and give us hope when we come to know them so well that they infuse our minds, and we see the events of our time as the biblical authors saw the events of theirs. We do this not by finding scripture passages to settle the hot button issues(it is possible to find scripture verses to support anything), but by recognizing and responding to the presence of God in the world about us, as the biblical authors did – in the newspaper and on television, in the faces of little children, our beloved pets, our family and co-workers, in the school lunchroom and at the supper table, in the noise of the street and sub-way, in the hospital and the prison cellblock.

Recognizing and responding to God is not always soothing. Sometimes God challenges and shakes us, raises questions we cannot answer, puts us with people we don't know and would rather not know. But it is God we follow, not our own wishes and whims. Living in response to the God of the scriptures, though often unsettling, brings encouragement that endures, and hope that never fades. *(Psalms 75, 76 * 23, 27; Wisdom 19:1-8, 18-22; Like 9:1-17)*

When I was a child, God and Santa Claus were mixed together in my imagination. According to the popular song, Santa was "making a list and checking it twice, gonna find out who's naughty and nice." God was likewise keeping track of my good and sinful deeds, and I envisioned Saint Peter guarding the gates of heaven armed with a huge ledger book. Here we find in Revelation words that fit this accounting model. Christ sends this message to the faithful in Ephesus: I see that you're doing a good job, but you have some black marks in the account book. "Repent, and do the works you did at first." There may be demerits in the book, but they can be erased through repentance and love.

As a child, I was astute enough to notice that even among the naughtiest of my schoolmates, no one ever actually got a lump of coal in the Christmas stocking. Santa had gifts for all. God has gifts of forgiveness and love for all.

Forward Movement Publications — 2011

February 2021

Dear Friends

Johann Sebastian Bach was arguably the greatest composer of all time. He lived a storied life, punctuated by tragedy. When he was a boy, he lost both his parents. Later, one by one, he would lose ten of his children and his wife. He spent time in prison.

He has frustrated his biographers, however, for he didn't tell his own story. He wrote no autobiography and had no interest in posterity. Bach thought *his* story, as a story, was of no importance. He never imagined that anything he wrote would survive him. And indeed for a hundred years he was entirely forgotten and his works were not performed.

The only story that mattered to him was Christ's story, and it was that he studied and proclaimed all his life. At the bottom of every composition, he wrote the letters "SDG" – *soli Deo Glory* – "To the Glory of God alone." Not to the glory of God and J. S. Bach, but to the Glory of God alone. Before he even began to put notes on paper, he first wrote the letters "J.J." for "Jesu juva": "Jesus help me."

Bach had *exchanged* his story for God's story for he understood that his hope lay not in any story he could invent but in the story of

The Anglican Digest is a ministry of the Society for Promoting and Encouraging Arts and Knowledge of the Church (a 501(c)3 organization 071-351665) at 805 County Road 102, Eureka Springs, AR 72632 Phone: 479-253-9701 Fax: 479-253-1277 E-mail: anglicandigest@att.net

Jesus Christ who loved him so much that he had died for him, who had defeated death, and who allowed Bach to look suffering, to look death, to look reality *squarely in the eye* in all its beauty and horror and strangeness and mystery.

The season of Lent is one in which we seek to do the same. This exchange of our story for God's story, and acting on its implications, is what Jesus was getting at when he said paradoxically: "For whoever would save his life will lose it, but whoever loses his life for my sake and the gospel's will save it."

This comes with every good wish and blessing.

+ Anthony Burton

The Right Reverend Anthony J. Burton
Board of Trustees

This incredible story was relayed to all who would listen and confirm our faith in God and especially in the Jesus of history. It is another of myriads of accounts of the power and necessity of faith.

This incredible story was relayed to all who would listen and confirm our faith in God and especially in the Jesus of history. It is another of myriads of accounts of the power and necessity of faith.

"Western Civilization"

Some of the secular and religious rulers of the time of the entrance of Jesus of Nazareth into our world had many prevalent ideas that ultimately not only needed to be changed but that the entrance of this personality into history led the way for them to happen. The changes precipitated ways of thinking and acting that became part and parcel to what we now know as Western Civilization. At the time of Jesus' teaching he was approached by some of the leaders of his society of the Roman Empire as to his authority. "When Jesus entered the Temple, the chief priests and scribes came to him as he was teaching, and said, 'By what authority are you doing these things, and who gave you this authority?'"

Referring to another thorn in the leaders' sides, Jesus said to them, "I will also ask you one question; if you tell me the answer then I will also tell you by what authority I do these things. "Did the baptism of John come from heaven, or was it of human origin?" And they argued with one another, "If we say from heaven, he will say to us, 'Why then did you not believe him?' But if we say, 'of human origin,' he would say, 'We are afraid of the crowd, for all are regarding John as a prophet from God.' So, they answered Jesus, 'We do not know.' And he said to them, "Neither will I tell you by what authority I am doing these things.'"

The Holy Gospel gives witness and explains who Jesus was as it became more and more clear as to the truthful authority that He taught and acted upon. From all of this, the early Doctors of the Church were able and determined necessary to formulate the Doctrine of the Holy Trinity wherein Jesus was actually God Himself in human form. God the Father, God the Son, and

God the Holy Spirit.

The new ideas brought to the individual and social order were more often than not, contrary to the norms of that place and time in history. The ruling civil and religious classes were threatened by these new ideas which challenged their control over the populace. Today, we take those ideas for granted but they were seen as radical at the time. Simply stated, His teaching was about love, compassion, mercy, rightful justice, forgiveness, and all the ways we now see as the "Will of the Father in Heaven." The conventional rules at that time were to just obey the authorities and trust their perspectives on wisdom. In the forward movement of Western Civilization, the teachings of Jesus became, by and large, the wisdom that guided education, law, science, and social order. Jesus was teaching about the love of God for each and every one of us. That God's will is to practice this kind of love and that mercy, empathy, compassion, and forgiveness are key to understanding the authority by which He has been sent to them, to us.

"Jesus answered them, 'truly I tell you, the (despised) tax collectors and prostitutes are going into the Kingdom of God ahead of you. For John came to you in the way of (God's love) righteousness, but you could not see it, and so do not believe him, but (the despised ones whom you feel are less than you) the tax collectors, prostitutes (and all in need of compassion, mercy, empathy, forgiveness)... saw and believed him, and even after you saw it, you did not change your minds and believe him.'" *(Mtt 21: 23-32)*

All this is to say that Jesus's authority was based on the love of God, and comes from God. If the human mind counts on its own authority without the entrance of God's love it is doomed to failure. Throughout the ministry and teaching of Jesus as recorded in the Holy Bible are stories, parables, actions, that related to the world the love of God as the principle authority to all thinking and actions.

Recently a young woman came to my office feeling deeply troubled. She was introduced to the Bible and church early on in life but in her teen years drifted away. Becoming pregnant at age seventeen, she and her boyfriend were married by a Justice of the Peace. Coming to me at age twenty-two, she felt a deep emptiness relating that her husband was not a believer in God, and she felt the need to bring God back into her life. We talked at great length. Jane's husband had a good job and she was apparently very talented and in need of some further education to compliment her God-given talents.

Talking through the many practical hurdles needed for both she and her partner she still expressed a need to somehow return to her childhood faith. She actually believed that God would and has already rejected her, and her feeling of spiritual emptiness was deep. Further counsel on the mercy, empathy, concern and forgiveness, and real love of God for her certainly helped her back to filling the gap, the missing piece in her life. She is back to the practice of worship in her church, reading the Bible, and raising her child in "the knowledge and love of the Lord" as stated in Holy Baptism. "It is our obligation to raise our children in the knowledge and love of the Lord." (*Book of Common Prayer*, pg. 304)

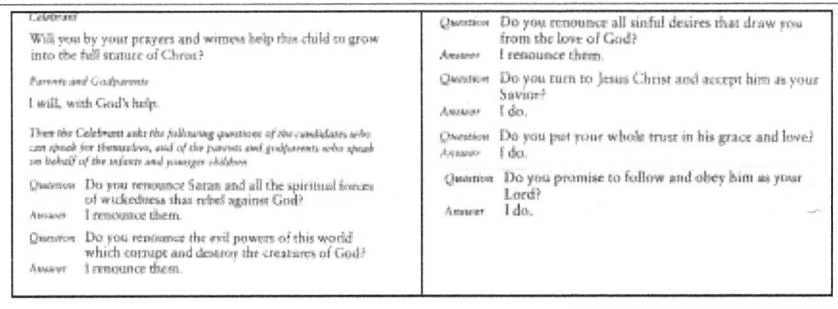

All this said, Western civilization grew and blossomed since the teaching authority of Jesus was recognized. Through the Saints, History and the Church, the physical, psychological, social, and spiritual needs of the human race were addressed. From the Dark Ages to the Middle Ages through the Age of Enlightenment to today, the teaching of Jesus became apparent in the advancement of hospitals, education, law, spiritual nature and social behavior; and that our physical health, psychological health, social health, and spiritual health are intertwined, one to the other.

If we eliminate our Spiritual selves as related to God, we find ourselves lacking the essential ingredient necessary for a healthful life. The nature of sin is that which is hurtful to you and to me. Without our God-given spiritual nature, which is love, we break down and so does all of society. The tyranny of sin is pain, destruction, and death.

At age twelve, according to the Holy Gospel, Jesus entered the great Temple in Jerusalem and boldly engaged the chief priests and the Pharisees in conversation. In no uncertain terms he told them that all their rules and authority was on the wrong track and actually wrong in their interpretation of God's love and Will for His Children, He told them that which we now know as "The Summary of the Law." That is "Love the Lord your God with all your heart, mind, and soul. And the second is to, "Love your neighbor as yourself."

A Distant Mirror

"Jeremiah"

Prophet (sixth century B. C. E.)

"The word of the Lord came to me saying,

'Before I formed you in the womb I knew you,

And before you were born I consecrated you;

I appointed you a prophet to the nations.'"

Jeremiah received his call to be a prophet in the year 625 B. C. E. His career was played out against the final years of the southern kingdom of Judah and continued for some time after the destruction of Jerusalem in 587 and the great exile to Babylon. His message was directed against the elite, the monarchy, the priests, and the official cult prophets who clung to the false assurance that nothing could happen to Judah so long as the Ark was safe in the Temple. Like other prophets before him, Jeremiah was sensitive to a deeper contradiction in the heart of Israel. The people had failed to comprehend that true faithfulness to God must be reflected in mercy and justice. To Jeremiah, the gap between the rich and poor of the land was a yawning gap in the covenant between the people and Yahweh. Under these circumstances, the official cult of Yahweh had become a form of idolatry. Short of some drastic signs of public conversion, destruction was inevitable.

Jeremiah preached this message for forty years. It didn't win him many friends. In good times he seemed like a harmless crank, but when conditions became ominous, Jeremiah's message sounded like treason or blasphemy. He was forced for long periods to go underground; he was flogged and put in stocks by the head priest of the Temple; he narrowly survived various assassination plots, one involving his own family. Once, he was nearly killed after being tossed into an empty well.

Ultimately, Jeremiah's message went unheeded and indeed his worst fears were realized. In 587 the Babylonians laid siege to Jerusalem for six months. Terrible famine befell the people. It all ended with a massacre of the royal family, the destruction of the Temple, and the burning of Jerusalem. Most of the population were carted into exile in Babylon, leaving only a few peasants to till the land. Our last glimpse of Jeremiah sees him being kidnapped by a band of renegades, a hostage to some petty intrigue. How and where he died is not recorded.

The following is a rewrite of the above account as if Jeremiah was speaking directly to the United States of America:

An Up-to-Date Look at Jeremiah
Jeremiah received his call to be a prophet in the year 1945 A. D. His career was played out against the final years of WWII and the changing, fearful but hopeful new World and continued for some time after the destruction of America and that world into Tyranny, and the great exile to hiding, until the ideas and ideals of Freedom rise again.

His message from long ago is now directed to the elite: powerful people assuming power over the masses; powerful Government and decision makers; religious institutions; and any modern-day prophets who assume the false assurance that nothing can happen to our republic so long as the idea of democracy, the Constitution, the Bill of Rights, and the system of checks and balances are safe in the halls of state and congress. Like other prophets before him, Jeremiah was sensitive to the deeper contradiction in the heart of our country.

The so-called Deep State looms as one of those problematic contradictions. It has become clear that those in control and so many of the people in general have failed to comprehend that true faithfulness to God must be reflected in mercy, justice, and truth. To Jeremiah, the gap between the rich and the poor, the powerful and the general populace, tyranny and freedom was the destructive gap in the necessary relationship between God and His people. Under these circumstances the official religion of God had also become another form of idolatry. Short of some drastic sign of public conversion, destruction was inevitable.

Jeremiah's long time of preaching this message didn't win him many friends. In good times, he seemed like a harmless crank, but when conditions became obvious and ominous as in the breakdown of the ideals that made us strong and truthfully productive, his message sounded like treason and blasphemy. Jeremiah and the truth being told forced him through lies, deceit and propaganda forced him into retreat and punishment. He narrowly survived various assassination plots, one involving his own family. Ultimately, the prophetic message went unheeded, and indeed his worst fears were realized. In 2020 A. D., the enemy laid siege of the nation for six months. Terrible famine befell the people of this once viable and God-fearing land.

Here continues Jeremiah's lamentation:

Jeremiah, a man in whose experience and consciousness the tragedy of the nation met full force with the tragedy of God:

> My grief is beyond healing,
> My heart is sick within me.
> For the wound of the daughter of my people
> Is my heart wounded.

His original call was marked by extreme reluctance. He experienced continuing tension throughout his life between his prophetic commission and the natural impulses of his heart. It gave him no pleasure to prophesy the destruction of Jerusalem. His suffering was compounded by the derision and persecution which greeted his pessimistic oracles. At the same time, extremely sensitive as he was to the feelings of God, he was haunted by the people's willful disobedience in the face of a disaster which he could foresee, but which he felt powerless to avert.

Yet, his commission as a prophet was not simply to "overthrow and destroy" but to "build up and plant." After the worst had happened, Jeremiah felt liberated at last to speak tenderly of hope and consolation. He wrote to the exiles in Babylon urging them to survive their captivity and to look forward to their eventual return. Transmitting the word of Yahweh, he said:

"The people who survived the sword found grace in the wilderness. …. have loved you with an everlasting love; there I have continued my faithfulness to you, again I will build you, and you shall be built, O Virgin Israel." Can we review and learn from our history so as to save our nation and make her better?

"It was the best of times, it was the worst of times, it was the age of wisdom, it was the age of foolishness, it was the epoch of belief, it was the epoch of incredulity, it was the season of Light, it was the season of Darkness, it was the spring of hope, it was the winter of despair, we had everything before us, we had nothing before us, we were all going direct to Heaven, we were all going direct the other way– in short, the period was so far like the present period, that some of its noisiest authorities insisted on its being received, for good or for evil, in the superlative degree of comparison only." (*A Tale of Two Cities*)

A Significant Revolution

"There never has been, there isn't now, and there never will be, any race of people on earth fit to serve as masters over their fellow men." (President Franklin D. Roosevelt) The American Revolution was a significant movement in history in that it introduced the idea of the capacity of individuals to think for themselves and likewise be in common with other individually able human beings. This would become a society of individuals "somehow" connected to a common source of information, or rather knowledge, which gave to them the incite and the power to become a productive society. The primary source of such an ability would have to be at the least reliable and at the most based on the best guiding principles.

This is the primary question to be answered. "What are those principles on which individuals must depend in order to both fathom one's thoughts individually and bring them to at least reasonable fruition together?" The idea that individual human beings were able to think for themselves and then to share those thoughts was revolutionary in history. The basic guide and source of this idea is the Holy Bible. This set of writings is about TRUTH being given to us by God and therefore giving each of us the ability to think for ourselves and be a more perfect society together.

This kind of experience is spelled out in the teaching of the Holy Bible and can be understood by all people. In an escape from tyranny our forebears brought this idea of freedom thereby freedom to a new place. The next question is where did that Bible come from? The American experiment in the Free Expression of individual thinking became the primary ideal of the new nation. Our earliest settlers escaped the tyranny of a despotic King in order to gain the freedom to think for themselves under the guidance of the love of God as taught them in the Holy Bible. They believed that each of us has the capacity to think and act for the good and well-being of all people.

The new United States Constitution provided the guidelines for protecting the basic rights and thinking of every human being. It was designed so that we can together solve the issues before us and continue to form a more perfect union. Faith in the God who gives to each of us guidance by the gifts of the Holy Spirit allows us to continue as a free people. The forefathers of this country knew this well and provided the Constitution to protect the belief in freedom" and its continuing implementation. President Ronald Reagan reminded us that in order to continue on this path of freedom we must teach this history and its "principles" to each generation forward. He warned that otherwise we could easily lose all the progress we have gained and fall back into that former tyranny over mind, body, and soul.

Again, recalling my own upbringing, the society we knew seemed peaceful and pretty much on the same page as far as our beliefs of being an American. The public school system was teaching the "3Rs" (reading, writing, and 'rithmatic) along with civics (our system of working together), history (from whence we have evolved), and, most importantly, our belief in God, the giver of all good gifts. There was a strong faith in our educational system in that it would help us to be the best that we can be, and a belief that we needed to be able to think and proceed in an open forum of free thinkers sincerely in search for TRUTH. I believe that most of us from that era of American and world history appreciated the basic as well as profound education that provided for us not only the ability to survive but to be enabled to think for ourselves and to thrive for the sake of all people and nations.

Of course, each of us and all of us together needed the guiding principles, education, and honest yearning and search for the TRUTH. Alongside the family unit, a public school system, and a basic belief in God, we were each enabled to learn and grow as individual thinkers and be productive in a good so-ciety. These instructions came from our families and the religious institutions which guided our belief system. Good, bad, and indifferent, the basics provided the tools we needed to grow and move forward. The debates of a two-party political format provided the needed (good, bad and indifferent) forum to struggle with the values of our basic beliefs. Belief in God and trust in each other were the glue which held us together.

Our parents (forefathers) and the men and women of our history have tried to continue to provide those tools of freedom with the responsibility to move forward in a healthy way. The Constitution, Bill of Rights, and the Rule of Law must continually guide us in the direction of a more perfect union. Prior to this revolution was a world and a history based on the power of a few over the masses of individuals supposedly under their care. Such a system produced a Tyranny over body, mind and soul. The teaching of the Holy Bible taught otherwise by bringing to the world and history a real Faith in a real God.

Under the tyrannical power of an insane King George III, the Pilgrims fled to this new land with the hope, prayer, and understanding of each indi-vidual's need to be free within the power and love of God. The Biblical idea is that God created us humans to be able to think as God thinks. The Bible says that we are created "in the image of God." The opposite of this is a belief that we are simply on our own and that there is no truth beyond our lone existence. The Bible teaches that human "vain glory" (the pride of thinking that my power over you is sufficient and all we have) is the ultimate evil the ultimate human sin. All evil and sin is contrary to the will of God and the TRUTH that sets us free! It is incumbent upon us to know our history (good, bad, and in-different); keep working for the revolution of Truth and being the best we can be for our own good and for the good of all!

We are called to continue to question our prideful motivations and ask ourselves if we are willing to do our best in search of the truth, and use the tools we have been given, to allow a healthful future to happen. May God help us! It has been said over and over again that, "Evil will persist and win if good men do nothing!"

With all this in mind, I am again reminded of those earlier years in which we were all seeking ways to go into a sound future. We all knew that we had to apply ourselves as best we could to make this happen. Early on in my own career I thought about becoming a Monk in the Church in order to devote my life to study. I am now thankful that I didn't follow such a path. Learning from sound schooling back then allowed me to realize that study and growing was everyone's responsibility no matter which vocation was followed. However, a life in the real world is for all of us as it was for me a challenge requiring great amounts of responsibility. My life out here in the real world has been a genuine challenge and a joy as well as unknown and unforeseen difficulties along the way.

So goes life and the greater mysteries presented in whatever path we choose to follow. How wonderful it is for me to enjoy my children, grandchildren, greater family, and friends. As far as the choice of a monastic life that was made by so very many devoted souls, I am truly grateful! I am most appreciative of all who have chosen such a path and the sacrifices it requires to be in honest search for that truth which brings peace beyond all human understanding. The monks teach the rest of us the absolute need for discipline, study, and prayer. For me, following several visits to two nearby monasteries, I realized that my temperament and enjoyment of the world outside was too alluring. In another section of this book, I wrote about "The Kiss," which totally defined my need and desire for conjugal love. Coupling my temperament along with belief in God and God's Will for all of us it was a no-brainer that solitary confinement was not something I could endure.

"The Law"

The definition of "law" requires a belief system which provides basic philosophic principles and values from which such law proceeds. For example, the law as understood in the Holy Bible counts on belief in God as portrayed within its own thesis. The thesis and the Holy Bible are of the Creation by a Creator from whom purpose, meaning, and law emanates. According to the Judeo- Christian Bible, the Law is given to us and comprehended individually and then corporately as a society. In other words, law is to be understood by each of us and then practiced societally. This is the meaning of free will. It means that each of us, individually, are capable of understanding the law, and thereby enabled to practice it. Jesus said simply, "The Law of God is love." He also said to, "Love thy neighbor as thyself." This encapsulates the meaning of free- dom. Freedom provides for us the ability to think for ourselves.

According to the Bible, the law is to be comprehended individually and from each of us practiced amongst each other. This is freedom. Jesus said to his followers, "You are truly my disciples if you live as I show you, and you will know the Truth and the Truth shall set you free." *(John 8:32)* Freedom is based on Truth and the law only enters in as the Truth is invaded, thwarted, or abused in any way. The Bible is all about Truth and the road to that Truth. The entire New Testament points to the Truth, freedom, and the embodiment of such on the Christ, the Incarnation of God. It is recorded that at age twelve, Jesus confronted the Pharisees and Saducees in their interpretations of the law. He essentially said that without Love the law becomes fruitless. He reminded them of the law of Moses summarized as, "Love the Lord your God with all your heart, with all your mind, and with all you soul is the first law and commandment. The second is like unto it... Love your neighbor as yourself. These are the first and greatest of all the Commandments."

The definition of "law" given in Webster's Collegiate Dictionary is this:

Law – n. 1a. A rule of action or conduct established by authority, society, or custom. b. A body of such rules. c. The control that ensues when such rules are enforced. 2a. The study and science of laws : jurisprudence. b. The profession of a lawyer. 3. The body of precepts that express the divine will as set forth in the Old Testament. 4. A formulation of a relationship that holds between or among phenomena for all cases in which the specified conditions are met. 5. A code of ethics or behavior. *syns: AXIOM, FUNDAMENTAL, PRINCIPLE, THEOREM – v. Regional. To litigate.

The definition of "freedom" as given in the dictionary is as follows:

Free-born adj. 1. Born as a free person and not a slave. 2. Of or appropriate to a freeborn person.

Freedman n. A man freed from slavery.

Freedom n. The state of being free of constraints. 2a. Political independence. b. Possession of political and civil rights. 3. Free will. 4. Facility as of movement. 5. Frankness or boldness of expression. 6. Unrestricted access or use.

The definition of tyranny and tyrant reveals the opposition to freedom and indiscriminate law:

Tyrannical – adj. being or characteristic of a tyrant or tyranny: DESPOTIC

Tyrannize – v. to exercise arbitrary oppressive power or severity

Tyrannous – adj. marked by tyranny

Tyranny – n. 1. oppressive power; oppressive power exerted by government; 2a: a government in which absolute power is vested in a single ruler especially: one characteristic of an ancient Greek city-state b: the office, authority, and administration of a tyrant 3: a rigorous condition imposed by some outside agency or force 4: an oppressive, harsh, or unjust act : a tyrannical act

Tyrant – n. 1a: an absolute ruler unrestrained by law or constitution; b: a usurper of sovereignty; 2a: a ruler who exercises absolute power oppressively or brutally; b: one resembling an oppressive ruler in the harsh use of authority or power

Slave and Slavery are the outcome of the sins or other tyrannies which plague and dehumanize the God-given way to Freedom.

Slave – n. 1. a person held in forced servitude; 2 disapproving: a person who is completely subservient to a dominating influence; 3 a device (such as the printer of a computer) that is directly responsive to another 4. drudge, toiler

Slavery – n. a: the practice of slaveholding b: the state of a person who is held in forced servitude c: a situation or practice in which people are entrapped (as by debt) and exploited 2: submission to a dominating influence; 3: drudgery, toil

It was our most famous and beloved president, assassinated by evil, who proclaimed and activated an abolishment to slavery.

Lincoln's Firm Signature

When the Emancipation Proclamation was taken to Mr. Lincoln by Secretary Seward, for the President's signature, Mr. Lincoln took a pen, dipped it in the ink, moved his hand to the place for the signature, held it a moment, then removed his hand and dropped the pen. After a little hesitation he again took up the pen and went through the same movement as before. Mr. Lincoln then turned to Mr. Seward and said, "I have been shaking hands since nine o'clock this morning and my right arm is almost paralyzed. If my name ever goes into history, it will be for this act, and my whole soul is in it. If my hand trembles when I sign the Proclamation, all who examine the document hereafter will say, "He hesitated."

He then turned to the table, took up the pen again, and slowly, firmly wrote "Abraham Lincoln," with which the whole world is now familiar. He then looked up, smiled, and said, "That will do." (Encyclopedia of 7700 Quotations)

7700 Quotations gives the following headings regarding the existence of God. Those titles include:

1. Glorifying God
2. The Call of God
3. The Existence of God
4. The Governing of God

5. The Guidance of God

6. The Love of God

7. The Omnipotence of God

8. The Omnipresence of God

9. The Omniscience of God

10. The Power of God

11. The Promises of God

12. The Protection of God

13. The Provisions of God

14. God's Strength – Our Weakness

If nothing else, the stories, testimonies, and experiences in such a book give adequate examples in the study of Law and anything else pertaining to belief. The subtitle of this book is "The Signs of the Times." In closing, I quote again one of many problems of the Good vs the Evil. Again, the Law is a way if not the way of correcting those problems which universally plague our human nature.

Psychiatrists and Sin

"Sin" does really exist, according to Dr. Karl Menninger. The famous psychiatrist is distressed that modern society tries to figure out its problems and talk about morality without ever mentioning the word "sin". He is convinced that the only way to raise the moral tone of present-day civilization and deal with the depression and worries that plague clergy, psychiatrists, statesman, teachers, lawyers, scientists, and ordinary folk, is to revive an understanding of what 'sin' is. (Encyclopedia of 7700 Quotations) And yes, "Democracy is based on the conviction that there are extra-ordinary possibilities in ordinary people." ("Freedom" in the Encyclopedia of 7700 Quotations)

American Law

Upon writing this brief on the philosophy of the law as it pertains to American law, I asked a close friend who is a district attorney, to provide for this book an outline of the same, as he sees it:

- The Constitution of the United States was adopted in 1788 and it is difficult to think of another document, tool, or product that has withstood time like our Constitution. This document has guided our country through periods of war, plague, turmoil, slavery, expansion, and conflict. Whether you believe that the Constitution must be strictly interpreted solely on the intent of the authors, or that it is fluid, flexible, and able to change with times, it is hard to image achieving the longevity, freedom, and prosperity of our great nation without it.

- The laws of our nation, whether local, state, or federal, are designed to be created with checks and balances by our separate branches of Government. Often times, we hear that change is "difficult," or that fundamental changes "take too long." This should be celebrated and respected to ensure that the pendulums of power do not swing too fast or furious in either direction.

  Laws provide the stability that support our society and economy. Laws impact every aspect of our lives from the food we eat, and the way we interact with our neighbors, to who we can marry.

- The laws of our nation cannot be respected on a part-time basis, followed or ignored based on personal convenience. The man who steals his neighbor's newspaper cannot justify the offense by rationalizing that he needs the newspaper more than his neighbor. We should all respect the rights of others in the manner that we want our rights to be respected. For example, if you want to maintain your Freedom of Speech, one should not decry that an opposing view is not protected simply to silence an opponent.

- When people speak about defunding the police or abolishing laws, they recklessly devalue the importance of laws in our society. I suspect that few demanding to defund the police have traveled to foreign lands that have little or no law enforcement. Imagine living in a world where someone could take possession of your farm simply because they wanted to, and had the power to do so, or where violent crimes had no repercussions.

- Those calling to defund the police or to end law enforcement have curiously been the same who immediately look for a lawyer or protection of due process if they have been accused of a crime.

- While societal norms are enough to keep most people from deviating from acceptable behavior, laws remain necessary to allow for repercussions for those who disobey. Most global citizens know through familial values and societal norms that you cannot spit on fellow pedestrians travelling on a busy street, however, we must maintain laws so that we can appropriately react to the outliers who deviate from those norms.

- The suspension of laws weakens our society and devalues their long-term value. For example, if the president and congress temporarily suspend immigration laws, it is hard to reinstate them and expect people to follow a law on Tuesday that was not enforced Monday. It also disrespects the people who followed the law and used the legal channels to build a better life for their family.

"Miss Taylor"

A boot in the pants was needed and given to me by our high school guidance counselor, Miss Taylor, back in those early years (1960 – 1963). The summons for me to go to the guidance office was a surprise as I had no idea why. It turned out to be a most significant conversation as Miss Taylor confronted me with most serious questions about my plans for the future. As I entered her office, she had a chair strategically placed for me directly across from her ominous and powerful looking desk. With a stern look but also a gentle smile, she asked me the critical question of my or anyone else's lifetime.

"What are your plans?" I meekly responded how well my older brothers Jim and Don were doing and planned to go to college as they did. "Well Warren," she said, "You'd better go look for a job instead! I am convinced that you do have a brain in your head and could be a whole lot better than your current grades now indicate. These grades will not enter you into any college!" Miss Taylor thanked me for coming in to see her and that was the close of that conversation.

About a year later, she approached me between classes in the corridor and said, "Warren, I see you are doing a whole lot better. Keep it up!" The rest is now history as such love and concern by one of my teachers gave to me the gift that I needed to go forward. I can also look back now with deeply felt gratitude for all the wonderful teachers I had in the schools of East Providence, Rhode Island.

There were 635 in my EPHS Class, and I now have the pleasure of seeing many of them in reunion and marvel at the successes of all of them. Each of us have reiterated our thanks to those teachers who truly cared about our well-being and the availability of a promising future ahead of us. There are myriads of stories that many have told of those ahead of them took the time and energy to love, care, and teach others "to be the best they can be". The following is just one of those and shows very well the meaning of it all.

The Teacher Who Pointed Outward

"Years ago, there lived in Switzerland a great schoolmaster whose name was Petalozzi. He was held in highest esteem and greatly loved, especially by the children who came under his character-molding influence. At his death, it was generally felt that a monument commemorative of his life of selfless service, should be erected so as to be an enduring memorial in the hearts of others.

The monument was erected. The day for its unveiling came. The sculptor had succeeded so well in reproducing the likeness of the schoolmaster that all who looked upon the statue hushed in reverence and admiration. The teacher was shown looking down upon the kneeling form of a little child whose uplifted gaze focused upon the face of the teacher.

Although the statue was a wonderful work of art, the teacher's most intimate friends felt that the sculptor failed to represent the dominant character and desire of the pedagogue—-not to have those he taught look with wonderment upon him, but rather upward to the challenging heights or goals as yet unattained, and to God, "the Creator of all good things." So, a change was made. At the second unveiling, all were pleased to see a kneeling child, looking not at the face of the teacher, but rather to the beckoning beyond." (Encyclopedia of 7700 Quotations)

With this in mind, I realize a need to interject some words of caution in a world that doesn't always give us the best reasoning and loving care to enable us to move ahead in the best ways possible. There is the reality of evil which thwarts Truth and does hamper and even tries to destroy that TRUTH.

The following story by teacher and writer Donald G. Barnhouse poses the question of problems related to evil. He said that "One of Satan's characteristic stratagems is to give those who believe that he does not exist an entirely wrong concept of what his true nature and character really are." He goes on to amplify this warning with some historical background as one example. "In the Middle Ages, when there were no radios, no magazines, no newspapers, no movies, no television, no telephones and none of the modern means of 'passing the time', the people were frequently amused by the 'miracle plays.' These were sort of religious pageants wherein religious stories were acted out on stage. In such pageants the audience learned to look for one character who was always dressed in red, wore horns on his head, and a tail dangling out behind him. His hoofs were cloven, and he had a pitchfork in his hand. The onlookers were quite thrilled when they saw this figure sneaking up on the hero and heroine. The idea arose that Satin (personification of Evil) could be called 'Old Nick', or even more mis-leading, 'his satanic majesty.' In all, this made the thought of Satin as being just a character who was slightly comical and even not real at all."

Further on in this book, I have more to relate on my thoughts regarding "The Problem of Evil" as well as my beliefs that love and TRUTH are also real and need to be followed in order to ward off the evils both within and all around us. I must also note here that my good friend and colleague Rev. Dr. Wilberforce Mundia received his Doctoral Degree from Boston University, his primary thesis being about "the problem of evil." Father Mundia was also an answer to prayer for me back in our earlier years as parish priests. In addition, it is important to say that The Holy Bible clearly states the difference between the realities of both the good and the evil. There is a whole lot more about Father Mundia further on in this collection of stories.

"Dr. William O. Martin"

Way back in my undergraduate studies (1963-1967), it was my good fortune to have had Dr. William O. Martin as a professor during my studies in philosophy and history. Under his tutelage I studied the work, philosophy, and stated, as well as hidden goals, of Karl Marx and Friedrick Engles. Marxism/Leninism was an expertise of his. Beliefs of my formative years as an American and as a Christian were bolstered by this study.

Even way back in the 1960s, Dr. Martin was shunned by some fellow professors due to his conservative beliefs, and his desire to warn us of the real threats of Communism. Such threats are clearly delineated in the agenda and writings of Marxism/Leninism. The actual works, which I read in entirety were frightening to me. They contained the primary agenda of "world domination" and the close of Western Civilization as we have known it.

Wishing I still had the thesis I wrote for his courses delineating forthcoming problems, I could more fully show how me as a nineteen-year-old student was thinking. I now see coming more and more the trends of our society in which Marxist plans for us are coming to pass. My thesis was about the upcoming computer age in which we could and would succumb to the active behavior of Communism. For example, the computer easily thinks for us, depleting our own God-given ability to think for ourselves. The more the computer thinks for us the more control it has over us. Communism is all about control of both the individual as well as the masses. This is in opposition to the Biblical teaching of Free Will which calls for us to think for ourselves in the light of God's Will for us. Human tyranny without God's will is the dire result of this Humanist philosophy.

A recent editorial in the Johnston RI Sunrise newspaper a Mr. Sam Parente wrote the following article. His fears of today's trends away from the beloved country we have grown to know and appreciate. His observation is that one entire political party has succumbed to the Marxist agenda:

> The states that comprise the Northeast section of the United States are populated by people who predominantly vote "Democrat".

Euphemistically, these states were called "Blue States". These states would probably change color to purple or red (ie. Independent or Republican) if these very same voters accepted my challenge to read Dismantling America by Thomas Sowell. Dr. Sowell is now an economist of the Hoover Institution at Stanford University. (His credentials can be easily checked by a quick search) This is hardly a far-fetched claim because the reader must be aware of the drastic change that is the "New Democratic Party" due to the takeover by far-left progressive leaders who now control the party.

Democrats who stay involved know exactly what has been stated here to be fact and if they really care about the future of this country, they should make a point to read the book. Dr. Sowell's message of the book is a serious concern to everyone, and all are strongly encouraged to read it as well. (Sam Parente, Cranston, R. I.)

It was way back in the sixteenth Century that the idea of Freedom began to widely take hold, especially in Western Civilization. Another well-educated colleague in ministry, Dr. Derek Zoyt, wrote the following article in the Oct 27, 2017, Blackstone Valley Express. The article is entitled "The Reformation: The idea that Changed the World."

This month marks the 500th anniversary of one on the most important events in modern Western Civilization: the birth of an idea that continues to shape the life of every human being today. In 1517, power was in the hands of the few and it was often corrupt, thought was controlled by the privileged and chosen, and common people lived rather bleak lives without hope.

Back on October 31 of that year, a poor and little-known German monk named Martin Luther nailed a list of ninety-five statements (called "theses") to the door of the church at Wittenberg, Germany, that sparked the revolution that would change everything. Luther's arguments launched the Protestant Reformation of the Church, which had a profound impact on Western culture – changing it at its core.

In addition to bringing reform to the Church, the Protestant Reformation also gave rise to the drive toward individualism, introduced the idea of freedom of religion, empowered the rights of the common man, and it launched the idea of the separation of church and state.

In many ways, if Luther's protest and the Reformation never happened, there would most likely be no pilgrims that would voyage from Europe in search of religious freedom and there would be no Puritans who would settle in our great Commonwealth. In fact, there would most likely be no America in the way that we know it.

Today, Luther's pounding critique against the church of his day still echoes around the world. At its heart, the movement that he and other reformers – like Ulrich Zwingli in Switzerland and John Calvin in France – set in motion called for reform in the church by going back to the Bible's core teaching about salvation.

The center of this teaching is often referred to by the Reformers (in Latin, which was the language of the church in that day) as the five solae: sola Scriptura – "by Scripture alone", solus Christus – "by Christ alone", sola gratia - "by grace alone", sola fide – "by faith alone", and soli Deo Gloria – "for glory to God alone".

Revolving around the fundamental truth that the glory of salvation belongs to God alone – not the church, Luther and the Reformers taught that the Bible alone – not church tradition or papal authority – has authority as God's Word to us, that Jesus Christ alone makes our salvation possible – there is nothing we can do to earn it, and that sinners are made right with God by grace alone and through faith alone – which are both gifts that God gives us. These teachings remain standing as the good news of salvation.

So, as we commemorate the Reformation this month, may we not only remember just how much of an impact it had on society religiously, politically, economically, and socially. Indeed, it was an idea that changed the world! But may each of us experience renewal and joy in understanding the depth of God's plan of salvation and his matchless love for us. Soli Deo Gloria!

"Threats and/or Opportunities:
The Law of God is Love"

A threat is, "an expression of the intent to inflict harm; a possible source of danger; or a warning sign." In the book *Games People Play*, the author describes in great detail how games are all too often played in that he or she will receive a desired result. Again, the end does not justify the means. This happens in relationships from two or more individuals; in the corporate world; in international relations; in the wide variety of political systems. The desired goal of all relationships should be the truth and trust that honesty and meaningful, rightly purposeful results will happen. All too often the goal is selfish and the opponent becomes the loser.

Selfish is defined as, "concerned only or primarily with oneself without regard for others." Hence, "self- centered", "self-seeking." Opponent is, "one that opposes another or others." In other words, the other becomes the adversary, falling into antagonism, and later to become war. In all this the rightful goal needs to be, must be, a mutual new search for truth and trust in the meaningful and purposeful outcome. I would call the breakdown of love and love's pure goals Evil. The dictionary definition of evil is "that which is morally wrong, bad, wicked; causing harm; injuries; a cause of suffering or injury."

When Christ was crucified he said, "Father, forgive them for they know not what they do." In the early history of Christianity, the many Saints and Martyrs spoke their understanding of the Truth and suffered the deadly outcome of evil as their love was not heard. They were pacifist in their practice of the faith. A pacifist does his/her best to reduce the tension that, if not reduced, ends in conflict. The dictionary definition of Pacifism is "opposition to war or violence as a way to resolve disputes."

The early Church struggled with the extremes of pacifism in that the question became "How far can we pacify to prevent the conflict before the ultimate need is to stop it?" This is where, by 500 BC, war was accepted as the last result after all conversation ceased and the evil would predominate and then dominate.

Limited war against the evil would become necessary to stop the evil and lead us back to the search for the Truth.

During my years in ministry, couples' conflicts were a regular problem in search of solutions. These conflicts prompted me to attend such meetings as Recovery Incorporated and Al-Anon. Individuals suffering from social phobias such as fear to be involved in outside activities with others was the healing process of recovery. Al-anon sought solutions for those suffering the disease of alcoholism in their significant other relationships. In Al-anon, the healthy significant other was most often brought to war against the evil in order to bring about the healing of the other.

The healthy partner needed to reject the evil of the disease by taking special care of oneself and turning away from the chronic evil. This is usually a most difficult process as the healthy partner desired the healing of the other. Ending such a relationship here becomes the only means to save oneself and precipitate the potential healing of the other. Tough decisions needed to be made to bring about normality and a return to the truth and healing. In Alcoholics Anonymous, individuals suffering these diseases are called to seek their Higher Power to defeat the problem and return to living a healthful life. The staid prayer of the Alcoholic is: "Lord, grant me the serenity to accept the things I cannot change, courage to change the things I can, and the wisdom to know the difference."

Earlier in these writings, the piece called "The Confessional" delineates the fact that we humans cannot get through life without help. Such help must be from each other along with such higher principles that guide us along the way. The purpose of confession is to provide a confidential place for honest, trustworthy dialogue wherein both the confessee and confessor find themselves humbly together and dependent on Love for the better outcome.

Facing the US and Today's world are serious evils which need attention:

1) North Korea as in a Dictatorship/Tyranny
2) Extreme Muslims, i.e. -ISIS; and any religious and political extremism denying personal development and freedom.
3) Agitation from Within (*an internal conflict here in the U. S. I. e. political agitation).

Jack's Penny Candy Store

Saint Paul very thoroughly reminds us that FREEDOM is based on TRUTH; that TRUTH is from God; and that such TRUTH will provide for us both FREEDOM and the responsibilities for such FREEDOM. "Seek the truth and the truth will set you free." It is also important to note that the entire Bible is dedicated to TRUTH and FREEDOM. The idea of human FREE WILL is pre-eminent.

In the current climate of history in the making, there are critical debates in the meaning of Truth, where it comes from, and how best to move forward. The debate is critical in that serious divisions of belief' have become divisive ways of thinking and hence divisive world views. These debates in belief and avenues to Truth include two major world forces in our world today. They are Atheist Materialism and Theist Spirituality. The one force believes that any higher principles of Truth are derived by our own making in a solely material world. The other believes that there exists higher principles derived from the reality we call God. It says that such Truth is given to us by God and thereby guides us forward. God is, therefore, the OTHER which is above each of us and all of us together. Truth exists and comes to us from beyond ourselves but can and does dwell within each of us.

In the current Marxist philosophy of Dialectical Materialism, there is a tenet which says that, "The ends justify the means." In other words, truth exists only by our own devising of it. We create our own truth and therefore anything goes according to our own devising. The question then arises as to "What end is sought and how is it achieved?" If the end sought is, "the good of all mankind," then the motive is pure. The next question is, "What are the means to this end?" The one force says that we create our own means to the end we prescribe. The other says that we seek higher principles above ourselves to reach the promised end. The result of the one world view is tyranny in that someone not relying on the other becomes the controlling factor. The other force relies on the given higher principles as the true guide forward and hence makes no room for tyranny. The next questions arise as:

"Who or What is in Control?"

"What is 'needed' for our Survival?"

"In What or in Whom can I and we Trust?"

"What is it that carries us forward or holds back our advancement during our lifetime?"

History is the primary resource given to help guide our direction into our future and development. The answers we gain from our personal history along with the broader picture are needed to guide the road we travel. It is the value of history that gives each and all of us together those focal points that we need to make the decisions we need to move forward. Whatever value system that has guided individuals and societies in history have been that which determines our thinking and our actions. This is tricky in that history comes to us from the eyes and interpretation of the beholder. Each of us and all of us together experience our lives and livelihood within the context of that system. If there come those times that we think out of the box so to speak, we find ourselves with questions to be resolved. For example, our religious up-bringing, and the laws governing those experiences can and often do call us individually and the system into question. Herein lies either the progress or the detriments of our lifetimes.

Thus, in our American society we have debates about our history and ways to go forward. This is the debate of politics. We must depend on knowledgeable leaders to help guide us in such debates. Our personal development exists within a brief lifetime and era of culture, circumstances, and the points of view given to us during that time span. Much is at stake as we look for guidance and direction, and we must be aware of the history that has brought us thus far.

I recall from way back as a young child many significant events and experiences which were milestones. First of all, there was Candy, Candy, Candy! And we did learn very early on that too much candy was not good for us and often had the tendency to make us very sick. We did 'learn' from our experience to seek help to get better. Yes, these kinds of experiences did help in leading me to choices made for good. But again, more help and guidance were needed. From whence does such help and guidance come in order for our health to survive and even to flourish?

One of these was JACK'S PENNY CANDY STORE. This wonderful place was visited more often than needed by me and my friends. Way back then, JACK'S was smack in the middle of our neighborhood. For me the store was mid-way between my home and my church. Here is where a significant event happened. Being dropped off to church and Sunday School by Mom and Dad, the walk home was a straight and easy one mile on the warmer days. It happened to be mid-LENT when key choices needed to be made that one sunny, warm, Spring Sunday. Frankie and I left Sunday School after being reminded again of the importance of LENT and had no other way home except going by JACK'S PENNY CANDY STORE. Most of us kids had given up our coveted candy break for the six long weeks of LENT.

During this span of sacrificial time we had our yearly MITE BOXES securely waiting at home for the coins that we promised to fill with the candy money. This Mite Box was brought back to church on Easter Sunday and destined to local and foreign needs of other children less fortunate than us. This was a most fulfilling experience full of promise and good will. But something happened at that time! Frankie and I both agreed that one stop at JACK'S wouldn't hurt anyone, and WHO would know?!

It was a long stretch without our candy fix. We could not resist the temptation! However, JACK, the candy man, asked us about our promises for Lent. He spoke to us about all the reasons he could muster up as to why we shouldn't use our hard-earned coins for that one slip of temptation. He reminded us that he would still be there after Easter but hopefully then we should have learned some important lessons and be much better off for it. For us Jack became a loving mentor far beyond our need for more candy. What a wonderful memory and key lesson in life and our hopeful journey ahead.

A Few Years Later

Moving my own timeline ahead a few more years, I'll not forget watching the news as a teenager in High School. I believe it was in 1961when I was in the tenth grade and a significant United Nations meeting was being broadcast. There in front of me was Soviet Premiere Nikita Khrushchev slamming his shoe on the podium and shouting with great anger and resolve, "WE WILL BURY YOU FROM WITHIN!" The President of the Soviet Union was telling the Western Democratic Republics, and most especially the United States and Western Civilization itself that Communism was to prevail and the world would be made one under that philosophy and rule.

To me, that was a terrifying threat rather than a mentoring promise of hope. Candy was being promised, so to speak, whether we liked it or not. There was no choice in the matter. To me this would be a different kind of LENTEN experience given by a not so reliable source or way of thinking and believing. It was at this turning point that I listened more carefully to the message being forwarded and decided to pursue it further. I needed to know what it was that Mr. Kruschev meant, believed, and was determined to pursue. This began my road to Philosophy, History, and later, to Theology. Instead of going to school to become a lawyer I decided to become a priest in the Church. I continue to have no regrets and thank my history, mentors, circumstances, and experiences which have brought me thus far.

During this time of study, I read all these works of Marx and Engels, the Bolshevik Revolution, and the pursuits of Leninist Communism. In this era of one lifetime from 1945 to now, we have gone from the Great Depression, WWII, and the ongoing discussion and divide between the Western Democracies and a threat of Global Communism. Twelve U. S. Presidents have served our nation, and the great debate continues. At this point in our time and era, our Nation has become more divided than ever. What is the problem that we must solve? What is the history that we need to learn so a that we can remain hopeful and move forward into a healthful future? In whom and in what can we TRUST?

Bolshevik Revolution: "We Will Bury You from Within"
The Bolshevik Revolution of 1915 brought the likewise singular rule of the Monarchy of Czar Nicholas of Russia to a halt. The so-called religious Monarchy of the Czars had extreme rule and power over the masses. The Bolsheviks replaced the Monarchy with equal or more power, the rule of a non-religious philosophy known as Marxism. Marxism is no other than another tyranny over the masses void of any religious belief system hence Atheism/Humanism. This is control of the masses with no Theism, Higher Power, Belief beyond human dimension, and, thereby, no higher principle to look to for guidance other than the philosophy, whim, fancy of the ruling person of a party.

No one or theory to praise or to blame for the outcome. Its power is confined to and contrived by human control void of any other resource such as a Higher Truth for its guiding principles. Whatever such a philosophy it chooses to utilize for its self-perpetuating needs or ends is all it has to go by. In this case, the ends would justify the means. In all cases, be it Monarchy, Marxism, freedom, or democracy, the means for promoting a better society's needs and beliefs must have guiding principles to be successful. This calls for a basis of TRUTH from which the principles utilized will give the needed results. If Atheism is based upon Truth, then so be it. However, if something other than TRUTH becomes the motivating principle then such would be the means to whatever end it would provide.

The framers of the new tyranny (which is as old as history can look back) now known as Marxism/Leninism/Socialism/Communism built that system on a philosophy of a little-known thinker/philosopher Ludwig Feuerbach from Germany of earlier years. Marx and Lenin actually re wrote this way of thinking and brought it into prominence as the basis for the Bolshevik Revolution. This philosophy was atheist and was the primary motivation used to end that which was the then Monarchy of Czarist Russia. Hence, this was the end of a tyrannical religious system and replaced by the equally and more tyrannical system of Communism. Ludwig Feuerbach followed by Karl Marx labeled Theology, or rather religious belief and faith as "the opiate of the people." And yes, so can any system be if not rightly understood and practiced. Again, what is the TRUTH? From whence does it come? What actually is our source of belief, strength, and rightfully executive power?

According to Marxism, the primary source of the Truth is science and such discoveries must be utilized to control the masses and all of society in order for wholeness and progress to be realized. Theology looks to the importance of Higher Truths as the guiding principles needed through any and all times of discovery and movement ahead. So, it is most important for science, law, government and all avenues to that better society to be guided by those higher principles.

As is the case with scientific discoveries, so it is with religion that both can be and have been utilized in mistaken ways such as control and power over others. This is narcissism in that one individual deems himself/herself smarter, better, and greater than others and thereby has the know-how and right to control the 'lesser" others. In this idea there needs to and must be a higher source of TRUTH, a principle to move us in a positive, healthful direction. Therefore, we must always test and weigh the results of our interpretations of both science and religion.

So again, the question comes forward as what is the Truth and where does it come from? Both can easily become a tyranny over the mind and soul of each of us and all of us together. In Marxist/Atheism the ultimate game plan is total control over the populace. Belief in TRUTH as perceived and taught in Theology has as its goal the belief that each of us has the ability to think and to perceive the TRUTH. The individual's ability to think for himself is based, and must be based on honest, humble search for the Truth. In our Judeo-Christian belief the Creator God is the source of that TRUTH.

In a previous section of this book titled *A Distant Mirror*, the Old Testament prophet Jeremiah is cited as an example of belief in the freedom given to us by God, or rather the God of Truth who calls all individuals and Societies into the idea and meaning of freedom and, hence, individuals and societies built on the knowledge of God, resulting in a healthy society.

It is not my intention here to give a thorough examination of the purpose and intent of the Bolshevik Revolution in Russia of 1915. However, I believe that a thorough study of that period will give needed information to our current times, and more especially to the American idea of freedom and how to protect that idea.

K. Marx   F. Engels   V. Lenin   *J. Stalin*

In the year 1961, Nikita Khrushchev of the former Soviet Union angrily stood at the podium of the United Nations General Assembly, slammed his shoes on the desk, and pronounced to the world that, "We will bury you from within." I was in high school and watched the entire tirade of the planned take-over of the world and the end of Capitalism. In his statements that notable day, Khrushchev told the world and more particularly the Western democracies that the Marxist Agenda was to take control of the world and all of society.

During this time in our current history, the Cold War was indeed a battle between Communism and Western democracy. Khrushchev seemed to actually believe that Communism was the answer for the advancement of society and needed to happen ASAP. Communism was calling for total control over everything and all people as opposed to Capitalism which called for a free market designed and controlled by free thinking individuals guided by history and laws to protect such freedom" The Democratic Republic, however needed guiding principles of truth based on Theology, belief in a power higher than itself in order to be able to survive and thrive.

In our lifetime, over these last one hundred years and more into the twenty-first century, there has been a continual debate and battle between the ideas of free thought and that of controlled thought by the powers that be. This is the ongoing battle between freedom and tyranny. Over the last several decades and even since the Bolshevik Revolution more than 100 years ago there have been periodic up-risings here in the U.S.A. prompted by the advocates for the over-throw of the American Government along with our belief and protection of our Democratic Republic. These basic beliefs are enshrined in our Constitution and the Bill of Rights.

It is therefore incumbent upon us to study and teach about these opposing forces in order to more clearly understand the threat being imposed and finding the best ways to reason with, debate, learn from or, in the end, combat such a threat. Marxism, Socialism, and Communism are based on total human power by the few, based upon Humanist philosophy. I believe we could begin with an understanding of the Holy Bible and such Truths given to us by God. The honestly given thoughts and debates over these matters must continue so that we can perceive the evil and continue to seek the TRUTH.

For example, from the Holy Bible is the following poignant quote from the ancient Book of Habakkuk 1:1- 4;2:1-4, which calls forth not only belief in God but also God's purpose and intention for the future of mankind:

O Lord, how long shall I cry for help, and you will not listen? Or cry to you "Violence!" and you will not save? Why do you make me see wrongdoing and look at trouble? Destruction and violence are before me; strife and contention arise. So, the law becomes slack, and justice never prevails. The wicked surround the righteous – therefore judgement comes forth perverted and justice never prevails. I will stand at my watch post, and station myself on the rampart; I will keep watch to see what he will say to me, and what he will answer concerning my complaint. The Lord answered me and said: Write the vision; make it plain on tablets, so that a runner may read it. For there is still a vision for the appointed time; it speaks of the end and does not lie. It seems to tarry, wait for it; it will surely come; it will not delay! Look at the proud! Their spirit is not right in them. But the righteous live by their faith. (Habakkuk 1:1-4; 2:1-4).

It is my belief, as expressed throughout this book, that belief and faith in God and the goals of our nation as ideally a God-believing nation are under siege by a philosophy and form of government that rules the populace by a strict agenda of human control. Such control is defined by a few, if not a singular human being guided by a philosophy that does not and will not acknowledge God's existence and presence in our pursuit of Truth. Such a strict and singular control over others have always been defined and experienced as tyranny.

Marxist/Socialist/Communism/ Atheism/ Humanism fall into this category. "Narcissism is a, if not the, primary culprit in that it pits one human being over the other in endless fighting for control. The Bible teaches that false human pride is the ultimate Sin, the ultimate evil, and the Truth that sets us free. (St. Paul).

The Webster's definition of "communism" is "An economic system in which production and goods are commonly owned. Communism is: a) a one-party system of government in which the state plans and controls the economy. "Tyranny" is, "A government in which the ruler has absolute power; the unjust or cruel exercise of power."

G. Washington   J. Adams   T. Jefferson   Abe Lincoln

The universal question throughout history is: "Are we alone or not?" Do we design our own future, or are there higher resources on which we depend? This question leads to the fact that we are not alone in the universe. As humans we at least have other humans upon whom we depend. The new question is, how much do we depend on others? Here-in is the basic micro human society- the family. Without the help of those who love and care for us, we could not survive or thrive. The famous pre-Bolshevik Revolution author as he saw the approach of a new tyranny in his land wrote: "If God does not exist anything is permissible."

In Fundamentals of Marxism/Leninism, a textbook prepared by Soviet scholars in Moscow and being used by members of the Communist Party throughout the world, and even more especially here in America, this statement appears: "Materialists (Atheists) do not expect aid from supernatural forces. Their faith is in man in his ability to transform the world by his own efforts and make it worthy of himself." (Encyclopedia of Quotations #734)

My first question here is, in whom do I trust to make ultimate plans for my life? What other man has such power?" Vladimir Lenin, the founder of Russian Communism said, "We will not accept into our membership anyone unless he is an active, disciplined, working member to one of our organizations." ("Encycl. of Quotations #731) So, I ask, did Lenin think that he was God and superior? Does his philosophy meet the criteria of true freedom? Who or what is Atheist Marxism?

The argument of human society is about the source of love upon which we need to depend on or to survive and ultimately thrive. Our world history from the beginning reveals a multitude of thoughts and processes as to how best to create, maintain, and advance the lot of being human and the organization of human society. At the least we need to know our history in order to go forward and create a better society. All of our presidents and other elected leaders are called to be honest in deliberation, protect our Democratic Republic and continue our sincerest pursuit of the Truth!

The reason I see a need to present some background about the Bolsheviks in modern-day history is to show that there is a marked difference in at least who is in charge here. Is there power that comes from God or are we alone in our own devising of the truth? The Bible tells us that the "sin of false human pride" is the downfall of human nature and healthy society.

An interesting aside on the results of false human pride is a question once asked of the great philosopher Socrates. When asked, "Why it was that Alcibiades, who was a brilliant and able man, and had traveled so much, and seen so much of the world, but was nevertheless an unhappy man?" Socrates replied, "Because wherever he goes Alcibiades takes (only) himself with him." Encyclopedia Of 7700 Quotations, #5578)

Here lies the dilemma: Do we put our trust in an Atheist philosophy which depends solely upon prideful humans who claim and proclaim his or her own power or truth? Or do we humbly seek truth from God who loves us? The Bolsheviks took control of Russia in 1915 via Marxist/Leninist Socialist/ Communism in order to advance and save society from tyranny. In reality it did the opposite and created a new tyrannical order. As said previously, Ludwig Feuerbach promoted this humanist-atheist philosophy and Karl Marx, and Vladimir Lenin forwarded this movement and the Communist state known as the U.S.S.R. was born. The political goal of Communism was for world domination and a controlled society throughout the world.

Today we hear the term "Globalism." Such Globalism is a theory of Communist design and pursuit. This has continued as a primary goal thus far into its history and promotional activities. I must note here that the Christian Movement in history has also devoted itself the promotion of belief in God by all people, at all times and in all places. This is also a global pursuit. This takes us back again to the ancient Israelites who brought the idea of God, Monotheism to light in the world.

Our ancient Hebrew ancestors known as the Israelites have promoted the idea that God the Creator not only exists, but also that He gives to us the love and power to move forward towards His ultimate goal. That ultimate goal is

God's love throughout the universe completed as stated "The Kingdom of God." Of course, such a philosophy or rather theology needs to be continually sought and reviewed for greater understanding and promotion as society and history advances.

The bottom line is the argument between Atheism and Theism. Are we on our own or does our ability to purposefully advance come from that higher power who we refer to as God? The answer is both, according to the Holy Bible. God created us in his image, giving us His power to freely make our own choices but only through the power of love. God's love is that which animates us and forwards us into a secure future. Again, we ask where might we go wrong in the midst of these opposing views, which are supposed to present the best solutions for history's future?

I (and many others) believe that the Bolsheviks use of Atheist philosophy was a flawed and dangerous attempt from the upstart. Marxism placed control into the hands of central human power and control... Communism. The Holy Bible Revolution also places the future into each of our hands through His Power of Love. Individual free will is born from God's gifts of love. That is, the gifts of the Holy Spirit. The gifts of the Holy Spirit teach and show us the avenue to truth as given to us by God our Creator.

I believe that the Bolshevik Revolution has raised havoc in its goal for world domination by distorting and even destroying the Gifts of the Holy Spirit and human free-will into the hands of Atheism and thereby misled human power and control over the populace, and every individual in society. This would be the end of our belief and practice of Freedom. Freedom is the ability to think for oneself, be responsible for such thinking, and to be enabled to promote such freedom to everyone. As some philosophers have said, "Human power corrupts, and total human power totally corrupts."

The primary sin of the human being is false pride wherein the corrupt power of one overtakes that of the other. Such is the battle for control. Such has become the Bolshevik Revolution. The Gifts of Love from God is the essence of the Holy Bible as known and practiced by, with and for, each of us individually. This releases us from the need to be in control, to be in fear. From God comes our wisdom and strength. In going forward with this message, I hope to present, in as few words and as best I can, the problems we face because of that Bolshevik Revolution.

During the decades following the Bolshevik Revolution, the philosophy of Marxist Socialism has been overtly as well as more deceitfully promoted toward the takeover of our American society along with the advancements of Western Civilization itself. In this case, I hope to make it clear that all philosophies in history are not all wrong in perceptions of making society better. So, it is with interpretations with the Holy Bible and our perceptions of truth from God. The need is to work towards the differences between the Good and the Evil no matter from which direction it is garnered. The point here is that truth needs to be recognized and then action taken from that direction. Hence a question such as, what is this philosophy, law, or scholarship based upon? We must divide the chaff from the wheat; the good from the evil.

The following message from J. Edgar Hoover's book *Masters of Deceit* outlines the deceitful promotions and forwarding of Communism/Socialism, in the task of destroying the American Revolution's promotion of the Democratic Republic. The American Revolution promoted and designed a society in which the Biblical idea of free will given by God is the basis of true human freedom. It is the truth practiced by individual believers which needs to be the basic rule of society and hence her rightful and healthful advancement.

"Mass Agitation"

(J. Edgar Hoover's book, *Masters of Deceit*)

The Communist Party's attack is geared to the wide variety of American life. Communism has something to sell to everybody. And, following this principle, it is the function of mass agitation to exploit all the grievances, hopes, aspirations, prejudices, fears, and ideals of all the special groups that make up our society, social, religious, economic, racial, political. Stir them up. Set one against the other. Divide and conquer. That's the way to soften up a democracy.

Here is the advice of a top leader giving instruction on how to spread the Party's influence:

Study your friends. See what they spontaneously talk about. What problems interest them? Is he an unemployed worker, skilled in his craft but without work? A storekeeper? Maybe business isn't so good. A trade-union man or a dairy farmer? What are their problems? A young man just out of school? Looking for a job? A member of a minority group? A young mother worrying about sending her child to kindergarten.

Unless each one of us grasps the meaning of this individual approach to every one of our friends and acquaintances, we are in danger of being ineffective.

Agitation must be carried on in specialized fields: among women, among youth, among veterans, among racial and nationality groups, farmers, trade unions. That's the responsibility of the Party commissions.

Consider youth, a prime target of communist attack. Communists start out with this major premise: American imperialism aims to create a corrupt, completely militarized youth - a 'gagged', 'scared' generation. This theme is expounded by word of mouth, in forums, in literature, in cartoons, hoping to exploit the lofty dreams of youth.

The approach always has two sides: (1) the deceptive line designed for public consumption, and (2) the real Party line designed to advance communism. Consider this deceptive line for youth:

- Increase trade with all countries, including the communist bloc, to provide "hundreds of thousands of new jobs for young people". *
- Outlaw all mass destructive weapons (atomic bomb) Promote universal disarmament and peace.
- Reduce military expenditures and repeal the draft.
- Repeal all repressive legislation" and "restore the Bill of Rights."
- Restore full academic freedom for students and faculties.
- Promote world-wide "youth friendship for peace and democracy," drop all bars to the travel of youth.
- Appropriate more money for schools, community centers, etc.

That is the line designed for public consumption. Sounds acceptable, doesn't it? But the Communists are not genuinely interested in improving the status of American youth.

For window dressing, they always support items desired by most of the people: lower taxes, higher wages, better housing, old-age security, higher farm income. These are thoroughly legitimate interests. To support these aims, and many others, is not to be a communist. The party is simply attempting to exploit such interests for its own selfish aims. They become party talking-points.

Behind this front, as in the call for world-wide youth friendship, more education, academic freedom, and so on, lurks the ulterior motive, the real party line. The attractive come along points are merely bait. Look closely to see how the adoption of these demands, as conceived by the party, would distort their true meanings and aid the communist cause:

"Restore the Bill of Rights" in communist language, means eliminating legal opposition to communism, stopping all prosecution of communists, and granting amnesty to those presently in jail. "Repeal the draft law" and "peace" mean curtailing our national defense effort and allowing Russia to become militarily stronger than the United States. "Increase trade with the Soviet bloc" means selling materials that could be used by the communist nations for armaments. "Restore academic freedom" means to communists that we should permit the official teaching of communist doctrine in all schools and that we should allow communists to infiltrate teaching staffs. If the communists had their way, America would be rendered helpless to protect herself. Incidentally, notice the communist use of the word restore, indicating that freedom is already gone, and the Party stands for its return.

With all this said, I look to my own fellow theologians, politicians, statesmen, philosophers, and all fellow human beings who struggle with truth and seek the betterment of every human soul and there-by society itself. One of my many favorites was Dr. Charles Krauthammer of recent notoriety whose compilation of thoughts on man and society was published soon after his death in 2019. His book is entitled *The Point of it All*. The following two articles point out how mis-in formation and lack of truthfulness lead us into failure. I now miss his regular TV appearances and articles as he did his wise and level best to keep us open minded and on the right track!

From Dr. Charles Krauthammer's book, *The Point of It All*

In the movie Sleeper, Woody Allen wakes up a couple hundred years in the future to discover, among other things, that scientists have found that tobacco is actually good for you.

Well, not quite yet. But how about eggs? After years of egg-phobia, we have learned that eggs might not be bad for you, after all. And that butter is healthier than stick margarine. Every month, it seems, some accepted nutritional fact is overturned.

We have come to expect that diet fashions, though promulgated with scientific authority, change like the seasons. What we do not expect is a change in hormone fashions. Hence the shock this week when a massive study of hormone replacement therapy in postmenopausal women had to be halted three years early because the estrogen-progestin combination appeared to cause an alarming increase in invasive breast cancer, blood clots, strokes and heart attack.

With that, the decades-old medical axiom about the protective powers of hormonal therapy was overturned in a flash. The reverberations were immediate. The company whose pill was being tested, Wyeth Pharmaceutical lost 24% of its value in one day. Millions of women are now frantically calling their doctors for advice on whether to continue.

Most shocking, perhaps, is the simple reminder of how contingent are the received truths of modern medicine. We know how pre-modern medicine got it wrong, from centuries of leeching and bleeding to lobotomies and shock therapies that destroyed the lives of so many psychiatric patients in the mid-20th century. But we think of modern science as infinitely more enlightened and more solid.

Not so. Less than a century ago, the most exalted scientific theory, Newtonian mechanics, was overthrown. Today it's successors, general relativity and quantum mechanics, have yet to be fully reconciled. Thirty years ago, the scientific consensus was that we were headed for global cooling. Today it is global warming. The only thing I feel reasonably sure about is that 30 years from now meteorological science will have delivered yet a new theory, a new threat, a new thrall.

The problem is that even the most sophisticated scientific studies are limited by method, by modeling, by sampling, and by an inevitable margin of error. Hence error and revision.

In medicine, because its solemn pronouncements are so widely propagated and so ingrained in people's lives, these revisions are particularly shocking. Yet common. When I was a kid, everyone got a tonsillectomy. It was a rite of passage. We now know that this was unnecessary surgery, indeed, worse than useless. We were routinely were given antibiotics for earaches. It now turns out that this did not hasten recovery, and in fact may have made us, and the population in general, more resistant to antibiotics.

For decades, breast cancer was treated with radical mastectomy, a disfiguring and deeply invasive surgery. The idea that many patients should instead be treated with lumpectomy was ridiculed for decades. It is now accepted medical practice.

My favorite myth is 98. 6. If there was anything solid in my medical education, it was that mean body temperature was 98. 6 degrees Fahrenheit. Well, in 1992 the Journal of the American Medical Association published a study that actually measured it. It turns out to be 98. 2 degrees. Where did the 98. 6 come from? From the German doctor, Dr. Carl Wunderlich. In 1868. No one had bothered to check it since then.

The myths go on and on. That infectious diseases had been conquered. (Then came HIV). That asthma is a psychological condition. That ulcers are caused by stress or stomach acid. For decades at mid-century, at the height of the psychoanalytic fad, the cream of the New York intelligentsia was sending its healthy children to five-day-a-week psychoanalysis.

So much nonsense. So much damage. Yet science has a hard time with humility. The rage today is regenerative medicine. Stem cells. Cloning. The growing, essentially, of replacement parts. It sounds wonderful, and it may yet turn out to be.

It is well to remember, however, that this is not the first panacea to be peddled. Yesterday, it was fetal tissue transplants for degenerative diseases and angiogenesis inhibitors for the cure of cancer. All of which looked wonderful on paper but have not panned out.

This is not to say that this embryonic research will not pan out. It is only to say that when you hear Senator Dianne Feinstein tell you that the research cloning her bill would promote will do wonders for your suffering Aunt Sarah, hold on to your wallet. She's talking about the speculative benefits from the most speculative of new technologies - at a time, when, until yesterday, science could not tell us the effects of the existing postmenopausal hormone therapy on known medical conditions.

For now, I'll put my money on Woody Allen. Sleeper discovers that hot-fudge sundaes turn out to be good for you, too

From Dr. Charles Krauthammer's book - The Point of it All The Myth of "Settled Science"

I repeat I'm not a global warming believer. I'm not a global warming denier. I've long believed that it cannot be good for humanity to be spewing tons of carbon dioxide into the atmosphere. I also believe that those scientists who pretend to know exactly what this will cause in 20, 30, or 50 years are white coated propagandists.

"The debate is settled", asserted propagandist-in-chief Barack Obama in his latest State of the Union address. "Climate change is a fact." Really? There is nothing more anti-scientific that the very idea that science is settled, static, impervious to challenge. Take a non-climate example. It was long assumed that mammograms help reduce breast cancer deaths. This fact was so settled that Obamacare requires every insurance plan to offer mammograms (for free, no less) or be subject to termination.

Now we learn from a massive, randomized study- 90, 000 women followed for 25 years - that mammograms may have no effect on breast cancer deaths.

Indeed, one out of five of those diagnosed by mammogram receives unnecessary radiation, chemo or surgery.

So much for settledness. And climate is less well understood than breast cancer. If climate science is settled, why do its predictions keep changing? And how is it that the great physicist Freeman Dyson, who did some climate research in the late 1970s, thinks today's climate-change Cassandras are hopelessly mistaken.

They deal with the fluid dynamics of the atmosphere and oceans, argues Dyson, ignoring the effects of biology, i.e. vegetation and topsoil. Further, their predictions rest on models they fall in love with: "You sit in front of a computer screen for 10 years and you start to think of your model as being real." Not surprisingly, these models have been "consistently and spectacularly wrong" in their predictions, write atmospheric scientists Richard McNider and John Christy - and always, amazingly, in the same direction.

Settled? Even Britain's national weather service concedes there's been no change -delicately called a "pause" - in global temperature in 15 years. If even the raw data is recalcitrant, let alone the assumptions and underlying models, how settled is the science?

But even worse than the pretense of settledness is the cynical attribution of any politically convenient natural disaster to climate change, a clever term that allows you to attribute anything -warming and cooling, drought and flood - to man's sinful carbon burning.

Accordingly, Obama ostentatiously visited drought-stricken California last Friday. Surprise! He blamed climate change. Here even the New York Times gagged, pointing out that far from being supported by the evidence, "the most recent computer projections suggest that as the world warms, California should get wetter, not drier, in the winter."

How inconvenient. But we've been here before. Hurricane Sandy was made the poster child for the alleged increased frequency and strength of "extreme weather events" like hurricanes.

Nonsense. Sandy wasn't even a hurricane when it hit the United States. Indeed, in all of 2012, only a single hurricane made US landfall. And 2013 saw the fewest Atlantic hurricanes in 30 years. In fact, in the last half-century, one-third fewer major hurricanes have hit the United States than in the previous half century.

Similarly, tornadoes. Every time one hits, the climate-change commentary begins. Yet last year saw the fewest in a quarter-century. And the last 30 years - of presumed global warming - has seen a 30% decrease in extreme tornado activity (F3 and above) versus the previous 30 years.

None of this is dispositive. It doesn't settle the issue. But that's the point. It mocks the very notion of settled science, which is nothing but a crude attempt to silence critics and delegitimize debate. As does the term "denier" - an echo of Holocaust denial, contemptibly suggesting the malevolent rejection of an established historical truth.

Climate-change proponents have made their cause a matter of fealty and faith. For folks who pretend to be brave carriers of the scientific ethic, there's more than a tinge of religion in their jeremiads. If you whore after other gods, the Bible tells us, "the Lord's wrath will be kindled against you, and he shut up the heaven, that there be no rain, and that the land yield not her fruit" (Deuteronomy 11).

Sounds like California. Except that today there's a new god, the Earth Mother. And a new set of sins - burning coal and driving a fully equipped F-150.

But whoring is whoring, and the gods must be appeased. So, if California burns, you send your high priest (in carbon-belching Air Force One, but never mind) to the bone-dry land to offer up, on behalf of the repentant congregation, a $1 billion burnt offering called a "climate resilience fund."

Ah, settled science in action.

And so, I state here and believe that we need to learn from our discoveries based on the sincere, honest search for the TRUTH. "But by the Grace of God."

From the Encyclopedia Of 7700 Quotation, I derive the following pertinent observations:

We will Bury You from Within: Nikita Khruschev

"In 1917, there were only 40,000 followers of Communism. But in 1925, their leaders met to formulate plans for the conquest of the world. In an address Lenin said: "First we shall take Eastern Europe, then the masses of Asia. After that, we shall surround and undermine the United States which will fall into our hands without a struggle - like an over-ripe fruit!"

At various times, Nikita Khrushchev boasted: 'Whether you like it or not, history is on our side. "We will bury you from within". And on American television in 1957, he declared: "I can prophesy that your grandchildren in America will live under socialism."

"It is estimated that in one year, three million young Communist missionaries are sent from Russia to indoctrinate the youths of the world."

· · ·

President Donald J. Trump

It is my considered opinion, along with millions of other patriots, that President Donald J. Trump came to the forefront of our history at the right time and in the right place. Because of his leadership, the questions of sound economic systems, patriotism, and a world picture of the strength and viability of the American Idea was restored. This needed to happen as we seriously and honestly debate in our search for the truth. He stood alone on the podium with little room to express this belief system. The door has been again opened for the debate to continue. It is so troubling to me and millions of others that this new beginning is thwarted by deaf ears not willing to give credence where credence is due. Yes, Evil is real and always seeks only to thwart the truth in order to gain for itself sole power and control.

· · ·

No Zeal for Membership

Vladimir Lenin declared that, "We will not accept into membership anyone with any reservations whatsoever. We will not accept into our membership anyone unless he is an active, disciplined, working member in any one of our organizations: We need to learn from history, the Holy Bible, and all who seek the truth in honesty, with facts, and with the humility to discern that which is the best for each and all of us together."

It is in this atmosphere today of serious political division that President Donald Trump was elected by the wider margin of the populace. It does seem to me that Mr. Trump came along at the right time and place of our history in that he sought to review our nation's history in order to restore that which made us a good society in the first place. It is up to us now to again interpret our history, and that which has guided us to this time of history. The debate must not be closed but rather opened further for the good of all.

"The Problem of Evil"

The Rt. Rev Geralyn Wolf of the Diocese of Rhode Island in an interview with the Providence Journal discussing issues of the Day 2014), especially those of perceived ethical and moral dilemmas stated that "...the identification of evil can be elusive and easily misstated..." For example, those issues such as abortion, drug use, relationship problems, the right to make choices for oneself, are all to be carefully weighed in the hope of resolution to a higher ground. To simply tag any problem with a universal statement of evil is simply not applicable. We need to draw upon all the resources thus far available from our history to come by the most reasonable answers as we can fathom in our decision-making process. Again, in whom, in what, and how do we find truth and the right answers in the midst.

In the Judeo-Christian Holy Bible, the problem of 'Evil' is initially stated in the story of Adam and Eve in the Book of Genesis. In essence, the story states that, "Human (man) has taken upon himself the knowledge of Good and Evil.". This translates to the primary sin we know as human pride. Human pride translates into a philosophy called Humanism, which eliminates the existence of God the Creator and makes man the sole proprietor of Good and Evil. In essence, without that Higher Power we call God, man becomes the creator of both the Good and the Evil. This leaves the sole interpretation of Evil, and therefore, sin, strictly in human interpretation. The problem arises here of the question of guiding principles as a needed guide for making the right or wrong decisions in all matters of individual and social policy and behavior. Again, where do we go for the TRUTH, the facts, and all other solutions to any of the problems that we face?

In Judeo Christian theology, it is essential to believe in and look to God, not oneself, for the difference between the Good and the Evil. In other words, the primary question is: can we get through life alone, without God, or is God essential in solving the problem of Evil, whatever evil happens to be, if it is at all?

A good illustration is that of the vocation of architecture. The goal and responsibility of an architect is to design that which allows all of us to safely enter, walk into or cross over. We must put our faith and trust in the ability and motivation of the architect. For example, we cross over bridges trusting the architect of that bridge. Following that faith and trust we need also to count on the building, the materials, and even those others who cross over the bridge with us. It takes an enormous amount of faith and trust for such events to happen! Otherwise, the bridge will collapse, or there could be a collision en route, or even worse, a suicide due to other breakdowns in life's journey. The bottom line is that the requirement of all architects, builders, and followers to be responsible in their multitude of vocations in order for us to have faith and trust in their designs and products.

The dictionary definition of "evil" is: "morally wrong, bad, wicked; causing harm, injuries; a cause of suffering or injury." In the first book of the Holy Bible, Genesis, the story of Adam and Eve stated the problem we face on each of our spiritual journeys. It shows that we as humans have the knowledge of both and good and evil, and therefore struggle with such knowledge. The Bible also teaches that we are given 'free will', thereby having choices to make between the good and the evil.

The famous twentieth century theologian Dr. John McQuarry posed a thesis on the problem of good, evil and free will. He states on his thesis "the Risk of Creation" that the principal Architect of Creation is that whom we refer to as God. He refers to the Bible's statement that, "God created us, His children, in His image." This means the free will is the gift of his image, and God wants each of us to choose between the good and the evil. The risk here is that we'll make wrong choices due to evil that can and does take over our ability to make right choices. We call this evil the Devil. Famous court cases forgave and exonerated some who claimed, "The Devil made me do it!" The risk here is: Do I choose the love of God, or do I go against His will for me and choose the Evil?

It is our choice to make, but also, we must face the outcome. According to McQuarry, God our Creator took a risk in making us "in His image" in the HOPE that our given ability to think for ourselves and make both right and wrong choices we would choose His love for us. In other words, God has given to us FREE WILL. It is our choice to make the right or wrong choices. The consequence is life or death. The bridge built by our creator is one that we can safely cross over. This will require our faith and trust in Him.

The Bible teaches us that the primary sin of our nature is pride. Good Pride is:

1. Proper respect for one's own dignity and work
2. Pleasure or satisfaction over something done, achieved, or owned…. a source of pride

The sinful or evil Pride to which the Bible refers as the "sin of Pride" is:

1. Excessive self-esteem
2. Conceit
3. "I don't need or want anything or anyone else unless it serves my purpose"
4. "I don't need God – there is no God but me"

The ultimate thesis on McQuarry's "Risk of Creation" is that "the Love of God will ultimately win this battle. Forgiveness, healing, comprehension, the power of genuine love, long-suffering, and the ongoing list of the gifts of the Holy Spirit will prevail and overcome the Evil of our sinful human pride that we can go it alone. How lonely is that?

"O God, your never-failing Providence sets in order all things, both in heaven and on earth… Put away from us, we entreat you, all hurtful things which can destroy us and give us those things which are profitable for us; through Jesus Christ our Lord who lives and reigns with you and the Holy Spirit, one God, forever and ever."

As a young priest at the age of twenty-eight, I was assigned as Rector of my first parish. In that parish was a very healthy list of current parishioners. After a while, I realized that many on that list were not attending church on a regular basis, and some not at all. I decided that I should visit everyone on that list, beginning with those not regularly participating. A frightening revelation happened at one of these visits. I made a phone call to initiate a personal visit, and that call was well-received and the visit was scheduled immediately.

As I entered, a very young child (around four or five years old) charged at me on his big-wheel bicycle, hit my legs and said, "Get the f*** out of my way!"

His Mom laughed and instructed Harry to go play in the other room so that "Father and I can talk." He obeyed, and our conversation proceeded. I didn't see this family again until several years later in order to arrange the baptism of their next newborn. The frightening revelation to me was that the love of God as practiced through each and all of us is going to be hard work, requiring the best in us to change the evil into the good. What do we teach our children? How do we teach our children? What are the resources available to teach our children? What might be the good and the evil in the mix?

Early in my chosen vocation as a priest in the Church, I was called by a parishioner to Baptize their dog. I explained why we need only to Baptize humans. Animals need not be baptized as they instinctively know how to survive soon after birth. Human Beings need continuous love, care, attention throughout life for both survival and to flourish. Baptism is all about belief in God, the reality of Truth, and the needed formulas to make Holy Baptism the viable route to follow. And so, states one of the prayers that preface the Bible Readings for that day in which such particular readings are given:

"Keep, O Lord, your household, the Church, (The people of God) in your steadfast faith and love, that through your grace we may proclaim your truth with boldness and administer your justice with compassion; for the sake of our Savior, Jesus Christ, who lives and reigns with you and the Holy Spirit, now and forever." The following stories reveal how evil imagination and worse, evil orientation, resulted in the breakdown of a safe society. These stories are from the Encyclopedia of 7700 Illustrations. (#1423, pg. 378)

"Pranksters in Shawnee, Oklahoma, took a stop sign away from a highway intersection and left it a half mile up the road. Chuckling as they drove off, they soon heard the results of their practical joke on the radio. The Rev. Clifford L/ Head, still in his thirties, was driving his station wagon filled with four other members of his family, passed through the intersection that had no stop sign at which point another car zoomed out of the warning-less side road and the fatal crash happened. The Pastor was killed instantly. His wife had both arms and legs broken. She and the children along with the other driver all had to be rushed to the near-by hospital for the much-needed emergency treatment."

"O God, from whom all good proceeds, grant that by your inspiration we may think those things that are right, and that by your merciful guidance may do them; through Jesus Christ our Lord, who lives and reigns with you and the Holy Spirit, one God, forever and ever." I always remember my Mom's words saying, "Try to keep from doing things you will later regret." Mom also said, among many helpful one-liners, "Tell the truth, or else the lie will follow you until the Truth is revealed, and it will hurt." Thank God for his forgiveness and comprehension… and "the truth will set you free" (St. Paul). We enter every Mass, Holy Eucharist, or rather "Prayer of Thanksgiving," with an opening collect toward forgiveness. "Almighty God, to You all hearts are open, all desires known, and from You, no secrets are hid. Cleanse the thoughts of our hearts by the inspiration of your Holy Spirit, that we may perfectly love you, and worthily magnify your Holy Name."

God's strongest saints have come to realize their weaknesses on each of their own spiritual journeys, and thereby have appealed to God for help and strength. One Sunday morning, as famous preacher Charles H. Spurgeon entered the pulpit to try to teach the meaning of the readings that day, a large crowd in front of him, he was overheard saying, "O God, help." Strong preacher as he was, he realized that he was insufficient for so great a task of relating the Gospel with power and conviction. He confessed to his listeners that such a task can only be done by the Grace and help of God with much forgiveness provided in the meantime. (Encyclopedia of 7700 Quotations)

"The Matter of Trust"

As I sit here watching the news, we are being told that Dr. Seuss is being flogged on the Town Common alongside of a new guillotine being constructed for lawless behavior as well as any who are disseminating mis-information to the people. Other such executions of extraordinary patriots are also now happening on the variety of commons across our nation. Stellar characters such as Thomas Jefferson, Theodore Roosevelt. Betsy Ross, Alexander Hamilton, and even Abraham Lincoln and Martin Luther King ae being erased from our history, thoughts, and memories.

Even as I stand here in defense of all the good people of history, I join millions of us who are also being condemned for these beliefs. I am glad that there are many of our obstinate children who continue to read these books for their wholesome enjoyment and education. It is sad to realize that so many other of our children have been brain washed into believing that Dr. Seuss was actually leading our children and all of society in the wrong direction. My question is, was Dr. Seuss intentionally trying to mislead the children and our entire culture? If there is indeed some evil intent inherent in Dr. Seuss, let's talk about it! To be disbanded without learning something good from such an experience is the real culprit and danger to our society. What is this current, so-called, WOKE anti-culture movement trying to do? Who is behind and organizing such a culture crippling, destroying events in our history? What are the intentions, purposes?

There are some who have ventured to tell me that, "The ends justify the means!" Actually, the Marxist/Leninist doctrine calls for regular use of this philosophy. In the case of the Dr. Seuss onslaught, it appears that there are other ulterior motives other than Dr. Seuss to bring about the destruction of our culture. Is this true? If so, what is the truth and how can we best learn from it? Is this actually a case of the ends justify the means? What, or in whom, can we trust as we question the principles that form our thinking and our culture?

I do not believe that any of us can trust anyone who actually believes such an absurdity as using any means to force and control an idea be it good, bad, or indifferent. All matters of TRUST must, must be of the TRUTH and must begin with each of us and from this standpoint we can learn and grow. In whom can we trust and what is the TRUTH? The following story represents the flaws of and need for trust in order for individuals and societies to be able to move forward in a positive, healthy direction. It states that individuals and society are inevitably flawed without TRUST and TRUTH as the necessary key to survival. The story is entitled: "Place No Confidence in Man."

The King of Italy and the King of Bohemia promised the Christian Reformer, during those uncertain and turbulent years of the Protestant Reformation in the1600s, John Huss's safe transport and safe custody. This was during "the age of enlightenment" along with the invention of the printing press and the upsurge of the education of the populace. Fr. Martin Luther was seeking respect from his powerful, controlling Church in Rome and the kings were gaining more and more power over their separating States. The many questions again were rising as to who was "in control" and who could be trusted. John Huss was an individual in the middle of this debate and seeking the "freedom" to express his beliefs. It was during this time that the Magna Carta in England was born and the "rights of man" formulated. To say the least, the questions of TRUST, TRUTH, and the idea of individual freedom was brought to the forefront of history. So back to Mr. John Huss and his conversation with the Kings of Italy and Bohemia. They both promised to him a safe journey and protection. They broke their promises, however, and Huss was martyred. The elected British parliamentarian, Thomas Wentworth, carried a document signed by King Charles I of England which read "Upon the word of a King you shall not suffer in life, honor, or fortune." Shortly afterwards, however, Wentworth's death warrant was signed by the same monarch. Wentworth's last words in life during his execution were, "Put not your trust in Princes". The bottom line to this account in the struggles of history and education is: "Put not you trust in man without your primary trust being in and this is our only route to Freedom. (Paraphrased from The Encyclopedia of 7700 Quotations)

- "When in doubt, tell the truth." Mark Twain
- "The trouble with stretching the truth is that it's apt to snap back." Saturday Evening Post
- "Half the fact is a whole falsehood." Old Proverb
- "Every man has a right to his opinion but no man has a right to be wrong in his facts." B. M. Baruch
- "Jumping at conclusions is not half a good exercise as digging for facts." Lutheran Digest
- "Time is precious but truth is more precious than time." Benjamin Disraeli
- "Facts do not cease to exist because they are ignored." Aldous Huxley
- "It is easier to believe a lie that one has heard a thousand times than to believe a fact that no one has heard before." Grit
- "When Aristotle, who was a Grecian philosopher, and the tutor of Alexander the Great, was once asked what a man could gain by uttering falsehoods, he replied, 'Not to be credited when he shall tell the truth.'"

(Above quotes from The Encyclopedia of 7700 Quotations)

In the Book of the Prophet Jeremiah we are reminded that, "We cannot put our trust in the children of man. They bend their tongues like bows to shoot their arrows of un-truth. They care nothing for right and go from bad to worse; they care nothing for me, says the Lord." *(Jeremiah 9:4ff)* In a study of the Bible there are hundreds of references to TRUST and the critical importance of trust in all of our deliberations. So, the question is now raised again, does the end justify the means? Can one trust any pronouncement which is not trustworthy and based on the honest facts, truth, and pure goals for the good of all involved?

Do the ends justify the means? Only if the means are based upon the TRUTH. Otherwise, No! Throughout history, the philosophical idea that "the end justifies the means" has rampaged entire societies and individuals alike. All societies ruled by tyrannical power - ruled by one person or a small group of those who claim to have all the answers to how best to govern - were always doomed to failure. Such an ideology that claims power over other ideas presented are destined to eliminate such a debate if it does not fully agree with that ideology. There is no debate or push back or reasonable thought allowed to question the rightness or wrongness of that controlling ideology. It has also been said in the challenge of any singular authority throughout history that, "Power corrupts and absolute power totally corrupts."

As one person or group takes upon himself / itself the right to rule or control all others according to that one idea there is no room left for learning, growth, and moving forward in the pursuit of TRUTH. Some actually believed that they knew better than anyone else and thereby had the 'divine right' to lead everyone else either to the perfect society or to have absolute control for their own self-centered fulfillment.

A contemporary, clear example of such a society and dictator is North Korea. This oligarchy was formed by one individual, the grandfather of the current dictator, who originally thought that Communism would bring about a totally controlled good society for the sake of all peoples. A psychological and spiritual history of this mis-led personality would reveal the evils of narcissism and the ultimate destruction of all peoples and societies. The definition of narcissism is: "excessive self- adoration and need to be in control, to perpetuate the same."

The goal of the Democratic Society is to allow free thought to flourish and thereby allow questions, learning and hopefully growth for the good of all. Such dictators in our current history have utilized such ideologies as Marxism, i.e. "Communist Ideology" as their tool for total control over the people over whom they are supposed to create a better society. History now shows how dangerous this can be and actually has been in all too many governments across the globe. The people under their charge have little, if any, say in the governance of themselves. They must do whatever they are told and simply follow orders whether it is good for them or not.

The fact is that the powers that be are just human beings who have taken upon themselves the right and privilege to satisfy their own perceived whims and desires. For them, in this case: The end justifies the means good, bad, and indifferent. This can lead only to self-destruction and if taken further, annihilation of both themselves and those of whom they are in control. No TRUST or TRUTH can exist in such an ideology and system of that ideology.

It was our own good President Abraham Lincoln who said that, "No man is good enough to govern another without the other's consent." President Lincoln also said that, "Those who deny freedom to others deserve it not for themselves and under a just God cannot long retain it." President Franklin D. Roosevelt said likewise that, "There never has been, there isn't now, and there never will be, any race of people on earth fit to serve as masters over their fellow man." A pertinent Epigram in the Encyclopedia of 7700 Quotations goes further to say that, "Liberty is always unfinished business." "If a nation values anything more than 'freedom' it will lose its freedom; and the irony of it is that if it is comfort or money that it values more, it will lose that too." This is all a matter of TRUST. The primary question again comes to the fore, in whom do we trust? The basic principle of any ideology or philosophy must be one's search for and then residence in the TRUTH.

One of the key problems with narcissism is its self-perpetuation guided by the belief that all truth is centered on this one individual and all must follow his/her truth as if he or she knew better than anyone else. Here is where we must call upon the Higher Principles as we together know them best in order to prevent such narcissism to take control of whatever questions we are trying to answer. Those principles are Truth and Trust. If somehow a divine entity is called upon for answers to these basic questions, that entity must be of the TRUTH and trusted for the answers. The answers and then the application of that "truth" needs to be trustworthy and hence trusted. Our God-centered belief is that TRUTH does exist and that it not only can be trusted but must be trusted. That truth perceived and given by trustworthy resources such as the Holy Bible will determine our resulting behavior. The resulting behavior of this belief is also the end justifies the means, but those means are determined by the TRUTH. The means are of and about the truth.

Another prime historical example of mis-use of the ends justifying the means was that of Adolf Hitler and his followers utilizing the most evil and destructive ideas for the sake of abusive power and control. The battle against such evil is always before us and all we have is the TRUTH and trust in that truth to combat it. For the world in which we live the ugly head of evil pervades and we must utilize the truth we are given by God and not relent or give in to its destructive power. Trust in each other is essential and that trust must have the TRUTH as guide for the advancement of all.

The question, of course, comes to the front again. What is the truth? From whence does it come and to whom is it given? To whom or to what do we trust and owe our allegiance? Joseph R Sizoo, a one-time pastor of the New York Avenue Presbyterian Church in Washington which Abraham Lincoln often attended, says he will never forget the day he held in his hands, for the first time, the Bible from which Lincoln's mother had read to him as a child. She had taught him to commit to memory many of its passages. It was the only possession Lincoln carried from Pigeon Creek to the Sangamon River. And book in my hand, I wondered where it would fall open. It opened to a page which was thumb-marked and which Lincoln must have read many times. It was the thirty-seventh Psalm, "Fret not thyself of evildoers…rest in the Lord, and wait patiently for him." *(Psalm 37:1, 7)*

(From #6923 of Encyclopedia of 7700 Quotations)

Abraham Lincoln was raised in a rural, poor environment, and his mother taught him the lessons of the Bible and to trust in the Lord. His belief in God and trust in the teachings given to him through the Bible were his guide and stay throughout his life as a youth and through his life as President of the United States. He was and is one of the most honest and trusted societal leaders of history. He was the epitome of a trusted teacher and leader based on his understanding of the truth and total need for humility, on his knees before the God of love.

One of my favorite periodicals is known as the *Anglican Digest*. It is encouraging to me that so many others of the Faith read this periodical dedicated to the search for the TRUTH. A pertinent article was written by The Right Revd. Michael Marshall, Honorary Bishop in the Diocese of London along with several other articles about the teaching and meaning of Lent, Holy Week, and Easter. These articles are found in the *Anglican Digest,* February 2021.

"The New Way of Life"
The Anglican Digest

As the seasons of the year travel from the death of winter to the newly transformed life of spring, so the Church of God, (at least in the northern hemisphere), invites the faithful to "walk the talk" of another journey of spring like transformation, from the death of the old to the transformed, new, abundant, and eternal life revealed once-and-for-all in time and space at Easter, in the person of the Risen Christ. Christians believe that the historical events of the three days of Holy Week (the Triduum) encapsulated what we term the "Paschal Mystery", and revealed once upon a time, the great cosmic mystery of all life, "hidden since before the foundation of the world," of what is true all the time, and until the end of time.

At this particular point in time, our world has undergone a "winter" of darkness and hardship, when many "hearts are failing for what is coming on the earth," and when many have been tempted to despair of a springtime of renewal and good news, any time soon. "The only trouble with the good news," says Frederick Buechner, "is that you generally have to find it all among the bad news," of which you could well say, there has been an abundance this past year, when, as the psalmist says, "There are many who are saying, who will show us any good?"

The annual liturgical pilgrimage, when Christians all over the world come together to walk with Christ the inner journey of the heart in Holy Week, could be especially poignant and relevant this year, as we seek to make sense of so much suffering which constantly threatens to be the dominating narrative of the human story. For, as Christians, we have another story to tell; some very different Good News to proclaim! It's the mega, over-arching story of an incarnate God, who, far from being above it all, is in fact our Emmanuel, - "God is with us," right here and now in the midst of it all and the mystery of it all.

Once and for all, Christ has been through it all, from heaven to earth and hell and back again, constantly inviting His aspiring disciples to follow Him on the Way to where, in the end, He alone makes sense of it all. With the bifocal lenses of the Paschal Mystery, we can begin to see what God can do and continues to do with suffering and death, and all our personal "Good Fridays" as in that bold and seemingly perverse claim of Julian of Norwich, "Even in the midst of personal suffering and the contemporary pandemic plague of her day, she could still boldly proclaim: "All will be well, all manner of things will be well."

Such a claim then as now, without the contradictory Evidence of the Paschal Mystery, would be insensitive and even absurd. But the Christian vision is not so much a question of what we see, but rather of how we see pain and suffering, death, and disaster. We need the bifocal lens of faith which sees the end in the means, the finished product of the new creation, even now, in the unfolding process, for only so we can ever hope in a painful world, where death, disaster, and despair masquerade as having the last word.

Yet, the first of those three days, paradoxically never referred to as "black Friday" but as "Good Friday," is annually celebrated not as the last word, but rather as the first word of a whole new narrative. For, with the benefit of hindsight, that momentous Friday is paradoxically perceived not as a tomb of death, but rather as the womb of that new, enriched, and abundant life which the Risen Christ longs to share with us, right here and now in the contemporary "winters" of our discontent. It's as though the bare and stricken branches of Calvary's Tree exemplify the hidden mystery of all trees and all life, whereby despair gives way to hope, darkness to light, the old giving place to the new by the One who faithfully promises to "make all things new."

However, we can only adopt this new way of life with any conviction if we can be, as those first Christians were - "witness of these things," following in the Way of Him who is the Way. In His way, we also, in our day, can triumph over suffering by seeing everything, light and darkness, sorrow and joy, death and new life, everything as that seamless tapestry, hand-woven by God with a pattern and purpose not yet fully disclosed from our present, limited perspective.

The Gospel of new life through death which Christ proclaimed and travelled was neither idealistic, nor pessimistic, but totally realistic: it recalls us to a spiritual re-awakening as men and women of the resurrection with "Alleluia as our song," and yet all the while also knowing, as Christ himself testified, that, "In the world you will have tribulation, but be of good cheer for I have overcome the world, and, strengthened by his Risen life and walking in His Way, SO CAN WE!"

It is important and interesting to note here that Saint Martin's Parish in Houston, Texas is one of the Partner Parishes in support of the Anglican Digest. This parish is the largest Episcopal parish church in the United States, with 9,600 members. It began in 1952 under the leadership of the Revd. Bagby. This parish now holds six celebrations of the Holy Eucharist every Sunday, in several different formats for the older, the younger, and families in general. They have fourteen Clergy and over 200 full and part time staff members. Deeply committed to outreach and mission, they commit 25% of the annual budget to service initiatives beyond their doors. How heartening and encouraging this is!

The following epigram well illustrates the meaning of 'humility' as known and practiced by many great leaders such as Abraham Lincoln.

- True humility is not to think low of oneself, but to think rightly, truthfully of oneself.
- A Christian minister once said, "I was never of any use until I found out that God did not intend me to be a great man."
- It is possible to be too big for God to use you, but never too small for God to use you.
- "God had an only Son, and He was a missionary and physician. A poor, poor imitation of Him I am, or wish to be." Livingston
- "A hundred times a day, I remind myself that my inner and outer life depend on the labors of others, living and dead, and that I must exert myself in order to give in the same measure as I have received and am receiving." A. Einstein
- "There is no king who has not had a slave among his ancestors, and no slave who has not had a King among his." Helen Keller
- Second Street is the first street in America. According to R. L. Polk and Co., publishers of city directories, Second Street is the most common street name in this country. Park Street is in Second Place. Third Street is third. Fourth Street is fourth. Fifth Street is fifth. Main is sixth. First Street – it is seventh! (#2315 Epigram Encyclopedia of 7700 Illustrations)
- Without humility before both God and man, there is no greatness.

Every time I've visited Washington D.C., I've gone first to Ford's Theater where our beloved Abe Lincoln was assassinated, then across to the house where he died. The blood stain on the pillow where his head found comfort was prominent. One cannot help but be brought to tears for the genuine soul of this great man. A 5th grade school trip brought me there for the first time." All of our children need to see such places of humble and biblically centered beginnings; read books of the honest, trustworthy people of history; and learn from whence truth emanates and look to the one's we can trust to guide us forward.

Psalm 118:9 states with clarity the need to trust in God: "It is better to trust the Lord than to put confidence in men. It is better to take refuge in Him than in the mightiest king." Saint Paul also admonished us with the following from his Letter to the early Christians at Corinth:

"The message about the cross is foolishness to those who are perishing, but to those who are being saved it is the power of God. For it is written, "I will destroy the wisdom of the wise, and the discernment of the discerning I will thwart." Where is the one who is wise? Where is the scribe? Where is the debater of this age? Has not God made foolish the wisdom of the world? For since, in the wisdom of God, the world did not know God through wisdom, God decided, through the foolishness of our proclamation, to save those who believe. (Christ is the wisdom of God, bearing the cross for us all). For God's foolishness is wiser than human wisdom, and God's weakness is stronger than human strength." (the Webster's Collegiate Dictionary defines TRUTH, and TRUST as follows:

TRUTH - 1. In accordance with knowledge, fact, or actuality; 2. The real state of affairs; 3. The state of being truthful, honesty.

TRUST - 1. Firm reliance on the honesty, dependability, strength, or character of a person or thing; 2. One in which faith or confidence is placed; 3. Something given into one's care for the benefit or interest of another; 4. The state or obligation given to anyone for the truth and good of all concerned.

Waiting in the Dentist's office on September twentieth, 2017, I picked up the local town paper known as the Uxbridge Times. The date here is important in that we struggle today as a nation with trends that work at confusing the populace and bringing our country down into ruin. The trend is obviously meant to formulate radical shifts on thoughts and ideas of the meaning of truth and control of the society. The so-called "Left-Wing Movement" is rampant and seeks only to change the focus of society into a Marxist Socialist State. In writing these memoirs and realizing the current trends I turned to the Editorial Page of the Times and there I read, "Dear Editor: "History tells us that democracy holds the seeds of its own destruction. The simplest example is apathy. Uxbridge today provides us with a perfect example. It is evident in the lack of voters willing to fill vacancies on many of the town's multi-member bodies. (Selectman James F. Dwyer).

The article goes on to show serious lack of will power and concern for the common good in that town. It also points out the lack of teaching on Civic Responsibility and teaching of the basic virtues of our society. I can also identify here with low attendance and participation in worship in the Northeast. Having traveled and lived in both the South and the Midwest, I found the churches full and vibrant. What's wrong? What happened here? Apathy and loss of a clearer understanding of who we are and how we behave is part of the problem!

A telling and favorite bumper sticker reads, "If you think education is difficult, try ignorance!" We have everything to learn from our history and it is essential for moving forward. Having studied the history of Western Civilization and Philosophy, I believe I've been given a solid base for an educated World View. Coupled with a Masters Degree in theology, my basic education allowed me to seek ordination to the Priesthood and thereby a way to teach and act according to the education afforded to me. Living in our free country and understanding the principles and construct of my nation allowed me to move forward in this vocation and pursuit.

Being born at the end of WWII gave me a background in patriotism and the struggles of reconstructing a world torn apart by that war and the goals of the political sides which contrived to fight for prominence. The two major sides now fighting for prominence and varying ideas for how to reconstruct a better world were the ideas of Democratic Republic and that of its opposing view, communism. The battle of ideas continues. The battle between total control of the populace known as the Communist Regimes and the free expression of an educated populace known as a Democratic Republic became the two opposing forces. The former Soviet Union controlled by the communist party in the east led by Russia was battling with the Democratic Republic of the United States of America and the west. This battle continues to this day.

I'll never forget Premiere Nikita Khruschev of the Soviet Union banging his shoes at the United Nations podium saying, in a fierce angry voice, "We'll bury you from within!" In other words, we'll change the minds of your populace into the ideas of the Socialist Republic and hence Communism. This has been happening and today is becoming more and more evident as the ideas of Marxism/Leninism gradually have crept into our thinking and actions. We as a people need to learn and know the difference between these two ideas promising to make the best society for all of the people. Ignorance and apathy are the evils which can make this happen.

The major difference between the idea which informs Marxism and the idea which forms Democracy is that treasure we know as Freedom. Freedom according to the West means that each individual has a destiny to think and act for himself/herself, whereas Marxism states that individuals do not have the capacity to think and thereby need strict controls. Both ideas need direction and control. In other words, the best route is to think rightly. Here is where we divide. In the West, belief in God and the guidance of the Holy Spirit and the history of the Holy Bible are the principles from which the Truth emanates.

In Marxism, the State and its rulers are the arbiters of that Truth and somehow know what is best for each individual and the collective whole body. Belief in the Holy Spirit and the existence of a loving God are not the source of all truth. Here is where the tyranny of the human mind being the source of the Truth rather than the human mind being guided by a Higher Power. In our society we call that Higher Power God. In the Marxist society there is no higher power other than the leader of the State.

In 1990, there were two televised interviews in the United States and on what then became the former Soviet Union. Under the leadership of Premier Nicolai Gorbachev, Russia was experimenting with the idea of Democratic Republicanism. The collapse of Soviet Russian Communism followed the Chernobyl nuclear power plant catastrophe. It also followed an intense but friendly informational conversation between President Ronald Reagan and Premiere Gorbachev in Reykjavich, Iceland. The gift to Mr. Gorbachev at the conclusion of this historic conversation was, "The Memoirs and Works of Thomas Jefferson."

Soon after this meeting of minds between Reagan and Gorbachev, an historic détente was established between the two opposing superpowers. In this early détente period, a specially aired program was developed for the public viewing of each nation. The respective programs were interviews by a Russian with American teenagers and the other by an American with Russian teenagers. The Russian students were selected from their elite teenagers educated by State teachers. The American teenagers were selected from those of our public school system. It just so happened that I luckily turned on my television at lunch time at the beginning of the Russian interview of Soviets hear in the U.S.!

The following is a brief of the interview led by Phil Donahue:

Mr. Donahue asked several key questions to the chosen teenagers after they had spent several months with American families. The questions were about their experiences here in the U. S. One of the key questions was about "belief in God". Many hands were raised. A fifteen-year-old girl obviously anxious to answer this question was called upon. Here is my brief recall of her answer.

"I thoroughly enjoyed my visit to America. I lived with a gracious and loving family, and they shared as much as they could of their day to day routine lives. They described themselves as a typical middle- class family in the mainstream of America. They attended worship of God. Took part in civic organizations; worked at their jobs and employment; and attended the public schools in their neighborhood." (Note here that she elaborated on her experiences in this venue.)

"To answer your question about belief in God, I'm anxious to share this experience now." (Just to note here that this fifteen-year-old Soviet child spoke fluent English). She went on: "In my country we do not give credence to any belief in any God such as you do here in America. The state is our higher authority. But I discovered on my visit here a wonderful sense of a stirring within myself from time to time. We went to their place of worship and the principle leader spoke about God and words from your Bible. You Americans are very fortunate to have such a belief system. The leader, called a Minister, uncannily touched upon that stirring within myself."

According to the belief, such a stirring comes from God. We also attended an international civic organization known as The Rotarians. It was fascinating to me that at the start of each meeting they called upon God to guide them in their thoughts, deliberations, and decision-making process. It was so wonderful to learn that the purpose of this group was primarily for relief to those in serious need around the world. They have even sent resources to Russia in times of serious need such as weather, medical or any such disasters. The latest disaster was the Chernobyl meltdown. I am sincerely grateful to Americans and to America for your genuine love and concern for everyone. This seems to come from the "stirring inside each of you."

There is a prayer among many that I want to briefly reflect on. Such prayers are pre-ambles to the weekly lectionary of Bible verses followed by most churches on particular Sundays of the church calendar. "Grant to us, Lord, we pray, the spirit to think and do always those things that are right, that we, who cannot exist without you, may by you be enabled to live according to your will; through Jesus Christ our Lord, who lives and reigns with you and the Holy Spirit, one God, forever and ever. Amen." (Prayer 14 of the Common Lectionary)

The following brief introduction is borrowed here from the daily meditation booklet called "Forward Day by Day." In this of many such resources on Christian thought, life, and actions is designed to help us to understand, appreciate, and live by Biblical teaching.

"Feast of Saint Boniface"

Saturday, June 8, 2005

Luke 18:15-30

"Good teacher, what must I do to inherit eternal life?"

I wonder what the young ruler was really asking Jesus. Did he truly want to know what he personally needed to do to gain eternal life, or did he want Jesus, upon learning all he had accomplished with regard to keeping the Torah, to simply say, "well done, thou good and faithful servant"? Did he want answers, or affirmation? Likewise, Mayor Ed Koch, the former Mayor of New York City, used to inquire of ordinary citizens, "How am I doing?" I wonder how he responded when someone replied, "Lousy!" or "So-so." Knowing a little about the character of Mayor Koch, I think he would have responded with a thank you and then say I'll try my best to do better. God help me! Later, I found his answer to the negative comment hurled at him. It goes this way:

"I don't know about you but I generally like to think that I'm doing a pretty good job of being a believer in the Lord and following His Spirit, but if the truth is told, I know there is a lot of room for improvement."

Jesus's answer to the young ruler is the universal answer to the question of ultimate harmony with God. "Get rid of whatever you love or worship more than God in your life." In the young ruler's case, it was many. What is it in yours?

Saint Paul said in his letter to the new church in Corinth as he was admonishing them to find their faith in God that, "He who sows sparingly will reap sparingly and he who sows abundantly will reap abundantly." This all emanates from the love of God within us. The opening prayer to the readings of the third Sunday in Lent asks, "Almighty God, who sees that we have no power within ourselves to help ourselves: Keep us both outwardly in our bodies and inwardly in our souls, that We may be defended from all adversities which may happen to the body, and from all evil thoughts which may assault and hurt the soul through Jesus Christ our Lord, who lives and reigns with you and the Holy Spirit, one God, forever and ever." (Book of Common Prayer, page 218)

In a recent pastoral interview, the young person (age thirty-one) who came to me with internal fears and resulting troubles, sought answers about belief in God, direction, and healing. She had been raised more or less in the faith, but in time, lapsed from the teaching. Married by a Justice of the Peace to a non-believer, she still looked to the knowledge and comfort of her faith. She wanted to somehow return and learn more of that which she now found missing within herself and the world around her.

She found some answers and comfort in our brief conversation but mostly learned that God would never reject her. She thought that her many perceived failures and hurts were punishment and that and that God would reject her. Not so! It is clear that we bring on our own punishment and hurts. However, during such times of separation from God and from ourselves with our faith and God's eternal love for us we can return and be whole again. He continually calls us back into syncopation with His un-dying love for us. From this interview my young friend not only felt better but went out desiring for a return to the love of God for her and her ongoing well-being. With this in mind I recall my dear friend and colleague saying to a penitent, "Remember that this a whole lot less expensive than a psychiatrist!"

In *the Common Lectionary Proper 21* is the opening "Prayer to the Readings" for October first which reads: "Oh Lord, you declare your almighty power chiefly in showing mercy and pity. Grant us the fullness of your grace, that we, in seeking your promises, may become partakers of your heavenly treasure; through Jesus Christ our Lord, who lives and reigns with you and the Holy Spirit, One God, for ever and ever, Amen."

Another friend following a pastoral encounter of penitence said that he learned again learned again that God is all loving and all forgiving… that He, above all others and all things knows how we feel. In Jesus, He has shown us in person empathy, compassion and all we need to return and move forward. The Church had become an invitation to the mysteries of love rather than an empty practice of rituals. God's intent and the Church's teaching is simply to guide us into the Peace which surpasses all human understanding.

"Personal Journeys"
An Incredible Interview

Working in my office at Trinity and St. John's parishes of Whitinsville and Millville Massachusetts, a phone call came through from a local high school and confirmation student seeking an audience with this local clergyman from a different religious denomination from his own. He sought other opinions as his way of completing his Confirmation requirements in his Roman Catholic background. My first meeting with Michael Wilkes took place on the beautiful spring day of April 17, 2019. This very bright, educated, and searching for truth young man was visiting area clergy and politicians with a battery of questions about religion and politics. I was enthralled and hoped for further conversation with Michael.

Michael explained that his inquiry was due to his current confirmation class in a local Roman Catholic church. I asked him if this inquiry was assigned to him. He said, "No!" and that his goal was "to learn about 'other religions' and their interpretations of church and theology." This began a new friendship for me and further fulfillment of my own desire for just this kind of conversation.

The following is Michael's own account of his spiritual journey, along with several of his articles printed in a local newspaper. I am hopefully encouraged by seeing searches for Truth in the up-coming generations as I see coming from Michael and recalling my own searching way back when I was his age.

Michael

Hello, my name is Michael Wilkes. I'm 16 and live in Whitinsville, Massachusetts. I was never a 'normal' kid by any standards. I have had an interest in politics since I was ten, I am trying to learn three languages, and I've always had a huge interest in theology.

I was born, raised, and baptized Catholic. While my parents brought us to church and CCD classes, they were never the real type of religious parents. My grandfather, on the other hand, was and is very religious. He is a Newborn Christian. One day I asked him for a Bible and he got it for me.

I was in seventh grade when I first started to study religion. Since I've been reading the Bible, there were many things the Church did that didn't make sense to me. For example, praying to Mary when in the Ten Commandments we are told not to have any graven images. I started to mark up my Bible with all these questions.

To get some answers about six months ago, I decided to talk to some religious leaders and hence my faith journey began. I talked to my Priest, Deacon and Bishop. I also talked to a Messianic Jewish Rabbi, Orthodox Rabbi, Newborn Pastor, Newborn teacher, and an Episcopalian priest. That priest just happened to be Fr. Warren.

Some leaders were not happy I was asking questions while others encouraged it. Fr. Warren and I have met a few times and talked many times over the phone. He has not only pushed my faith journey forward but inspired me to ask more questions. I have found the more I question, the deeper my faith becomes.

One of the reasons I continue to ask Fr. Warren questions is because he explains them in a logical way that makes complete and total sense. Out of asking these questions, a true friendship has sprung up. While I am certain I am leaving my Catholic faith and I don't know where I will be going, I do know because of people like Fr. Warren, I will always be welcome in their church.

· · ·

Letters to the Editor: Time for Tracy!
November 2018

Dear Editor,

Almost anyone who knows me also knows how politically active I've been this election season, especially for a fifteen year old. I've worked on 9 different campaigns. Many people ask me why I've been so politically involved and I give them the same answer, Tracy Lovvorn.

One night over the summer, I tuned into my favorite local show, The Gary Rosenberg Show. That week Mr. Rosenberg had Tracy on as a guest. After listening to her for an hour, I could clearly see she was the right candidate to be our Congresswoman. A few days later, I joined the Tracy Lovvorn for Congress Campaign. As I said earlier, Tracy is the right candidate for the job and I'm hopeful after reading this you will feel the same.

Before we dive into Tracy's policies let's take a look at our current Congressman, Jim McGovern. Congressman McGovern has been in office for 22 years! Since 2010 he's run unopposed. In 20 years, he has only passed 8 bills! 6 out of the 8 were renaming a government building. Congressman McGovern supports higher taxes, sanctuary cities, and is a progressive socialist. He also votes with Nancy Pelosi 95% of the time.

Meanwhile, our district is the most conservative district in all of Massachusetts. It's clearly time for a change, and Tracy is the change we need! While Congressman McGovern has voted to increase taxes on small businesses, Tracy owns her own small business in Grafton, which helps improve the local economy. Along with being a proud business owner, she is also a proud wife, mother, health care provider, operations manager, and has even uncovered fraud. In 2009, Tracy stood up to corruption and big business fighting corporate Medicare fraud, waste, and patient abuse. Tracy's actions resulted in millions of dollars to go back into the Medicare Trust Fund. Her courageous actions have helped change the way rehab services are billed in the skilled nursing environment, which is a more fair system to the elderly.

Tracy is also a huge supporter of legal immigration. She feels that at this time in our nation's history, it's very easy to come into this country illegally, but not legally and that is what she wants to change. Tracy believes to combat this epidemic we need to reform our visa system, since 40% of all illegals are visa overstays. She also feels we should strengthen our border with walls, fences and guards to protect our citizens. She has said she wants to work with the current administration in order to solve this problem.

Tracy has said her number one priority is to bring more attention to the health and safety of the youth. Today in America kids are killing themselves, drinking, doing drugs, harming others, along with becoming obese. She once said, "As a mother and as a healthcare professional, I bring to the table heartfelt concern and the ability to work toward defining and addressing root causes which can ultimately result in the development of solutions."

Another position on Tracy's agenda is term limits. She supports term limits for a few reasons. Number one, they help prevent corruption in Washington, so actual work can be achieved. Number two, they help prevent people from making a career out of politics. Finally, they allow new ideas to be injected into our government. Tracy has said she would like to expand the congressional term to three years and allow a candidate to serve two terms.

Jim McGovern has been in office for 22 years and has nothing to show for it. What is there left for him to do? To tell you the truth, like so many other people in the 2nd Congressional District, I have no idea. As Dr. Joseph Warren, President of the Massachusetts Congress once said, "On you depend the fortunes of America. You are to decide the important questions upon which rests the happiness and the liberty of millions yet unborn. Act worthy of yourselves. " I am a strong believer that we the Americans of today are ready to act worthy of ourselves, to take back our government. How do we start, you ask? By selecting the right people who represent us, and I like so many others believe that candidate to be Tracy Lovvorn.

-Mike J. Wilkes, Northbridge
President of the Class of 2021
Working on the Tracy Lovvorn for Congress Campaign
Working on the Ryan Fattman for State Senate Campaign
Working on the Baker Polito Campaign
Working on the Geoff Diehl for Senate Campaign
Working on the Mike Soter for State Rep Campaign
Volunteer at Mass Victory

. . .

Letter to the Editor: Flat and Fair

Dear Editor,

April 15th, Tax Day... I challenge you to find me one person who likes paying taxes. Politicians, like Bernie Sanders, say we should pay more in taxes than we currently pay. Our Founding Fathers never envisioned us paying taxes. Income tax only became a law due to our 16th amendment that was ratified in 1913.

Today in America we talk about how the wealthy "should pay more" or "don't pay their fair share" when as a matter of fact, this couldn't be more incorrect. When we talk about the top 1% of Americans we expect them to be making $50,000,000. The top 1% of Americans make $400,000+. According to census data from 2015, the upper middle class of Americans (the top 10% or above) make between $100,000 - $350,000 per year. A study done by CNN shows people that earn $133,000 a year pay over 80% of all Federal Income tax. This is insane! All people talk about is taxing the top 10% when the top 10% aren't all millionaires. So what do we do to solve this travesty? Believe it or not, there is a fair and simple solution, it's called a Flat Tax.

What is a Flat Tax, you ask? It means that everyone pays the same percentage of money in taxes. For our purposes, we'll be following Senator Rand Paul's tax plan at 14.5% (the bare minimum our government needs to survive). It doesn't matter if you make $50,000, $500,000, or $50,000,000, you pay 14.5%. This system is a more fair way to tax because the wealthy still pay more in taxes but aren't being overtaxed. With a Flat Tax, we could abolish Income, Payroll, Corporate, Luxury, Capital Gains, and Property tax. Now I know what you're thinking, "If we abolish all these taxes, how will the government get money?" According to studies done by the Tax Foundation, if we abolished Income Tax, Payroll Tax, and ended Corporate welfare and replaced it with a Flat Tax of 14.5% we would create about 2,000,000 jobs! This would put more money into our private sector allowing the economy to grow.

As I mentioned, this would also abolish Corporate welfare. Multi-billion-dollar companies can't get out paying anything in taxes. So, no matter how many lawyers and accountants a company may hire, they won't get out of paying the 14.5% Flat Tax. This also means mom and pop stores will no longer be paying 40% in taxes. Everyone pays the same percentage, this way it's fair.

Everyone will be able to file a simple tax return on one page, saving you time and the government money. When we get rid of Payroll Tax any household making under $35,000 would automatically save $2000! You would have more money to spend on your family and reinvest back into the economy. Additionally, under a Flat Tax, only people above the voting age (18 years of age) would be taxed. No more students, like myself, would be stuck paying the FICA work tax. I'm only 15 and don't have the right to vote but I have a job so I have to pay taxes. As of now, the government is committing taxation without representation.

I'm not saying a Flat Tax would be perfect and some adjustments would need to happen, but it is a much better system than the current. In the words on Senator Rand Paul, "This will shake up Washington and Wall Street no doubt, but I'm not running for their approval, I'm running to take our government back."

Senator Paul is correct, creating a Flat Tax is the first step in rebuilding our government and bringing liberty back to our nation.

Mike Wilkes, Uxbridge

. . .

Opinion Editorial: Sign me up for the Libertarian Party July 2018

During elections in the United States, we are often plagued with two choices, Republicans or Democrats. I often ponder, how did our nation become so divided? The Republican Party of today, is not the party of Lincoln and the Democratic party of today is not the party of Kennedy. Both parties, have left the values of being American. While there are still good politicians on both sides who value country over party like Mike Warner, John McCain, Susan Collins, and John Kasich, most politicians only look out for their special interest groups. This is wrong! This isn't what America was founded on, and like many Americans, I'm fed up!

Being 15, I started to research what political party I affiliate with. I've always loved politics and for many years I considered myself a Republican, however, over the last year and a half the Republican party has been distant from its core values. I ask you what ever happened to the Party of Reagan, Eisenhower, or Coolidge. Truthfully, I don't know. I'm sure many Republicans and Democrats feel the same way as I do. Upon my research, I found there is a political party that the majority of Americans identify as and they don't even know it. This party is the Libertarian Party.

The main philosophy of being Libertarian is simple, freedom. We as Libertarians believe if what you're doing can't hurt anyone, it's your God given right to do it. We believe in a small federal government that is fiscally conservative while socially, we're more liberal or independent. I'll give you an example of how our current government is wasting our tax money. A grant of $700, 000 was given to study autism. However, instead of the money being used to study autism your government decided to spend the $700, 000 to study Neil Armstrong's statement when he landed on the moon. Did he say "One small step for man", or "One small step for a man"? Your government spent $700, 000 studying the preposition "a" instead of studying autism. To add insult to injury the federal government never came to a conclusion. Libertarians, like myself, hate taxes because there is much waste in their spending.

Instead of paying ridiculous amounts of money in taxes, Libertarians want a federal Flat Tax, so everything is flat and fair. Libertarians are for balancing budgets. Every minute our national debt goes up by $1 million! We want to balance the budget, debt, and the deficit by cutting government spending. Many Libertarians are in favor of abolishing many government agencies, such as, Housing and Urban Development (HUD), Department of Education and privatizing Social Security. We absolutely want to privatize as much of the government as we can.

When it comes to social issues we're more lenient. We are strong advocates of freedom of speech, we believe that you should be able to criticize your leaders. We support stem cell research and we feel marijuana should be legal and run it like a business.

Republicans and Democrats both vote for wars, Libertarians don't. We feel we should stop sticking our nose in other countries business. Most of the time when we topple regimes an even worse group takes over. A perfect example was Saddam Hussein. He's now dead because of the U. S. and ISIS is now in control of the region. Don't get me wrong, if the country is attacked we should go to war, but when the U. S. starts poking it's face through the curtains of another country for no reason, then we have a problem.

Many people reading this are probably Libertarian and don't even know it. All you have to do is believe in a small, transparent government that allows people to make decisions. Allow people to keep the majority of the money they make and the money the government takes, it goes towards necessary spending. When you can privatize something, you should. As a future politician, I really do hope that the Libertarian party can one day be as prominent as the Republican and Democratic parties. I want to make that change, not for myself, but for America.

-Mike Wilkes

"Pandemic 2020: COVID 19- World-Wide Disaster and/or Opportunity"?

Why would I search for answers to such things as the problems and hopes in calamity, disaster, human failure, death, and even evil itself? I have been writing this book for more than 10 years now and the experiences shared span my lifetime. One of the most recent challenging events thrust upon us is the Covid-19... the Pandemic 2020. This is to both good and ill affect how we go forward into the future.

We are currently struggling with The Covid-19 Pandemic and the many questions as to how we survive its devastations as well as how best to go forward in reasonable ways for the good of all. "What happened?" "Why did it happen?" "What are the results of this catastrophe?" "What can be done?" "What shall we do?" The questions, concerns, fears, and out-come are now for us to solve with sanity and hope. As I write this piece now our Nation has only hours to go before a long-awaited Presidential Election that will set us on the on-going path of making decisions towards our future. We pray that the electorate will have the combined wisdom to bring forth wise leaders who will to the best of their ability help us move forward.

We human beings are somehow handed the power to solve this problem. So, what's new? Earthquake, fire, flood, wind, disease, good and evil are ours to face on this fragile tiny island Earth that we call home. We must listen! We must act! My own world view is again challenged as I look to God in belief that He is present to help us to solve this problem. In such a belief we are not alone and totally on our own in the universe or in this time and circumstances presented. The philosophies of Atheism teach that our power is totally based within each of us and with no other resource to draw upon other than ourselves alone. In other words, it is up to me/us alone to solve whatever problems we face. Again, as a Christian, I believe that God is with us at this time and will be our guide through this challenging time, as well as all such challenges that we face individually and together as a People. Bothe answers have the element of the truth in that we have freedom to choose, and we have facts, education, and all the tools necessary to help us solve such problems. Where do we turn? Which way do we go? Are there principles that will help guide us along?

Throughout recorded history, the experiences and events of our lives invite the question of both the reality of God as well as His presence in the events and situations we each and together face. It seems terribly unfortunate that all too many of us have short memories of the important events and experiences of history which should have informed our future and betterment. We should, must be especially cognizant of how and why such events of our past were handled. History has surely shown us the results of our decisions, our actions. For this reason, it makes good sense to see the best and the failed attempts of history and belief to follow through in this process.

Again, key influences have informed and affected my own world view as to how best to seek solutions to the problems that confront us. I do, however, recognize that our personal, more immediate, experiences are not forgotten and have the greater influence on our lives. For example, a positive example of events of influence in my history happened at the tender age of five years when Uncle Bill, recently home from WWII, took me to the Fourth of July parade with a flag in hand and said to me: "Georgie, this is all about our beautiful country and your precious Faith and Freedom." He went on to say that the design of this nation was built upon Faith, Trust, and the pursuit of the good of all people throughout the world. Hence, this Parade and celebration of Thanksgiving" in spite of a war which seemed to be necessary to ward off the prevalent evil. Of course, Uncle Bill said this in simpler terms for a five-year-old to more easily comprehend. But the message was clear, and I certainly took it to heart. Thank you, Uncle Bill! This is the reason why it has become more and more clear and dear to me as to how important family, history and all who love and care about is essential to our personal as well as collaborative future.

Therefore, accurate history learned in school is essential. I purposefully use collaborative as opposed to collective future, as I believe that each of us has the ability, to a greater or lesser degree, to think for ourselves and thereby gain insight, truth and wisdom by our sharing such things with one another. The term collective connotates a singular point of view with no further discussion.

In this time of the Pandemic of 2020 (COVID-19), we have much to think about along with purposeful ideas to share in the hope of gaining more insight, clearer wisdom, and the continued search for truth in the more expedient fight with such diseases in the future. I would welcome information that truthfully and factually shares insights into our human actions to all of our common problems.

It is so important to mention here that the Crucifixion of Jesus of Nazareth was a pandemic of long ago but meaningful to this day and forever. After all, it was the common enemy we know as evil that killed Truth on the cross at that fateful time of world history. A crumbling but still corruptly powerful Roman Empire was wrongfully spreading its own evil intentions into the world. The power and goodness of God in this Jesus was a threat to all in that power driven and tyrannical society. The Roman Empire had become a long lasting, corrupt government when it lost its honest search for truth and corruption ensued.

How timely it was for God to come among us in the person of Jesus of Nazareth to confront the face of Evil. The only way we can continue to comprehend this history is to learn it over and over again, one generation to another. The only way to prevent the evils of history to repeat themselves is to be aware of them and work at preventing them with all we've learned and keeping to an honest search.

Proverbs 4:23
"Above all else guard yourself as evil will try to consume your life…"
"Search the truth and do your best to tell the truth."

Proverbs 3:21
"Have two goals: wisdom – that is, knowing and doing right – and common sense… They keep you safe from defeat and disaster and from stumbling off the trail. With them you can sleep without fear You need not be afraid of disaster of the plots of wicked men."

Also, listen carefully and don't take everything at face value. For example, On October 30, 1938, there was an evening broadcast about an invasion of Martians in N. Y. City. A woman anxiously dialed the N. Y. City bus terminal to get information on the next departure out of the city.

"Hurry, please!" she cried. "The world is coming to an end, and I am not ready. I have so much else to do!"

Yes, she was seriously misled by the false broadcast which was a reading from the famous Orson Welles' The War of the Worlds.

So realistic and convincing was the problem that she and over a million other Americans believed that an invasion from Mars was landing and they were as tall as skyscrapers. The crowd was panic-stricken. (II6959 Encyclopedia of 7700 Illustrations)

A great plea goes out these days as it has been generally mounting since I can remember: "Please, save our Nation from lies, deceit, and any who see power and control over others as their goal. Make us, again, a truth-seeking people and trustworthy as our initial forefathers had envisioned."

In theory, as opposed to atheist philosophy, we are not alone, but a real higher power is our resource beyond ourselves and helps to guide us in all problems to be solved. In other words, we are not alone and with God we work together for all solutions. My own world view is based on my Christian faith in God. This does not necessarily negate other theistic beliefs but rather gives credence to belief in such Higher Power.

In my world view as a Christian this latest Pandemic has not only shown my need for God's love but also much needed ways for all of us to solve the problems given herewith. In other words, we are not alone, and there are solutions. The Holy Bible teaches and shows historic examples of such a God who is with us throughout our lives and circumstances. We are not alone!

The title of this book, BELIEVE WHAT?! intends to show God's love at work in life's experiences. The best I can do is share my experiences and hopefully show why I believe God has been a presence in all of them. Again, these are un-embellished experiences except for my belief that God has been in all of them.

The following articles were written in our local Trinity and Saint John's Lenten Parish Newsletter. These articles were written long before the Pandemic's wrath became more and more apparent. The articles convey a belief system that became needed and clearer when the realization of its forthcoming impact became apparent several weeks later. Note that the other articles in that particular quarterly Newsletter reflect our Lenten and Easter beliefs as we normally see them from year to year. Little did any of the writers know that they would directly be about the oncoming soon to be disaster called COVID-19.

The Climate Issue

The climate change question is also on the forefront of today's political and scientific debates. It is true that the many issues of history, human solutions, and this fragile island we call the Earth have always and must continue to be at the forefront of concern among all others. The question again arises as truth vs. fiction, facts vs. misinformation. As President Reagan said about the solving of our concerns. "Verify, Verify. Verify." Trust in truth, facts, and the experiences of history must be drawn upon in order to go forward. In the past, for example, the Earth has experienced major as well as minimal changes. We can now look back to find similarities and differences and better determine solutions. A political debate is not enough without the facts being accurately presented.

From Trinity – St. John's Lent-Easter Newsletter
From the Pastor's Desk

Healing and Eternity

The message of the Christian Easter is the Resurrection. Not only did Jesus rise from the dead but all God's children are destined for Eternity. Along with this promise is the message of the entire Bible that our Resurrection begins during one's lifetime on this fragile home we call Earth. The Bible's message is one of healing. This is all about Resurrection. Healing is needed for our entrance into Eternity. For example, Moses led the Israelites from the Tomb of Tyranny into Freedom. Their requirement was this newly found freedom was to believe in, and follow, God's Will for us. This is the beginning of healing and thereby release of each of us from the Tombs of Darkness. The Tombs of physical malady and all the psychological, social, and spiritual maladies that harm us need healing. This becomes our Resurrection from death and our entrance into Eternity.

As Christians we believe that Jesus is the door to healing in that He not only taught and lived such healing with us but also rose from this life into new life in Heaven. All the human infirmities due to the reality of evil and the consequences of sin were brought into sharp focus by the Jesus of history. Jesus became the pivotal point in bringing total healing to the world as our goal and purpose became just that. Eternity begins with the power of God the Holy Spirit in us. Since this pivotal event of God coming among us and becoming one of us, physical, psychological, social, and spiritual healing became the primary message to the world and our history.

As we celebrate Easter, we give thanks to our Creator (God) for release from all the tombs that prevent our healing and becoming. With the Resurrection of Jesus those early Apostles witnessed a new body, and the ultimate creation of our human soul into eternity. If you notice the sincere smile of anyone who truly loves and cares about you, you have gotten a glimpse of eternity and our resurrection from the dead. Fr. George Warren +

Message from Sr Warden
"The Meaning of the Cross of Ashes on Ash Wednesday"

Wondering why a small, dusty cross anoints the foreheads of Christians once a year? Ash Wednesday marks the start of Lent, a 40-day period of penance for Christians around the world. It always falls on the Wednesday six and a half weeks before Easter, which Christians believe is the day Jesus was resurrected.

The origins of Lent trace to 325 CE, when it was more commonly used as a preparation phase for Baptisms. The holiday's length is an homage to Jesus Christ's 40-day fast as he traveled through the wilderness after being baptized and before he began his ministry. This period is considered by Christians to be God's test of Jesus' spirituality and ability to withstand temptation.

Today, Christians use the holiday both to repent and reflect. The ash cross marking observers' foreheads is meant to represent morality and penance for their sins. It is applied by a priest during a morning mass, often along with a small blessing: "Remember that you are dust and to dust you shall return." Many choose to keep it on all day. The ash is made from the burned palm leaves used during the previous year's Palm Sunday, which commemorates

Jesus's arrival to Jerusalem. It's believed that residents welcomed him by waving palm fronds.

Ash Wednesday sets the tone for Lent, which is considered a time for self-improvement. Originally, Christians observing Lent were allowed only one meal a day and were forbidden from eating meat or fish during the entire period. This tradition was relaxed by Roman Catholics around World War II. While some still abide by a strict version of the fast on Fridays during Lent, many instead choose to give up indulgences like alcohol and social media. Lent ends on Easter, more than six weeks after Ash Wednesday. (Sundays are not counted in the 40-day observation period).

Eastern and Western churches use different days to mark the start of Lent. In the west, Ash Wednesday opens the holiday. In the Eastern Orthodox churches, Lent begins on the Monday seven weeks before Easter and Ash Wednesday is not observed.

-Mitch Palmer

"Coronavirus" By Susan Stone

It's warm out, shouldn't be... strange, strange winter and no snow! But we'll pay for it in July, meaning it will be warmer or hotter than usual. Oh no, what is going to happen and then, there is the coronavirus. What if I get it, what if Tom gets it – worried about the family, especially T. J. and Erik in Quincy and Boston, respectively. Worried, especially about Erik on the T, and all the other people who may not have washed their hands, sneeze prolifically all over the train, and just don't get it. They don't believe it's real – there is no Coronavirus. I actually heard one woman say there is no virus – it's a democratic ploy – fake news.

So, who is better off, the people who think it's 'fake' and go blithely through life carelessly coughing and sneezing everywhere they go because, after all, it's not real! Or the worriers, who do everything right but still worry and worry. Oh, and we can't get hand sanitizer anywhere.

Tom and I are in the biggest category, not the millennials, not the children (thank God), but the old and weary. My kids and grandkids all tell us not to go out, to use hand sanitizer, which we can't get, and just generally beware. So, is the boogie man behind this? Will I ever go out for lunch again, which is the best part of my week? Maybe we should just have the house hermetically sealed and then we can wave through a cloudy plastic at people we think we see. Ah, well.

I think we have all forgotten something. God has not left. I know this because I talk to him every day. He is God. The only God who is in control of my life. The God I praise and love and who loves me beyond my understanding. I don't know why he does, but he does. It is hard to comprehend sometimes, well not sometimes, but a lot of the time. So, despite Coronavirus, He is there, He loves us and cares for us and wants us to know him. Why, well, it has to do with His Son, Jesus. You remember, the Son who died on the Cross for us, rose again, and went on to be with the Father. (I would have loved to see that reunion).

So, no matter what, Coronavirus, other sickness, job loss, He is here and always will be until we go to see Him and the Father. I'm not ready for that or I don't think I am, but His Will is enough for me.

Lent 2020: A Call to Prayer, Fasting, and Repentance Leading to Action
(An Invitation from Presiding Bishop Curry to Turn and Pray on Behalf of our Nation)

As the season of Lent approaches, Episcopal Church Presiding Bishop Michael Curry invites Episcopalians and people of faith to turn and pray on behalf of our nation.

In times of great national concern and urgency, people of faith have returned to ancient practices of repentance, prayer and fasting as ways of interceding with God on behalf of their nation and the world. This is such a moment for us in the United States.

On Ash Wednesday, I will join with other Christian leaders observing this Lent as a season of prayer, fasting and repentance on behalf of our nation, with continued fasting each Wednesday until the Wednesday before Advent begins.

Our appeal comes during a time of profound division and genuine crisis of national character. This is not a matter of party or partisanship, but of deep concern for the soul of America.

The group of religious Elders who share this commitment – the same group that over a year ago published the "Reclaiming Jesus" statement – includes Evangelical, Roman Catholic, mainline Protestant leaders. While we hold diverse political affiliations and positions on many issues facing our country, we find common ground in two shared convictions:

First and foremost, we are committed to Jesus Christ as Lord, and his way of love as our primary loyalty. Second, because we love our country, we are concerned about its moral and spiritual health and well- being.

For me, this call is rooted in my personal commitment to practice Jesus' Way of Love, by which I turn, learn, pray, worship, bless, go and rest in the way of our Savior. Especially now, drawn together by love, hope and concern, and recalling the wisdom of our ancient traditions, I am grateful to join others in the spiritual practice of prayer, fasting and repentance for our nation. If you feel called to join others in this practice, the invitation is attached. The full text, together with the "Reclaiming Jesus" document can be found of the Reclaiming Jesus Website. Let us pray:

Almighty God. We humbly pray that we may always prove ourselves a people mindful of your favor and glad to do your will. Bless our land with honorable industry, sound learning, and pure manners. Save us from violence, discord, and confusion, from pride and arrogance, and from every evil way. Defend our liberties, and fashion into one united people the multitudes brought hither out of many kindreds and tongues. Endue with the spirit of wisdom those to whom in your Name we entrust the authority of government, that there may be justice and peace at home, and that, through obedience to your law, we may show forth your praise among the nations of the earth. In the time of prosperity, fill our hearts with thankfulness, and in the day of trouble, suffer not our trust in you to fail; all which we ask through Jesus Christ our Lord. Amen.

Your brother,

The Most Rev. Michael B. Curry, Presiding Bishop and Primate

The Episcopal Church

"Keep the Faith: Our Faith is not a Fairy Tale"
By Bishop Doug Fisher
Worcester Telegram - Posted Jan 25, 2020, at 3:01 AM

"What do you think is the most important verse in the entire Bible? Not your "favorite" verse but the "most important" verse? People of faith will have many different opinions.

My seminary professor, Michael Himes, said it is Luke chapter 3, verse 1, and I agree with him.

In the 15th year of the reign of Emperor Tiberius, when Pontius Pilate was governor of Judea, and Herod the ruler of Galilee, and his brother Philip ruler of the region of Ituraea and Trachonitis, and Lysanias ruler of Abilene, during the high priesthood of Annas and Caiaphas, the word of God came to a man named John son of Zechariah.

That is the most important line in the entire Bible because it tells us that our faith is not a fairy tale. It is not "once upon a time…". It is not "a long time ago in a galaxy far, far away…" No. In this time and in this place, the word of God came to this person. Our faith is based on God's story joining our story here on earth. Our faith is real. Our faith may be mystical, but it is not abstract.

God who reveals Godself to John, and to the Hebrew prophets before him, and to Jesus and Mary and the apostles, that God continues to offer us guidance through the Spirit here and now. The Spirit has not retired and moved to Florida. The Holy Spirit is still with us.

In your life, what is the Spirit saying? Where is God leading you? Especially, if you are in a spiritual wilderness, how is God present to you now? How is God's love present to you now? And, as the Presiding Bishop of the Episcopal Church, Michael Curry, says so clearly, "if it is not about love, it is not about God."

What is the Spirit saying to you in this time and place and what is the Spirit saying to the Church and to society? There is so much good in our world. I see so many small and large acts of kindness and generosity.

The conclusion of Bishop Fisher's article in the Worcester Telegram of January 25, 2020, was a new call to the Church and to society to seek the guidance of the Holy Spirit at all times but most especially for help in Times of Trial. He points out the good in human beings and how both great and small acts of kindness and generosity do bring about all that is needed and especially in these times of crisis.

Bishop Fisher has championed issues such as Environmental Care and the problems of Violence in Society. My own deep concern in discussing politically difficult issues such as these is that we continue to honestly and openly seek facts and statistics and thereby promote healthful solutions to such problems.

My own considered opinion in these current issues and debates is that we do not lose sight of already given laws which protect the rights and responsibilities of each of us as provided in our Constitution and Bill of Rights. New pushes for "government controls" and even elimination of such rights is being challenged, I believe, beyond the given reasons for making those changes in the first place. I clearly do not trust much of the political motivations behind such changes. Our Forefathers designed our Constitution with the pure intentions of providing the "individual's" rights and obligations for self-protection as well as all "freedoms" of each of us as described in Holy Scripture. Those forefathers planned such rights and obligations as they understood God's Will. We must continuously review the comprehension and intentions of those who sought only to protect our rights as individual human beings with the Holy obligations of protecting all of us as "free People". Today's encroachments of more Government Control are, I believe, further encroachments on the freedom and responsibilities of each of us. This discussion and debate need to continue in our search for TRUTH in all matters. The real issues such as Environmental Care and Violence in society are indeed real ones but need very careful consideration as to how and why we make these major decisions by and for each of us and all of us together.

In times such as these a likely question about God comes to mind. "How does God speak to us here?" God said to Moses, "I AM" Exodus 3:6

"Belief and Prayer"

Following Easter, the Christian faith leads us to an understanding that we are called to be a Resurrection People. In other words, in the light of the Holy Bible, and more especially, all that the Jesus of history brought to us in teaching and action, there is a future – and more so, an eternal one. Life becomes a forward movement into the future. Rising from the dead, we become alive in him. Our actions then rise to the fulfillment of God's Will for us and promises to us.

Following Easter comes the Pentecost, Memorial Day, and our nation's celebration of freedom from mass tyranny, the 4th of July. In the Pentecost, we are reminded of God's personal relationship with us as the Holy Spirit comes to us. On Memorial Day, we honor those who came before us, those who prepared our journey forward. And yes, on the Fourth of July we give thanks for our nation's hope to foster and protect our Freedom to be the best we can be.

As Biblical people we are called to pray for Freedom, as God has provided for us. In this year of political debate and elections we look to God for guidance and help. We are called to pray together for our nation:

By the Reverend George Warren

Litany of Thanksgiving
For the Nation

Almighty God, giver of all good things:

We thank you for the natural majesty and beauty of this land.

They restore us, though we often destroy them.

Heal us.

We thank you for the great resources of this nation. They make us rich, though we often exploit them. Forgive us.

We thank you for the men and women who have made this country strong. They are models for us, though we often fall short of them.

Inspire us.

We thank you for the torch of liberty which has been lit in this land. It has drawn people from every nation, though we have often hidden from its light.

Enlighten us.

We thank you for the faith we have inherited in all its rich variety. It sustains our life, though we have been faithless again and again.

Help us, O Lord, to finish the good work here begun. Strengthen our efforts to blot out ignorance and prejudice, and to abolish poverty and crime. And hasten the day when all our people, with many voices in one united chorus, will glorify your holy Name. Amen.

Book of Common Prayer, pg 838-839

A General Thanksgiving

Accept, O Lord, our thanks and praise for all that you have done for us. We thank you for the splendor of the whole creation, for the beauty of this world, for the wonder of life, and for the mystery of love.

We thank you for the blessing of family and friends, and for the loving care which surrounds us on every side.

We thank you for setting us at tasks which demand our best efforts, and for leading us to accomplishments which satisfy and delight us.

We thank you also for those disappointments and failures that lead us to acknowledge our dependence on you alone.

Above all, we thank you for your Son, Jesus Christ, for the truth of His Word and the example of His life; for His steadfast obedience, by which He overcame temptation; for His dying, through which He overcame death; and for His rising to life again, in which we are raised to the life of your Kingdom.

Grant us the gift of your Spirit, that we may know Him and make Him known; and through Him, at all times and in all places, may give thanks to you in all things. Amen.

(Book of Common Prayer, pg. 836)

"Paddling through Lent – and Life"

Lent is a time for restoring balance to our lives. The Eskimos practice balance as they venture into freezing Arctic waters in little boats. If you've ever paddled a kayak, you know how easy they are to tip. Thankfully, kayaks are just as easy to turn back upright.

That isn't a bad image for Lent – or for life as a whole. Whatever spiritual disciplines we adopt, if we succumb to temptation, it's no biggie. One of the lessons of Lent is that, as long as we're traveling light, it takes only a quick twist of the paddle to right us. That paddle twist might take the form of a quick but heartfelt prayer: "Jesus, set me straight again!" Or it might mean some extra time set aside for quiet meditation with God. Don't get worried if your spiritual discipline fails now and then. Just let Jesus help you get upright once more and keep paddling!

- Adapted from Carlos Wilton, in Homiletics

A Lenten History Lesson

Though the date of Easter varies, the majority of the Lenten season occurs during March. In fact, the word Lent comes from the Anglo-Saxon words lenctentid (meaning "March") and lencten (meaning "Spring"). The first reference to Lent dates back to 325 AD, in one of the 20 canons decreed at the council of Nicaea. By the eighth century, Christians started observing Lent, and a tenth century monk named Aelfric connected the use of ashes and the "Lenten fast" to the pre-Easter period.

Lent lasts forty days to represent Jesus' time in the wilderness, when he was tempted by the devil. The six Sundays that occur between Ash Wednesday and Easter Sunday aren't counted as part of Lent; instead, as the traditional day of worship, they're considered mini-Easters.

Easter Around the World

Easter traditions are important, but they vary widely. While Americans dye hard boiled eggs, Kenyans carve soapstone eggs and present them as gifts in banana-fiber boxes. In Bermuda, locals fly homemade kites on Good Friday – a tradition that began when a teacher illustrated Christ's ascension to heaven using a cross-shaped kite.

Ethiopian Christians observe a fifty-six-day fast from meat and all animal products. On Easter, they dress in white to worship in churches decorated with handmade fabric. Then they feast with non-Christians on roast chicken, goat, and rice. In France, church bells are silent between Holy Thursday and Easter to observe Jesus' Passion. According to legend, the bells grow wings and fly to Rome to be blessed, returning on Easter with chocolate and presents. In one town's main square, chefs make a giant omelet with 4,500 eggs to feed 1,000 people!

See(k) First

On Facebook, I can "follow" as many people as I want, viewing their messages, photos and activities. But I can choose only thirty to "see first" – that is, to prioritize in my news feed. As of this writing, (Facebook changes often), if my "see first" list is full and I want to add someone new, I must "un-prioritize" someone else.

That leads me to ponder bigger matters: I often claim to follow Jesus, but what might I need to "unprioritized" to make him not just a priority, but the priority in my life? To what do I devote time and attention but ought to let go to follow Christ more closely? What activities, behaviors, and values do I need to not just bump from my "see first" list, but "unfollow" or "block" entirely? Perhaps they are antithetical to discipleship or simply take too much time away from prayer, Scripture, and service.

This dilemma isn't unique to the digital age. Facebook parlance is about what we "see first," but in Matthew 6:33, Jesus says, "Seek first the kingdom of God and his righteousness." (ESV, italics added)

-Heidi Mann

Charles Krauthammer

At this writing, I'm missing one of my favorite journalists and commentators, Dr. Charles Krauthammer. For many years I have trusted this famous intellectual's opinions because of his honest summaries of current political events. One thing I most trusted was his ability to "see the devil in the details". His primary concern was to decipher political agenda as it distorted the facts, the truth for political ends. Here again we see, "The end being used to justify the means".

The following two brief articles from his latest book, Charles Krauthammer, put together by his son soon after Dr. Krauthammer's death in the springtime of 2019, shows the glaring misuse of scientific fact for political ends. I now miss his regular TV appearance and articles as he did his wise and level best to keep us open- minded and on the right track!

The Myth of "Settled Science"

I repeat: I'm not a global warming believer. I'm not a global warming denier. I've long believed that it cannot be good for humanity to be spewing tons of carbon dioxide into the atmosphere. I also believe that those scientists who pretend to know exactly what this will cause in twenty, thirty, or fifty years are white- coated propagandists.

(These two pertinent articles are recorded in the "Jack's Penny Candy Store" article forward in this book.)

Common and Extraordinary Ethics

After all, the topic ethics and morality can't be covered in a few words or even in a library of explanations, but our ethics and behavior are with us day in and day out. The questions are, "Who or what are we answerable to?" "Who or what do we affect in our decisions and behaviors?" Here I offer several stories regarding rightful behavior and outcome.

The College Professor

Some years ago, my first year of philosophy in undergraduate studies. The course was Ethics. The professor made a chart of the class and asked us to sit in the same seat at each session for the entire semester. In this way he was able to get to know us and to be enabled to give us a grade after our final exam. At the end of the semester he got to know us well and had a good idea how to grade each of us. The quality of the grade was very important to all of us as the cumulative average would clearly affect each of our future pursuits.

Just before the final exam, one of us stole the name and seating chart of the professor. Before the exam, which would be in the coming weeks class, he asked that the one who removed his chart would please privately and anonymously return it. No-one confessed. We all received an "F" (Failure) for that course. What a lesson on Ethics and Morality.

A Seminary Test

A class of Seminarians in a theological graduate school out somewhere in the Midwest were about to take their final exam in order to be enabled to go back to their respective Bishops for ordination to the Priesthood. The Seminary was in an inner-city section where crime and poverty were rampant. Unfortunately, because of the dangers to life and property, the door needed to always be locked. Of course, the twenty Seminarians were very anxious about the forthcoming 'final' exam and wanted it to be over. The examining priest announced the time and place of the exam and that at 10:00 A.M. the doors would be locked. Everyone except one scrambled to be there well before that lock down time. At the entrance door was an intoxicated, smelly, obviously hurting man. He was begging for help and all said that they would come to his aid after the critical four-hour examination inside. The last student with two minutes left to get inside for the test, stopped and went directly to the aid of this sorely hurting individual. The door locked and the priest-to-be missed the test.

The next day the professor of theology announced the results of that extraordinarily important test of vocation. Nineteen failed, and the one locked out passed the exam. Come to find out the poor man at the door was an actor. That was the primary part of a long exam. Another lesson on life's goals and personal pursuits was learned. Nicholas of Myra (See the Story of Benjamin). Many stories of our beloved Saint Nicholas have swept the world since he was born way back in the 300s AD in the ancient Roman Empire.

Freedom vs. Tyranny

Throughout recorded history, the primary struggle of human society has been the battle between tyranny and freedom. The Webster's Dictionary describes "tyranny" as, "The controlling power of one over the other; a government in which the ruler has absolute power; the unjust or cruel exercise of power; a state of severity; rigor."

The same dictionary defines "freedom" as "The state of being free of constraints; Political independence; Possession of political and civil rights; Free will; Frankness or boldness of expression; Unrestricted access or use.

Freedom as addressed in these writings are about the ability and availability of each of us to think and act according to our God-given free will. In other words, God provides each of us and all of us together the power and responsibility to make right choices.

I wish to now add to this definition the Biblical definition of Free Will, which is, God's gift of Freedom to the individual human being. In other words, God's Will for us is to be the best we can be with the knowledge and the power to make the best choices. President Franklin D. Roosevelt once said, "There never has been, and never will be, any race of people on earth fit to serve as masters over their fellow man."

Another anonymous quote states that, "If a nation values anything more than freedom, it will lose its' freedom; and the irony of it is that if it is comfort, control, power, or money that it values more, it will lose that, too." Another said that, "Democracy is based on the conviction that there are extraordinary possibilities in ordinary people." Under the title of "freedom" in the Encyclopedia, Signs of the Times, it notes that "a global survey of political and civil liberty indicates that personal freedom has diminished in the 1970s for eighty-five million people in seven countries." The assessment was made by Freedom House, a New York based non-profit organization that rates nations as either free, partly free, or not free.

Sixty-six countries with forty-two percent of the world's population were termed "not free". The survey listed 1 percent fewer people in the "free" category than a year earlier. (Encyclopedia of 7700 Illustrations – Signs of the Times).

President Ronald Reagan warned us that, "If we neglect to teach our children the history and values of our freedom, we'll lose them to tyranny." This paraphrase of our President relates to the slow but steady deterioration of our values and freedom in our nation today. In my opinion, the ongoing search for the more perfect society is dependent upon our comprehension of the meanings of freedom and tyranny, and our continual pursuit of Truth.

The Holy Bible is clear about the path of Truth. Such a path includes Belief and Faith in God, human Freedom, and the Sin of Pride that leads to our destruction. The following Epigram from the Encyclopedia Of 7700 Quotations describes this meaning of Freedom further:

"Liberty is always unfinished business." - The Ethical Outlook

"Those who give up essential liberty to purchase a little temporary safety deserve neither liberty or safety." - Benjamin Franklin

"If a nation values anything more than Freedom, it will lose its freedom; and the irony of it is that if it is comfort or money that it values more, it will lose that too." - Doubleday

"There never has been, there isn't now, and there never will be, any race of people on earth fit to serve as masters over their fellow men." - Franklin D. Roosevelt

"Democracy is based on the conviction that there are extra-ordinary possibilities in ordinary people." - Friendly Chat

"G. K. Chesterton once said that it is often supposed that when people stop believing in God, they believe in nothing. Alas, it is worse than that. When they stop believing in God, they believe in anything."

Dostoevski remarked in his book CRIME AND PUNISHMENT

that "If God does not exist, everything is permissible."

"Jesus then said to those disciples, "If you continue in my word, you are truly my disciples, and you will know the truth and the truth will set you free." (John 8:32)

Charles M. Houser said much about truth, freedom, and faith in God. He said that, "Atheism never composed a symphony. Never painted a masterpiece. Never dispelled a fear. Never healed a disease. Never gave peace of mind. Never dried a tear. Never established a philanthropy. Never gave an intelligent answer to the vast mystery of the universe. Never gave meaning to man's life on earth. Never built a just and peaceful world. Never built a great and enduring civilization."

"Half a fact is a whole falsehood." - Old Proverb

"Every man has a right to his opinion, but no man has a right to be wrong in his facts."- Baruch

"Time is precious, but truth is more precious than time." - Disraeli

"It is easier to believe a lie that one has heard a thousand times than to believe a fact that no one has heard before." -Grit

(Encyclopedia Of 7700 Quotations)

In the ongoing concern and work of our nation, most especially as we hope to be a people of integrity and always in search for the Truth, we must always examine our own decision-making processes for both the good they must promote as well as the mistakes which need review and correction. The following account regarding our decision-making process should be noted and tested as per the rules of law and our Constitution.

As I now move along with the theme of freedom's need and responsibility to fend off the many encroachments of tyranny I use the example of President John F. Kennedy's stand- off with Premiere Nikita Khrushchev in the Cuban

Missile Crisis of 1962. The Soviets had sent a flotilla of ships filled with missiles for delivery in Cuba. These were offensive missiles to be aimed at the United States. This was the time of the Cold War between the Western Democracies and the eastern Communist bock of States controlled by Soviet Russia. I remember this 'incident' well, along with my fellow high schoolers. We were in class and all terrified. President Kennedy announced to the Russian Premiere that if those ships did not immediately turn around and head back to the Soviet Union the United States would have to retaliate by force. Those ominous ships turned around and headed back to their home port and that particular crisis terminated.

The Cold War continued! This particular incident brought us close to a world-wide devastating confrontation. Each of our countries had nuclear warheads directed towards each other and if used the world would have ended. It was during this time that a policy now known as the Executive Order of the President was brought into existence. Its purpose was for "Emergency Use Only" to provide protection from such a foreign threat to our Nation. Since then the Executive Order became useful and used by Presidents for other than immediate danger problems. This in itself became a problem as it gave such singular power to the President without the rightful, lawful avenues of further discussion and acts of congress. Thus, a singular person being the president had taken on unilateral power far beyond its original intended purpose.

To my knowledge, this expansion of such power has not been adequately reviewed for needed corrections. It seems now to be the case that any given president can utilize this power for whatever he or she chooses. This is dangerous ground as any particular political party or philosophy can be set forward at any given time for its own will and purposes. I'm not clear as to how such power can be checked and corrected at this time without reasonable debate, the protection of law, and the good of our nation and each of us within it.

My source of information says that "The emergency measures set forth by the late President J. F. Kennedy still stand. They became part of the vast array of Executive Orders when they were signed on February 16 and 27, 1962. Those emergency documents provide that the President, and any succeeding President shall have complete and final dictatorial control. The Executive Orders are to be carried out through the Office of Emergency Planning, and they may be put into effect in "any time of increased international tension or economic or financial crisis." So all-inclusive are these orders that a listing of them is provided here:

THE EXECUTIVE ORDERS

Executive Order # 10995 – Take over all communications Media.

Executive Order # 10997 – Take over all electric Power, Petroleum, and Gas fuels and minerals.

Executive order # 10998 – Take over all food resources and farms [including farm machinery].

Executive order # 10999 – Take over all methods of transportation, highways, seaports, etc.

Executive order # 11000 – Mobilization of civilians into work forces under governmental supervision.

Executive order # 11001 – Take over all health, welfare and educational functions.

Executive order # 11002 – Postmaster General [member of President's Cabinet] will operate nationwide registration of all persons.

Executive order # 11003 – Takeover of all airports and aircraft.

Executive order #11004 - Take over housing and finance authorities to relocate communities, to build new housing with public funds, designate areas to be abandoned as unsafe, and establish new locations for populations.

Executive order # 11005 – Take over all railroads, inland waterways, and public storage facilities.

Executive order # 11051 – Designate responsibilities of office of emergency planning, give authorization to put all other executive orders into effect in "Times of increased international tension or economic, or financial crisis."

[Encyclopedia of 7700 Quotations # 1117].

I believe that it should, must, be our immediate concern and legal responsibility to watch and review all Executive orders for purpose, legitimacy, trust, truth, constitutionality, rights, and responsibility of all citizens and on goes the list of reasons for the protection of the nation, freedom, legitimate government in the light and darkness of both freedom and tyranny. I hope that current as well as future leaders will take the time and responsibility to study such matters of freedom and tyranny for the sake of each of us and all of us together. All of us need to be aware of such Executive orders so that we can intelligently and truthfully discuss and debate such orders for the protection of our nation, the world, and the idea of freedom.

"Majority rule is dangerous. All the great injustices of history have been committed in the name of unchecked and unbridled majority rule." The late Senator James A. Reed, of Missouri, in one of the most forceful speeches ever delivered before the Senate, observed with great truth: "The majority crucified Jesus Christ; the majority burned the Christians at the stake; the majority established slavery; the majority jeered when Columbus said the world was round; the majority threw him into a dungeon for having discovered a new world; the majority cut off the ears of John Pym because he dared advocate the liberty of the press." (Encyclopedia of 7700 Quotations)

Katherine

"I sought the Lord, and he answered me. He delivered me from all my fears." *(Psalm 34:4)* At age thirty-seven, after the birth of my third child, I was hospitalized for three months with serious postpartum depression. What had started with postpartum hormonal changes and sleep deprivation led to years of requiring sleeping pills every night to ensure a nights' rest. For a long time afterwards, the inability to sleep became a trigger and a marker to me of the stress in my life and a warning that fear and depression could be lurking around the very next corner. It was a torment.

Even though I had had the daily practice of prayer and reading my Bible and talking with the Lord Jesus for years, the problem of fear of not sleeping persisted. It had been my habit even before my last child's birth, whenever I couldn't sleep, to open my Bible and read until I was comforted and peace returned. One night, several years after her birth, I remember being in my living room, again, not able to sleep, and hearing, not an audible voice, but the voice of the Holy Spirit in my spirit reassuring me that he was healing me of this problem of not sleeping.

Back upstairs in my comfy bed, I fully expected to go right off to sleep. When morning came I was altogether surprised that I had not slept at all. I had simply been resting in the arms of my Heavenly Father. I knew then that my Gracious and Loving Father had freed me from a besetting fear – the fear of not sleeping – the fear of becoming ill again – the fear of the one whose octopus tentacles sought to paralyze and strangle with suction-like grips – a many-armed beast.

Now I realize that however much I sleep or don't sleep is not my concern. I am to trust God for enough. It's not even my responsibility, and being awake at night can be a wonderful time for prayer. Thirty-seven years later, I have been awakening to the truth that like all of the Father's children, Christ's followers, the Mighty Army that God is raising up, we are to become like David who, pretending insanity before Abimelech and fearing for his life, wrote the words of Psalm 34: "I sought the LORD and He answered me; He delivered me from all my fears." Over and over in this Psalm, David writes that when we cry out, the LORD hears, and He answers us and delivers us. His angel even camps around those who fear Him.

What a lesson and a reminder to me from thirty-seven years ago: that the LORD who delivered me from fear of not sleeping and depression, etc. is here now, and desires to deliver me (us) from every fear – fear of COVID, fear of loss, fear of death and persecution, fear for our families, every fear. Him only are we to fear! Rejoice now with me as we praise Him!

Katherine
August 20, 2020

P. S. I fully expected God to heal me of not sleeping. But instead, He healed me of the FEAR of not sleeping – so much bigger. He truly does more than we can ask or imagine.

A Spiritual Journey

It is told that the great and famous St. Augustine of Hippo was an only child, raised by his mother and wealthy merchant father. His confessions reveal that being spoiled in an opulent, comfortable, not to be concerned environment provided him a slow beginning to understanding the real world out there. He later found the Lord after a long life of searching in all the places where God actually was present but he didn't see it! At the end of his life Augustine said: "I have not known anything until I've known thee, God!"

Another most famous saint of history was Nicholas of Myra. Nicholas' dad was also a wealthy ship merchant who provided vast amounts of wanted but not necessarily needed goods to the world throughout the Mediterranean and beyond. During this time of history, from the late 200s into the 300s, Christianity was outlawed as a "threat to society and the Emperor" during that time of a secular, crumbling Roman Empire. Nicholas' father was not a Christian, but his mother was. He was raised by his Mom on the study of the life of Jesus of Nazareth. All of this had to be done in secret with the instructions to live by this faith without talking about it. However, St. Nicholas, from early childhood, made regular visits to the sailors on his father's ships and told stories of Jesus amongst the sailors. They adored this special child. As an older teenager he was ordained by the secret society of Christians, and later became a Bishop.

Still visiting the sailors throughout his life, he convinced them to deliver goods to the poor of Myra during the night before the Winter Solstice. He was arrested for this "act against the Empire," sent to prison, and died of starvation almost a year later (325 A. D). Many of us now call him Santa Claus. Many in Europe still celebrate the Feast of St. Nicholas at Christmastide.

We are all on a faith journey whether we know it or not. God seems to be always reaching out for us to return. The famous contemporary theologian Dr. John McQuarry said in *The Risk of Creation* that God took a risk in this love creation by creating us and giving us free will to choose our path and that love would win..

Tamara

On this day back in 2010, I had surgery to remove a cancerous, golf ball-sized tumor from my brain. The first miracle was that it was discovered before I had a major seizure. Second miracle was that I had a phenomenal brain surgeon. Third miracle was I didn't have any handicaps after the surgery, when so often, that is the case. The list of miracles is endless!!! However, in that moment, and many years afterwards I didn't see the miracles and I was extremely bitter. If I'm being honest, I was mad at God. How could he let this happen to me? I was jealous of other people who had so-called normal lives. I stuffed my emotions and shut people out. I definitely had to work (and pray) my way back to where I am today spiritually—through acceptance, gratitude and humility.

I don't regret that this happened in my life. I now believe that nothing happens in God's world by mistake. Today I feel a deep sense of gratitude, peace, and serenity. Perhaps I can help another person and that's why I'm still here. Or maybe bad things sometimes just happen. The key is, I don't need to figure it out. I can just pray every day for knowledge of God's will and the strength and power to carry that out, one day at a time. It's not often that I make long-winded comments, but I needed to put this out into the universe today. I am beyond blessed and grateful for the life I have today.

A good friend of mine, David Small, wrote the following account of his "Faith Journey."

"Religious Life History "

I have been a son, husband, father, student, musician, soldier, researcher, friend, mentor, volunteer and career food safety professional. I was baptized July 19, 1947 at St. Mark's Episcopal Church, Augusta, Maine and confirmed December 13, 1959 at St. John's Episcopal Church, Portsmouth, New Hampshire. Growing up in a strong Episcopal family (my paternal grandfather being a devout Episcopalian), I went to Sunday School, participated in the youth group and was an acolyte from an early age through graduating high school. The key influential people during this time were my parents, my maternal grandmother (although she declared she was never baptized), high school teachers, clergy and the astronaut Alan Shepard.

Attending college was a liberating experience studying science and philosophy in the 60's. The freedom to actually question the existence of God! Looking back now I realize that this questioning, this straying from God's love, actually was part of my faith journey. I remember reciting the creation of the universe via the Big Bang theory to a friend's mother my freshman year, never thinking what was prior to the Big Bang. How naïve. Now, I can't imagine that black "black void" without the presence of God.

Graduating college, I enlisted in the Army. My life changed. I was away from the security of home; my world was chaos. I grew up fast. After military service I was fortunate to find a place of employment. The company not only offered me a position but also offered to send me to graduate school (from which I graduated in 1978). I was on a good track! However, I was in a spiritual desert, had not attended church in a while, and was really out of touch with God. The year was 1972 and I felt it was time to renew my relationship with God. The only way I knew how was to return to my Episcopal roots.

In September of 1976, I married a wonderful Irish Catholic woman in an ecumenical service at St. Luke's Roman Catholic Church, Westborough, MA. Prior to being married, we had been going to both St. Stephen's and St. Luke's. We were getting involved in a new religious experience and sharing our past religious backgrounds, which were quite similar. We became involved in developing the ARC covenant between St. Stephen's and St. Luke's. Spending a lot of time at meetings and worship, things were much different in those days – no cell phones, no laptops, no kid's soccer – we had much more involvement with the under 30-somethings. I went from a spiritual desert to a flourishing of church activity. We continued until 1983.

In April, 1983, we were blessed with our first child, a beautiful daughter. Because Fran was a RC and her family had a strong Irish Catholic heritage, our children (a second daughter was born in 1986) were to be raised in the RC Church, a fact that did not bother me as long as they had the opportunity for a solid Christian education. Fran and I attended St. Luke's through the 90's to ensure we set an example for our children. When our children were in high school, almost ready for college, they drifted away from church, and at that time also, I stopped going to St. Luke's.

Our parents and Fran's oldest brother passed in 2002, 2003, 2004, 2009, and 2010. This left a large void in our lives, especially Fran as she had been the primary care giver and advocate for all. I learned a great deal more about the strength of her character during those years and realized how blessed I am to have her as my wife, a partner who has supported me for over 37 years. From her actions, I learned how important it is to be an unselfish, caring attendant for those who cannot care of advocate for themselves. She exemplifies the Ministry of Presence.

After my father passed away, the first of our parents, I wandered aimlessly for seven years, searching for answers. Perhaps I was really searching for the right questions to ask.

Then one Sunday I returned to St. Stephen's. Fr. George, the interim priest at that time, was a wonderful mentor who gave me something for which I was looking – not answers, but where to look for questions in search of my answers. He directed me to Education for Ministry - EfM (I am in my third year). From that point on I have been moving forward in understanding my faith.

Reading the Bible one night, I came across James 2:26 and realized the connection between my efforts to reduce hunger in our society and my own spiritual journey – to me now the two, faith and works, are inseparable. This has since been reinforced through other Scriptures, specifically Matthew 14:16 - Jesus said to them, "They need not go away, you find them something to eat;" you being the operative word, I knew then that the Scriptures were speaking to me. Retirement has afforded me the freedom to pursue my hunger relief efforts.

Prior to retirement I spent close to 40 years in the food business as a food safety professional. During that time, I volunteered as a technical liaison between my company and the NE Food Bank Network for approximately twenty-three years, during which time I was a member of the Board of the Worcester County Food Bank for 12twelveyears. Currently I serve as one of the two Board Vice Presidents of the Community Harvest Project (CHP), a nonprofit organization that grows and harvests fresh fruits and vegetables for hunger relief efforts in Worcester County. In 2013, CHP provided 320,000 lbs. of produce to aid hunger relief through the Worcester County Food Bank.

As a volunteer at the Worcester County Food Bank, I assist in the meat recovery program and in training volunteers. Over the last year, I became involved in Our Father's Table, a program to provide hot meals to marginalized people in our local area, sponsored by an ecumenical faith group. Continued involvement with the hunger relief organizations, along with study and reflection through EfM, has greatly increased the impact of Jesus' words in Matthew 14:16 and has played a major role in my calling to seek ordination. Through ordination I believe I can better serve those who are food–insecure, while concurrently bringing their situation to the attention of the church and to motivating and inspiring the parish and our community to action.

My parish discernment process was not easy as many direct, thought-provoking questions were asked of me. Yet, at the same time, all members of the committee were supportive of my desire to seek ordination. Since my intentions have been made known to the parish, I have received words of support and know that I am being upheld and will continue to be upheld by the prayers of many in my parish community. This show of support confirms for me that I belong to a solid Christian family at church and have a support structure within my circle of friends. But, most importantly, I have the support of my wife and a family that is steadfast and unconditional.

Although retired, I am financially sound. I believe that each one of us desires to support organizations that we believe mitigate suffering in our world. I believe my donations, along with others, can make a difference in mitigating hunger, even if it is only in Worcester County. Donations to the church are spread among many organizations and not only provide practical relief, but also spread the Good News, a mission that is much needed in today's world. I am well known by the Church Treasurers and Finance Committee for doing my part to support the mission of the Church.

I have continued feeding my hunger for spiritual knowledge by joining various Bible study groups, participating in Holy Week and Easter Liturgy, continuing in EfM, becoming a lector, an active Vestry member (Stewardship), and leading Morning Prayer Services during Advent.

For the last four months, I have been meeting regularly with a spiritual director. The experience has been exciting and rewarding. She has helped me to understand where and when God has spoken to me through others and that introspective prayer is my personal, quiet time with God. I look forward to continuing this journey, guided by my spiritual director.

My calling remains to work on hunger relief efforts in Worcester County. Through ordination, I believe that I can strengthen those efforts while, additionally, spreading the Good News, and motivating those within the walls of the Church to come and see, to step outside, and to do God's work in our community.

David K. Small
December 2, 2013

"Mitch"

I can break down my spiritual life into distinct timeframes, the first being from my birth until I was about ten in 1963. During this time my earliest memories are going to church in Pennsylvania with my grandparents. I remember being in Christmas plays and Easter pageants with other children. Despite the fact that I only saw these other children once or twice a year, I was accepted and made to feel part of the group. I didn't really know what I believed, if anything. Because my father was in the Navy, we moved around a lot, but the one constant was spending the holidays in Pennsylvania. These are my earliest church memories and experiences.

In the late 1950s, we lived in Norfolk, Virginia and Salem, Massachusetts, and I remember going to Baptist Churches where my parents were very involved. I don't know exactly what I felt or what I believed, I just know that it was expected that Sunday morning was spent in church. After my father got out of the Navy in 1963, we moved to Connecticut and that's when I really became involved in church and began to develop my own beliefs and thoughts about God and Jesus and what it all meant.

In 1966, at age twelve, I became a Christian. At this point I made the Baptist Confession of Faith and was baptized into the church. It was at this time that I took my first Communion because in the particular Baptist Church we belonged to, you were not allowed to have communion until you were baptized.

During this time, I was very involved in church youth group, at one point in the capacity of a youth preacher. I gave my first sermon when I was sixteen years old. It was also at this time that I felt the first tug of a call from God. I became interested in liturgical churches. I had a paper route and one of the customers was a Lutheran minister. He asked me if I would be interested in working in his Bible School playing games and doing activities with the younger children. I said yes, and so, for a week, I spent my mornings outside playing football and badminton, then at the end of the day going in for a short service. As it was a Lutheran service, it was liturgical. I was hooked. It was like nothing I had ever experienced before. I loved it.

Because of this, I began to lose interest in the Baptist Church and the low Church style of worship. However, being a teenager, I couldn't convince my parents to let me go anywhere else except to the church they belonged to. I got around this by dating a lot of Catholic girls and would go to Mass with them on Saturday nights just to experience the Liturgy. This is how it was for the rest of the 60s and into the early 70s.

In 1971, when I went away to college, I stopped practicing any form of religious activity. I never lost my faith, but I didn't practice it, either. If anything, it was nothing more than lip service when I was home on school holidays and over the summer. I would call out to God when I was in trouble, but if things were going well, God was the furthest thing from my mind. This went on for about eleven or twelve years. During this time, I attended a Catholic college and would occasionally go to services, but not very often. When I did attend church, it was to go to a liturgical service.

I got married for the first time in 1982 to a woman I had met in college who was a very devout Catholic. While I wouldn't go to church with her, I felt at this time that I needed to start going back to church. I found a small Lutheran Church in Quincy, MA. Once again, I was hooked, but this time it was both the theology and the liturgy. I was confirmed in the Lutheran Church and became very active as an LEM and as an usher. I continued in this church until 1992. At that time, my first wife and I split up, I moved away, and again stopped going to church. We eventually divorced, and I was on my own. Since we have a daughter and I had agreed that she would be raised Catholic, on the weekends when she came to stay with me I would take her to Mass. While I really wasn't practicing at least I was going. I attended the Episcopal Church in Framingham, Massachusetts for a while but ended up leaving due to church politics. I went to another Lutheran Church for a while, but again, things got in the way and then I stopped going again. This lasted until 2006.

During this time, I got remarried and my current wife is not of our faith. She is, however, extremely spiritual and very supportive of my spiritual journeys. So, in 2006, I convinced her to go to Saint Paul's Episcopal Church in Hopkinton, MA with me. We went for the first time on Palm Sunday and by the second Sunday of Easter I really felt I'd found a church home.

The Rector and I became good friends and once again I began serving as LEM and acolyte. I served on the vestry in the roles of Junior Warden and was director of the stewardship program for three years.

I reaffirmed the baptismal vows from my Lutheran confirmation with Bishop Tom Shaw in 2009. At the Rector's urging, I taught the confirmation class in 2011. I felt the tug once again that God wanted me to do something more than what I was doing. I felt that He wanted me in a ministerial role. I thought the diaconate was the way to go and I began to explore becoming a deacon in the diocese of Massachusetts.

At this time, I began to take my spiritual life much more seriously and began to get up early every morning to spend time with God in daily devotions. I was encouraged to explore the diaconate process by a dear friend who is a Deacon (and who graciously agreed to be my spiritual director through my earlier Priesthood discernment process) and our parish Rector, although he thought I was more suited to be a Priest than a deacon. Father Mike and I had many discussions around this as we made a pilgrimage together to the Mont St. Michel Monastery in July of 2011. This is when I really started a discernment process. I also had discussions with a friend who is in the diaconate program in Western Massachusetts and she also felt that I had the heart of a priest, not a deacon. In 2015, I met with Father John Stubbs and we discussed these feelings with an eye toward whether it made sense for me to pursue ministry as an ordained priest. We concluded that this was the right path to pursue and while there were no promises, it made sense for me to follow this path and see where it took me.

I was not accepted for study for the priesthood, but Father John spoke to the Bishop regarding this decision. While the Bishop could not override the committee decision he did grant me a license to preach and a license to be a Lay Worship Leader. I have used these at both Trinity and St. John's regularly since then. The call to ordained ministry has never gone away. This call is just as strong today as it was earlier. I feel that this opportunity presented with Father John's retirement is a door being opened by God for me to answer this call.

If it turns out not to be the proper use of what God has given me, I just want to be the best layperson I can be and can serve Him, my parish, and the diocese to the best of my ability.

"The Great Dane"

We love our pets! One of my favorite bumper stickers reflects a great truth for many of us: "My dog rescued me." Popular charities among many of us are The Humane Society and the very many other local rescue leagues that save animals from abuse.

The true story mentioned here is personal on several levels. Some years ago, the Rives side of our family went to the homestead in Shrewsbury, Massachusetts to celebrate Thanksgiving. Grammy and Gramp were always such beautiful hosts. There we were, John and Kim with Clay and Tammy; Pete and Sue with Jason and Jesse, Peach and me with Joel, Addie and Brian, and Grammy and Gramp. At that particular Thanksgiving, Uncle Mike was, I believe, stationed in Cambodia as a U.S. Emissary.

During our pre-dinner munchies and glass of wine, Uncle John announced that he had just adopted a Great Dane puppy. Before coming in earlier he had placed the new puppy into Gramp's brand new VW Beetle. We wondered how Gramp was able to get in and out of that Beetle. Excited with the announcement of Uncle John's new dog, we all filed out to see both the new car and the small Great Dane puppy. Evan as a puppy, this handsome dog could not possibly fit into such a tiny car. Here is what we found... a cute little dog, smiling and wagging his tail in a small VW with no interior furniture. The dog had totally torn to less than shreds, the entire interior of Gramp's brand-spanking new VW.

The rest of the story is history. Other than Gramp, the rest of us rolled on the tarmac in laughter and tears. Gramp was not happy! Insurance did not cover family destruction. A wonderful, recent NovEl (2013) entitled The Shack by William P. Young, tells of an abducted child, her wonderful pets, and her joyful time in Heaven with her loved one's past, and hope for the future. This heart-wrenching story calls us into the promise and hope of life everlasting and the continued closeness with those we love, including our pets. How could there be a Heaven without our pets, loved ones and all? Over the years the church celebrates the Feast of Saint Francis of Asissi, who loved all creatures and saw a soul in all of them. On that day, we have "the blessing of animals". When asked from time to time as to why animals are not baptized as we are, the answer is, "Animals do not need to be baptized. They have no sin!"

. . .

A Visit from Santa Claus

Oh yes, the surprise visit from Santa Claus! On a Winter day in Shrewsbury, MA. A raging blizzard was howling outside. Gramp insisted on delivering a timely gift to a neighbor. I offered to go along just in case the small VW got stuck in the rapidly accumulating, un-plowed snow. Sur enough, we slid into a ditch en route. Looking around as Gramp frantically tried maneuvering out of the ditch I saw Santa approaching. I then told Gramp that Santa would come to our rescue. He didn't take such a wise crack lightly until, indeed, there was Santa knocking at his window and offering to help. Together were able to get moving again. We managed to get back home and the gift was not delivered until sometime later.

More Stories

There are many stories for all of us to share both for learning and the betterment of ourselves. These stories as we have perceived them can be both serious as well as humorous and both. As a matter of fact, we need a whole lot more humor in that none of us is perfect and probably in all that we do can find the humor of it all. Such humor teaches us both humility as well as understanding of each other and, thereby, forgiveness.

I'll never forget a recent wedding that was halted for a goodly space of time because the photographer did not follow explicit instructions. The photographer is not to interfere in the process and solemnity of the ceremony. During the marriage ceremony in question, the relatively young female photographer jumped to the front of the Altar rail as the reader was in the middle of the second reading of I Corinthians 13th chapter: "One may have all knowledge to move mountains. And all the wisdom of the world, but the most important of all these it Faith, Hope and Love, and greatest of these is Love."

There in the middle of the aisle between the Altar and the Reader at the Lectern was the photographer lying prone and face down on the floor with her tights halfway down her cheeks. The reading stopped in the midst of this experience; no one dared laugh; and I gently and as discreetly as possible guided her back to the place she was meant to be. No more was said about the incident either there at the church or at the reception afterwards. After a brief and stunning delay, the ceremony was completed.

Many years ago, during my years as curate in St. Barnabas' Church, Father Olsen and I were celebrants of the funeral of a dear loved one. Funerals are the necessary and needed obligation of the parish priest. It was a blustery, cold winter day and the newly fallen snow was very deep, having been a several days storm. The Committal Service following the Mass was at the small and little used historical cemetery near-by.

The hearse could barely fit as it struggled up the narrow dirt path. Fr. Olsen and I, fully dressed in ceremonial attire, sat together in the car directly behind the hearse. As we simultaneously opened the side doors (usually an attendant would open them for us but there was little to no room for that to happen) and exited only to find ourselves under the car, feet connecting, and unable to get out from under. The ice was slanted and slippery. Finally, with much help, we were extricated and able to complete a very brief Committal Service. The funeral director said to us on the way home, "Only the two of you could have found yourselves, fully garbed, under a hearse, foot to foot!"

Speaking of the three important observances in the Church: Baptism, Marriage, and Funeral, there was the time we were remembering Miss Mary Taylor. Mary was over a hundred when she passed, and she was the oldest and longest in years communicant of the Trinity Parish in Milford, Massachusetts. During the ceremony there was a loud knock at the side door of the Sanctuary. Two-year-old Brian there as we opened the door, with his pants down to his ankles, crying, and saying, "Mom, I need you to wipe my bum!"

Mary Taylor would have been in hysterics and honored by this intrusion into her ceremony and her entrance into eternity. In her last years of this life, Mary had slowly lost her cognitive abilities in that dreadful disease we know as Alzheimer's. However, during that time funny occurrences also happened that were true to Mary's character and great sense of humor. While in the nursing home Mary was informed that I was going to visit her in a little while. When I arrived there was Mary, stark naked except for her typical white gloves, Sunday hat, and prayer book. Startled and at a loss for words, all I could say was "Hi Mary!" Her response was, "I'm going to church."

At a wedding reception back in the fun days with Father Olsen at St. Barnabas' Church, we were seated around the periphery of the Veterans Hall in E. Greenwich, Rhode Island during the cutting of the cake time of the reception. Fr. Olsen fell asleep, as he often dozed at other events. While holding his lit cigar in his hand, his hand fell, hit the leg of the lady next to him... There was a scream, and everybody looked to see what the commotion was about. Fr. Olsen was awakened and asked me what was going on! He was oblivious to the entire incident and the reception went on as if nothing significant had happened.

. . .

In those earlier years, the Ecumenical Movement was flourishing. Christians were enjoying a wonderful and fruitful dialogue following centuries of a divided Church. In the early 1970s, Bishop Mc Vinney was the Bishop of the R. C. Diocese of Providence, Rhode Island He was an old-fashioned Prelate in that proper décor and manners were of the utmost importance He was doing his best to accommodate this new relationship with the Protestant churches.

I believe it was a difficult as well as interesting journey for him at that time. The Bishop hosted a Religious Service and social gathering of the various denominations at the Cathedral in Providence. It was packed to the brim. In the middle of that memorable service and just after a superb homily by the Bishop, he disappeared from the Sanctuary. All of a sudden over the newly installed speaker system was the sound of the Bishop relieving his bladder. He neglected to turn off his microphone. Returning to the Altar he was oblivious to the fact that we all heard the commotion from the lavatory. The beautiful ceremony proceeded. I never heard whether or not anyone told the dear Bishop of that incident.

· · ·

At a wedding in Trinity Parish, Milford, some years ago, I was reading from the Gospel of St. John. It was a widely chosen Gospel reading for weddings. The Gospel clearly states how we are called to give our lives for our friends. Everyone heard me say how we are called to "give our wives for our friends." To this day I am reminded of this bold statement by me in the Church, as if this is what the Truth is. Such mistakes can surely be made and there is much humor and learning in it all.

· · ·

The Famous "Bumper Sticker" Incident

When my children were little, they were gradually taught the important do's and don'ts of getting around the obstacles that would eventually confront them. "Life is chock full of obstacles which, if possible, should be avoided." In other words, "Don't touch the hot stove or you'll get burned!" Inevitably, by our need to experience, the warnings are not always successful. The experience needs to happen in order for the learning to become complete.

Way back then, Joel spotted some outrageous bumper stickers and asked me to purchase some of them for the car bumper. I had to refuse and also explain why. Some of those messages were not appropriate both for one's character as well as one's health. End of story… until…!

That next Christmas, under the tree, was a gift for me from Joel! I again explained that, although it was very funny, I could not place it on the car bumper. He took it into hiding, and it was hidden for several years until it surfaced on the front of his new Boom Box. Boom Boxes were a combination of radio, cassette player, and recorder, which one carried around on his travels. They were very popular on the streets, on the beaches, etc. back then. This was long before the cell phone era.

So, this is what happened. Joel's first Confirmation class was to be held. I asked for the use of his Boom Box. When we arrived at the church, I noticed the bumper sticker on the Boom Box. Asking him to remove it, he did, and flung it onto the seat of the car, and we went ahead for the class. During the instruction time I was called out to the emergency room of the Milford Regional Hospital. Upon arriving, they were already a flood of ambulances and police there, in response to a serious, multiple vehicle accident. During this time as I was trying to help throughout the area, a kind police officer approached me with the bumper sticker. It had just fallen off the seat of my pants. The Police Officer thoughtfully but knowingly said, "Is this yours, Father?" Everyone had seen it pasted in perfect order on the seat of my formal suit pants: "Who farted?"

During my early childhood, my brothers Jimmy and Don, along with our close cousins Joyce and Barbara, brought me to Crescent Amusement Park in Riverside, Rhode Island. This was the time of my first ride on a roller coaster. Don placed himself in the front car and the rest of us sat in the cars behind Don. With some trepidation, along with the excitement of this initiatory ride, I sat with Cousin Joyce in the last car. There were several other riders in the middle of it all. Soon after the ride began and as it was making the first climb before the sudden terrifying decline soon the happen a horrible gas from the front enveloped all of us except the perpetrator. That gas remained with us throughout the ride. Don still denies his involvement and tells us that all he remembers is that the rest of us behind him moaned, groaned, and laughed along with the screams of that memorable roller coaster ride. We all survived, and life went forward as it would and should.

SO MANY STORIES TO TELL!

"In Conclusion"

Way back in 1967, as I was beginning my four-year journey in Philadelphia for graduate work in theology, I got on a bus to center city. The goal was not necessarily to see another city but rather to enjoy the famous huge soft pretzel which began there at Rittenhouse square. With one dollar to spend, I was able to not only accomplish the mission but also return with twenty-five cents. What an extraordinary trip that was! Sitting on a park bench and enjoying the pretzel a much older gentleman came along and sat beside me with his pretzel.

Soon after a brief spell of small talk, the saga began. He asked me if I had yet visited the famous Wanamaker Department Store just across to the far side of the park from our park bench. I let him know that I had only twenty-five cents left to spend so couldn't consider that adventure. He said, "Oh no! Just go inside and take it all for what it's worth." He then proceeded to tell me the story of John Wannamaker. He told me how as a young boy John was raised in a row house just outside of the inner city. Wannamaker had even less than one dollar if any extra to spend. John's Mom and Dad attended a local church and he went to Sunday School. There were Bibles for sale one day, but John was unable to buy one.

After complaining to his parents, his Dad gave him a job of shining his shoes so that he could save up for the expensive book being sold for five dollars. Wannamaker saved those pennies, finally got the book, and with the help of his teachers, from then on, he read it with delight. The rest is history. Wannamaker not only developed the famous Wannamaker Department Store but also several other of the business stores surrounding Rittenhouse Square. He became a much-loved human being, and a philanthropist at that. The gentleman there with me proceeded to direct me to the home of the original Liberty Bell just a block away. How extraordinary for me to have spent my dollar on that journey into the heart of Philadelphia. I came to find out that at least two of the churches in the city were built through the generosity of John Wannamaker.

From my considered point of view over the last several decades, it appears that there has been a critical loss of all too many of the principles and values that have guided and allowed us growth and a system of belief towards an honest, healthy, and solid culture. To me, our American culture has been built on a solid foundation with truth and freedom as our common belief and goal. My own choice to study and be ordained as a priest in the Church was built on the culture within which I was raised and educated. The Judeo/Christian belief in a Creator we call God became, for me, the basis in which such principles and values of our culture would find adequate guidance in our ongoing search for the Truth. The idea and questions of FREEDOM are, in my mind, critical to our forward movement individually and together as society.

With this in mind I share an historical account dating back to the crumbling Roman Empire some 300 years after the birth of Christ. It says that the wealthiest man in the area of Rome was Croesus. Croesus was probably in his fifties and taking stock of not only his enormous wealth and power, but he was also being cognizant of the fact that he was growing older. He also worried about the failing atmosphere in his once powerful country. At that time, he had been witnessing a large number of Christians coming out of hiding and fearless of the massive persecution of so many of them. They were actually being used as sport in the Arena as the crowd watched them mauled by lions.

The Christians were clearly not very popular amongst the masses but were giving powerful messages that were beginning to make everyone think about life, death, and the crumbling world around them. They were realizing that corruption was rampant even in the places of influence that once made them a great society in the first place. They knew their history. It became clearer and clearer that evil was pervading, and the sins of humans were bringing about their downfall. At that time, the well-known philosopher and teacher, Thales, was also giving out warnings and admonishments to their weakening society. Croesus went to Thales and asked him the following universal question: "Who, or what, is God?"

Thales told Croesus that he needed some time and deliberation in order to return with some answers to such a profound and pertinent question. The famous early Church theologian, Tertullian, learned about the inquiry of Croesus to Thales. He wrote to them the following answer: "There", he exclaimed, "is the wisest man in the world and he cannot tell you who God is. But the most illiterate, simple laborer among the Christians knows God, and is ready and able to make Him known to others." (Encyclopedia of 7700 Quotations #522o)

Saint Tertullian was one of the early Church Fathers who formulated Christian theology in those tumultuous times of the failing Roman Empire and the rapidly growing Church of history. Not long after the Resurrection, and the Pentecost, the earliest disciples of Jesus wrote the New Testament of the Bible. Unafraid, they moved forward in both giving their experiences of the historical Jesus and spreading the Word as far as possible. They met much opposition and argument as to who this Jesus really was, but through all the turmoil the Church was born, and grew, and thrived throughout the world.

It is interesting to note here that the Christian calendar of observance (Advent, Christmas, Epiphany, Lent, Easter, the Pentecost, to the Feast of Christ the King) places three important observances directly following Christmas Day. They are St. Stephen, Deacon and Martyr, on December 26; St. John, Apostle and Evangelist, Dec 27; and The Holy Innocents Dec 28th.

St. Stephen was a young advocate of Jesus, and probably of a poorer and less educated background. While Stephen was being stoned to death by an angry mob, he repeated Jesus' words from the Cross on that fateful Good Friday: "Father, forgive them, for they know not what they do." St. John the Evangelist, a Greek scholar and convert in the early Church, authored the Gospel according to St. John. The Holy Innocents were those children who were slaughtered within two years of Jesus' birth because the Roman Empire thought that its power and authority were being threatened. It was, as history has shown, the danger of absolute power by any human being.

Even at that time, soon after the birth of Christ, there was a sense of hope against all hope in that era, as well as in our own. Power, control by a few, tyranny over mind, heart, body and soul, was being questioned. Ultimately this new wave of hope brought an unfailing Jesus to his death on the Cross. But Easter happened and here we are!

St. Basil of Caesarea, another of our early Church Fathers in the fourth Century A. D. said the following to the Church and to the world:

O human, what should we do with you? When God remains in the heights, you do not seek Him. When He comes down and converses with you through flesh, you do not receive Him. But how will you be brought into affinity with God when you seek explanations? Realize that God is in the flesh, for this reason: because the flesh that was cursed needed to be sanctified; the flesh that was weakened needed to be strengthened; the flesh that was alienated from God needed to be brought into affinity with Him; the flesh that had fallen in Paradise needed to be led back into Heaven.

Jesus said, "Blessed are those who believe, but have not yet seen." (John 20:29). Jesus said, "The meek shall inherit the earth."

The famous young nurse, Anne Sullivan was called in to care for the child, Helen Keller, who was born blind, deaf and mute. It was Anne who stayed with that once unruly Helen throughout the rest of their lives. The light, peace, grace, and power of God's love was found in that relationship. Beneath the high altar of the Cathedral of Saints Peter and Paul in Washington, D. C., the remains of Ann and Helen are interred in that crypt chapel beneath the High Altar. Inscribed on the chapel crypt are the following words: "With all this said I believe that the idea of 'Freedom' is our goal and our responsibility. Throughout recorded history the greatest battle has been that between tyranny and freedom."

The Holy Bible takes this further as defining freedom in terms of God's gift of free will, given to each of us according to His Will and Purpose for all humankind. Each of us are Free in that we are the best we can be in the context of His purpose for us. That purpose is the Love of God. The Truth emanates from this point. As Jesus said to the Scribes and the Pharisees that time in the Temple at Jerusalem. "The Law of God is Love! Love the Lord your God with all your heart, mind, and soul; and Love your neighbor as yourself. This is the Law and the Commandment." Jesus was twelve years old when he spoke to those Leaders of the People.

President Franklin D. Roosevelt once said that, "There never has been, and never will be, any race of people on earth fit to serve as masters over their fellow man." Another anonymous quote states that, "If a nation values anything more than freedom, it will lose its freedom; and the irony of it is comfort, control, power, or money that it values more, it will lose that too."

Another said that "Democracy (one's free expression of his thoughts in honest dialogue) is the primary ingredient in search of the Truth." It is true that "There are extraordinary possibilities in ordinary people."

In the Encyclopedia of 7700 Quotations under the subject of freedom and titled "The Signs of the Times", it is noted that, "A global survey of political and civil liberty indicates that personal freedom has diminished in the 1970s for eighty-five million people in seven countries. The assessment made by Freedom House, a New York based non-profit organization that rates nations as either free, partly free, or not free. Sixty-six countries with 42% of the world's population were termed as *not free*."

Beginning in this century President Ronald Reagan warned us that, "If we neglect to teach our children the history and values of our freedom, we'll lose them to tyranny." This paraphrase of the President's thoughtful and provocative words was in relation to the slow but steady deterioration of the values and freedom we have long cherished in our nation. Yes, in my opinion as expressed throughout the documents of this book, that it is incumbent upon us in a free society to continue with the wisdom so far given to us to seek the TRUTH in all honesty and sincerity.

In my considered opinion, the Holy Bible is clear about the path of Truth. Such a path includes and is dependent upon Belief and Faith in God, the freedom to express and debate that which we believe, and the humility to learn and grow. As the Bible also teaches, it is the sin of false pride that prevents our ability to move forward. The famous G. K. Chesterton once said that it is true that when people stop believing in God, they fall on themselves, and anything becomes permissible. Fyodor Dostoevsky in his book CRIME AND PUNISHMENT pointedly notes that, "If God does not exist, everything is permissible."

Charles M. Houser said that, "Atheism never composed a symphony, never painted a masterpiece, never dispelled a fear, never healed a disease, never gave peace of mind, never dried a tear, never established a philanthropy, never gave an intelligent answer to the vast mystery of the universe, never gave meaning to man's life on earth, never built a just and peaceful world, never built a great and enduring civilization."

Jesus said to his disciples, "If you continue in my word, you are truly my disciples, and you will know the truth and the truth will set you free." (John 8:32) The Church's Common Lectionary provides a complete and organized study of the Holy Bible. As we follow this study each Sunday for three years beginning with Advent and ending in Christ the King, we shall have studied and come to fathom the Will of God for us. In conclusion of this book I repeat the readings for the seventeenth Sunday after the Pentecost (second year B) as it sums up for me the message I have wished to convey in this collection of writings.

The UNGODLY by their words and deeds summoned death; considering him a friend, they pined away and made a covenant with him, because they are fit to belong to his company. For they reasoned unsoundly, saying to themselves, 'short and sorrowful is our life, and there is no remedy when a life comes to its end, and no one has been known to return from Hades. Let us lie in wait for the righteous man, because he is inconvenient to us and oppose our actions; he reproaches us for sins against the law, and accuses us of sins against our training. He professes to have knowledge of God, and calls himself a child of the Lord. He became to us a reproof of our thoughts; the very sight of him is a burden to us, because his manner of life is unlike that of others, and his ways are strange. We are considered by him as something base, and he avoids our ways as unclean; he calls the last end of the righteous happy, and boasts that God is his father. Let us see if his words are true, and let us test what will happen at the end of his life; for if the righteous man is God's child, he will help him, and will deliver him from the hand of his adversaries. Let us test him with insults and torture, so that we may find out how gentle he is, and make trial of his forbearance. Let us condemn him to a shameful death, for, according to what he says, he will be protected.' Thus they reasoned, but they were led astray, for their wickedness blinded them, and they did not know the secret purposes of God, nor hoped for the wages of holiness, nor discerned the prize for blameless souls.
(The Wisdom of Solomon 1:16-2:1, and 12-22)

PSALM 54

6 "I will offer you a free will sacrifice * and praise your Name, O Lord, for it is good.

7 For you have rescued me from every trouble, *

and my eye has seen the triumph over the foes."

JESUS AND THE DISCIPLES passed through Galilee. He did not want anyone to know it; for he was teaching his disciples, saying to them. 'The Son of Man is to be betrayed into human hands, and they will kill him, and three days after being killed, he will rise again.' But they did not understand what he was saying and were afraid to ask him. Then they came to Capernium; and when he was in the house he asked them, 'What were you arguing about along the way?' But they were silent, for on the way they had argued with one another who was the greatest. He sat down, called the twelve, and said to them, "Whoever wants to be first must be last of all.' Then he took a little child and placed that child among them; and he took the child into his arms and said to them, 'Whoever welcomes one such child in my name welcomes me, and whoever welcomes me welcomes not me but the one who sent me. *(Mark 9:30 – 37)*

"This is your lot, the portion I have measured out to you, says the Lord, because you have forgotten me and trusted in lies." *(Jeremiah 13:25)*

Socrates taught for forty years, Plato for fifty. Aristotle for forty, and Jesus for only three. Yet the influence of Christ's three year ministry infinitely transcends the impact left by the combined teaching from these men who were among the greatest of all antiquity. Jesus painted no pictures; yet some of the finest paintings of Raphael, Michelangelo, and Leonardo DaVinci received their inspiration from Him. Jesus wrote no poetry; but Dante, Milton, and scores of the world's greatest poets were inspired by Him. Jesus composed no music; still Haydn, Handel, Beethoven, Bach, and Mendelson reached their highest perfection of melody in the hymns, symphonies, and oratories they composed in His praise. Every sphere of human greatness has been enriched by this humble Carpenter of Nazareth. (Henry C. Bosch. Encyclopedia of 7700 Quotations)

Episcopal Seminary Chapel, West Philadelphia, Pennsylvania

Saint John's Church

Millville, Massachusetts

Designed by Richard Upjohn

Dedicated in 1848

PARISHES SERVED

The Church House, Diocese of R. I., South Providence, Postulant, 1965

Saint Barnabas', N. Philadelphia, Pennsylvania, Seminarian, 1967 – 1969

Church of the Redeemer, Bryn Maur, Pennsylvania, Seminarian, 1969 – 1970

Saint Barnabas', Warwick, Rhode Island, Curate, 1970 – 1975

Trinity, Milford, Massachusetts, Rector, 1975 - 1992

Saint John's, Sutton, Massachusetts, Rector, 1992 – 1997

Saint John's, Millville, Massachusetts, Rector, 1998– 2002

Saint Mark's, Warwick, Rhode Island, Rector, 2002 – 2008

All Saint's Parish, Newport, Vermont, Interim, 2010

Saint Stephen's, Westborough, Massachusetts, Interim, 2011 - 2012

Saint Phillip, Putnam, Connecticut, Interim, 2012 – 2016

Grace Church, Oxford, Massachusetts, Interim, 2018, 2019

Saint John's, Millville, Massachusetts, Interim, 2019 –

Trinity, Whitinsville, Massachusetts, Interim, 2019 -

V. N. A. and St. Camillus' Hospice, Team Pastor, 1990 – 2002

Haitian Mission, Food for the Poor, 1997

LOVE

CREATES

Phoebe S. Main, Age Nine

AND
HERE WE ARE!

www.ingramcontent.com/pod-product-compliance
Lightning Source LLC
Chambersburg PA
CBHW051256120626
46547CB00015B/1966